After Year Zero
Geographies of Collaboration

Annett Busch
and Anselm Franke

Essays

Anselm Franke
Annett Busch
John Akomfrah
Denis Ekpo
Lotte Arndt
David Murphy
Clare Davies
Nida Ghouse
James T. Hong
Shirin M. Rai
Travelling Communiqué
Kodwo Eshun
Łukasz Stanek
Marie-Hélène Gutberlet
& Tobias Hering
Stacy Hardy
Bisi Silva
Bongani Madondo
Max Annas
& Gary Minkley
Charles Tonderai Mudede
Fred Moten

Preface

The histories and developments of African and European societies have always been profoundly interrelated. It is for this reason that, from its inception, the Haus der Kulturen der Welt (HKW) has worked with African artists and intellectuals, examining and questioning the reciprocal interactions between the societies. The institution set itself the goal of opening up a German and European-related discourse, of decentering European perspectives, and addressing relationships of structural violence and power asymmetries existing between the societies.

In the process, postcolonial discourse, as initiated by a series of African and other non-European intellectuals, was an essential source of ideas. In recent years the aim has been to translate this discourse into a society which, for a long period, had negated its colonial heritage or actively denied it, primarily locating the dark side of its history in German National Socialism. This promoted a focus on German national history, even amongst critical German intellectuals. Furthermore, the goal, then as now, is to pursue the postcolonial discourse—which has its roots in the decolonization processes of the twentieth century, stimulating public debate primarily in the Anglophone world of the 1970s and 1980s with its first significant contributions—in a world in which the limits of power and the exercise of violence are being partially re-articulated or realigned.

As both active agents and passive stakeholders in these processes—which as a rule are described using the term globalization—the task is to continually establish historical points of reference as standards by which to judge and evaluate today's developments.

In this spirit, I would like to draw attention to three of the HKW's projects which have significantly influenced the institution's thinking.

In "Black Atlantic", a project largely inspired by Paul Gilroy, although developed together with many others, the HKW explored the history of exploitation, oppression, and slavery which has shaped the Americas' and Europe's relationship to Africa for centuries. The project made it clear that the slave trade not only promoted the political, and above all economic development of Europe and the U.S., but that the mobility of black African societies, especially in the twentieth century, was essential to the cultural and intellectual developments which exerted a decisive influence on European centers such as Paris and London.

In a certain sense this led into the project "The Short Century", which Okwui Enwezor developed together with the HKW. In "The Short Century", Enwezor explored the history of independence and liberation movements between 1945 and 1995, illustrating how a new historical subjectivity emerged from the African liberation movements which fundamentally questioned the universal claims of European hegemonic thought.

Enwezor's comprehensive project "The Short Century" formed the point of reference for the detailed analysis of "In the Desert of Modernity", in which Marion von Osten, Tom Avermaete, and Serhat Karakayali, using the example of Casablanca, analyzed how colonial Morocco was used as a laboratory for the development of modern European architecture. In the process, European architects studied local architecture, adopting some of its essential principles and utilizing what was, from their perspective, a non-culturally defined space, reconceptualizing the strategies developed in North Africa within the context of a European modernity which presented itself as autonomous of colonial experiences.

All three projects addressed both the logics of violence and power asymmetries of the past, as manifested in the reciprocal interactions between Africa and Europe, while simultaneously altering the fundamental European perspectives through the inclusion of the black protagonists.

Finally, "After Year Zero", which was developed for the HKW by Annett Busch and Anselm Franke following their Goethe-Institut enabled workshops on "Matters of Collaboration" in Algiers, Dakar, Johannesburg, Paris and Brussels in 2012 and 2013 and presented at the HKW in 2013, explored aspects of the emerging postwar world order, and decolonization in relation to the aftermath of fascism. It juxtaposed the Iron Curtain with the Color Curtain as different topographies of historical memory that informed political geographies. And it juxtaposed the 1957 Congress Hall in the center of Berlin, an icon of re-education and US-led liberal humanism that now hosts the HKW, with the 1955 Afro-Asian Conference in Bandung, Indonesia that marked a major milestone in decolonization, discussed here in the context of a century of Pan-Africanist congresses that instigated African independence. As an exhibition and platform for multiple discussions, "After Year Zero" became a forum for an urgent debate on the fundaments of global relations and the narrative-imaginary framing of history.

Bernd Scherer

Preface

For the team of the Museum of Modern Art in Warsaw, hosting the exhibition "After Year Zero" and collaborating with the Haus der Kulturen der Welt on this publication is a natural consequence of our interest in emancipatory discourses and the critical reading of dominant narratives: their reinterpretation and rewriting. Established in 2005, the Museum focuses on the questions of transformation, so important in Poland. Our institution attempts to construct its own narrative through comparing an array of contemporary transformation experiences in various parts of the world, highlighting their emancipatory and transgressive character. A pivotal moment in building our own narrative came with our confrontation with the question of the tension between the East and the West in the context of the changing configuration of power in the aftermath of the Cold War. Symbolically, the year 1989 became the starting point of the Museum's collection. What is more, the exhaustion of the idea of the West is investigated within the project "Former West", initiated by BAK in Utrecht with the Museum as an active participant. The acknowledgement of the illusionary character of the suppression of barriers after the collapse of the Berlin Wall, and above all the limitations of promises offered by the Western postmodern project, was a key formative moment for the work of the Museum.

The starting point for "After Year Zero" is the Bandung Conference held in April 1955. That gathering demonstrated the solidarity of the states of Africa and Asia and attempted to establish an agreement beyond the idiom of the Western political culture. The goal of "After Year Zero" is to map emancipatory postcolonial discourses. The project seeks to imagine the world differently—beyond universalism based on Western values and the reality after the Cold War. It also highlights the fact that, apart from the Iron Curtain, there is also a Color Curtain that existed and continues to exist until the present day. Even though it was supposed to disappear symbolically around 1960, when liberation movements in Africa gained momentum, the Color Curtain can still be observed, while the consequences of long-standing racial divisions remain poorly articulated and do not influence the language of politics. What is at stake here is the contemporary shape of relations between Europe and Africa. Imagining a potential common future and a different division of power becomes a necessity in the face of the tragedy of growing inequalities between the continents and the loss of interest of the EU in the problem of African emigration. The curators of "After Year Zero" argue that the major obstacle blocking a new opening are the ruins of old ideas: progress, modernization, nation state—ideas that continue to lie at the foundation of the European order, but at the same time retain an inextricable historical link with colonialism and exclusion. Disassembling the old frames is a necessary process to start a dialogue based on partnership. Yet, it is not enough to raise awareness of the historical deficits and contemporary consequences of the project of modernity. We need to locate the sources of alternative narratives. This is the reason why the exhibition and the publication gather the traces of alternative political projects, structures and networks of contacts that emerged in Africa and in migrant environments. The project looks for those traces in niche magazines, documentary films, and works of art.

Research of this kind has already been conducted before—even if on a slightly marginal basis—within the Museum's narrative. Among other texts, this publication includes an essay by Łukasz Stanek, published within a research program that concerned the activity of Polish urban planners and architects in African and Asian countries (the "brotherly help" between socialist states), initiated by the Museum in 2010 (within the project "Warsaw under Construction"). Later, those designs and projects in Africa and Asia became one of the sources of inspirations for Polish postmodern architecture. Postcolonial studies have always formed part of larger projects carried out by the Museum, such as "Modernologies" curated by Sabine Breitwieser in 2010, and the seminar on "blackness", run by Fred Moten within a program devoted to contemporary performance art in 2014.

However, the greatest hope that the Museum invests with regard to research for "After Year Zero" concerns the inspirations that this research might offer to the local rewriting of identity narratives and raising awareness of the usually transparent frames that surround fantasies related to the contemporary era. The contemporary humanities in Poland have witnessed a number of symbolic turning points. For the Museum narrative, the most important of them are two texts that compel a revision of the history of the Polish community and infringe on the hitherto recognized foundations of cultural coordinates. The book *Fantomowe ciało króla. Peryferyjne zmagania z nowoczesną formą* [The Phantom Body of the King. Peripheral Struggles with Modern Form] by Jan Sowa from 2011 is an attempt to transform the historical narrative that concerns the unique form of Polish statehood based on "Nobles' Democracy". Sowa shifts the focus of this narrative to the history of serfdom—the enslavement of the majority of the rural population in the realm of feudalism and an economy based on agriculture; a situation that continued to exist until as late as the mid-nineteenth century. In his book *Prześniona rewolucja* [Over-dreamt Revolution], Andrzej Leder portrays a post-feudal society that undergoes modernization as if without its own will and awareness—through passive participation in the destruction of the elites of the former feudal society, witnessing the Holocaust, and accepting the imposition of the dictatorship of the proletariat by the Soviets in 1945. Leder demonstrates the passive attitude of the majority of the population to postwar modernization—or indeed revolution. The struggle against national narratives in the field of historical studies is an introduction to the search for a language that will be able to describe the contemporary era of global capitalism, an era that we have entered with a weak sense of our own subjectivity and unclear ties with modernity—a domain of the elite, destroyed by the war and Stalin's postwar terror—as well as the resulting cultural alienation. Therefore, the question of the possibility of creating new universal emancipatory projects is a very interesting question in the Polish context. Equally fascinating are the theoretical and artistic challenges that concern the way of looking for sources of alternative narratives.

Joanna Mytkowska

Introduction

Annett Busch and Anselm Franke

"How to start?" "I was very tempted to copy John and start with an image."[1] Echoes of beginnings. Algiers, June 22, 2012. There is always a beginning before a beginning. In Algiers 2012 we set up our first workshop in the framework of a project under the title "Matters of Collaboration", which was made possible by a grant from the Goethe-Institut. The exhibition "After Year Zero" again developed out of this series of workshops and nomadic discussions held in Algiers, Dakar, Johannesburg, Paris, and Brussels. In the workshops, dedicated to critically engaging historical and contemporary relations between Europe and Africa, two radically different aspects of "collaboration" have been explored: collaboration with an enemy or adversary, and collaboration as the creation of common ground and the making of political imaginaries, as "working together", literary translated from the Latin *co–laborare*. The double-edged term "collaboration" consistently puts into question colonial modernity's identitarian and "Manichean" logic (Frantz Fanon) and its long afterlives in the present day. It directs attention instead to a grey zone, characterized by the in-between and at the same time by radical asymmetries of power. "Collaboration" also draws attention to relations between individuals and frameworks and systemic parameters that they undermine or transform.

If we follow the close reading by Marie-Hélène Gutberlet and Tobias Hering of *Come Back Africa,* which "is famed today as having been the first film in the collection of Arsenal—Institute for Film and Video Art in Berlin" one can see how the beginnings, endings and the returns interfold and how many entangled routes an archive can provide. Gutberlet and Hering are both part of the broad and multilayered project "Visionary Archive" which is similar to "Travelling Communiqué", a project which "reads" the photographic archive (1948–80) of the Presidential Photo Service of the "Yugoslav partisan leader and statesman Josip Broz Tito"; their main concern is to question the myths of beginnings to reconnect the present with the past through the unpredictable richness of a documentary image—and not to illustrate history. The filmmakers Yervant Gianikian and Angela Ricci Lucchi on the other hand have worked for many years with lost and salvaged archives. They draw the archival image into the present by re-filming it; their work on history is a work on the image. "The historical image in their work is both forensic evidence, and haunting, hallucinatory presence of the past." In "After Year Zero" in Berlin they showed private archives, drawings and a four-channel installation also based on archive materials from the attack of Mussolini on Ethiopia in 1935, the beginning of the Second World War on African soil.

In "Lotus Notes" Nida Ghouse imagines beginnings (Tashkent 1958, Cairo 1962, Beirut 1981) alongside the literary magazine *Lotus*, a magazine for Afro-Asian writing, from a moment and place where one didn't want to think about history: "I am in Cairo. History is impossible.

1 See the lectures by John Akomfrah, Jihan El-Tahri, Kader Attia, Bongani Madondo, The Otolith Group and many others, including discussions, at http://www.mattersofcollaboration.net.

The year is 2012." But the gaps and black holes, the images of history and historic images have to be renewed and invented.

We have tested, questioned and stretched the notion of collaboration across different overlapping fields, such as economics and politics, language and literature, cinema and music. Most of the artists in the exhibition as well as authors in this publication have participated in the discussions on collaboration. The essays reflect, in their heterogeneity, different threads of vivid discussions which, again, began in Algiers with a take on the concept of Négritude, proposed by the filmmaker and artist John Akomfrah. It was not so much the intention to pick up a historic philosophical debate but to search for a connective, and in this sense powerful name for visible and invisible, transnational and coded collaborations across a clearly framed political agenda, which got lost and needs to be invented anew. This lecture on Négritude and the following debate[2] became a kind of reference point for following discussions, and this publication. The essays by the academic researchers Lotte Arndt and David Murphy supplement this programmatic attempt with historic excursions, while Denis Ekpo argues for the necessity of a "Post-Africanism" in an "attempt to pull Africa and Black America out of the Africanity tunnel so that we can be fully reconnected to the infinite, problem-solving creativity of the global world process." With the notion of Négritude the question of a possible and impossible universal came again into play, a concern which unfolds explicitly in the contributions "The Universal Project" and "Universal Pictures" but also echoes throughout the body of all texts.

The disparate essays are connected through another thread which is the research on historic journals and magazines. During the preparations for the exhibition "After Year Zero" in Berlin we realized all of a sudden that the main source for our favorite texts and quotes were various Pan-African journals and magazines, mostly from the African Diaspora. The connection to historic moments was filled with immediacy and the breath of promising but also fragile beginnings often noticeable. The follow-up of the exhibition in Warsaw and this present publication gave us the opportunity to open and deepen the research on little-known historic magazines from the African continent and the African Diaspora. The format and potential of mostly cultural and vanguard magazines is understood as a periodical and often temporary intervention against hegemonic voices. These magazines were often set up under precarious circumstances as a collaborative artistic form of organizing discourse, critique and self-expression, but also as a format which renders possible the necessary task of creating a new language to talk about art, life and politics.

"Do Magazines Do Culture?" The question raised by the writer and editor Rajat Neogy in the 24th issue (1966) of the legendary magazine *Transition* that he founded at the age of twenty-two in Uganda, has been taken up by the music journalist and social critic Bongani Madondo who replied with a "yes.... sometimes" and with a glimpse of his own biography remembered through magazines such as the South African edition of

2 Also online at http://www.mattersofcollaboration.net.

Rolling Stone and early issues of *Vibe.* It seemed to be the right moment, something was in the air. We encountered surprisingly enthusiastic responses and a rich pool of academic research on the same topic which has been carried out recently. Instead of even trying to represent the full range, we followed the experiences and preferences of the authors. Titles such as *Souffles, Transition, Lotus, Tricontinental, New Culture, Staffrider, Black Images, Black Orpheus, Présence Africaine* open up to wide networks of transnational collaborations, a labyrinth Clare Davies follows in detail in her essay "Geographies of Solidarity", taking the Moroccan magazine *Souffles* from the early '60s as a starting point. "Many of these journals no longer exist", writes Stacy Hardy in her essay on South African magazines during apartheid. "This does not matter. What matters is that they did exist and that their energies, ideologies and imagination live on in work that is published in other journals on the continent today."

As most of the artists in "After Year Zero" in Berlin took part in the workshops they also took part in the curatorial process and most of them produced special work in the context of this project. John Akomfrah explored the notion of independence, another "year zero", as a space of dependencies, not yet overcome, through his new piece based on *Transfigured Night* by Arnold Schönberg itself inspired by a mystical love poem from German romanticist Richard Dehmel. His three channel work *The Unfinished Conversation* invoked the formative years of Stuart Hall and his coming of age as a public intellectual, seeking out currents and convergences between a single life and history, particularly in the 1950s, the decade of significant migration from the Caribbean to England, but also the decade of the Korean War, of the Suez Crisis that brought the world to the brink of a Third World War, the insurgency in Hungary and the breaking away of the European left from Stalinism and the USSR. The Otolith Group developed a work on postage stamps produced in Ghana between 1957 and 1966, assembling them into a political calendar of Pan-Africanist imagery. In his contribution to the publication "Statecraft: An Incomplete Timeline of Independence Determined by Digital Auction" Kodwo Eshun takes on the role of a critic who writes about a piece he has conceived himself as an artist, and *In the Year of the Quiet Sun* is a kinomuseum of Pan-Africanist Pop art.

For "After Year Zero" in Berlin, Kader Attia produced a work based on the collection of African "tribal" objects housed in the Vatican, invoking the role that religion and missionaries played in the colonial scenography. In Warsaw he contributed with *Silence's Injuries*, slides showing a series of West African LP covers dating from the African postindependence era, on the basis of which he reads the history of blues against the grain. Music, another thread which was fundamental in the workshop in Johannesburg, developed together with Max Annas who here explores the notion of African Jazz, also through a series of LP covers. The word "Jazz" appeared in many names of African music bands throughout the continent who played many different genres of music other than jazz and seemed to be more a statement of Pan-Africanism as an imaginary project full of polyrhythmic tones.

The timeline of the exhibition ends with an interview with influential African National Congress (ANC) organizer Victor Moche by documentary filmmaker Jihan El-Tahri. Moche had edited the magazine *Sechaba* from various places in exile, and spoke of the intricate "geographies of collaboration" that had made the work of the ANC possible, clandestinely and officially, across the continent and the world. And the exhibition began with yet another screening by Jihan El-Tahri, called *Flag Moments* that depicts the celebrations of independence across various states in Africa. And it includes a discussion by ANC spokesperson Jessie Duarte recalling the quarrels around the state dinner in 1994—an official event marking the end of apartheid. Here, it seems as if African anticolonial aspirations had finally been fulfilled throughout the continent, coming full circle from the first Pan-African congress in 1900. But this state dinner also symbolizes, just like the entire history of decolonization, that an exit from one frame is not necessarily a step onto new and blank territory.

The exhibition was expanded in scale at the Museum of Modern Art in Warsaw after the Berlin edition of "After Year Zero". The diversity of artistic media ranges from painting, with two works by Daniel Kojo Schrade from his *Afronauts* series, and photography including Kiluanji Kia Henda's triptych *Redefining the Power*, which plays with the power of representation in appropriating monumental leftovers of the colonial past. Different lines of flights toward a future that has to be invented, rather than awaited.

We would like to thank all the participants of the "Matters of Collaboration" workshops, and those who helped facilitate them. We are also deeply indebted to the artists and authors in this publication, as well as the teams at the Goethe-Institut in Algiers, Brussels, Dakar, and Johannesburg that supported and hosted us, and the teams and collaborators at both the Haus der Kulturen der Welt in Berlin and the Museum of Modern Art in Warsaw. Last but not least, our deepest thanks are reserved for Heidi Ballet, who has not only co-organized this endeavour with us from its outset, but has also been instrumental in gathering and organizing research.

The Universal Project

Anselm Franke

Although in what follows the meaning of "Europe" is not restricted to the geographical, let me begin with the immediate and physical: Far from being the medium of exchange it was once, the Mediterranean Sea that separates Europe from Africa geographically now constitutes a "solid" barrier,[1] a highly surveilled frontier, a zone paradoxically both of control and abandonment, gradually turning the rift between Europe and Africa into the grave of tens of thousands each year. The circumstances surrounding this mass grave are a continuation of what Frantz Fanon, speaking of African life under colonialism, described as "life at a discount [...] perpetually haunted by death."[2] It is at the same time symptomatic of a larger phenomenon and silence; of the narrative-imaginary vacuum, the incapacity to speak the present, the lack of a universal project and political alternative to transcend particular struggles and unite the minoritarian, to ever reach a critical mass powerful enough to dismantle the hegemonic language of "economic rationality", used chiefly by the techno-managerial discourse of the EU and its allies and collaborators.

When talking about the relation between Europe and Africa, we thus think of the Mediterranean paradox: a wall that is liquid. Yet this also means to emphasize that no separation ever succeeds to completely subjugate reality to its standards and grid: the real will always remain a liquid medium of unpredictable currents, and people will always follow these currents as much as go against them (they somehow reach their destination—this has been called the "autonomy of migration"). But on the other hand, the logic of division yields real, catastrophic effects.

Western modernity played out on the back of Africa through the slave trade and colonial subjugation. Not only did the allegedly universal values of the colonizer loose their currency in the colonies, this hypocrisy gradually added up to a momentous collective lie, whose spell has not yet been broken. The "idea of Africa" as a negative foil played as much a constitutive role for the rise of Europe as did the institution of the slave trade. The universal values of Western modernity, in Achille Mbembe's words, were built upon the "condition nègre"—the specter of modernity. Colonial modernity has been built on this scission, erecting its positive, universal face on its negative projection, Africa. What is being argued here is that this division, this "constitutive outside", this "underside" of European universalism, beleaguers the present. The way it stands today in the way of a future global imaginary, echoes, by way of inversion, the famous colonial imaginary, according to which Africa was not only lacking in the universal (Hegel), but constituted an outright barrier to modernity that "obstructs universal life" (Victor Hugo)[3] and hence needed to be overcome—which meant being taken possession of.

1 I borrow this expression from the project "Solid Sea" by the group Multiplicity, produced for documenta 11, Kassel, in 2002. See http://www.stafanoboeri.net/.

2 Frantz Fanon, *Towards the African Revolution*, trans. Hakoon Chevalier (New York: Grove Press, 1964), 173.

3 Victor Hugo, "Discours sur l'Afrique", in *Actes et Paroles, Vol. 4* (Paris, 2002).

The rift that separates Europe from Africa will forever remain a universal symbol for the colonial at large. It stands both for a separation and an entanglement. Modernity, here understood in the broadest sense as a discursive and ontological matrix (determining a certain set of choices), has been "from the start a north-south collaboration".[4] And after nominal independence, colonized subject and colonizer do not get rid of each other, but go separate ways. However, there are few languages for this entanglement and history of "collaboration", by which the modern world was produced in the colonial encounter, because most language does not reflect the entanglement, but enacts the separation. And the same counts for images, and hence for the cognitive maps we have of the world. There is little common ground for imagining a non-identitarian, global future today, because the former colonial hegemon and the former colonial subject do not share the same map or memory. And as long as there is no shared memory, there is no ground on which a horizon for a common future can be staked out.

"After Year Zero. Universal Imaginaries and Geographies of Collaboration" was a project dedicated to such a possible shared memory and its antinomies, crafted from the "countermemories that contest the colonial archive".[5] It held that this shared memory must be a memory of the liquid barrier—the Mediterranean today, the Middle Passage at the outset of modernity. And it held that in order to counter the phantasm of fixed and pure identities, it must be a memory of "geographies of collaboration"—embracing both the negative and the positive meanings of the term, the collaboration with an enemy, and the building of alliances, commonality betrayed, and constructed, and mobilizing them as device to unsettle divisions and clear boundaries in the topography of thought, particularly in a present in which, as Frantz Fanon had foreseen, the boundaries between colonizer and colonized are being increasingly blurred. Such memory then must be a memory of the *framework* that is shared, which both perpetrators and victims have in common, and in which both of them always have agency, the radical asymmetries of power notwithstanding. And it must be a memory of the rift itself, a memory that breaks open the separating line, and demonstrates that the two sides do not exist separately from each other, and that everything happens in this in-between, in translation, circulation, conflict and misunderstanding. This is arguably a memory that is painful, a memory that returns, again and again, to the scene of the crime. This return to colonial subjugation as primal scene of modernity is necessary in order to bring into view the continuities and ruptures pertaining to this framework, and how it conditions the set of choices in the present. How can the separation in memory, being so often intangible and a matter of implicit meanings and the workings of representation, become explicit, without inadvertently affirming, as happens so often, the very divides one seeks to bridge?

Perhaps never before has this division been so tangible as in the two major lines of division that have characterized the twentieth century:

4 Jean Comaroff and John L. Comaroff, *Theory of the South. Or, How Euro-America is Evolving Toward Africa* (Boulder: Paradigm Publishers, 2011), 30.

5 Kodwo Eshun, "Further Considerations on Afrofuturism", *The New Centennial Review* 3, no. 2 (Summer, 2003): 287–302.

the Iron Curtain on the one hand, and the Color Curtain on the other. The Color Curtain: This is how American novelist Richard Wright re-phrased W. E. B. Du Bois' original 1900 description of a racially divided world with the term "the color line", when he was reporting from the 1955 Bandung Conference, a quintessential event of decolonization tantamount for the birth of project that was the "Third World." The two divides have come to stand for two different frames of reference: the Iron Curtain determining the twentieth century historico-political understanding of the northern hemisphere with its closely related, yet competing universalisms, and the Color Curtain as the historico-political frame based on the experience of colonialism and racism, where European ideas of the civilizing mission and the white man's burden as universal history have been experienced, at best, as "negative universal history", since there is no universal history that "leads from savagery to humanitarianism, although one indubitably leads from the slingshot to the megaton bomb."[6]

Juxtaposing these two "divides" brings to the fore the degree to which they determined the new world order that emerged after 1945, characterized by the confrontation of Eastern and Western blocs and the Cold War on the one hand, and decolonization on the other. It is the dissonances, blind spots and omissions that emerge between these two different historical topographies and their respective universalist projections and ideologies, that inform current political fault lines and debates on universality. For the politico-historical topography of the northern hemisphere, fascism and Nazism have acted as the major benchmark, as the negative foil against which the postwar global order was to be constructed, as the bastion of civility cast against the barbarism that had spread in Germany, and was based either on liberal humanism, or socialism. For the individuals and nations that gathered in the Indonesian city of Bandung in 1955 to conceive of independence for more than 2 billion people of color, this reference to the crimes of fascism, too, was important, and yet far less central, since it was inscribed into a continuity of colonial and imperialist crimes:

> *There was no Nazi atrocity—concentration camps, wholesale maiming and murder, defilement of women, or ghastly blasphemy of childhood—which the Christian civilization of Europe had not long been practicing against colored folk in all parts of the world in the name of and for the defense of a Superior Race born to rule the world.*[7]

W. E. B. Du Bois had been among the organizers of several Pan-African Congresses and other events that ultimately prepared the path to Bandung, and eventually, to independence. He was present at the very first congress, organized by black West Indian barrister, Henry Sylvester-Williams, of Trinidad, practicing in London, and in 1945, he was honorable president of the Fifth Pan-African Congress that took place in Manchester. Bandung takes place at a crossroads set against the backdrop of the ideology of Pan-Asianism, which had been captured by Japanese imperialism and left a bloody trail in Asia, and a Pan-Africanism that had yet to unfold. Immediately after the end of the

6 Theodor W. Adorno, *Negative Dialektik* (Frankfurt am Main: Suhrkamp, 1966), 314.
7 W. E. B. Du Bois, *The World and Africa* (New York: International Publishers, 1947), 23.

Second World War, the fifth Pan-African Congress of Manchester called for the end of colonial rule in Africa. Its main organizer had been George Padmore, and its secretaries were Kwame Nkrumah, the founder of the Republic of Ghana that became independent in 1957, and Jomo Kenyatta, later president of Kenya.

For those congregating in Bandung, the year 1945 and its immediate aftermath showed for the second time that the promise of self-determination had been broken, even though over 1.2 million soldiers recruited from the African colonies had fought alongside the allied powers to liberate Germany and Italy, and millions more had been involved in Asia to defeat Japan. In 1919, it had been Woodrow Wilson's promise of the right of self-determination of all people that had been betrayed by the European powers at Versailles, and now, for a second time, the promise of self-determination invoked to secure the loyalty of colonial people in the war effort, as written in the Atlantic Charter drafted in 1941, in which the allies laid out the foundations of the postwar order. When Aimé Césaire declared in 1950 that "Europe is indefensible",[8] he put into words a widely felt sentiment, which had gradually taken shape ever since revolutionary France had turned its back on revolutionary Haiti, had swelled during the First World War, and which would now be further inflamed by the insistence of the imperial powers on keeping their colonial possessions, despite the foundation of the United Nations in 1945 and the new humanist rhetoric. Hence the promise of self-rule, after 1945, could only be redeemed through violence. The independence of the Philippines and India led the way into decolonization. But from Vietnam to Algeria to Kenya, it was brutal violence that has shaped the future postcolonial state and its relation to the former colonial power.

The Bandung Conference then brought together an alternative trajectory of world events organized by intellectuals and activists of color who had been subjected to forms of colonialism, racism, and oppression. The conference was a model of collaboration of the soon-to-be de-colonized "Third World," signaling an anticolonialism that, at the time, was ready to fully embrace modernization and national development. But it positioned itself both outside the "spheres of influence" and the ideological confrontation of the Iron Curtain. Bandung had laid the foundations of various organizations of Afro-Asian solidarity, which played a crucial role in asserting the sense of solidarity among colonized and formerly colonized people for the decade to come. In 1957, the Afro-Asian Peoples' Solidarity Conference (AAPSC) took place in Cairo—an organization that would also be called the "peoples' Bandung".

In the run-up to independence, it had above all been subjects of the French colonial empire, such as Aimé Césaire, that had indicted the false universalism of colonialism, and called for a different universalism: "My conception of the universal is that of a universal rich with the particular, rich with all the particulars, a deepening and a coexistence of the particulars."[9] The journal *Présence Africaine*, founded by Alioune Diop, became the focal point of a movement called Négritude, in which another prominent voice was Léopold Senghor from Senegal, who understood

8 Aimé Césaire, *Discourse sur le colonialisme* (Paris: Edition Présence Africaine, 1955), 32.
9 Ibid.

Négritude as a necessary step to a fuller universalism, as had already been predicted by Sartre in his 1948 introduction "Orphée Noir": Négritude is a negation in a dialectics that leads to a "civilisation de l'universel," which consists of a symbiosis of civilizations.[10]

By 1960, more than half of African nations had become independent. This was the so-called "Year of Africa." But the same year already saw a turning point in affairs, with the dawn of the Congo Crisis, and soon, the murder of Patrice Lumumba. In 1963, the first assassination of a president (Sylvanus Olympio of Togo) inaugurated what would become a long series of military coups across the continent. In the 1970s, the Portuguese revolution at home led to a last wave of independences, but soon after, the structural adjustment programs imposed by the IMF for debt relief would devastate already fragile economies. Kwame Nkrumah, the major proponent of Pan-Africanism, who would be deposed by coup himself in 1966, had warned in 1965 that formal sovereignty will not be enough to realize equality, and delineated what he called neo-colonialism, by means of which African states would economically remain subordinated.

Furthermore, the boundaries that postcolonial states had inherited as the borders of their national territory were based on colonial divisions and frontiers. From India to Africa, in different forms, this became one of the haunting questions of decolonization, as the newly independent states inherited the underside of the political tradition of the sovereign, territorial nation-state with a monopoly of violence, as formed in the Peace of Westphalia in Europe: The "minority question," which had left a monstrous trace of violence on the road to the naturalization of the European nations. The universality-in-the-sign-of-difference proclaimed in Bandung often fractured against the backdrop of the mobilization and construction of tradition and ethnicity as apparent demands to create the imaginary narrative-horizon of the nation.

For the European left, after (and insofar) it broke with Stalinism, these two frames of reference resulted in an internal fracture, with antifascism and anticolonialism becoming the benchmarks for two conflicting political horizons: the former gradually replacing anti-imperialism with antitotalitarianism and human rights, and, in seeking to uphold a progressive universalism that was attacked by the other side as Eurocentric, interventionist and neo-colonial, siding with the U.S.; the latter increasingly embracing cultural relativism while maintaining alliance with anticolonial and anti-imperialist movements despite their increasingly identitarian and fundamentalist nature. What, we may ask, is so compelling here that it makes such a choice inevitable? Can there not be, between totalitarianism and colonialism, a "shared sense of catastrophe"? On what grounds would we be able to refuse a choice between two evils? Does such a choice in itself not present a double bind, enacting a well-known pattern, under the long shadow of the "Manichean" logic of colonialism?

1945: The liberation from fascism, year zero for Germany and Europe (the phrase coined from the film by Roberto Rossellini). "After Year Zero" first materialized in the Haus der Kulturen der Welt (HKW), the for-

10 Jean-Paul Sartre, *Black Orpheus*, trans. S.W. Allen (Paris: Présence Africaine, 1976).

mer Congress Hall of West Berlin, built in 1957 as a gift from the U.S., and situated in sight of the Reichstag and the border with East Berlin. In this site, literally built in the wasteland of the centre of Berlin, the "year zero" represents the capitulation of the fascist Axis powers in 1945. The city symbolic of Nazi terror, Berlin, now became symbolic of the Iron Curtain.

"After Year Zero" set out to question the continuities and discontinuities in the world that emerged after 1945, the "hour zero" of Europe. Because along the lines outlined above, 1945 meant at least two different things: On the one hand, the broken promise of self-determination, on the other, the rescue and reconstruction of Western civilization. The price that had to be paid for the rescue of Western civilization after its collapse into terror and industrial genocide, concerned the gap between the rhetoric of universal values, and the racist practices of exclusion and disenfranchisement. The genocidal impulse of colonial culture, which drew its legitimacy from the equation of difference with inferiority, now had to be neutralized. This reconstruction was proclaimed against the immediate backdrop and the sheer monstrosity of the crimes of the Nazi regime. The violence of annihilating alterity, emblematized by the White Terror and Nazi genocide, was the immediate context that made it possible to establish a new architecture of global institutions, with "genocide", among other things, being recognized as a capital crime in international law, and with the refutation of racism in the hands of UNESCO on the grounds of a new scientific consensus on evolution and the legitimate and illegitimate usages of "race".

The "breakdown of civilization" at the heart of Europe thus had instigated a new universalism in international politics promoted by the West. But it presents a version of history that stays firmly within the European domain. Nazism, rather than being placed in a continuum with European imperial politics, then constitutes an absolute exception, a civilizational setback, within an otherwise progressive history of modern universality and emancipatory politics. At stake here are the narrative-historical *resources* through which identity, legitimacy, and consensus is (and can be) crafted, and the role that breaks and continuities in civilizational narratives have. By framing the Holocaust as absolute evil, the escape from which must be organized by civil society at all times and costs, post-Second World War universalism isolated the genocidal politics of Nazism and thus of colonial modernity. This allowed for "history" not only to remain firmly within the dominion of the West, but largely helped to secure the integrity and continuity of Western historical narrations of itself. Concessions were to be made: the West has had to recognize "the necessity of encountering different cultures by means other than the shock of domination and conquest".[11] The acceptance of "cultural difference" became a hinge in this operation, despite or because of its de-politicizing tendency, which could neutralize asymmetries of power in the sign of "culture".

The creation of the concept of "culture" as the valve of difference allowed the other domains of universality and hegemony to go unchallenged, among them, chiefly, the universality of modern science. What had previously been the narrative of the civilizing mission, now, was

11 Craig Owens, "The Discourse of Others, Feminists and Postmodernism," in *Beyond Recognition: Representation, Power, and Culture* (Berkeley: University of California Press, 1992), 166.

repackaged and objectified in a techno-scientific discourse of progress. It is from this that the discourse of "development" stems. This amended, inclusive self-narration of Western civilization now seemingly cleansed from its regressive, fascist side, however, has been erected upon the exclusion of colonial history, continuing the categorical exclusion of the colonial sphere as the suppressed foundation of Western universality.

For the non-European world, 1945 was the beginning of a new era in which the authority and legitimacy of Western dominance had been radically called into question. The Color Curtain and the Iron Curtain: these divisions invoke different versions of modernity, different lineages and continuities, which have to be brought into a relation with each other if we are to wrestle from them the horizons of universality. The Soviet bloc adhered to the narrative of class struggle as universal history. This yielded a dynamic, but ideologically closed conception and interpretation of world events. The West, on the other side, championed its universalism of capitalist liberties by trying to separate liberal humanism from the genocidal side of modern civilization. Any too close a connection between the Nazi-genocide and the histories of racism and colonial genocide had to be avoided: the monstrosity and particularity of the Holocaust had to be treated in isolation, as absolutely unique. This was also the precondition for the ability of the U.S. to position or fashion itself as an anticolonial power. The Holocaust acted as symbol of absolute evil from which any civil society must escape at all costs. This became the basis of universalist humanitarianism and its interventionist agenda in the second half of the century.

Colonialism and capitalist modernity had resulted in a de facto universalization. Two historical benchmarks epitomize this closing of the circle: In the late nineteenth century, European colonialism, after the scramble for Africa, had covered the last white spots of the map. And in the middle of the twentieth century, in the aftermath of the disasters of fascism and with the looming threat of a nuclear holocaust, it was the founding of the United Nations that was to fulfill the need for a global order, on the way to a global civil society It is above all the legacy of decolonization on which the fate of this civil society hinges. Currently, we are witnessing a slow awakening from the post-Cold War imagination of a borderless world, where the phantom-universality of capital has successfully hidden, at least in the dominant media-imaginary and if only for a brief moment, the proliferation of segregation and exclusion. It is the continuous working of the logic of division and identitarian inscription, which underlies the necessary return to a universalist politics in the present.

At the same time, it is a near-consensus now that any intellectual or political project that aspires to wholeness, universal validity or totality is grossly inadequate in the conditions of postcoloniality. And yet, there is a growing urgency for a project that is capable of bringing diverse struggles together, without, at the same time, eliminating their particularity and difference. In the past decades much progressive intellectual work in academies has been dedicated to the deconstruction of universals and truth-claims, to decentering of Western perspectives and the unspoken normative center, through which, as Slavoj Žižek has pointed out, the Western subject could claim a "direct, unmediated access to the dimension of universality."[12] This struggle against truth claims and the false universality of disciplinary and colonial culture has significantly altered the terrain of representation and thought. But as Dipesh Chakrabarty has said, "analysis does not make it go away."[13] The "provincialization" of Europe, too, knows two competing interpretations: one that seeks to relativize and particularize Eurocentrism, and another, which "underlines the need for an extension and displacement of the borders of theory beyond Europe, as a condition of possibility of an authentic universalization."[14] It has become increasingly important to probe the possibilities of such an extension. After decades in which intellectual work has insisted on the critique of hidden universalist assumptions—the need to accommodate difference and incommensurability, and to tell other stories—there is a sense that what had once been an invitation had perhaps too quickly and prematurely turned into a conclusion, and that the place previously occupied by universal signifiers had been abandoned too quickly, without insisting that it is from the "other story" that the universal dimension needs to be rebuilt. According to Mbembe, "Black criticism has long argued that, in their drive for sovereign mastery over the world, Western powers mask a particularism that is characteristically formulated in terms of universalist values. Yet it is a universalism that is premised on a racist conception of what constitutes the human."[15] It seems certain that abandoning the quest for what Immanuel Wallerstein has called the unfulfilled promise of a truly "universal universalism"[16] today, will only further fuel the disintegration into minoritarian positions, their commercialization or worse, essentialist identity politics, and weaken the capacity of global struggles to establish common ground.

Rather than assuming the year zero of 1945 to be a radical break, "After Year Zero" attempted to explore the "tacit but basically unmodified racial hierarchy" that "is still being articulated inside all the belligerent chatter about culture and civilization that followed on from Cold War geo-political formulations."[17] It is precisely because these hierarchies have become implicit that it is necessary to address the question of universality—as a means to making the frames and resources explicit. "After Year Zero" therefore turned to the histories of decolonization, to the Black Radical Tradition, and the emergence of the Third World. The project treated these histories in a partial and speculative manner: What mattered to us was not an encyclopedic treatment of certain histories, which is in better hands elsewhere. We aimed at challenging frames and working on the picture of history and the topographies of thought, against the backdrop of a cosmopolitan future being lost to the phantom universality of capitalism and its continuing logic of division: the partisan today is often

12 Slavoj Žižek, *Ein Plädoyer für die Intoleranz*, trans. Andreas Leopold Hofbauer (Wien: Pasagen Verlag, 2009), 59.

13 Dipesh Chakrabarty, "Postcoloniality and the Artifice of History: Who Speaks for 'Indian' Pasts?" in *Representations*, no. 37 [Special Issue: *Imperial Fantasies and Postcolonial Histories*] (Winter, 1992): 1–26; 2.

14 Matthieu Renault, "The Idea of Muslim National Communism: On Mirsaid Sultan-Galiev", *Viewpoint magazine*, March 23, 2015, http://www.viewpointmag.com/.

15 Achille Mbembe, "Faces of Freedom, Jewish and Black Experiences", *The Wiser Review*, July 2004.

16 Immanuel Wallerstein, *European Universalism: The Rhetoric of Power* (New York: New Press, 2006).

17 Paul Gilroy, "Postcolonialism and Cosmopolitanism: Towards a World Understanding of Fascism and Europe's Colonial Crimes", in *After Cosmopolitanism*, eds. Rosi Braidotti, Patrick Hanafin, and Bolette B. Blaagaard (London: Routledge), 112.

channeled into ethnic and other identitarian forms, in which the histories of terror continue to write themselves.

And this logic of division, certainly, has been a defining factor in the fate of anticolonialism and the postcolonial. Yet for precisely this reason, it is also the place, metaphorically, from which a universalist imaginary can and must be articulated. Universality ought not to be disavowed, but must be constructed on different grounds. "Universal history matters", says Susan Buck-Morss in her much discussed treaty on Hegel and Haiti,[18] pointing to the repressed colonial dimension of the Enlightenment and its root metaphor, slavery. Not only did she point to constitutional and continuous repression of this dimension in European collective memory and historiography, at a moment when, to name but one example, a revisionist new national law has been enforced in France prescribing teachers to present the former colonial presence of France, particularly in North Africa, as positive and progressive; she also expresses a growing sentiment with regards to a renewed importance of universality (without, however, making quite explicit to what ends). Any such renewed claim to the universal, rather than being a system of positive values, must be measured by its exclusions. It must be based on a "shared sense of catastrophe", and an awareness of the entanglement—a shared awareness, of the degree to which this matrix, as Fred Moten and Stefano Harney point out (following Aimé Césaire), harms and dehumanizes not only the victim, but the perpetrator alike.[19] It is in this sense of a quest for a common ground that Achille Mbembe has recently referred to the "claims for a possible universality"[20] as common claims, disavowing the idea of a disentanglement of a non-European from European thought.

Exhibitions, especially the encyclopedic modern museum, have often been accused of producing an "illusion of full identity", of full knowability, following an age-old equation according to which, in Western history, knowledge and representation are equated with objectification and mastery. Thus exhibitions often turn history itself into a thing. A complex set of relations is reified and encounters us as objectified phantasm. Against this power of reification stands the relational, dialogic power of an art that does pacify the inevitable conflict of being part of intolerable structures through "universal" images, representing a common but empty set of "human" experience. The work that had been brought into the constellation of *"After Year Zero,"* then, did not seek reconciliation or stabilization. Rather, they seek to open up the processes of meaning-making towards their other side: the side of the relational truths of embodied history. The "unconscious" of history is then exteriorized and becomes both sensuous and material. Time is turned into space: history here becomes a diagram of structural conditions, transformative forces, and lived relations. An exhibition then is like a mental topography, a landscape of emotions and thoughts, and of their structural underpinnings and narratives.

18 Susan Buck-Morss, *Hegel, Haiti, and Universal History* (Pittsburg: University of Pittsburg Press, 2009).

19 Fred Moten and Stefano Harney, *The Undercommons. Fugitive Planning & Black Study* (Wivenhoe: Minor Compositions, 2013).

20 "Interview with Achille Mbembe," *Transversal, European Institute for Progressive Cultural Policy*, issue 10, 2013, http://www.eipcp.net/.

Such exhibitions focus not on the dead object and the representation of the historical fact, but on the life of forms. They renounce dry formalism—empty universals and the ossified aspects of language—and seek to make contact with the struggle that brought about a particular form, its living grounds. Forms are alive when their inert capacity to make a difference becomes the active foundation for consciousness that exists in tension and non-identity with the world. It is the life of forms that makes possible a particular form of life. This holds for all human culture: we do not only make our media, but our media also make us. Like recursive figures in drawing, this is the backdrop against which figuration takes place.

In exhibitions, such "figuration" refers to the making and remaking of collectives. Exhibitions are testing grounds for different forms of "being-with", projections of possible communities and collectives. The backdrop or "ground" here refers to the available cultural resources and their ability to reflect a common experience, to construct a common language, to provide common ground.

Universal Pictures: A Dialogue between a Future People from the Desert

Annett Busch

During the film, when we tied Aaron, I thought of Lumumba. And when Moses said: "Let him free!" we no longer see Aaron (he is already off-screen), we de-framed him during this last sentence ("Für seine Freiheit, dass es ein Volk werde" [For their liberty that they become a people]), in order to re-frame Moses. And Moses destroys Aaron, but, in doing so—and this seems obvious, at least I hope so—Moses destroys himself, although he is right in sending the people back into the desert, adding: "In der Wüste seid ihr unüberwindlich und werdet das Ziel erreichen" [In the desert you are invincible and will achieve the goal].
—Jean-Marie Straub[1]

"Non-reconciliation is also a way of making and producing films. It is the stubborn refusal of all the forces of homogenization," wrote the film critic Serge Daney in 1977 in *Cahiers du Cinema*[2] on the Paris release of the film *Moses und Aaron* from Jean-Marie Straub und Danièle Huillet. Twenty years after 1945, *Nicht Versöhnt oder Es hilft nur Gewalt, wo Gewalt herrscht*, a radically accentuated treatment of Heinrich Böll's *Billiard um Halbzehn* produced in 1965, is the filmmakers' harshest ever protest against the falsity of a presumed, longed-for Year Zero.

Between the ostensibly abrupt cutting of images in high-contrast black-and-white, which are not assembled according to the rules of classical filmic continuity which expends much effort in making the cuts as seamless as possible, a historical continuity emerges, namely that of the collaborators, profiteers, and co-perpetrators of the Nazi regime who continue their work in the new Federal Republic.

"Non-reconciliation: that is, neither the union nor the divorce, but their double possibility."[3] This dialectical tension finds its expression as an intractable political stance in every successive Straub-Huillet film, as a "resistance against a false aesthetic."[4] The programming of a double feature composed of *Moses und Aaron* (1974) and *Ceddo* (1977) from Ousmane Sembène as the opener for a conference accompanying the exhibition "After Year Zero" in Berlin, was the product of a vague but sustained intuition that the meeting of these two films could produce a third thing: Something new, something different. And so it did. The task was to track down exactly what it was that unfolded over a period of more than four hours, in which spaces, sounds, and images entered into a new relationship. Two sources could be of assistance here. Firstly Serge

1 Jean-Marie Straub and Danièle Huillet, "Conversation avec Jean-Marie Straub et Danièle Huillet (Moise et Aaron). Par Jacques Bontemps, Pascal Bonitzer et Serge Daney", *Cahiers du Cinema*, no. 258/259, (1975): 8.

2 Serge Daney, *A Tomb for the Eye (Straubian pedagogy)*. http://www.sergedaney.blogspot.no.

3 Ibid.

4 Ute Holl, *Der Moses Komplex—Politik der Töne, Politik der Bilder* (Zurich/Berlin: diaphanes, 2014), 57.

Daney's critique of the film *Ceddo* in which he refers to *Moses und Aaron*—if only in parentheses:

> *Thus the people in* Ceddo *lose their freedom (the village), their lives (the king), their blinders (the princess.) But there is worse.* Ceddo *is the story of a putsch, with the intrusion of religion into politics (as in* Moses und Aaron, *for instance) and the transition from one type of power to another. But it is also the story of a right which is lost: the right to speak. A right but also a duty, a duty but also a pleasure, a game.*[5]

And secondly a book published a few weeks ago, *The Moses Complex* from the media analyst Ute Holl, in which she undertakes an extrapolation of the potency of the Schönberg opera, and above all, the films of Straub and Huillet, into the present.

Moses und Aaron and *Ceddo*, two films, two peoples at a turning point where power is renegotiated and time is set to zero. "*Ceddo* is a Pulaar word that designates in one way or another those who resist slavery. That means those who 'conserve the tradition.' The Ceddo are 'the people of refusal.'"[6] The people in *Moses und Aaron* are confronted by a similar and yet completely different problem. It is the abstractly maintained choreography of the spoken positions, the appeal, the invocation in the midst of a barren landscape, which connects the two films, above all in their direct confrontation. The people remain on the sidelines as a choir, challenged to make a decision between Moses and Aaron in their bids for leadership. The people have lost their patience, they call for an understandable, perhaps all too easy answer. Moses refuses to treat the people as fools. "They must grasp the thought", said Moses, the "ineffable, ambiguous thought", and this thought must not be falsified, for example, by the image. However, Moses lacks the words. He needs a mouthpiece, a translator, Aaron—and every translation is also a falsification and an appropriation. "The problem of advocacy disrupts the exodus and makes the people intractable. Everyone counts. However, no one speaks for themselves."[7]

> *If the imam wins, it is not because he is militarily stronger, it is because he introduces an element which will cause the traditional African power structure to implode. And this element is a book, a book which is recited: the Koran. Between the beginning and the end of the story told by Ceddo, what has changed is the status of speech.*[8]

The preparations for the exhibition "After Year Zero" were accompanied by the red thread of a debate, namely of confronting, once again, the cumbersome concept of universalism, rejected so many times in the past: To erect universality, the process of universalization, criteria of general validity, as both requirement and challenge, as a means to avoid the trap of cultivating geo-cultural niches. Who lays claim to the title of universality, and from where? Dialectical tensions

5 Serge Daney, "Ceddo", originally published in *La Rampe*. http://home.earthlink.net/~steevee/Daney_ceddo.html.

6 Josie Fanon, "In the Name of Tolerance: A Meeting with Ousmane Sembène", in *Ousmane Sembene: Interviews*, eds. Annett Busch and Max Annas (Jackson: University Press of Mississippi, 2008), 114.

7 Holl, *Der Moses Komplex*, 31.

8 Daney, "Ceddo".

emerge between distancing and laying claim, between abstract and concrete. How does the concrete manifest itself in abstraction and an abstract level in the concrete image? What kind of images are these? Does universalization describe a process of detachment from social and local contexts, or does it point instead to the viewers' limited powers of observation? Finding a language for that within the image which is not readable, but visible and audible, requires translation.

The question of translation is posed in a number of ways. From the beginning it has accompanied every cinema which one has become accustomed to call "African cinema", a cinema which was far more present as text, description, and film criticism, than as film actually on the screen. In Europe and the U.S. it has primarily generated politically motivated texts, often in harmony with a language of solidarity in support of the liberation movements in the Third World. These texts have, if at all, translated the content, and accordingly, reduced the films to their political or emancipatory content and, albeit with good intentions, promoted niche formation and the perception of otherness. At the same time the young cinema of the African continent was characterized by distancing gestures, employed as a means of countering colonial and postcolonial image politics with something of its own, of whatever nature. There are very few film critics, for example Serge Daney, who, long before the term "World Cinema" was coined, identified and established unexpected connections on the formal level, retrieving African and Latin American cinema or Asian cinema from the periphery which, above all, is determined by production conditions—inscribing it into the center of a universal medium. Cinema, pure and simple, with all its variety and difference, its genres and division of labor:

> *Every "form" is a face looking at us (...) And only the one who has been struck early enough by formal violence will end up realizing—at the end of his life—how this violence is also "content". And the moment will always come early enough for him to die cured, having traded the enigma of singular figures of his history for the banalities of a "cinema-mirror-of-society" and other serious questions with no answers. The form is desire; the content is only the background when we are gone.*[9]

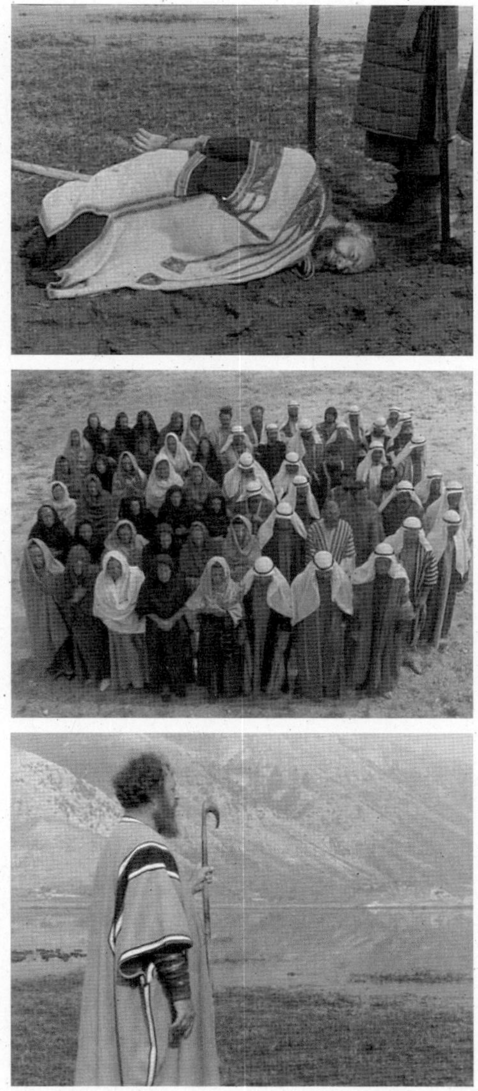

Jean-Marie Straub and Danièle Huillet, detail from—*Moses und Aaron,* 1974.

The potential universality of the medium consists in the assumption that the production of sound and image is based on a series of decisions, the choice of lens, the framing, original sound (or not), soundtrack, diegetic or extra-diegetic music. The decision making processes and their implications may be as diverse as cinema itself, and are often confused with the category of the "gaze" (a term from literature[10]), and the associated vehement critique. There is

9 "Serge Daney, The Tracking Shot in Kapo," *Senses of Cinema.* http://www.sensesofcinema.com. The article was first published in *Trafic,* no. 4 (P.O.L. Editions, 1992).

10 Claire Denis in a film seminar in Munich, Filmmuseum 2009.

virtually no one that has understood the relationship between sound and image, noise, speech, and music as an ethical question with such sustained rigor as the filmmakers Jean-Marie Straub und Danièle Huillet. "When we wrack our brains for months at a time in order to discover how to frame Moses in the third act, questioning this ten times over, then we ask ourselves what does the eye mean in this context? Nothing!", stated Danièle Huillet in an interview.[11] For Daney the question of the position of the camera is also connected with the question: What is an antifascist image? It is necessarily a created image, an image that is not destined to exist, which constitutes the opposite of images of power, which is directed at the power and not at the victim; power is also inscribed in this position. The retrospectively created image, which raises an objection to history and the writing of history is not documentary and not from the archive.

Ousmane Sembène and Jean-Marie Straub and Danièle Huillet have created historical images, on the level of image and tone. The bodies are in dispute with the voice and the song. The voice remains present, even when its body is not visible, it remains in contradiction, as sound, song, even when the words are virtually unintelligible, as in the case of *Moses und Aaron*. A negotiation is not articulated through speech, the spoken word, but through the presence of voice, volume, and resonating body. With Straub and Huillet it is Schoenberg, with Ousmane Sembène it is Manu Dibango who adds an extra instance to the historical layers. The use of xylophone, saxophone, and electric guitar catapults the people, who are in the process of being enslaved and disempowered, into a future present, and past, of the 1970s. Schoenberg, in the case of Straub and Huillet, adds, with his twelve tones in their egalitarian arrangement, a sensitive openness to Moses' tenacious efforts to preserve the complexity of thought, together with a manifest play of clouds filmed in an amphitheatre in Abruzzi. What can be uttered, thought, shown? What kind of image is capable of recording and reflecting the complexity of a thought? In *Ceddo* images and masks constitute a threat as they stand for reproduction: a multitude of images, many gods, and a people that claim its autonomy—at least for a short time—through images which it has created itself. While Moses sings against the simplification generated by the image, the golden calf, light, wind, and clouds which will never abide by his laws, drone, framed by a simple, static, and simultaneously moving image, embedded in a natural spectacle. Moses, wracked with self doubt, must enforce the laws of his tablets, but will never issue the law as a command. While in *Ceddo* the prohibition of images by the Imam is issued as an order, culminating in the practice of repetition and recitation.

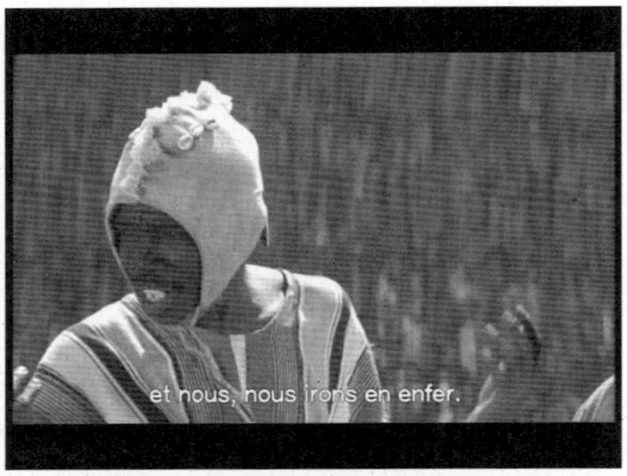

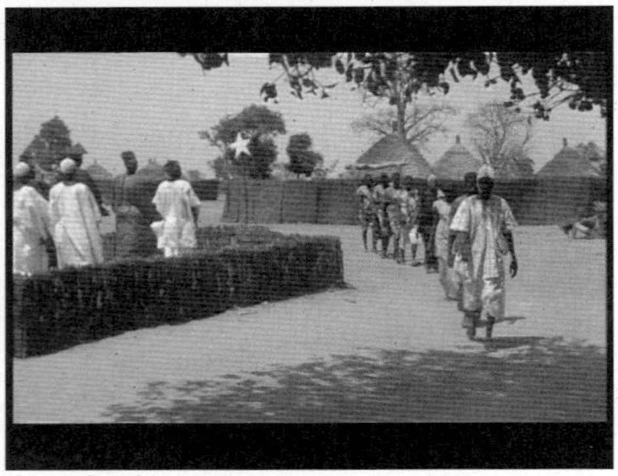

Ousmane Sembène, detail from—*Ceddo*, 1977.

In the case of both Sembène and Straub and Huillet, the connection to the local is established through the locality, the precise selection of the

11 Straub and Huillet, "Conversation avec Jean-Marie et Danièle Huillet (*Moise et Aaron*). Par Jacques Bontemps, Pascal Bonitzer et Serge Daney" *Cahiers du Cinema,* no.258/259, (1975).

film location (as well as the manner of speech). In this sense, abstraction works against representation, thus establishing a common basis within which to rediscover itself in the image. Showing a village, a non-urban piece of land, not in order to emphasize difference, nor to formulate the theme of a sociological question in relation to the city, but as a rural landscape understood as a theatrical setting that fades out the diversity of the urban, while simultaneously speaking of concrete conditions. By these means the history of a village becomes universal, as a chamber play, which with its specific micropolitics points to macropolitics, without investing a supposedly universal, global politics with general validity. It remains a relationship of forces that acts in variety of directions, and accordingly, must be negated or laid claim to.

Ceddo and *Moses und Aaron*, produced at virtually the same time in the mid-1970s, at a time when the French film magazine, *Cahiers du Cinema*, in the spirit of political radicalization, enforced a prohibition on images for a number of years, merely adorning its cover with titles and text, still belong to a "world with cinema," as Serge Daney formulated it in *Tracking Shot of Capo*. In distinction to a "world of television,"

> *...where, otherness having more or less disappeared, there are no good or bad ways to manipulate images. These are no longer "images of another" but images among others in the market of brand images. And this world that no longer revolts me is precisely the world "without cinema," meaning without this sense of belonging to humanity through a supplementary country called cinema. And then I see clearly why I have adopted cinema: so it could adopt me in return. So it could teach me to tirelessly touch with my gaze the distance from me at which the other begins.*[12]

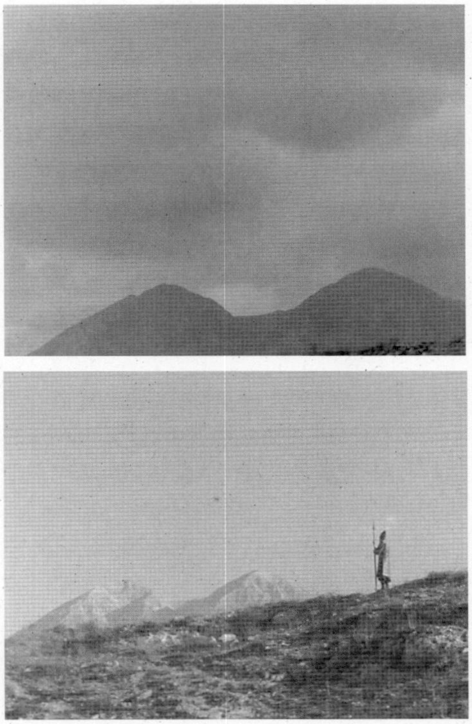

Jean-Marie Straub and Danièle Huillet, detail from—*Moses und Aaron,* 1974.

Ute Holle wrote a book about one film, *Moses und Aaron*, which no longer exists in the form in which she remembers it as, a 35 mm copy.

> *...I was recently in the Regenbogenkino in order to "introduce" 2 of Straub's films (without which they can't be understood). Unfortunately there was no one under 55 there! (...) In Kassel there were around 100 people in the cinema watching Straub from 9:00 pm to 3:00 am. The copy of* Moses und Aaron *was almost completely red. For many of them the dedication to Holger Meins was more important than anything else...*[13]

So wrote Harun Farocki on October 31, 2012 in an e-mail to Ute Holl. Both films have long been available on DVD and probably have more viewers than ever before—and that is good. However, what is lost is a background noise. Together with Straub, Holl writes of two central ideas—decision and nomadic life:

> *The cloud proves to be a structure reciprocal to the burning bush. Under no circumstances must it become a sign, as Aaron wants it*

12 Daney, *"Tracking Shot of Kapo."*
13 Holl, *Der Moses Komplex*, 346.

to be: "a sign for the people" (act II, time code 1089–90), instead, as Moses calls for, it must remain in the recursive openness of the meteorological, thermodynamic temporality of becoming, beyond the image, like the desert. Then comes the dual crossing: Cut and camera angle. "L'idee de Moise, c'est que la traversée du désert est sans fin. C'est l'idee du nomadisme, tout simplement."[14]

The becoming-universal of an image as the visual manifestation of a sophisticated, expended fabrication—as resistance against communication.[15]

14 Holl, *Der Moses Komplex*, 341.

15 Gilles Deleuze, "Having an Idea in Cinema (On the Cinema of Straub-Huillet)," in *Deleuze and Guattari—New Mappings in Politics, Philosophy and Culture*, eds. Eleanor Kaufman and Kevin Jon Heller (Minneapolis: University of Minnesota Press, 1988). See also: http://www.ofapeoplewhoaremissing.net.

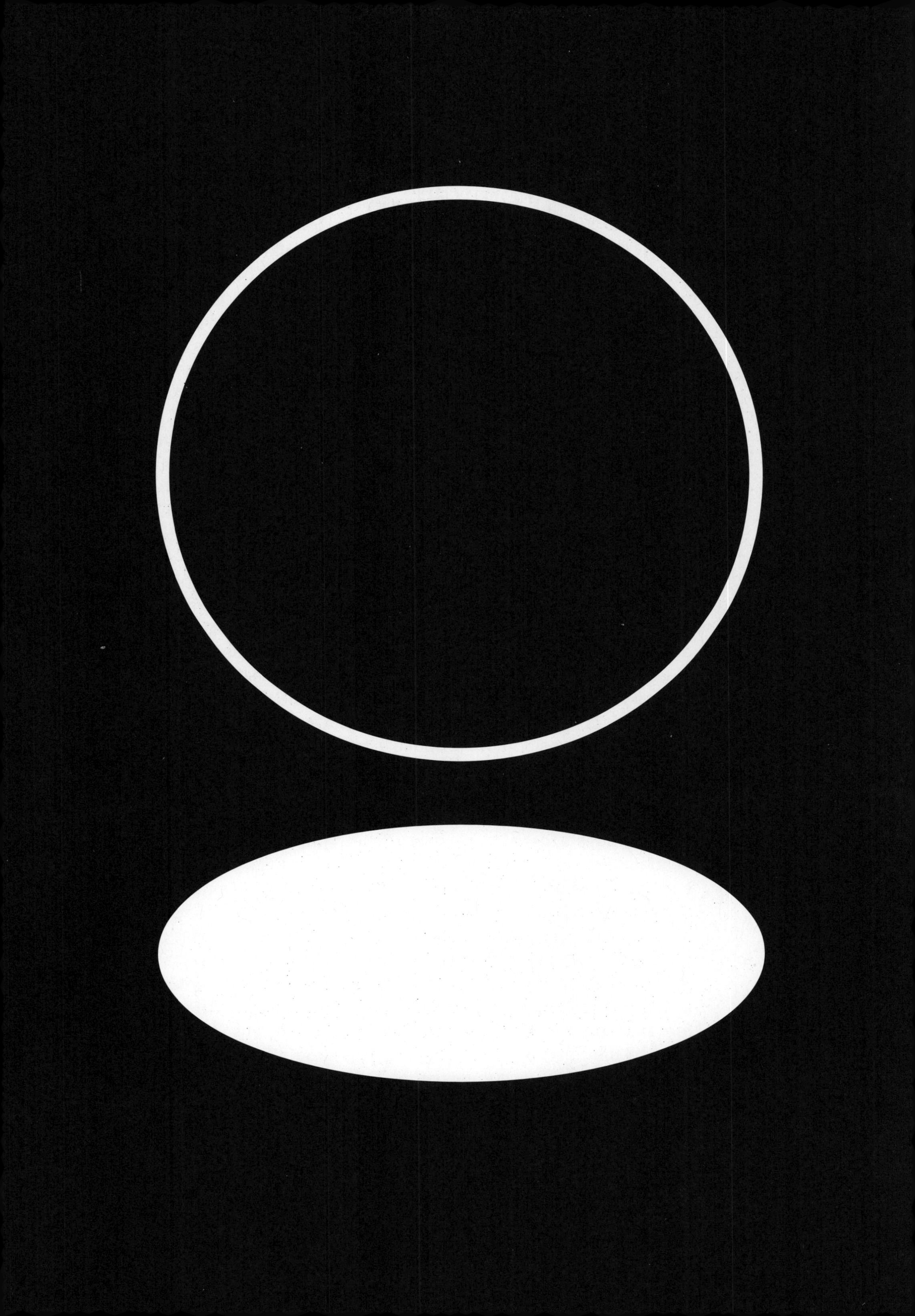

Négritude as a Concept of Collaboration?[1]

John Akomfrah

Why Négritude? Before I answer this question allow me to first offer two images from two of my favorite films, which might help to situate my argument in relation to Négritude. The first is from David Lean's great film *Doctor Zhivago* (1965). Yuri Zhivago (Omar Sharif) returns to the house that used to belong to the family. When he arrives there is a kind of "inappropriate presence" in the house as the property had been commandeered by the *Soviet*, the council in that region, and turned into tenements. As the commissar approaches Zhivago he states, "Comrade, your house is too large for one family and it has been taken over, now all these families are living in it." And Zhivago, who does not retaliate, replies, "Yes, yes ..." The commissar asks Zhivago what he thinks of the situation. Zhivago begins, "I think it is ..." but there is a silence before he continues—and this silence is very important to what I am about to say—"I think it is ... just." In the English language the word "just" belongs on the side of legal-speak, so Yuri Zhivago is not saying that he thinks it is right, because right would involve him being in agreement with it, he is saying simply that the situation is "just." Secondly, "just" suggests that, given the imperative of the moment, it was the only answer to give: it is "just" that the *Soviet* should take the family house, but not because he agrees with what has happened, not because he wants it to happen, but because it is "just." Thirdly, "just" suggests a certain emotional relationship to the proposition: we propose to take your house, what do you have to say about it? And the emotional relation is one of distant proximity: Zhivago seems to say that I agree that this must happen, but I am not in agreement emotionally, so I will stand aside and offer you a statement which suggests that at least I give you my consent, if indeed consent was needed; but since consent wasn't needed because you've gone ahead anyway, I give you my consent after the fact, which is simply to say it is something you must do, you have done it, and I will go along with it.

The reason I want to suggest to you this visual idea of "distant proximity" in relation to Négritude is because Négritude is a historical fact, a series of propositions: the fact is that even if I do not share all of its precepts and suppositions it still has a presence, which means therefore that I must at least concede to that presence. This is something that goes to the heart of the critique of Négritude, because at its heart the critique of Négritude suggests that it does not have a presence. My dispute is with the denial of presence rather than with an acceptance of Négritude. That is the first image.

The second image is from the opening scene of Andrei Tarkovsky's *The Mirror* (1975). A man whose identity is unclear, who the viewer has not yet met and doesn't see again, walks up to a woman, who the viewer

1 This text is an edited transcript of a talk given as part of the workshop series "Matters of Collaboration," (http://mattersofcollaboration.net/) held at the Goethe-Institut, Algiers on June 22, 2012, organized and funded in collaboration with the Goethe-Institut, Brussels

sees occasionally, but whose status in the film is uncertain: is she the mother of the character or not? It's not clear for at least half of the film, but it slowly becomes clear that, yes, she is the mother, the maternal character in this film. She is sitting at the edge of a forest near where she lives, when the man walks up to her and asks her whether she knows how he can get to such-and-such a place. The scene is an impossible one, however, because it doesn't appear to be the sort of place where one could get lost—it looks like a field, and anyone who has managed to navigate a pathway through it, one thinks, can't possibly be "lost." Anyway, the point is that the scene clearly has been set up in order to illustrate an idea. And the idea is simply this: a man walks up to a woman to ask her directions and the woman replies that she doesn't know. He walks away, and as he is walking away a wind, which comes from right of frame and crosses the frame, disperses the grass very beautifully. So the wind gets up and then passes, the man stops and turns around, and he turns around in such a way as if to suggest that he knows something has happened, but he can't see what has happened. He turns around to acknowledge the presence of something, but it is clear from the way in which the man stops, the length of time, the duration of his stillness, and the manner in which he turns around, that Tarkovsky is suggesting the presence of something more than just the wind. It is the suggestion, I am proposing, of the phantom; these unseen guests that are said to haunt landscapes, of which we are aware and know that they are around, but we don't necessarily see them. We feel their presence, but we don't see them. Négritude for me is one of those phantoms.

The presence of a phantom in West Africa suggests inappropriateness—that the burial of the deceased has not been performed appropriately, maybe somebody did not pour the right water or make the correct eulogy, something has been done inappropriately. This is the only way that phantoms in West Africa are able to "live" and remain in the netherworld between the living and the dead: they walk among the living because somebody did not respect the formalities and the rituals of exorcising the dead from the space of the living.

I want to commandeer, or if you like, steal this metaphor to talk about Négritude, and argue that it was not buried appropriately. The problem of Négritude for people of my generation, I'm talking about the people who came of age in the 1970s, is simply this: when we started taking notice of the concept of Négritude the movement apparently had already been "superseded" and outlived its use value; Négritude was no more, and yet it was clear to me and to others that Négritude was still the unseen guest at several tables, because many of the assumptions of Négritude continued to be part of discussions even though it was not named as such. For me, Négritude has to be one, at least one of the inescapable routes we take, precisely because we are talking about collaboration. Négritude is one of the collaborations in the African political imaginary that suggests to me an affinity with what we are trying to do. But I want to put that aside for a moment and concentrate first on the burial of Négritude and then you will see what I mean.

When the first of Négritude's founding documents, the collection of poetry, was published in 1948, the movement died one of its three deaths.

Many writers have suggested that Négritude's first death was that proposed affectionately by French philosopher-writer Jean-Paul Sartre, who was responsible for writing the introduction to this first Négritude collection. Imagine that the person asked to write the introduction for the book actually puts it to death. Sartre's statement in his introduction was to become one of the key critiques of Négritude—it was incorrect, but nonetheless stuck. The critique by Sartre stated that Négritude was necessary for a moment in time and that it was specifically because Négritude was necessary that it spoke in a language Sartre coined "anti-racist racism." Négritude, Sartre argued, was both necessary and possible to overcome, once its key fault was corrected. The key fault of Négritude according to Sartre was its essentialism. Négritude was essentialist because it tried to suggest that there was an essence to Africanity. Of course this is wrong, because we all know there is no essence to anybody, but that is the whole point of antiracism according to Sartre. So in 1948, Sartre accepted Négritude intellectually, but predicted that in time Négritude would go away, or at least the presuppositions of Négritude would go away. This was the first critique, which worked on the basis that Négritude was essentialist.

The most recent critique of Négritude—and as far as I'm concerned one of the most interesting aspects among all the critiques of this aesthetic, political, and cultural movement—starts on the basis of a compliment, but one in the form of what is known in English as "damning praise," which in fact is equivalent to the kiss of death. This critique, offered by the Créolité group, asserts: we accept the premise that in the beginning Négritude allowed the marriage between Europe and Africa to take place. However, as a result of that marriage, Creolization has taken place and we have transcended and moved beyond Négritude. We have become Creole and as we have become Creole we don't need Négritude, particularly if Négritude is speaking of an "essence." So Négritude was dismissed by the Créolité group for its lack of hybridity: they viewed it in terms of one fixed, unified bloc that had met another unified bloc, so that on the one hand there was European identity and then on the other Négritude. Now the time had come for these two blocs to come together to create the new world: voilà, goodbye Négritude, welcome Créolité. Négritude was not hybrid enough.

The third critique actually is probably more familiar to many of us: it is not strictly speaking a critique as such, and it might be seen as kind of an insult to call it one at all. It's a sort of literary slight-of-hand, a means of dismissal by way of a snigger. The English, for example, are very good at deploying this sort of put-down, whereby the suppressed laugh means that one can dismiss something without necessarily having to say why one is dismissing it. And that critique, if one can call it that, starts with the Nigerian writer Wole Soyinka's very famous phrase that, as "A tiger does not proclaim its tigritude", why then do we, of African descent, need Négritude? I perceive this as a forced universalist critique of universalism, because the assumption behind what Soyinka is saying is this: look, it is self-evident that we are all human beings whether black or white, it is self-evident that the African personality is a human personality, so why do we need to spell it out? One can hear the sneer behind the assertion that there is no need to spell it out because it is self-evident. Well, I would argue that there are very many people who might want to dispute that snigger and I am one of them, because I do not agree that it is at all self-evident that we are all seen as human beings. Certainly if the self-evidence behind that statement was once true then it was only historically accurate for a very short time. Bear in mind that Soyinka makes the tigritude comment in around 1967 or 1968, and that only around two years before that the Voting Rights Act had been passed in America, which was seen as the last piece of the jigsaw in the acceptance of the African diaspora as part of the human family because until 1965 that had not been obvious at all. In fact, therefore, for most people of the diaspora, especially in the American context, it was not self-evident at all that they were viewed as human beings. Legally, juridically, the black diaspora was not seen as part of the human race, because if you are seen as a human being you hold naturally conferred rights, including the right to vote, etc., but before August 6, 1965 blacks in the U.S. did not have those rights. So I dispute the extent to which first, this "self-evidence" was always the case or second, the extent to which this "self-evidence" was universal, i.e. apparent to everybody all of the time. Soyinka was constructing a historically specific argument in order to damn something which, even by then, was three decades old.

Now to return to the question, why Négritude? In 1969, at the Pan-African Conference held in Algiers, the Beninese philosopher Stanislas Adotevi voiced another critique of Négritude, this one built on the basis that Négritude did not sufficiently account for change. Claiming that Négritude was too conservative, Adotevi argued that it was the extent to which Négritude stressed the "African" that rendered it unable to stress other sociopolitical issues such as class, and so on. In other words he was saying that Négritude was too politically conservative, that is, neither socialist nor Marxist, and as it was not Marxist it was therefore unacceptable. In 1969 this was a very persuasive argument, all one had to do was criticize something for not being Marxist and then it was up to the accused to spell out where there might be an affinity between their argument and Marxism, because otherwise they were damned. Adotevi's stance therefore is perfectly sensible for the time, a time when Marxism was one of the key paradigms and all the radical thinkers in Africa felt they had to have a relationship with it. In some ways Marxism's relationship to contemporary Africa and African thought is probably similar to the relationship that Négritude had once had with the Africa of the time: slightly anachronistic and a telling presence, but not a central one, and by no means a defining paradigm for political discourse in Africa.

I believe that a number of the critiques of Négritude were incorrectly prescribing a death; in fact, having already made a misdiagnosis they were falsely describing a death. The documents relating to Négritude make this clear when understood in context. In 1944, as the world became aware that Europe was caught up in the throes of barbarism, a certain self-immolation was taking place in Europe. A group of young men, some of whom were part of that war effort, Léopold Sedar Senghor for instance, decided that they would secede from the universalist project. Thus it was a highly conscious decision to take up a position vis-à-vis the ongoing political developments in Europe. The secession was a planned distancing: in his long poem *Return to the Native Land* (1947), Aimé Césaire states very clearly that we are moving away from you (Europe) and your barbarism, you (Europe) and your killings. Négritude, first and foremost, was a set of accusations against the universalist project, which said: we do not take your version of universalism seriously; we do not take it seriously because it is fraud; the rhetoric for your version of universalism clearly has not included everybody. Remember, this is six months before the end of the Second World War, just before it was announced that six million people had been gassed in concentration camps in Europe: were these people not human beings? And why would a person who is part of the minority not very consciously and very deliberately say to Europe, I really don't want to be part of your game, I want to play somewhere else. Why not, in 1945?

That is one element of the context for Négritude, but two other very interesting points within the literature about the death of Négritude are worth noting. One relates to something I have already mentioned and that is the way in which Négritude became a collaborative project between different parts of the African world, nuanced, endlessly returned to, changed to suit circumstances, and which concerns a comment Césaire made in 1977. Many of the documents on Négritude suggest exactly this sense of evolution, whereby every time these radical thinkers opened their mouths they demonstrated how they were trying to take account of what was happening around them, incorporated the changes into their discourse, and readjusted what they meant by Négritude. For example, Césaire's critics had obviously made it known to him that they rejected Négritude because they thought it was essentialist. But Césaire argued that Négritude—and it was the first time that anybody had actually pinpointed the collaborative nature of the movement—was an attempt by people from different parts of the black world to share in a common heritage, a common historical memory. It is important to appreciate that the Négritude movement was not a group of people entering into a debate blindly arguing from the stance that we are all Africans, but that it was the basis for a collaboration whose aim was to bring people together. Thus it is also important to note Césaire's argument that the African peoples have certain historical memories in common, *historical memories*, not biology, not history, but historical memories in common. So from the very beginning of Négritude there was an attempt to use it as the fulcrum of collaboration. This sense of collaboration was inbuilt into the project of Négritude.

The other point relates to Senghor's position on Négritude quite late on in the debate, when he says something really quite interesting at a conference in Italy. He states that he, other members of the Négritude movement, other Africans, see themselves as Euro-Africans, products of both the African continent and Europe, thus when they argue Europe has reason and Africans take that reason and that Africa has feeling and Africans take that feeling, he is not suggesting literally that Europe is reason and Africa is feeling, what he is saying is that in Africa the "Other" is *embraced:* "We *embrace* the 'Other'" were his very words. And so the feeling to which Senghor is alluding is one *constructed* between

Africa and Europe. What he is saying then is: we *embrace* the "Other," the "Other" of Europe, and so if you suggest that your culture is more about reason, then by implication—and this is the dialectic that I have been arguing should be borne in mind—you are saying that there is a part of the world that is the "Other" to European reason. And if that is the case then we accept that we are from that world. In other words, the "feeling" that Senghor is talking about is embracing alterity, embracing the "Other," which Europe had banished as being outside itself. However, he is not saying that this is "natural," meaning that Africans are naturally "feeling" people and Europeans "naturally" have reason, but he is making this statement within the overall discourse about the discursive regime of Europe. This is Europe, seen clearly as the powerful entity, that has used this regime to map the world in order to suggest that all matters of the intellect belong to Europe. And this means that Africa must, by implication, embrace the "Other," the alterity of that regime, which is "feeling." And so Senghor is arguing that when all of this is brought back into the mix, Négritude does not then take it and say submissively: we are happy with feeling, you can have reason. No, they bring that back into the mix in order to reconfigure the basis for a dialogue that could take place between Africa and Europe. This is very important because, to me, it seems that this is the only honest thing that one could say about Négritude which has any value for us now. Sometimes people want to bypass false universalism, but clearly at any one time there are investments as to where we are coming from. Négritude says let's speak about these investments, let's make them clear as the basis of our dialogue with each other.

These are some of the reasons why I think Négritude is still worth consideration. I think it was wrongly buried and frankly, I feel that the reasons it was buried are inaccurate, because I think Négritude continues to resound. The reason why I think Négritude hangs around and walks among us still like a phantom, is this: of all the projects to have come out of the African political imaginary, for me, Négritude is the one philosophy that appears to still "have legs." Although it is not specifically mentioned by name, as such, it does seem to be the one philosophy that haunts African popular culture, certainly almost all of pop culture in the new world. It is not clearly spelt out, but it tends to come out in a kind of it's-a-black-thing-you-wouldn't-understand kind of way, but nevertheless that *is* a black thing you wouldn't understand, which is the lingua franca of most hip hop culture, most youth culture, which relies much more on Négritude than on any of the other political imaginaries, or indeed any of the other political collaborations, whether between Malcolm X and the Nation of Islam, W. E. B. Du Bois and the organizers of the Manchester Congress in 1945, or indeed the longest lasting political relationship between the journalist and Pan-Africanist George Padmore and the African nationalist Kwame Nkrumah; most of these do not still resonate now. There are political institutions in existence that are the result of these collaborations, but Négritude and the language of Négritude still walks in a way that the other radical movements of this time do not any more, and so this is why I believe Négritude is still worth discussing in the context of collaboration today.

Passions of Blackness and Imperatives of a Post-African Imagination: Re-reading *Black Orpheus* and *Black Images*

Denis Ekpo

Whoever wants to relive the inaugural ferment and passions that created Négritude/black consciousness; whoever wants a retrospective peep into the unusual racial-cum-cultural energies that drove artistic creation, ideology discourse and cultural politics in Africa and the black Americas in the second half of the twentieth century, should just reread early issues of these flagship Pan-African journals, namely, *Présence Africaine*, *Black Orpheus*, *Black Images*, and *Free Lance*.[1] In these iconic archives of pan-black historicist experience and awareness, one can easily reconnect with what it felt like, from the 1950s to the 1980s, to be a black man living in Africa and in the Americas, and what it was like writing about blackness in the Americas or celebrating Négritude in Africa. Apart from serving as the barometer of the Pan-African intellectual/cultural atmosphere of the period, these journals are undoubtedly first rate sociological documents for the study of postwar dynamics of black thoughts, politics and art. *Présence Africaine,* subtitled *Cultural Journal of the Negro World*, launched in 1947 in Paris, covered the postwar Negro world from the unusually fertile and hectic Francophone vantage point. *Black Orpheus: A Journal of African and Afro-American Literature*, published at Nigeria's premier university, The University of Ibadan, was created by two famous German Africanists, namely, Uli Beier and Janheinz Jahn. Its first issue appeared in 1957, the year of Ghana's independence and the heyday of anticolonialism, cultural nationalism, Négritude and Pan-Africanism. *Black Images* first appeared in 1972, published in Ontario, Canada, and was perhaps the most radical in its pursuit of the Pan-African blackness agenda. *Free Lance* was created in Ohio in 1950 as a journal of African-American poetry and prose. All four journals had, despite the diversity of voices and perspectives, one common underlying purpose and focus, namely, re-educating both the black world and the non-black world on the predicaments, misrecognised triumphs and on-going challenges of the black race in a world that had in the past almost completely disqualified it and in the present was yet to be fully at ease with it. However, for reasons of space and analytic depth, only the two of these four journals, *Black Orpheus* and *Black Images*—considered the most representative of the major shades of blackness/Négritude politics—will be examined more closely. In this retrospective on *Black Orpheus* and *Black Images*, I want to focus on the shift from the exuberant, polemical, activist passions of blackness/Négritude of the '60s and early '80s (which these journals cover) to the post-Négritude self-questionings and search for alter-

1 *Présence Africaine*, founded by Allioune Diop in 1947, published in Paris; *Black Orpheus: Journal of African and Afro-American Literature*, founded by Uli Beier in 1957, published by the General Publications Sections, Ministry of Education, Ibadan (First issue 1957, last issue 1993); *Black Images: A Critical Quarterly on Black Culture*, editors Lennox Brown and R G Murray, Toronto, Ontario (published five issues between 1972–73); *Free Lance*, Publication of The Free Lance Poets and Prose workshop, Ohio (published between 1960–69).

natives of the '90s (which they don't talk about). As I will argue that the seeds of later post-Négritude doubts were already sown in the extreme oppositional passions of the Négritude/blackness paradigm, the essay will center on the birth of Post-Négritude/post-African imaginaries out of the very womb of Négritude/blackness. But first, how did *Black Orpheus* and *Black Images* inscribe the black/African predicament?

The Passions of Blackness/Africanity

Black Orpheus and Black Images, in their very titles, proudly and unapologetically advertize their almost exclusively Negro-centric preoccupations: one is a critical quarterly of black culture, the other, a journal of African and Afro-American literature. Though overtly culturally oriented, they managed to cover directly or obliquely, through the medium of art and ideology, virtually all issues of relevance and interest to the fate of the Pan-African world. Core worries arising from the existential imperative to defend, illustrate and uphold the hitherto denigrated values of black culture and civilisation form the background for the study of the arts, ideological discourse and liberationist activities that framed the emergence and evolution of pan-black cultural and political consciousness. Negro-African arts—literature, poetry, paintings, music dance and other performance arts are carefully documented, studied and mostly inscribed as mirrors of the many predicaments of black men and women all over the world and as creative markers and vehicles of emancipatory cultural politics.

However, despite the commonalities in the core preoccupations of both journals, their largely dissimilar sociopolitical contexts of conception, production and circulation lead to significant differences in each journal's construction of and response to the predicament and passions of blackness. Thus while in *Black Orpheus,* African culture is captured at the celebratory cultural nationalist moment of a recently rediscovered or reconquered treasure, namely Négritude, in *Black Images,* black culture in the Americas is framed as being almost always in an uncanny state of crisis. The theme of the first issue is titled "Black Cultural Crisis in Canada."[2] The lead paper written by black playwright Lennox Brown, captures the essence of the near permanent crisis that is said to haunt the very existence of black culture in the Americas. According to him the source of this crisis is not just some happenings in the recent past or any current conjuncture of antiblack forces; the source according to him is history itself along with the fatality of its endless repetitions. For the black man in the Americas, "to know this history is painful; not to know it is disastrous"[3] he reasons. To illustrate the fatal hand of history on black culture, he recalls the story of two white merchants who in the '70s were convicted for "selling contaminated meat already condemned by government officials to blacks because, they said in court, 'negroes can eat anything.'"[4] To Lennox Brown, black culture in Canada and in the Americas as a whole is encircled by a history that managed to leave behind this kind of action and especially the response by these white men almost two centuries

2 Lennox Brown, "Black Cultural Crisis in Canada," *Black Images* 1, no.1 (1972).
3 Ibid., 4–8.
4 Ibid., 4.

after the abolition of slavery and despite civil rights. The workers/builders/defenders of black culture, especially the artists, writers and intellectuals, cannot but feel caught in the stench of a history that is still bent on contaminating almost everything black: "The black writer still smells the stench of this meat. He sees worms forming in the intestines of the victimised children. He also sees the slave trader mentality of those white merchants. This is his cultural reality."[5] In Lennox Brown's view, this episode is nothing but the allegory of the black predicament in the Americas; it encapsulates not only black cultural reality but also the pathological history that over-determines it. Above all, it preprograms the black intellectual, artist and writer to a special historical task of black cultural/political emancipation.

Although Brown's description of black cultural reality appears unduly apocalyptic, his panicky and alarmist tone is paradigmatic of *Black Images*' entire inscription of the passions of blackness in the Americas. For his tone here chimes with, or sets the tone for the general resistant ideological orientation and activist scholarship format of the journal. As black culture and history are here configured essentially in traumaphiliac and victim-centered crisis-ridden terms, it stands to reason that only resistance-based artistic engagement and scholarly activism can rise to the task of rescuing and healing blackness in the Americas. Hence the choice of themes, works of art, historical episodes, black heroes to commemorate and exalt, white villains to excoriate etc., appears a priori dictated by the imperative not only to fight the unrepentant enemies of the race but also to chart an emancipatory path out of the hidden and overt pathologies of black culture.

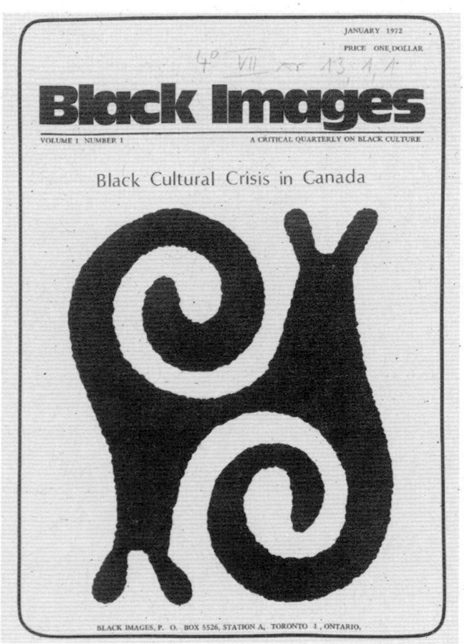

Cover of *Black Images* 1, no. 1, January 1972.

Thus besides devoting several issues to celebrating and redignifying survivals of old African cultures and traditions in the new world, including such colorful trans-Atlantic survivals as voodoo in Haiti, Brazil and Cuba, *Black Images* in several issues dwell performatively on the lives, thoughts and works of universal black emancipators such as Marcus Garvey, Anta Diop and of course Frantz Fanon.[6] But before I return to the reason for the overwhelming visibility given to these radical Pan-African troika, I want to examine how *Black Orpheus*, situated at a different geopolitical spectrum of the black predicament, also represents the same passion of blackness.

In *Black Orpheus*, though Africa was still under the same spell of Pan-African euphoria that envelops *Black Images*, the context of the reception and celebration of blackness/Négritude here was significantly different. Négritude having been rediscovered, codified and vigorously affirmed, independence acquired or about to be, the need for the earlier polemical and accusatory identity politics had by now somehow subsided making way for a mostly celebratory inventory of Negro-African values and traditions. The focus of the writings in *Black Orpheus*, from its first issue in

5 Ibid., 5.
6 *Black Images* devoted volume 1, no. 3 &. 4 to Frantz Fanon and Cheikh Anta Diop while volume 1, no. 2 reproduces in full Marcus Garvey's speech titled "The Negro's Fullest Part".

1957, is on the documentary stocktaking of African values as expressed both in traditional folk arts and in the new forms of writings done in European languages. The primitive paintings and sculptures rescued from tribal shrines and pagan altars that survived missionary idol burnings, are proudly put on display with a great deal of cultural nationalist pomp. Uli Beier's paper titled "Shango Shrine" not only reconstitutes in all its pagan awesomeness the beliefs, rites and rituals surrounding this famous Yoruba god of thunder, but brings from colonialist disqualification the exquisite primitive genius of great works of sculpture that embodied each facet of the multifarious powers of the fearsome god.[7] Many other Africanists as well as African cultural nationalistic academics publish their reports on their anthropological rescue missions in West African and Caribbean artifacts, folk poetry, paintings and sacred art objects. Then works by Négritude poets, especially poems by Senghor, David Diop, and Bernard Dadie are translated and published. A lot of attention is paid to the anticolonial novel, particularly those of Mongo Beti and Ferdinand Oyono.[8] Significantly, despite some Anglophone misgivings regarding the cultural value of Négritude (following Soyinka's sally that a tiger does proclaim its tigritude but should rather show it by pouncing on its prey), *Black Orpheus* seems unbothered in its coverage by any alleged Anglophone/Francophone divide on the question. The documentarist/celebratory trend continues until the 1970s when the editorial team became completely Africanized and emphasis naturally shifted to the study of postindependence writings and art as well as black American writings and culture.

What is noteworthy about the early issues of *Black Orpheus* is the absence from its pages of the militant pathos—the alarmist sense of African culture in a state of emergency requiring urgent revolutionary salvage work and in need of messianic figures—that one finds in almost every article in *Black Images*. However, Negro-African culture experienced as either Négritude or black consciousness, is given absolute centrality by the two journals. But while *Black Images* sees Négritude with the eye of Aimé Césaire as a powerful weapon of war, in *Black Orpheus*, Négritude is received in the more conciliatory Senghorian sense as a settled ensemble of the values of black civilisation in Africa and the Americas. The two journals also report on the major Pan-African cultural events of the 1950s through the 1970s. Thus the first and second congress of black writers and artists that took place in Paris and Rome in 1956 and 1959 respectively, are fully covered by the two journals. But while *Black Images* highlights the ideological oppositions between radical black intellectuals like Anta Diop and moderates like Senghor (agreeing with the former and rejecting the latter), *Black Orpheus* is content to merely report on the proceedings of the two congresses.

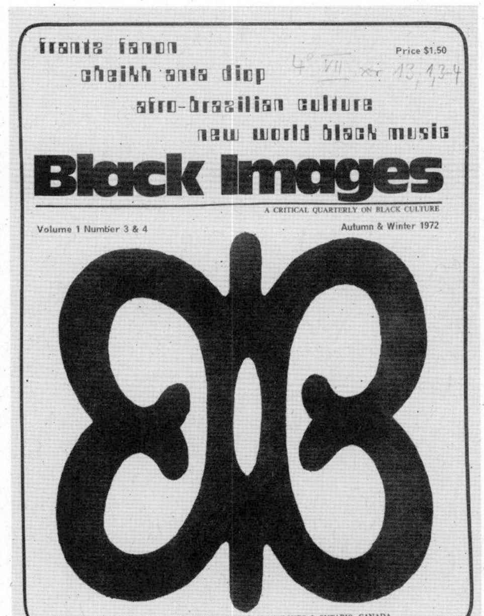

Cover of *Black Images* 1, no. 3 & 4, Autumn & Winter, 1972.

7 Uli Beier, "Shango Shrine", *Black Orpheus*, no. 4 (1957): 30–35.
8 Uli Beier, "The Novel in the French Cameroun", *Black Orpheus*, no. 2 (1958): 42–52.

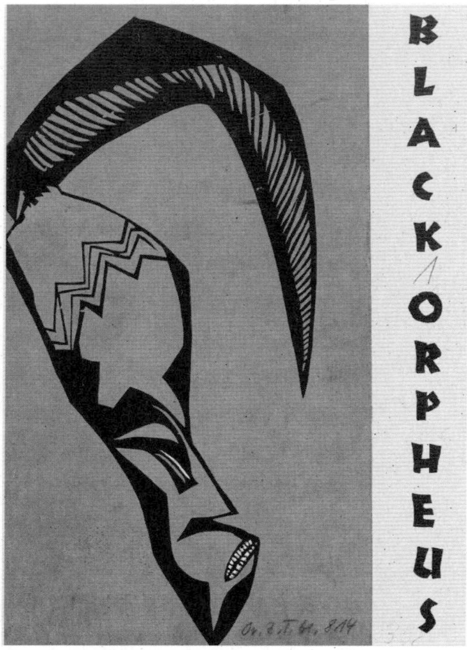

Cover of *Black Orpheus*, no.1, September 1957.

As stated before, it is in the choice of black emancipatory voices/master thinkers as well as in the place accorded their thoughts that the two journals mark their almost opposing approaches to the blackness theme. In *Black Images*, the works of Marcus Garvey, Anta Diop and Frantz Fanon are documented and analyzed exhaustively with an obvious hagiographical reverence.[9] Despite obvious differences, what these three Pan-African master thinkers have in common is the very strong belief that there is a fundamental black predicament created by the three historic enemies of the black race, namely, slavery, colonization and racism. While Garvey and Diop defend a fundamentalist and radical conception and practice of blackness, Fanon promotes a more universal but no less radical psychology of race and identity politics. In response to colonial racial theories about Africa, Diop postulates in his influential *Nations nègres et culture*,[10] an African origin of civilization through the demonstration of the black sources and agency of Egyptian civilization. Diop sees Négritude as "a fighting philosophy for strong men"[11] and is therefore highly critical of the conciliatory gestures of Senghor's Négritude. He excoriates alienated or assimilated Africans who try to escape their African heritage by appropriating an alien culture. Garvey's race politics went so far as to propose total racial/cultural separatism for blacks and, or, their massive repatriation to Africa. *Black Images* deliberately recalls and highlights these rather extremist views of these black leaders ostensibly because the journal seeks to canonize them as models of current theory and practice of black liberation. Interestingly, there is no serious study devoted to any of these figures in any issue of *Black Orpheus* that I have so far read. But that does not mean that their voices were not important or well heard in Africa; it may just reflect the non-revolutionary, more self-assured and balanced scholarly policy *of Black Orpheus*.

The Impasse of Négritude

The 1950s through to the 1960s mark the period of innocence of Négritude in Africa and of black consciousness in America. *Black Orpheus* responds to this innocence of Africanity by publishing articles ranging from African creation myths to the role of ancestors in Senghor's poetry.[12] For *Black Images* the period of innocence extends until the '70s. Between 1972 and 1973, its five extant issues wax Pan-African in its radical black consciousness coverage. Topics vary from "African Sources of New World Black Music" to the "Swahili Image Today".[13] However, by the '70s the passion of blackness along with the vogue of Négritude had already started

9 R.M. Lacovia, "Frantz Fanon: A Rehabilitation of our living dead", *Black Images* 1, no. 3 & 4 (1972): 47–62.

10 Cheikh Anta Diop, "Nations nègres et culture", Présence Africaine (1955). See also: *The African Origin of Civilization* (Chicago: Chicago Review Press, 1989).

11 Cheikh Anta Diop, quoted by James E. Spady in "The Cultural Unity of Anta Diop", *Black Images* 1, no. 3 & 4 (1972).

12 Uli Beier, "The theme of ancestors in Senghor's Poetry", *Black Orpheus*, no. 5 (1959).

13 Laz Ekwueme, "African sources of in New World Black Music", *Black Images* 1, no. 3 & 4 (1972).

to wane. Vigorous denunciations of Négritude had appeared. Stanislas Adetovi's *Négritude et Négrologues* and Marcien Towa's *Leopold Sedar Senghor: Négritude ou Servitude* had turned the Senghorian edifice of Négritude inside out.[14] Towa claimed that Senghor's Négritude was no more than a shameless neo-servitude to French cultural imperialism. Adetovi's grouse was that Négritude was merely a wishy-washy Europeanized reflection on the Negro rather than the revolutionary weapon it was supposed to be. Although Sartre had tried to salvage it by calling it "an anti-racist racism", a minor term destined to disappear in a new synthesis of a world without race or class, it was realized that Négritude's antiracism was not an overcoming of racialist essentialism; it was still racism reversed, internalized and made no less destructive of the human in the black person. To many others on the Fanonian left, Négritude only amounted to naturalizing the powerlessness of the colonized African as a virtue rather than mobilizing it for the immediate overthrow of colonial rule. The Fanonians emphasized Négritude's mystifications on Africa; its unscientific character as a description of the state of Africa. By this they failed to realize that Négritude was first and foremost a mythologization of Africa. As a master narrative, Négritude was mostly a constative description of what we think we are by virtue of our being Africans and black. However, Négritude also wanted to be above all a performative doctrine, a self-description which told us what to believe, how to act on Africa and on the world, the inspiration for the actions we took and the choices we made. It is Négritude's performative claims, i.e., what it inspired Africa to do, what Africa did under its spell, that opens it up for a more enlightening critique. In this, regard we can say that Négritude's conceptual vulnerabilities started to show the moment it exceeded poetry and myth in order to become a metapolitics sponsoring not only cultural nationalism but decolonization and later, the African Path to development, African socialism etc. It became clear that Négritude as a performative metapolitics did indeed drive Africa but mostly to negative outcomes. The African path to development became a path to hunger, poverty and chronic underdevelopment; African socialism led straight into blood kleptomaniac dictatorships. The common black soul animating all black/African peoples amid differences of tribe and tongue or religion was not strong enough to prevent or stop periodic inter-tribal massacres and could not save the newly independent states from chronic conflicts and instabilities. Thus the impasse of Négritude was mostly performative: all the fine feelings about Africa's communal values and the mystical brotherhood of black souls, all the Senghorian theories on black emotivity and participatory cosmology did not translate into any visible economic or political positivity that could legitimate the Négritudian worldview.

Post-Négritude Blues

Thus Négritude died essentially because its performative force brought negative outcomes, meaning that Négritude was a maladaptive doctrine out of sync with how the modern world works. However, performativity was hardly the reason why latter-day postcolonial deconstructionists

14 Stanislas Adetovi, *Négritude et négrologues* (Paris: Le Castor Astral, 1998); Marcien Towa, *Léopold Sedar Senghor: négritude ou servitude?* (Yaoundé: editions Clé, 1971).

sought to overthrow it. Unlike the leftists who criticized its lack of a veritable revolutionary force, the deconstructors emphasized Négritude's discursive essentialism. And so most of the post-Négritude movements in art and theory that rose up in the '80s attempted to salvage Africa from the essentialism of Négritude's/black consciousness's identity politics. And so from the '80s the vogue of poststructuralism's dissolving of metaphysical and essentialist thoughts led to postcolonial theory's generalized deconstructive onslaught on the ontological categories of Négritude/black consciousness. It was realized that identity politics constructed on such categories as nativity, African soul, blackness etc., amounted to a mere reversal of the same colonialist essentialism. Without changing the metaphysical structure of the discourse, Négritude's anticolonialism was a replication of the same colonialist logic. And so Négritude, under the spell of postcolonial theory, lost its strong nativist or countercolonial innocence for, compelled to speak in the forked tongue of French postmodernism, it could only avow its linguistic constructedness (out of the very material of the colonial ratio) as well as the aporias, ambivalences, the differences etc., that traverse all its founding categories; especially Africanity, black soul etc.

A more current and trendy postmodern inflection on Négritude is Afropolitanism. The term was launched and popularized by Taiye Selasi in a 2005 article titled "Bye-Bye Babar".[15] The idea arose out of the great difficulty of trying to define Africanness for a generation of diasporized, heavily hybridized Africans with floating identities: "this one lives in London but was raised in Toronto and born in Accra; that one works in Lagos but grew up in Houston, Texas. Home for this lot is many things—they belong to no single geography but feel at home in many".[16] She invented the term "Afropolitan" to describe those migrant Africans born or raised elsewhere that have African blood or at least a drop of it, but who are culturally cosmopolitan. They are both Africans and cosmopolitans. The term caught on and became very fertile in the domains of fashion, culture marketing, art and art theory. One addict saw it as "Africa's contribution to shaping globalization".[17] It also spawned several intellectual debates. Mbembe recuperated it for academic cultural theory by seeing as the new post-Négritude subject position most appropriate for Africa's global migrants. But what really held Mbembe's interest in Afropolitanism was what he called the promise of thinking Africa and Africanness outside the racialized categories in which Négritude and other black consciousness discourses and art have been held captive. However, Mbembe's academic canonization of Afropolitanism did not stop him in his latest book, *Critique de la raison nègre*, from elevating the "nègre" to the status of the newest cosmopolitan liberatory principle and resistance agency against new forms of global neo-capitalism. His postmodern jeremiads on the negrè as the embodiment of history's wrongs does not however appear to sit well with his earlier praise of Afropolitanism's promise of freedom from the tyranny of race and victimhood.[18]

15 Taiye Selasi, "Bye-Bye Babar", *Lip Magazine*, 2005.
16 Ibid.
17 Minna Salami, "Can Africans have multiple subcultures?", *Ms Afropolitan Blog*, April 3, 2013.
18 Achille Mbembe, *Critique de la raison negre* (Paris: Editions la découverte, 2013).

Perhaps the most radical, even countercultural, post-Négritude/blackness movement in art and culture is Afrofuturism. The term was first coined by Mark Dery in 1993. According to Wikipedia, "Afrofuturism is a literary and cultural aesthetics that combines elements of science fiction, historical fiction, fantasy, Afrocentricity and magic realism with non-Western cosmologies in order to critique not only the present day dilemmas of people of color, but also to revise, interrogate and re-examine the historical events of the past". Ytasha L. Womack speaks of a post-black era in which art, aesthetics, culture deviantly breaks out of the fossilized black mystique in order to explore multiple futures for black people in the U.S.[19] Afrofuturistic art thrives on deviant beauty or the sci-fi grotesque as art. It is art that seeks to disturb everything including reason and social morality. So characterized, Afrofuturism is not so different from extant extreme forms of postmodern experimental art, the type of art that Roger Kimbal calls "art without beauty". What still justifies the prefix "Afro" is that Afrofuturism, despite its surrealistic burning of idols, is still anchored in some form of identity politics: it is said to have "a great reverence for ancestors and ancient societies" including references to "Egyptian deities and other African traditional religions".[20] It is however in music that the over-the-top posturing of Afrofuturism is most visible. Anchored mostly in the hip hop phenomenon, Afrofuturistic music is an anti-establishment cultural movement by black underclass urban youth against all they consider wrong in the U.S. and in the world as a whole. One writer calls the cultural switch enacted by hip hop as "the change from a black consciousness to gansta/thug mentality".[21] If that is the case, the question is in what sense does Afrofuturism amount to a shifting of black consciousness to a more global self-understanding more suited to the social and political challenges black youths are facing in the U.S. today?

In both Afropolitanism and Afrofuturism there is no doubt a clear determination and will to move away from the ideological and discursive rigidities of Négritude/black consciousness. A lot of motions, noise, gestures and new words have been launched to signify post-Négritude changes in art and experience, and the self-understanding of black and African persons living in the twenty-first century. The trouble with these loud and self-important post-Négritude things is not the seriousness of purpose or the will to succeed but their outcomes. Consider Afropolitanism, the so-called promising bold new merger between Africa and the cosmos. Can it really live up to the postracial liberatory promise that Mbembe and others find in it? I recall the earlier merger promised and promoted by Senghor's *métissage culturel* between African culture and modernity, i.e., between say, African magic and Europe's scientific rationality. It was to a large extent that cultural cross-breeding that brought about the syncretisms as well as hybridizing processes that landed Africa in the current development-eroding postcolonial disorder and chaos. To be sure the new merger between Africanity and cosmopolitanism/

19 Ytasha L. Womack and Derek T. Dingle, *Post-Black: How a New Generation is Re-defining African Identity* (Chicago: CUP, 2010).

20 Ytasha L. Womack, "Afrofuturism: An Aesthetic and Exploration of Identity", *IEET blog*, January 4, 2012.

21 Rakhyt, "Hip Hop and Afrofuturism: the seeding of the consciousness field", *AFROFUTURISM Blog*, April 26, 2001.

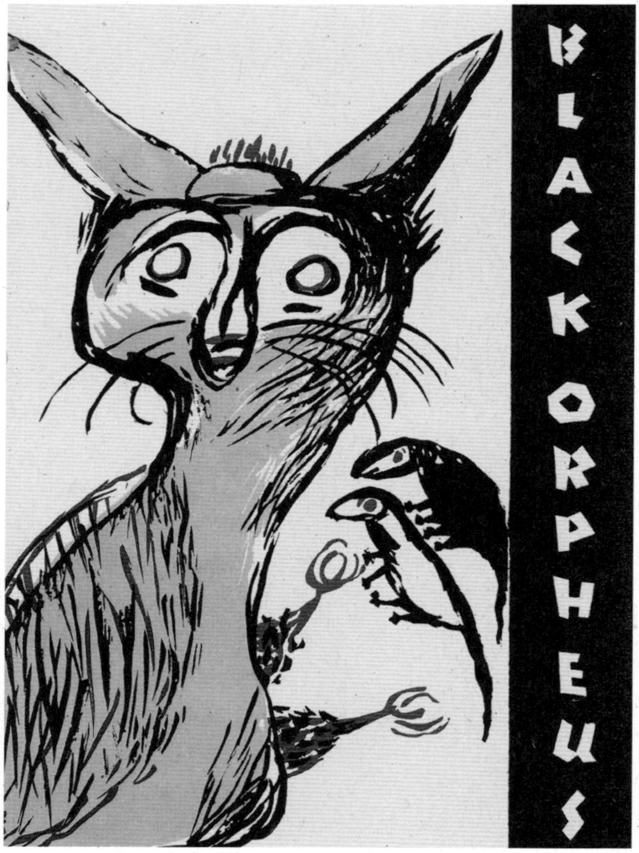

Cover of *Black Orpheus*, no.11, 1962.

globalization is merely a postmodern collage rather than the old program of the Africanization of modernity. However, as a new thought process Afropolitanism is still at best a neo-hybridity and as such, it portends even worse outcomes for Africa. Afropolitanism sponsors mostly a mind-set of frivolity and cut-and-paste flightiness that is profoundly impervious to the mental seriousness and cultural discipline demanded by the imperative to restore Africa to sociocultural order, non-hybrid rationality and disciplined scientific approach to progress. An Africa that has not even fully begun to exploit the resources of older rational modernity for its orderly growth has no business dissipating its cultural energies trying to experiment with postmodern subrational thoughts, cultures and art. As a people from a late-and-bad starter continent, you don't become "a co-shaper of modern times" by latching principally onto the glossy surfaces of the postmodern world such as fashion, African pop or marketing kente-accented laptop bags in New York. You do so primarily by mastering and getting into the technology driven power games that drive wealth creation in the global economy. If the people of the West and other developed places seem to find so much meaning in and a lot of satisfaction from the glossy surfaces of modern things, it is mostly because these people have largely finished their world's work: they have conquered hunger, disease and ignorance. Now their most serious concerns are play and entertainment; they derive infinite gratification from postmodern art, hip hop, exotic African cultures and outlandish premodern religions. For us in Africa, it should be work before entertainment, serious thinking before Afropolitanism, real art before Afrofuturistic madness. As Emma Dabiri says, in Afropolitanism, "African progress is measured by the extent to which it can reproduce a western life-style now without having to physically be in the west".[22] That makes Afropolitanism a highly misleading way of thinking Africa. Africa's progress can be measured principally by the extent to which it can feed itself and stop begging.

As for the super radical countercultural movement called Afrofuturism, the question is whether the advertized consciousness shift articulated mostly through gangster-thug mentality indeed constitutes a shift away from the rigidities of the old blackness paradigm or simply a regression far below the least rational idea of blackness ever imagined? No doubt Afrofuturism in music and visual art may actually fit into the postmodern tempo of anything goes as art and have thus been able to galvanize enormous youth energy the world over. This may be good for the

22 Emma Dabiri, "Why I am not an Afropolitan", *Africa is a Country Blog*, January 21, 2014, http://www.africaasacountry.com.

black and world youths. However in this essay, I am not only describing what is; I am evaluating the various thought patterns and cultural movements of the black world in regard to their abilities to insert or reinsert the black world more fully and profitably into the universal world process from which we usually claim history i.e., from which other people had tried to exclude us. I note that all the post-Négritude movements in art and intellectual discourse are gesturing towards a postracial postcolonial world the attainment of which will enable the black man in Africa and in the Americas to fully unfetter and optimize his universal human potential. Accordingly, I am interested in examining whether in all these post-Négritude intellectual and art movements, the mind of blackness, the Négritude ideal has been sufficiently restructured, shifted or changed to enable the black man to reach his cultural goal or whether it has been simply further disempowered. In Afropolitanism and Afrofuturism, has the blackness paradigm been sublated? Has the human consciousness of the African/black man been expanded, improved or has it been further confined, trivialized and further misaligned with the world?

The Post-African Turn

As noted much earlier, Négritude had defined Africa as a being rather than a becoming; Africanity became a permanent condition rather than a contingent resting place or a temporary subject position; blackness became an existential predicament rather than a color among others. Post-Négritude theories and artistic consciousness tried to move beyond Négritude's epistemological strictures by teaching Africanity and blackness to speak in the forked tongue of French postmodernism or in the futuristic street dialects of hip hop. The trouble with these post-Négritude Brownian motions is that while they try to move beyond the archaic essentialism of Négritude, they do not dare to question the legitimating ground of all discourses of negro-African self-consciousness, namely, the very idea of Africa, the structuring principle of Africanness, that ur-principle that underlies and fertilizes all gestures of a specific negro-African self-awareness. Realizing the fatal tendency for post-Négritude discourses, art and aesthetics to merely throw coquettish postmodern or new-age bandages onto the real wounds of the African/black condition, I think that unless Africa or Africanity, the very foundation of black/African self-and-world-interpetation, was questioned, deconstructed and reconstructed, we will continue to move around in circles of self-deceit, thinking that we are making intellectual and cultural progress. The post-African turn arises out of the decision to go down to the bottom and question our most prized myth, the ground of our identitarian pride and of our endless race worries, namely, the very idea of Africa that founds the notion of black/African predicaments and the discourses that seek to solve them. The post-African starting point is that the value—the utility, necessity—of Africa/Africanity as used in all our preferred self/world interpretations has become questionable, is due for questioning and for total deconstructive overhaul. We know that the name Africa as used in Pan-African self-narratives is far from being just a geopolitical marker, a location on the globe. Recuperated from earlier colonialist invention, Africa was reinvented by us as a unique locus of traumatic memories and of unfinished vengeance. If today evoking Africa or Africanity still affords Africans and people of African descent a deep emotional and identitarian gratification, it is because not only do we unconsciously relive the grand traumas that framed its history and sense of self, but also because we feel a sense of anticolonial/antiracialist vengeance against Europe/ white men who colonized Africa and enslaved many Africans. Africa still stands as the sacred symbol of black vengeance against enemies of the black race. On account of such a massively traumaphiliac-cum-vindictive symbolic efficacy of the name Africa, we never really even imagine the possibility of questioning it, its genealogy, its utility as a permanent marker of who we are and want to be. The task of post-Africanism is to lift the stone-cast sacred mental/ cultural taboo around Africa's neck so we can truly interrogate Africanity/ blackness and allied narratives as well as question their value in the postimperial, postracializing context of the globalised world. The post-African thinker starts by recalling that Africanity was created and marked by the arrival of Europe in Africa. In other words coloniality is the condition of possibility and of articulation of Africanity or Négritude. In black America, slavery and its aftermath are the reason for the rediscovery of Africa and the creation of Negroness or blackness as the archracial/cultural resistance category. In asserting Africanness or blackness, we have managed to successfully repress its generally reactive, oppositional genealogy; we have forgotten its nature and form as a negative resentment construction; we have turned it into an inviolate self-definitional positivity of our being and becoming. Our normative idea of Africa, though born out of anticolonial/ antislavery resistance, anger and revenge, has been ratified as the sole idea of Africa, indeed the only possible one. Of course we post-Africans recognize and applaud the historical role this negatively-constructed Africa played as the inspiration and trigger of anticolonial/ antiracial struggles of the past. We acknowledge its contingent value as archintellectual weapon of war against colonial civilizational disqualification of Africa. But we are saying that what has remained ominously unthought and unread in this triumphant idea of Africa is that it frames and enacts Africa as a permanent archvictim continent whose every creation can only be a reaction; Africanness/ blackness as an existential predicament from which we can't really escape. Whether as the essentialist Black Mother of Négritude and Negro-renaissance cultural romanticism, or as the postmodernized plural entity of post-Négritude, Africa has been standing before us like a sacred hieroglyph harboring specific ancestral wisdom, cultural/artistic splendors, uncommon riches and beckoning on all of her children all over the world. This mystery "Africa my Africa" the poets never stop singing about, hiding secrets of an African way of life, African path to development or African solutions to Africa's problems, now stands before the post-African gaze totally disrobed as a dumb abstraction, neither good nor bad, but supremely indifferent to our frantic searches for common ancestral formulas for Africanizing modernity, democracy and development. It is now time to lay waste to these massive psychological/cultural idols that have lain upon our imagination and hampered the growth, cultural health and the unbounded human creativity of the human spirit in the black man of

Africa and the Americas. For us, this accepted idea of Africa, Africanness and blackness is perhaps the greatest unconscious limitation we have placed on our infinite human imagination, including on our capacity to create and design alternative Africas that could even serve us better in today's global space. The Africanity paradigm and the mind-set it engenders take us straight into what Stephen Smith terms "a negrologie", the logic of unconscious separation from the modern world, a pathological temptation of withdrawal into an essential self.[23] It is above all a logic of victimhood, blaming others and outer circumstances for our woes, always trying to evade self-responsibility and mistrusting and suspecting modernity, especially capitalism seen as a perpetual western conspiracy to undo Africa and the black man. To a post-African, given that the global world process is infinitely greater than the Africanity/blackness tunnel we speak from, Africa's redemption cannot begin until we manage to reengineer our minds out of Africanity so that we can reintegrate and embrace the infinite openness of the global world process.

Post-Africanism does not believe that post-Négritude movements in art or theories have what it takes to effect the fundamental mind-set/worldview changes that Pan-Africa needs. The retention of the prefix Afro in Afropolitanism and Afrofuturism is proof that the radicality of these self-styled postmodernizing movements is merely chic. Despite the faddy cosmopolitanism, boundary-erasing moves, free-floating *mixities* and fluidities these movements flaunt, the prefix Afro still points them to unconscious identitarian yearnings, because it remains a boundary fixer, an ontological thought-stopper, and a separation-from-the-world reflex. All the fake postmodern cosmopolitanisms conceal an unconscious yearning for an African specificity, the same old struggles for recognition, the same barely-hidden tension and anxiety for a special kind of global visibility. Post-Africanism seeks a total redemption of Pan-Africa from all these hidden struggles, anxieties and inner worries that have afflicted all African self-narratives and cultural politics hitherto. For us there can be no true and full recovery of our global creative freedom so long as these secret anxieties, tensions and hidden resistances that afflict our thought patterns, feelings and art are not detected and removed. The post-African idea is that it is counterproductive to want to start something new on Africa without changing the old. All post-Négritude movements merely built on the same un-deconstructed Africanity ground of Négritude, the same mind-set and emotional foundation of Négritude; thereby they are merely putting new wines into old bottles or carrying clean water into an already polluted source. At best post-Négritude further masks the nature of the maladaptive Africanity foundation; at worst, it renders it malignant and impervious to new cures. How does post-Africanism hope to change the old bottles of the African/black predicament before introducing the new wines of postmodern global world-transforming wisdom and creativity? How do we post-Africanize the mind—the thoughts, beliefs and feelings—of Pan-Africa?

The root causes of the predicament of Africanness/blackness are the historical traumas of slavery and colonization that Africa and Africans

23 Stephen Smith, *Negrologie-Pourquoi l'Afriquemeurt* (Paris: Calmann-Levy, 2003).

suffered at the hands of white Europe and white America. Africanity and blackness were created as the sole possible responses to these traumas. We have been conditioned to believe that these traumas that mangled our collective psyche, identity and historical memory were caused by these episodes themselves. Post-Africanism says that the traumas that created Africanity and black consciousness are not really slavery and colonization; they were created and borne by our particular responses to slavery and colonization. This means that if we could manage to change the responses, we can reconfigure our collective historical memory and also mitigate the traumas or remove them altogether. I note that the African and black American cannot really overcome Négritude, Africanity or blackness because, in the case of the African, he is still fundamentally an anticolonialist, and in the case of the black American, an antiracist, antiwhite man of resentment. He cannot overcome anticolonialism, antiracism or antiwhiteism because his historical consciousness is still overwhelmingly tied to and over-determined by a traumatic view of history; especially of the defining episodes of slavery and colonization. So for the mind of Pan-Africa to move beyond Négritude and change for the better, we must find a way to substantially change the received traumatic or traumaphiliac reading of slavery and colonization.

A Post-African Re-reading of Slavery and Colonization

I recall Lennox Brown's view of black history as both painful and disastrous—"knowing it is painful, not knowing it is disastrous". He no doubt arrived at this bleak conclusion because as a black American, he strongly believes that black history embodies the very traumas that are still causing pain and disasters. For the post-African, it is not necessarily so. To be sure everybody knows that the historical circumstances that produced black America were difficult and barely imaginable for the man of today. The memory of slavery probably still jars on the psyche of many a black American today. However, the error is to think that this condition is a fatality of black history. For us, it is only a fatality of a certain reading of black history; it ceases to be such a fatality the moment that history is read differently. Similarly, as Africans, we have been conditioned by our protracted anticolonial culture to think only one dimensionally, i.e., wholly negatively about colonization. We have never been taught to consider the possibility that we needed to have experienced colonization so that we could learn vital, growth-bearing, world-changing lessons about life and the common world we share with other peoples and races. In both cases, it seems that the earlier master-thinkers of the black condition (those that *Black Images* uphold as the eternal guides of Pan-Africa) had a lot to do in fostering the persistence of our negative, traumaphiliac account of slavery and colonization. Fanon in particular taught Africa to view colonization as the greatest crime committed against Africa and the source of Africa's postcolonial underdevelopment and smallness. He also formulated a theory of slavery and race that suggests that many behavioral neuroses, such as self-hate, sadistic violence, etc., are the inevitable psychic escape route for many blacks caught in the slavery-race social complexes of the Americas.

However, although Fanon's alarmist account of slavery, race and colonization has taken hold on our Pan-African historical and political imagination, Post-Africanism believes that the Fanonian account, popular as it is, has been mostly counterproductive: it has become an aggravation of, rather than a cure for the many maladies of our received historical and cultural consciousness. As a post-African interested in the search for cures, my task is to look beyond Fanon and Mbembe for alternative accounts of our historical pasts that not only unravel hidden inner wisdom of events but also furnish Pan-Africa with new inspirations and models for a mind-set switch. One such alternative reading is provided by Hegel's idea of the "cunning of reason in history"[24] According to Hegel, it is like the god of history or reason, which governs world history and the major events in it, mostly operates cunningly by leveraging men's passions, greed and ambition as a trigger for great actions whose hidden purpose they are not aware of but whose effects world history uses to drive great changes in the world. In other words, world history often uses great evil actions by great evil actors to move the history of the world from one stage to another. The colonization of Africa, (like the colonizations of some other places], is a good case of the cunning hand of world history making use of the cupidity and rivalries of newly industrialized Europe to cause them to scramble for Africa—apparently for selfish national aggrandizements, but in the process, opening Africa up and connecting it to the world. From a Hegelian point of view, Africa which had been wrapped up within itself, isolated from the theatre of world history, had to be routed out of anthropological slumber by the conqueror's cannon shot; she had to suffer colonial violence, brutality, domination, exploitation etc., as the price for being opened up and attached to world history/modernity. The violence, injustices, exploitations, subjugation and domination attributed to colonialism are crimes only in regard to what Hegel terms "school master morality", whereas in the supramoral logic of world history, these are only the means for bringing Africa out of isolation and making it an integral part of the world.

On this alternative account, it becomes clear that the idea of colonization as a gruesome crime against Africa has persisted in our collective historical memory only because we have listened exclusively to Fanon and his heirs. We have learned to seal our ears with wax to any alternative account. But if we manage to move from Fanon to Hegel, we quickly realize that colonization was the universe's most economical, albeit painful way to fast-forward long isolated Africa into world history. The argument that colonization is the source of Africa's underdevelopment does not arise: it wasn't the task of colonization to develop Africa. Its world historic role was to open up Africa and show her the road to modernity and development. It was Africa's responsibility to take or not take the colonial road to development. Thus for the post-African, it is not a question of how Europe underdeveloped Africa; it is a matter of how Africa, unlike Asia, failed to leverage colonization to develop itself.

In the slavery episode, unlike colonization, the cunning hand of world history is less easily detectable. The gruesome sufferings of the

24 Hegel's idea of the "cunning of Reason" is found in his book *The Philosophy of History*, trans. John Sibree (New York: Dover Publications, 2004), section 3, subsection 36.

Middle Passage, the abject miseries and brutalities of plantation life, the deprivations of post-Abolition, the endless pains and humiliations, make of slavery in the Americas a barely imaginable enactment of man as beast to other men. And yet since world history/ the universe allowed it, we must still try to seek a world historical purpose behind even so unspeakable a means. Here the Biblical story of Joseph in Egypt provides additional evidence of Hegel's cunning of world history. When his bothers sank to the dust begging him for forgiveness for having sold him into slavery, Joseph told them something close to this: "you meant it for my harm; God meant it for our good. God used you to preserve us for posterity". The African seller, the white buyer and the white plantation owner all meant slavery for the bodily and psychic harm of those helpless Africans in chains. But the cunning of history intervened and through the crucible of great pains and suffering, turned it for the long-term good of the African American. Through slavery, the African in the U.S. was preserved and allowed to participate in the edification of the greatest experimental civilization ever built by man. Through slavery, Africa gave not only her sweat but a soul to a mechanical civilization that otherwise would have perished of her soulless materialism. Today, just try to imagine the U.S. without African Americans! To be sure, still recalling how their ancestors landed in north America in chains and in the hold of a ship is still gruesome enough. They would have preferred that that their ancestors, like the ancestors of the whites or of Obama had come to America of their own volition. Of course that wish was not fulfilled. But has such a black American considered the cunning hand of providence that used slavery to cause him to be in America rather than being left behind in Africa as the offspring of an unsold African? Today a good number of the offspring of the unsold African eking out a living amid the hunger, conflicts, wars and disorder of Africa would wish that their ancestors had also been sold because, according to a quote I read in the web sometime ago, "the worst day in America is still better than the best day in Africa". Pondering this, the black American will realize that although there are still challenges for the black man in the U.S., where he is now, what he is now, is perhaps the best possible outcome for him. A black man who still finds it difficult to get over the trauma of slavery and racism should ponder the cunning of providential wisdom that used the sufferings of slavery to cause him to escape the fate of Africa.

What Hegel's cunning of history and Joseph's wisdom of the unseen better future have in common is to enable the radical expansion of consciousness, the breaking out of the confines of a received moralistic view of things, the stretching of historical memory to the point where it begins to embrace its long-repressed no go areas. Through Hegel's expanded rationality of world history, not only can we Africans and black Americans totally reconfigure the historical memories of slavery and colonization, we can more importantly exit the traumatic memories by rediscovering in them buried positivities and advantages that pan-black culture had conditioned us to be blind to. Thus post-Africanizing our reading of slavery and colonization shows that: [1] The story of slavery, like the fact of blackness, is not a burden or an existential predicament unless we allow it to be. We allowed it when we gave an exclusively traumatic meaning to it. We can unlearn the trauma by changing the story the way Joseph changed the story of his captivity into one of divine preservation for posterity. Once we have understood the cunning hand of world history in ordering human affairs, what is left for the black American is for him to quit bleeding from old scars so that he can practice what Nietzsche calls *amor fati* i.e., love of fate, accepting what is, what the past was and loving it. The black man who practices amor fati frees up his energy for creative uses, for the things he can change. The opposite of amor fati is remaining stuck in resistance patterns of thought, victimhood and a perpetual accusation of external circumstances. To me, staying put in resistance and victimhood is the real enemy of the freedom that black Americans yearn for. [2] Colonization has been seen as the source of Africa's postcolonial burden because we failed to see the cunning hand of history that sought to use colonization to quicken our entry into modernity and development. The post-African refers the hard-core Fanonian who still holds this archaic anticolonial view to the ex-colonized countries in Asia who have successfully modernized. He suggests that rather than still blame colonization for the persistence of Africa's woes, we should blame the persistence of the anticolonial mind-set that has blinded us to the historically proven advantages of colonization in good hands.

The move from Négritude through post-Négritude to post-Africanism is necessitated by the imperative to save Pan-Africa from its acquired racial/cultural self. The Africanity myth common to both Africa and black America may still be fertile for resistance thinking, victim-centered art and theory but it is not good enough for harnessing the infinite riches of the imagination of the global citizen of today. Post-Africanism is an attempt to pull Africa and black America out of the Africanity tunnel so that we can be fully reconnected to the infinite, problem-solving creativity of the global world process.

Decolonization in Adversity: Cultural Constellations through the Prism of *Présence Africaine*[1]

Lotte Arndt

A day after the attack on the satirical newspaper *Charlie Hebdo* and the hostage-taking in the kosher supermarket in eastern Paris in 2015, several official speeches brandished like a shield the values of the French Republic and "civilization" that needed to be defended against "barbarism." The satirical magazine was transformed into a sacred symbol of freedom of expression and enlightenment—principles that are declared the pride of Western society, to be defended against the enemy at all cost.

In this belligerent scenario that functions through binary oppositions, the selectivity of French universalism remains unmentioned. Yet while claiming to be "blind" to differences, the history of Republican liberty has long been colored.[2] The racial, classist, gendered and cultural codification of the French nation is inextricably linked to its colonial history. It is within this context that the struggle for decolonization occurred and can now inform us. Obviously, historical conditions have changed since the first half of the twentieth century. However, today's muted social divisions and the difficulty of formulating unifying, transnational projects of emancipation—urgent more than ever to counter fundamentalist closures of all denominations—urge us to reflect on the ongoing exclusionist structures, and to trace them back to the time when Paris was the capital of one of the largest colonial empires.

On the eve of independence, the shape of the nation-state and the territorial delineation of borders had not yet become fundamental postcolonial conditions—the possibilities of historical invention still seemed endless. Guadeloupian writer Maryse Condé recalls the unifying period of the journal *Présence Africaine* prior to African independence in the 1960s:

> *...[T]here was a wonderful, generous dream in those days. The dream of a black world which would not be broken up into distinct nations by the colonial languages and various colonial systems of governments. A black world which would speak through one voice, through the univocal voice of its poets and writers. A black world which would recover its dignity and pride.*[3]

While the writer highlights the idea of the cultural unity of a "black world"—opposing cultural continuity to the historical carve-up since the slave trade, and artistic redemption to political violence—other movements were forging Third World alliances, demanding self-determination

1 This article was first published in *Qalqalah, a Reader #1*, edited by Bétonsalon—Centre d'art et de recherche and Kadist Art Foundation, Paris, March 2015. Thanks to Virginie Bobin, Mélanie Bouteloup and Élodie Royer. A first draft of this paper was presented in the frame of "Action! Painting, publishing!", closing exhibition and public events that finalized the residency of Marion von Osten at Laboratoires d'Aubervilliers in Summer, 2012.

2 Sue Peabody and Tyler Stovall, eds., *The Color of Liberty. Histories of Race in France* (Durham and London: Duke University Press, 2003).

3 Maryse Condé, "Order, Disorder, Freedom, and the West Indian Writer", *Yale French Studies*, no.97, part 2 (2000): 155.

while seeking allies among those ready to support them by force of arms if necessary. Rather than emerge as a history of indivisible and unambiguous oppositions to colonization, the work of decolonization preceding independence was accompanied by difficult negotiations, during which political and artistic movements transformed the tools of domination into concepts for a new project for society.

I will examine some of the constellations through which these laborious projects were mapped out in issues of *Présence Africaine,* a journal founded in 1947 (and accompanied by a publishing house since 1949) in Paris by the Senegalese intellectual Alioune Diop. Through the prism of the journal—the quest for a future postcolonial language developed amid the backdrop of that colony's mainland—there appeared what could be called *adversarial constellations*: within the policy of unity that *Présence Africaine* defended as its guiding principle,[4] some fundamental fault lines emerged. The journal presented itself as a forum where cultural strategies would be shaped, where both impasses and breakthroughs could be outlined. To refer to Michel de Certeau, I propose to read the work undertaken by the journal as a *construction site of the future in confined spaces*:[5] in other words, the incessant effort to surpass social assignations while being conditioned by one's environment and by the power struggles of one's time.

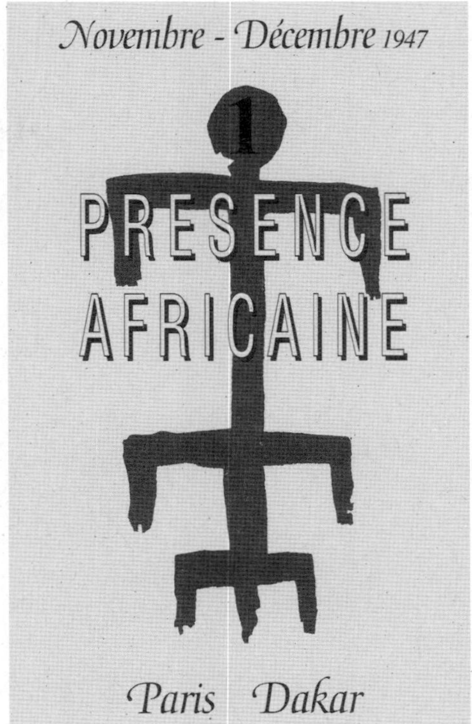

Cover of *Présence Africaine* 1, 1947. Reproduced by permission of Présence Africaine

Building an African Presence in Paris

Présence Africaine was founded in Paris, which in the 1920s had become a nodal point in the creation of a black transnational movement[6] and internationalist alliances,[7] following the Bandung Conference held in Indonesia in 1955, an event integral to the Non-Aligned Movement and a crucible of nationalisms seeking independence.

"The role of Paris was both fascinating and deeply ironic," writes Tyler Stovall. "After all, the city was the heart of one of the world's great colonial Empires, a place where anonymous French officials supervised the subjugation of millions of black Africans. Outside of Marseille, London, and some other British cities, one could not find a more diverse black population anywhere in Europe."[8] Ironic indeed because "French

4 For an ample presentation of *Présence Africaine*, see Sarah Frioux-Salgas, ed., "Présence Africaine". Les conditions noires: une généalogie des discours", special issue of *Gradhiva*, no. 10 (2009), 2009), accompanying the exhibition "Présence Africaine" (curator: Sarah Frioux-Salgas), Musée du Quai Branly, 2009–2010. I would like to thank Sarah Frioux-Salgas for her generous comments, and for the views of the exhibition *Présence Africaine* at the Cheikh Anta Diop University, Dakar, 2011.

5 De Certeau speaks of cultural work as a "proliferation of inventions in limited spaces" in *La culture au pluriel* (Paris: Seuil, 1993), 13.

6 Iris Schmeisser, *Transatlantic Crossings between Paris and New York. Pan-Africanism, Cultural Difference and the Arts in the Interwar Years* (Heidelberg: Universitätsverlag Winter, 2006).

7 See Brent Hayes Edwards, *The Practice of Diaspora. Literature, Translation, and the Rise of Black Internationalism* (Harvard: Harvard University Press, 2003); Michel Fabre, *La rive noire. De Harlem à la Seine,* (Paris: Lieu Commun, 1985).

8 Tyler Stovall, *Paris Noir: African Americans in the City of Light* (Boston: Hougthon Mifflin, 1996), 90.

colonialism and primitivism [thus] paradoxically combined to foster a vision of Pan-African unity."[9]

The decolonization movements drew upon tireless processes of translation: both in the literal sense of a policy of multilingualism—to allow information and literature to travel between colonies—as well as in the wider sense of the translation of ideas.[10] A forum for testing proposals and forms, the journal laid the foundation for a "counterculture of modernity,"[11] which progressively challenged France's universalist position and demanded full civil and cultural participation for the colonized. Cultural unity and solidarity—formulated at times in racial terms, at other times in anticolonial terms—were key instruments in this pursuit.

In this context, one can speak—to quote Edward Said and Brent Hayes Edwards—of "adversarial internationalization," which both authors describe in terms of "the attempts to organize alliances to challenge the prevailing discourses of Western universalism that were simultaneously adversarial in themselves, structured by political disagreements and differences of lived experiences."[12]

Labor of Transformation

In the early years of *Présence Africaine*, the evolving discourses it published were conceived in close exchanges with the positions elaborated by the researchers at the Musée de l'Homme [Museum of Man]. A precursor being the Musée d'Ethnographie du Trocadéro, the museum was founded in Paris for the 1937 World Fair. Its purpose was to present humanity in all its anthropological, historical and cultural diversity. *Présence Africaine* shared with the researchers of this institution a unifying concept of humanity and the according of value to "cultural difference." The concept—vaguely complementarist—posited that an absence of African cultural preservation impoverished the whole of humanity; African renaissance should therefore be based on the recognition of the "black genius."[13] An extension of German Romanticism, which considered the distinctive character of a "people" to be found in its cultural "genius", the movement advocated the work of invention on the basis of difference: it stated that it is in the *expression gathered in its creations* that "a people's" distinct share of humanity can be found. Studies by German anthropologist Leo Frobenius and Belgian missionary Placide Tempels' *La Philosophie bantoue* (the first book to be published by *Présence Africaine* in 1949) pursued the journal's celebration of African cultural specificity.

However, the cultural valorization of the African continent on the basis of ethnographical knowledge was from the very start caught up in a relationship of transformation. Having become emblematic of the pluralist enterprise of *Présence Africaine*, the multiple semantic layers enclosed by the symbol of the journal offers a good example.

9 Ibid.
10 See Edward Said, "Travelling Theory" in *The World, the Text, and the Critic* (Harvard: Harvard University Press, 1983), 226–47.
11 Paul Gilroy, *The Black Atlantic. Modernity and Double Consciousness* (London: Verso, 1993).
12 Edward Said, "Third World Intellectuals and Metropolitan Culture", *Raritan* 9 (1990): 31.
13 Alioune Diop, "Malentendus", *Présence Africaine*, no. 6 (1948): 6.

The symbol was inspired by a Dogon stone painting made famous by French ethnologist Marcel Griaule's studies on the cosmology of the Dogon. During the Dakar-Djibouti mission, the last of the large-scale expeditions financed by the French government between 1931 and 1933, many objects were "collected" in often asymmetrical conditions, and would subsequently make up the collection of the Musée de l'Homme.[14] The artifacts became material indicators of the cultural uniqueness of a group. While valorized, these groups became reified as objects.[15]

It was within this context that writer Michel Leiris participated in the choice of the symbol for the journal.[16] A surrealist, Leiris was a member of the patronage committee of *Présence Africaine* and an occasional contributor to the journal. In his articles at the time, egalitarian humanism and a fascination for Otherness as an invigorating alternative to the petrification of European societies went hand in hand. Leiris was hopeful with regard to ethnography; in 1930 he described it as a "magnificent science" capable of placing "all civilizations on an equal footing, considering none among them more valuable than another. [...] It is the most generally human because it is not limited."[17] Although his position was anticolonial, he nonetheless agreed to participate in this sizeable national expedition that "definitely pursued political and economic colonial interests."[18] The expedition led him to distance himself from the ethnologists' approach: after returning from the Dakar-Djibouti mission, he published *Afrique fantôme* [Phantom Africa], a critical and self-reflexive travel diary that by virtue of its subjectivism was a turning point in ethnographical writing.[19]

The ambiguities of the participant extended to those of the collected objects. In the course of their celebration and interpretation by researchers from the Musée de l'Homme, the Dogon artifacts and drawings became ethnographic objects par excellence. At the same time, they were appropriated for African cultural affirmation. The symbol of the journal—a drawing copied by Marcel Griaule during the expedition—turned into a symbol of the African voice in the heart of the colonial capital. As Salah Hassan rightly points out, cultural signifiers do not stay fixed throughout their successive interpretations. Having become the symbol of the journal, over the course of the 1950s the drawing detached

14 On the role of the Dogon in building French identity, see Irene Albers, "'Passion Dogon.' Marcel Griaule und Michel Leiris. Die Geheimnisse der Dogon [und der Franzosen]," in *Black Paris. Kunst und Geschichte einer schwarzen Diaspora,* eds. Bettina von Lintig, Kerstin Pinther and Tobias Wendl (Wuppertal: Peter Hammer Verlag, 2006), 161–180.

15 "When statues die, they enter art," declares the narrator in *Les statues meurent aussi* [Statues Also Die], a film commissioned in 1953 by *Présence Africaine* from Alain Resnais and Chris Marker. The filmmakers describe thusly the mutation of these artifacts, objects both esthetic and informative of their "culture of origin" that constitute the material collection of representations of Africa in Europe. See Peter Bloom, "La subversion des hiérarchies du savoir dans 'Les statues meurent aussi'" in *Zoos humains,* ed. Nicolas Bancel, Pascal Blanchard et al. (Paris: La Découverte, 2002), 355–61.

16 Frioux-Salgas, 2009, 10.

17 Michel Leiris, "L'œil de l'ethnographe", *Documents* 7, no. 2 (1930), 407.

18 Simone Ott, *Schwarz hat so viele Farben. Afrikanisch-französischer Kulturtransfer im frühen 20. Jahrhundert* (Frankfurt am Main: Peter Lang, 2009), 284. Retrospectively, he offers some quite harsh criticism of ethnography: "I was not let down by Africa but by ethnography. [...] I thought upon leaving that, thanks to ethnography, I would be able to leave my own skin, and get inside the skin of others, so to speak. However, I realized that I did not change in the least, and that if among the people I met I did make some friends, it was not the ethnographical study that created proximity between us." Michel Leiris, "Les Africains ont aussi le sens du beau, Entretien avec Irmeline Hosmann", *Afrique, magazine de L'Afrique et de Madagascar,* no. 69 (1967): 34.

19 Michel Leiris, *Afrique fantôme*, rev. ed.(1934; repr., Paris: Gallimard, 1981).

itself from Griaule to become an "image of resistance for African cultural and political identity."[20]

These entanglements confirm that it was not only the primitivist appropriation of African artifacts that was integral to Western modernity. In fact, ethnological discourses and primitivism themselves constituted a space for action within the project of decolonization. In this sense the cultural transformations of modernity emerged as a "two-way traffic"[21] that transformed every aspect of the colonial relationship.

In *Présence Africaine*, the valorization and reinterpretation of African artifacts and the magnification of an African imagination[22] became tools central to the construction of a counter-modernity. On the cover of an issue of *Le musée vivant* in 1948—co-edited by the director of the APAM,[23] French art historian Madeleine Rousseau and the Senegalese researcher Cheikh Anta Diop—the abolition of slavery in 1848 is juxtaposed with "the evidence of black culture" in 1948. The issue was given an introduction by Communist writer Richard Wright; his combative words were followed with a totally different text by Michel Leiris, who provided a whole list of attributes that likened Africa to an "ethnographical present,"[24] immutable and eternal, constructed as the direct opposite of Europe.[25]

Présence Africaine gradually abandoned its quest for European recognition to take up the development of tools for self-representation. To give an example, the first two meetings of the Congress of Black Writers and Artists organized by *Présence Africaine*—in Paris in 1956 (at the Sorbonne, the hub of French culture) and in Rome in 1959—were accompanied by posters designed by Pablo Picasso. The painter embodied more than anyone else the ambiguous role that primitivism played in African cultural affirmation: while attributing value to African artifacts, especially to masks,[26] he showed a disinterest in their creators and contexts.[27] Asserting the "exorcist"[28] potential of "black art" as the only thing of consequence in the advent of Cubism, he declares to have found "everything I need to know about Africa [...] in these objects."[29] Using the encounter

20 Salah Hassan, "Inaugural Issues: The Cultural Politics of the Early *Présence Africaine*, 1947–55," *Research in African Literatures* 2, no. 30 (1999): 205.

21 Kobena Mercer, "Introduction," in *Cosmopolitan Modernisms*, ed. Kobena Mercer (Cambridge: MIT Press, 2005), 21.

22 Bennetta Jules-Rosette, "Conjugating Cultural Realities: Présence Africaine," in *Surreptitious Speech. Présence Africaine and the Politics of Otherness (1947–1987)*, ed. Valentin Yves Mudimbe (Chicago: Chicago University Press, 1992), 14–44.

23 The *Association populaire des amis des musées* [People's Association of Friends of Museums], founded in 1936, with links to the Musée de l'Homme, directed by Madeleine Rousseau.

24 Johannes Fabian, *Time and the Other. How Anthropology Makes Its Object* (New York: Columbia University Press, 1983).

25 Michel Leiris, "Message à l'Afrique," *Le musée vivant* (1948): 5.

26 According to Guillaume Apollinaire, Picasso explains, "My greatest artistic emotions were those I felt when suddenly the sublime beauty of the sculptures made by the anonymous artists of Africa appeared before me. These works, passionately spiritual and rigorously logical, are the most powerful and beautiful of what the human imagination has produced." See Georges Braque et al., *Braque, Matisse, Picasso. Opinions sur l'art nègre* (Toulouse: Toguna, 1999), 10.

27 On the subject of Picasso and primitivism, see Ott, *Schwartz*, 51–90; Daniel J. Sherman, *French Primitivism and the End of Empire. 1945 to 1975* (Chicago: Chicago University Press, 2011).

28 See Klaus Herding, *Pablo Picasso. Les Demoiselles d'Avignon: Die Herausforderungen der Avantgarde* (Frankfurt am Main: Fischer, 1992), 42.

29 See Benoît de l'Estoile, *Le Goût des Autres, de l'Exposition coloniale aux Arts premiers* (Paris: Flammarion, 2007), 233. Michel Leiris observes: "Picasso never cared about ethnography! Alright, he appreciated certain African objects but it was a purely esthetic appreciation. He did not concern himself with what it could signify." Michel Leiris, *C'est à dire. Entretien avec Sally Price et Jean Jamin* (Paris: Editions Jean Michel Place, 1992), 24.

between Picasso and Guyanese modernist Aubrey Williams as an example, Simon Gikandi describes this ambiguity well. He begins by highlighting Picasso's apparent ignorance of Williams' artistic practice—a painter like him—preferring to comment on his "fine African head."[30]

The poster for the first congress features the head of a young man, shown in profile, crowned with a wild olive branch. It is in fact a portrait of Jacques Césaire, the eldest son of Aimé Césaire; the portrait accompanied one of the poems in the collection *Corps perdu* by Césaire, illustrated by Picasso.[31] The two men had met at the (communist-leaning) World Congress of Intellectuals in Defense of Peace, held in Wrocław in 1948. Romuald Fonkoua, the current publication director/editor in chief of *Présence Africaine*, offers a double interpretation of the image: for him it represents the victory of African intellectuals and athletes, but also sacrifice—the Christian crown of thorns.[32] The reading becomes even more convoluted if one takes into account that the African intellectuals who gathered at the conference in Paris appropriated the painter's fame for their own cause and, adding a caption to the poster, imposed their own interpretation. The words—verses borrowed from *Cahier d'un retour au pays natal* by Aimé Césaire—read:

> *...what I want*
> *is for universal hunger*
> *for universal thirst*
> *to summon it to generate*
> *free at last, from its intimate closeness*
> *the succulence of fruit*

Accompanied by these verses, the portrait on the poster represented, symbolically, the affirmation of the colonized, and embodied the aspirations of a subject.

Yet the history of the appropriation remains convoluted. In 1956, Aimé Césaire left the PCF (French communist party) after writing a furious "Letter to Maurice Thorez" in which he asserted that communist solidarity did not take racism and colonialism into account. At the conference in Rome in 1959, Picasso created a second poster that seems to have come from the movement for peace: it depicts a circle of small figures, each a different color, harmoniously holding up a globe. On the eve of independence and in the middle of the Algerian War, there was a noticeable absence of any kind of militant statement from the image. Instead, emphasis was placed on the unity of humanity and a message of pacifism. Here, the partial disconnection of the flow of communication between solidarity movements in emerging Cold War blocs and struggles for decolonization becomes apparent.

In Rome, Picasso was not the only one to make a poster—South African artist Gérard Sekoto produced a second one. Born in 1913 in South Africa, Sekoto had worked with his compatriot Ernest Mancoba, a member of the avant-garde group CoBrA (created in Paris in 1948). Sekoto participated in both *Présence Africaine* conferences, and contributed

30 Simon Gikandi, "Picasso, Africa, and the Schema of Difference", *MODERNISM/modernity* 10, no.3 (2003): 455–80.

31 Romuald Fonkoua, *Aimé Césaire* (Paris: Perrin, 2010), 213.

32 Ibid.

often to the journal. A figurative modernist painter, he gradually turned towards Négritude at the end of the 1950s. In 1966, he participated in the First World Festival of Black Arts, co-organized by *Présence Africaine* in Dakar. His positions evolved considerably during the last years of the decade preceding independence: in 1957, he advocated artistic universalism, asserting that art did not accept the color line. Artists were free to create as they pleased, without being confined by predefined affiliations. However, two years later, in a piece entitled "Responsibility and Solidarity in African Culture" that appeared in *Présence Africaine,* he argued that the African diaspora should return "to Africa from time to time to draw inspiration from spiritual sources that have nothing to do with Western influences."[33] Here, Africa becomes "the origin," in opposition to Western influences. The poster he conceived for the conference in Rome exudes the influences of Négritude.[34]

The choice of posters and logo accentuate the slow transformation of signifiers carried out during the decade preceding independence. Alliances were often fragile: though the journal's African editors managed to appropriate the fields of ethnography and primitivism, they were nonetheless subjected to forced Eurocentric and racist readings. When *Présence Africaine* formed its patronage committee, anxious to have access to a European support group capable of championing the journal to the French authorities, intellectuals such as Jean-Paul Sartre, Marcel Griaule, Jean Rouch, Michel Leiris and Emmanuel Mounier (note that they were all men) were invited to join. To take the example of Mounier (the publication director of the eminent humanist review *Esprit*), his *Lettre à un ami africain* [Letter to an African Friend] that appeared in the first issue exuded such paternalism that Alioune Diop responded to him five issues later, in an editorial furiously rejecting all forms of tutelage and condescension.[35] The relationship between the two men was definitely strained.[36] This event confirms the difficult negotiations that marked the period since the alliances between African and European intellectuals that created a "we" beyond racial divisions, to the violent conflicts that erupted out of the pressing demands for equality.

It seems that 1955 was a decisive year with respect to the change of direction at the journal, and exemplary of the constant changes that occur in hegemonies. As noted by Salah Hassan, the relative weight of the three main ideological formations present in the journal—liberal humanism, Pan-Africanism and communism—was redistributed around 1955.[37] Up until that point, liberal humanism, based on the projection of a universal civilization, dominated.[38] From 1955 onwards, political Pan-Africanism, nationalism and connections with non-alignment became

33 Gérard Sekoto, "La responsabilité et la solidarité dans la culture africaine", *Présence Africaine,* no. 27–28 (1959): 264.

34 See Christine Eyene, "Sekoto and Négritude. The Ante-room of French Culture," *Third Text* 105, no. 24, issue 4 (2010): 423–35.

35 Alioune Diop, "Malentendus", *Présence Africaine,* no. 6 (1948): 4.

36 Philippe Verdin, *Alioune Diop, le Socrate noir* (Paris: Lethellieux, 2011), 127–57. This did not stop the journal from publishing a moving obituary in its special issue 8–9, in 1950, following the intellectual's sudden death.

37 Hassan, "Inaugural Issues," 195.

38 Even if earlier radical positions can be found—for example, in the special issue on work in Africa, coordinated by the French communist writer and sociologist Pierre Naville in 1953.

more prevalent.[39] In the summer of 1955, the liminal piece *Notre nouvelle formule* [Our new direction] declared that all articles would be published as long as they "concern Africa, do not betray either our antiracist, anticolonial determination, or the solidarity of the colonized."[40]

Blurred Forms

Présence Africaine gradually shifted from a humanist concept that saw "culture" as the creative expression of humanity as a whole to a more staunch anticolonialism. Thus, to resist "colonial negation"—a term employed by Romuald Fonkoua to designate the denial of equality that was the basis of the colonial regime—the journal generally did not advocate a particular aesthetic or ideological orientation. The policy announced by Alioune Diop in the first editorial was to consider publishing work by all "men of good will." Indeed, among contributing artists there was a wide variety of positions: those of the Nigerian modernist painter Ben Enwonwu who was highly critical of abstraction, which he considered to be an easy seduction by the West,[41] and that he countered with "nka," the Igbo (a language and people in Nigeria) concept of art as fabrication, or craft;[42] or the filmmaker Ousmane Sembène, who trained in the USSR and chose the path of social realism; or Haitian architect Albert Mangonès, who, after studying in Brussels and New York, asserted that colonization had destroyed architecture in Africa and left in its wake only the shantytown. Consequently, he explained, an African modernism needed to be invented, based on an analysis of the needs of populations, and following the expertise of modernist architects like Frank Lloyd Wright and Le Corbusier.[43] In 1955, in a debate on national literature that pitted French surrealist Louis Aragon against Aimé Césaire, followed by various *Présence Africaine* authors against each other, Césaire rejected the prescription of an aesthetic form in the name of the revolutionary cause; he favored instead a syncretic composition that he named after the fugitive slaves who rebuilt a society on unknown and hostile territory: "marronner" [to maroon]—a position that required the development of an invented aesthetic for an emerging future.[44] The literary forms in the journal seemed to free themselves more easily from academicism than did visual art. Beyond that, the business of cultural decolonization was partial on yet another level: it presented itself as almost exclusively male. The writer Richard Wright was the only one to point out, in fact, at the conference in 1956, the absence of women among the speakers.

While the concept of culture as the expression of the creative faculty of humans guaranteed an extreme diversity of positions, it also prevented a more militant policy that could have made the journal a tool

39 Hassan, "Inaugural Issues," 194.

40 Alioune Diop, "Notre nouvelle formule" *Présence Africaine,* no. 1–2 (1955): 6.

41 Ben Enwonwu, "Les points de vue de l'Afrique sur l'art et les problèmes qui se posent aujourd'hui aux artistes africains" in *Premier festival mondial des arts nègres. Catalogue,* ed. Société africaine de culture, Unesco, Republic of Senegal (Dakar, 1966).

42 When Okwui Enwezor, Salah Hassan, and Chika Okeke-Agulu founded their journal on contemporary African art in the U.S. in 1994, they chose "nka" as its title.

43 Albert Mangonès, "Architecture et civilisation négro-africaine", *Présence Africaine,* no. 27–28 (1959): 286–91.

44 James Clifford, *The Predicament of Culture. Twentieth-Century Ethnography, Literature, and Art* (Harvard: Harvard University Press, 1988), 180.

in the development of a specific aesthetic proposition. On the other hand, the positions all had in common the search for new forms of expression for the creation of a new Africa. Following Elisabeth Harney, who argued against adopting "such blanket terms such as abstraction from a European modernist hermeneutical framework,"[45] we should analyze the processes of borrowing, sharing and reconfigurations in the context of asymmetrical power.

Along with independence came the political divisions of a world henceforth carved out by the Cold War and neocolonial strangleholds. *Présence Africaine* participated in the organizing of large African festivals (Dakar 1966 and Lagos 1977) that replaced the conferences of the 1950s in Europe. Many contributors to the journal also attended the Pan-African Cultural Festival in Algiers in 1969. Yet ideological divisions were strongly felt at these festivals organized within the remit of nation-states, with differing, at times contradictory, geopolitical affiliations.[46] In 1966 in Dakar, *Présence Africaine* took charge of organizing the World Festival of Black Arts, and published its proceedings. However, because of political differences, many artists—Miriam Makeba and artists from Cuba, Guinea, and Algeria, to name a few—were absent.[47] Whilst the Afro-Brazilian painter Wilson Tiberio (who had lived for a long time in France) and poet Léopold Sédar Senghor were working in tandem in 1956, their paths split soon after. Tiberio became a militant tricontinentalist during the 1960s; he still attended the conference in Dakar in 1966, but was deported afterwards by president Senghor due to his political stances. While Senegal built the Musée Dynamique, thus anchoring its postcolonial modernity in Ancient Greece, the Pan-African Cultural Festival in Algiers, with its parades and performances, celebrated "ancestral" popular culture. And when Alioune Diop sought a place for *Présence Africaine* in the organization of the Festac 77 in Lagos, pursuing the idea of a united vision of the continent, the clashes that emerged with the heads of this regional power in full national expansion were such that he left the country outraged. The African unity voiced from the diaspora of Paris or the Caribbean was now at loggerheads with the national realities, rivalries and geopolitical affiliations of African countries. The adversarial decolonization extended well beyond independence, and was now being negotiated within the context of a network of nation-states that had become the condition for postcolonial independence.

Translated by Francesca Devalier

45 Elizabeth Harney, *In Senghor's Shadow: Art, Politics, and the Avant-Garde in Senegal, 1960–1995* (Durham NC: Duke University Press, 2004).

46 Cédric Vincent, ed., *Festivals et biennales—machines ou utopies?* (Paris: L'Harmattan, 2008).

47 See the virulent criticism by Abdallah Stouky: "The World festival of Black Arts, or nostalgia for Négritude", *Souffles*, no. 2 (1966): 41–5.

Black Internationalism in Interwar France[1]

David Murphy

La France Noire

The history of black culture in France in the interwar period has long been dominated by accounts of jazz, Josephine Baker and the *vogue nègre* of the 1920s; of Aimé Césaire, Léon-Gontran Damas, Léopold Sédar Senghor and the birth of Négritude in the 1930s. Over the past three decades, groundbreaking academic research[2] has uncovered the writings and activism of another largely forgotten group of black militants from the 1920s. This research never managed fully to displace the dominant narrative regarding this period, especially in the mind of the general public. However, a spate of recent cultural artifacts in France—from exhibitions to publications to documentary films—have sought to position the history of what is now commonly termed "La France Noire" within a wider historical framework that extends beyond the wave of mass migration that began during the *Trente Glorieuses*.[3] Pap Ndiaye's *La Condition noire* (2008), a genuine media phenomenon (which saw the text misleadingly dubbed "the birth of black studies *à la française*"), devoted a chapter to exploring the history of black people in France. In late 2009, the "Présence Africaine" exhibition at the Quai Branly Museum in Paris gave prominence to a group of pioneering black activists from the interwar period[4] (as did the special issue of *Gradhiva* that accompanied it).[5] In late 2011/ early 2012, Pascal Blanchard, a leading figure in the ACHAC collective of scholars, was involved in two initiatives that made a point of beginning their historical narrative well before the Second World War: his co-edited collection *La France Noire* (2011), a handsomely produced *beau-livre*, promptly sold out in the run-up to Christmas (has the story of blackness in France attained the level of acceptability that allows it to be offered as a stocking filler?), and he co-authored the documentary film, *Noirs de France* (2012), which served as a televisual companion to *La France Noire* and was screened to audiences over three weeks on France 5. The material highlighted in these various forums was not new, but the impact of these high-profile cultural events was to create a sense of a lost history at last being rediscovered.

1 This work was supported by grants from the British Academy and the Carnegie Trust for the Universities of Scotland. Published as "Defending the 'Negro race': Lamine Senghor and black internationalism in interwar France" in *French Cultural Studies* 24, no. 2 (2013): 161–73. Copyright © 2013 by SAGE Publication. Reprinted by Permission of SAGE.

2 See Philippe Dewitte, *Les Mouvements nègres en France 1919–39* (Paris: L'Harmattan, 1985); C.L. Miller, *Nationalists and Nomads: Essays on Francophone African Literature and Culture* (Chicago: University of Chicago Press, 1985); B.H. Edwards, *The Practice of Diaspora: Literature, Translation and the Rise of Black Internationalism* (Cambridge MA: Harvard University Press, 2003); B.H. Edwards, "The shadow of shadows", *Positions: East Asia Cultures Critique* 11, no.1 (2003): 11–49.

3 D. Thomas, *Black France: Colonialism, Immigration and Transnationalism* (Bloomington: Indiana University Press, 2007).

4 For a description of the exhibition and its aims, see Présence Africaine: a forum, a network, a movement: http://www.quaibranly.fr.

5 See S. Frioux-Salgas ed., "Présence Africaine. Les Conditions noires: une généalogie des discours", special issue of *Gradhiva*, no. 10 (2009).

One of the central recurring figures at the heart of these accounts of black France in the 1920s is Lamine Senghor, a Senegalese veteran of the First World War, who emerged in the mid 1920s as the best-known and the most influential black anticolonial activist of the period. In his writings and activism, Senghor combined a communist-inspired critique of empire with an attempt to forge a shared sense of black identity across disparate groups within France and more globally. This article will chart the trajectory of Lamine Senghor's brief career as an activist from 1924 to 1927 (he died of tuberculosis in November 1927, having suffered serious lung damage when his battalion was gassed at Verdun in 1917), as a means of exploring the possibilities for black advocacy in 1920s France.[6] At the same time, the story of Senghor's activism and ideas will serve as a platform from which to assess briefly, in the conclusion, the more celebrated advocacy of blackness by the Négritude writers of the 1930s. Lamine Senghor and his fellow activists of the 1920s, such as Tiémoko Garan Kouyaté and Max Bloncourt, are generally perceived as representatives of a failed movement, the positive dimension of their work limited to their role as precursors to the successful black movements of later periods. However, it is my contention that we cannot simply dismiss Lamine Senghor's project because of its "failure". As Frederick Cooper, the renowned historian of francophone Africa, has argued in another context (the collapse of a federal project linking France and Africa under the Fourth Republic): "the failure ... is explainable, but explainable does not mean that failure was inevitable and that the attempt is a minor detour along the path of history".[7] The case of Lamine Senghor offers us an important historical vantage point from which to examine some key issues that remain of central relevance today. Should the black community seek equality through its own independent pressure groups or through strategic alliances with mainstream political parties? And how does one engage with issues of racial (or religious) equality within the terms of the purportedly color-blind and secular Republic?

The Diagne–*Les Continents* Trial

On November 24, 1924, Lamine Senghor made his entry onto the French political scene when he appeared as a witness for the defense in a libel trial, at the *Tribunal de Paris*, which for a few days at least thrust several key black actors to the forefront of public debate in France.[8] The antagonists at the heart of the trial were the most (in)famous black Frenchmen of their day. The plaintiff, Blaise Diagne, had developed an international profile over the decade since he was first elected deputy representing the *quatre communes* of Senegal in 1914, as is illustrated by the political capital he deployed in hosting W. E. B. Du Bois's 1919 Pan-African Congress in Paris; the main defendant, René Maran, was

6 This article is inspired by a wider research project that includes a critical edition of Lamine Senghor's writings (Senghor, 2012) and an intellectual biography to be published in 2014.

7 See F. Cooper, "From imperial inclusion to republican exclusion? France's ambiguous postwar trajectory," in *Frenchness and the African Diaspora: Identity and Uprising in Contemporary France*, eds. C. Tshimanga, D. Gondola and P.J. Bloom (Bloomington: Indiana University Press, 2010), 117.

8 See A.L. Conklin "'Who speaks for Africa?' The René Maran-Blaise Trial in 1920s Paris," in *The Color of Liberty: Histories of Race in France*, eds. S. Peabody and T. Stovall (Durham, NC: Duke University, 2003), 302–37.

author of the Goncourt-winning *Batouala* (1921), a novel whose anticolonialist credentials rested primarily on the staunch critique in its preface of French colonial practices in Central Africa.[9] In reality, very little separated Diagne and Maran in terms of their fundamental attitude to French colonialism: both believed profoundly in France's *mission civilisatrice* and they argued for the full assimilation of black people into French culture. However, as with so much of the racial politics of the 1920s, the fault line between the two men centered on the "dette du sang" that France was deemed to owe to its colonial troops who had played such a vital role in the First World War. Over 130,000 black African troops had participated in the war with over 30,000 killed, and Diagne had played a crucial role in recruitment, especially in the latter stages of the conflict.[10] In January 1918, he accepted an invitation from Clemenceau, desperate for the extra troops that might finally bring the war to a successful conclusion while limiting the loss of further French lives, to lead a recruitment tour in French West Africa. Given the title of Haut Commissaire de la République, Diagne was greeted in the colonies with the pomp and ceremony normally reserved for white dignitaries from the imperial center, which initially enhanced his reputation amongst France's many black subjects and its few black citizens. However, by the time of the libel trial in 1924, Diagne had become a figure of hate for some, especially amongst black activists: promises made about black participation in the war leading to reform of the colonial system, as well as increased access to rights and citizenship, had proven illusory; for many reformist and radical black groups, Diagne had sold out to colonial interests.[11]

It was in this context, in October 1924, that Maran published an article titled "The Good Disciple", in the black newspaper *Les Continents*, in which he accused Diagne of having received "a certain commission for each soldier recruited".[12] Similar accusations had previously appeared in the mainstream French press but an indignant Diagne regarded the publication of such claims in a "black" newspaper as a danger to his reputation as an advocate for equality. *Les Continents* was the newspaper of La Ligue Universelle de Défense de la Race Nègre (LUDRN), founded by the colorful figure of Kojo Tovalou Houénou, a lawyer and dandy, the son of a prosperous Dahomean merchant (he claimed that he was in fact a descendant of the mythical King Behanzin). Although Houénou was a great admirer of Marcus Garvey and his United Negro Improvement Association (at the time of the trial, he was actually in the US where he met Garvey and addressed the UNIA convention), LUDRN and *Les Continents* shared little of the Jamaican's radicalism. In the terminology of the

9 As most commentators have noted, the novel itself is far more ambiguous in its representation of Africa than would appear from a reading of the preface.

10 According to Michel (2003), over 200,000 sub-Saharan African troops were raised during the war but only about 130,000 saw active service in France. In the interwar period (in the absence of reliable historical research), the estimates for the number of troops who saw action and the numbers killed were vastly over-inflated: for example, Lamine Senghor and other critics of the war regularly claimed that over 100,000 had been killed. The debate still rages between historians regarding the extent to which African soldiers may have been used as "shock troops" in order to spare French lives.

11 See G.W. Johnson, *The Emergence of Black Politics in Senegal: The Struggle for Power in the Four Communes, 1900–1920* (Stanford CA: Stanford University Press, 1971).

12 L. Senghor, "La Violation d'un pays et autres écrits anticolonialistes," presented by D. Murphy ((Paris: L'Harmattan, 2012), 109–10. The original article was unsigned but Maran later acknowledged authorship.

times, LUDRN was "anticolonialiste" in the sense that it called for the reform of the colonial system; it did not call for the independence of the colonies. It was thus closely aligned with the position of the moderate French left (SFIO) and the Ligue des Droits de l'Homme: indeed, Félicien Challaye, one of the Ligue's most powerful orators also appeared as a witness for the defense in the libel trial.

In late 1924, Lamine Senghor occupied a far more radical position in relation to empire than LUDRN, and his testimony presented French society with a troubling image of the *tirailleur sénégalais.* The arrival of vast numbers of African troops on French soil had led to a significant transformation of the vision of the African in the popular imagination: in place of "the savage", the image spread of "the good tirailleur, this big child" who smilingly served France (most infamously in the imagery for the Banania powdered chocolate drink). However, Lamine Senghor's intervention projected the tirailleur sénégalais as a man who had been radicalized by his experiences and who would now devote himself to the denunciation of colonial injustice:

> *Instead of attempting to prove precisely how much the great slaver trader [Diagne] received for each Senegalese he recruited, they should have brought before him a whole procession of those blinded and mutilated in the war. [...]*
>
> *All of these victims would have spat in his face the infamy of the mission that he had undertaken.*[13]

Senghor had already been a militant for several months in the Union Intercoloniale (UIC), an organization created by the Parti Communiste Français in 1921 with the aim of providing a forum in which a broad transcolonial front against empire might develop. Although nominally an independent group run by and for representatives of the colonized peoples (Nguyen ai Quoc, the future Ho Chi Minh, was one of the most active members of the group in its early stages), the UIC was in fact controlled by the PCF's Comité d'études coloniales. In the columns of the UIC's newspaper, *Le Paria*, were to be found the most violent denunciations of empire of the period. What made the UIC particularly menacing was the group's communist provenance, for the Communist International (or Comintern) of 1920 had adopted a resolutely anti-imperial stance and it was increasingly pressuring communist parties in the imperial nations to adhere to the party line.

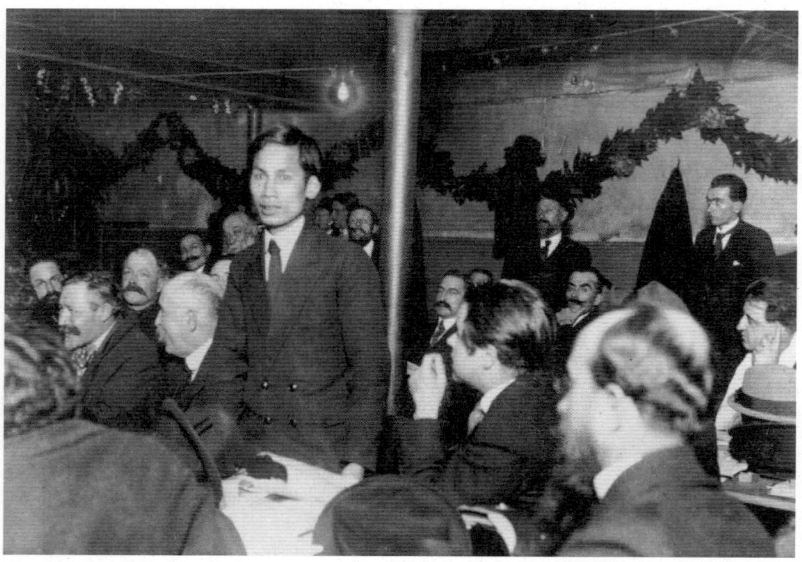

Ho Chi Minh at the Congress of Tours, France, 1920. Reproduced by permission of Art Resource, New York.

13 Ibid., 33–34. Unfortunately, the *procès-verbal* of the trial was lost in a fire in the municipal archives in the 1970s; however, Lamine Senghor wrote an account of the trial for *Le Paria* from which I have cited here. The model of the *tirailleur* who is blindly loyal to France is to be found in *Force-Bonté*, an autobiographical work by Bakary Diallo, published in 1926.

Although one might legitimately question the good faith of the Comintern in its anti-imperialism, the fact cannot be underestimated that communism was the sole metropolitan movement of the mid–1920s to call for the independence of the colonies: in the eyes of its colonized members, the UIC represented the potential for fruitful alliances in the imperial center; while for the French authorities, the movement was a potentially subversive revolutionary force that needed to be closely policed.

Why though did the young Senegalese communist come to the defense of a bourgeois reformist newspaper? Lamine Senghor appears largely to have been motivated by his status as a war veteran, something that would remain central to almost every article and speech he would write. The fact that he had fought for France made it that much more difficult for the French authorities to dismiss him as a subversive, a fact that surely did not escape the PCF leaders who decided to promote him within the movement's ranks. Also, in 1924, the Comintern had called on communists to seek alliances with all anticolonial nationalist movements: and, as Philippe Dewitte, the leading historian of black movements in France in the interwar period, has argued, the Diagne–*Les Continents* trial was perceived as an opportunity to create a united anticolonial front.[14] This united front would only last a few years but it is in this context that we must situate Lamine Senghor's activism. The newspaper lost the trial but, as was indicated above, the incident cemented a profound change in the perception of Diagne: previously seen by many blacks as a defender of his race, his status as a deputy constituting proof of the promises of assimilation, he now came to be regarded as a traitor to the black cause. For the radical black movements of the next few years, Diagne was the *bête noire*, often caustically dismissed as a *nègre blanc* or, in an echo of the charge made against him by Maran, decried as a *négrier*: he became virtually the sole figure around whom disparate black groups could unite in opposition. There is a major irony here of course in hatred of a black leader, one who had hosted the 1919 Pan-African Congress to boot, acting as a unifying force for more radical black movements. In reality, though, such maneuvers would become a mainstay of national and transnational black politics throughout the twentieth-century, as the pioneers of one era were decried as Uncle Toms (or worse) by younger, more radical generations that followed. When Lamine Senghor launched a black movement in 1926, the group would insistently refer to itself as "la jeunesse nègre", positing their radical position as a generational break with a conservative, older black leadership. But would this bring about a radical break with the assimilationism of their elders?

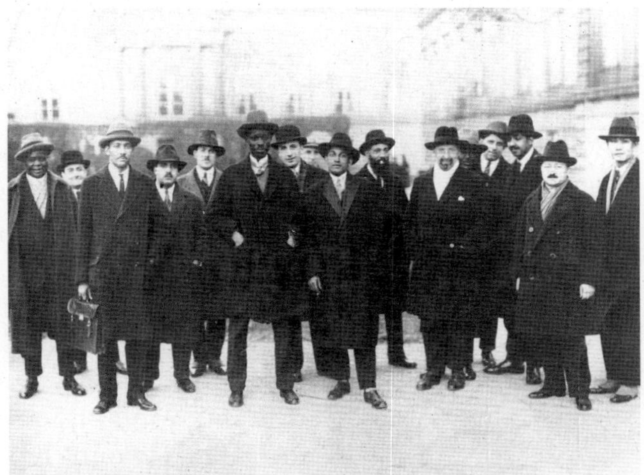

Portrait of Lamine Senghor, J.T. Gumdede and other delegates that attended the 1927 League Against Imperialism Congress in Brussels in February 1927.

14 Dewitte, *Les Mouvements nègres*, 91.

L'Union intercoloniale: Building a Transcolonial Front against Imperialism

In the aftermath of the trial, Lamine Senghor became a mainstay of UIC activities and a regular contributor to *Le Paria*. He wrote about strikes in French West Africa, projecting black and white workers united against their capitalist bosses and condemning forced labor in the colonies as a new form of slavery. However, his most significant contribution was in seeking to forge alliances with representatives of other colonial movements, based on the principle that the transnational reach of empire must be met with a transcolonial front of anticolonial resistance.

In late 1924 and throughout 1925, the PCF, responding to the Comintern's policy of building alliances with nationalist movements, carried out its most sustained anticolonial campaign when it sought to organize resistance to the colonial war in the Rif Mountains of Morocco.[15] The most zealous advocate of the Comintern's anticolonial line within the PCF was Jacques Doriot who saw in the resistance of the Moroccan indigenous leader, Abd el-Krim, against Spanish and French domination of the Rif region, the perfect occasion for the PCF finally to prove its anticolonial credentials to an increasingly impatient Comintern. When Abd el-Krim won a remarkable victory over the Spanish colonial army in September 1924, Doriot and Pierre Semard sent a congratulatory telegram on behalf of the Jeunesses Communistes (published on the front page of *L'Humanité* the following day), which expressed the wish that "after its definitive victory over Spanish imperialism, it will continue, on partnership with the French and European proletariat, in its struggle against all imperialisms until the liberation of Morocco is complete."[16] Doriot's notoriety increased when he suggested in parliament on February 4, 1925, that French troops in Morocco desert rather than fight their "proletarian" brothers in the Rif.[17] It seemed at last as though the PCF was fully embracing the Comintern's anticolonial agenda but, in reality, much of the PCF hierarchy was reluctant to lend the campaign its full support.

In contrast, Lamine Senghor threw himself wholeheartedly into the campaign against the Rif war, appearing at countless rallies alongside French communists, particularly Doriot and Paul Vaillant-Couturier, as well as prominent UIC members, such as the Antillean Max Bloncourt and the Algerian Hadj Ali. It was during this intense period that Senghor appears to have developed his extraordinary skills as a powerful orator. There was a concerted attempt (particularly by Doriot) to present Abd el-Krim as a proto-communist figure, seeking to create a modern republic, although this was by no means a move unanimously welcomed in communist circles, including the UIC where the likes of Bloncourt and the Haitian Camille Saint-Jacques privately argued against lending support to a "backward" tribal leader such as Abd el-Krim.[18] Lamine Senghor

15 See D.H. Slavin, "The French Left and the Rif War, 1924–25: Racism and the Limits of Internationalism," *Journal of Contemporary History* 26, no. 1 (1991): 5–32.

16 Senghor, "La Violation d'un pays," 121.

17 Ironically, the Rif war was won by the French primarily with the help of colonial troops, which meant that Doriot's fraternization strategy was largely irrelevant to conditions on the ground.

18 The wariness expressed by these UIC members is emblematic of a debate that dates back to the Comintern conference of 1920 over whether alliances with nationalists were useful in the context of anticolonial struggles (as Lenin argued) or whether they were fundamentally misguided (as the Indian Marxist M. N. Roy argued).

adopted the "official" Comintern line and promoted an alliance between all those engaged in anticolonial struggle: for instance, in his one (revealingly titled) article on the question for *Le Paria*—"The Riffian people are not the only ones. The oppressed of the world are with them"—he begins by linking the events in Morocco with the communist-nationalist revolt in China. However, his contributions go way beyond Doriot et al., in thinking through the specific nature of the uprising in the Rif, in particular articulating the potentially revolutionary nature of Islam and its role in fomenting anticolonial revolt:

> *The eyes of Islam, in particular, are turned towards the struggle unfolding between the valiant people of the Rif and the might of French militarism; the whole Islamic world, carried along on a wave of enthusiasm, is watching this victorious march towards independence.*
>
> *In light of this, French capitalism, which oppresses tens of millions of Muslims, screams in despair and rage.*[19]

Whereas Doriot "translates" the actions of the Rif rebels into a proto-communism, Lamine Senghor regards the sense of despair and oppression felt by the Islamic world as sufficient motivation in itself for their revolt. Indeed, his analysis of the role of Islam in popular resistance to Western military intervention is couched in terms that resonate with our own contemporary post-9/11 world:[20]

> *With its usual hypocrisy, [French imperialism] presents the success of the Rif armies as the prelude to an Islamic crusade against the Christian world.*
>
> *Islam, represented by 300 million slaves, crushed under the heel of different European imperialisms, thus receives the label of "Barbarism" while European capitalism becomes "Western Civilization."*[21]

The Rif war is not the result of a Samuel Huntington-style "clash of civilizations" but rather the understandable resistance of a colonized people to external domination. Indeed, there is considerable hypocrisy in the demonization of Islam, for it is a "spiritual force" that France itself had recently tried to win over to its cause:

> *Can French imperialism not recall that France itself has built in Paris a mosque demanded by the faithful so that it could attempt to bring the spiritual force of Islam under its tutelage and rally its "partisans" under its flag?*[22]

Senghor here refers to the decision taken by parliament in 1920 to build a mosque in Paris, giving state recognition to the contribution of France's Islamic subjects to victory in the First World War; the parallels are striking with the Sarkozy government's (2007–12) schizophrenic attitude towards Islam with approval accorded to state-sponsored groupings while Islam more generally is demonized.

19 Senghor, "La Violation d'un pays," 35.

20 See, for example, the arguments made regarding Muslim protests across the globe against the anti-Islamic film circulated on the internet in September 2012. "The only surprise is there aren't more violent protests," *The Guardian*, September 19, 2012, http://www.theguardian.com/commentisfree/2012/sep/18/violent-protests-blowback-us-intervention.

21 Senghor, "La Violation d'un pays," 36.

22 Ibid.

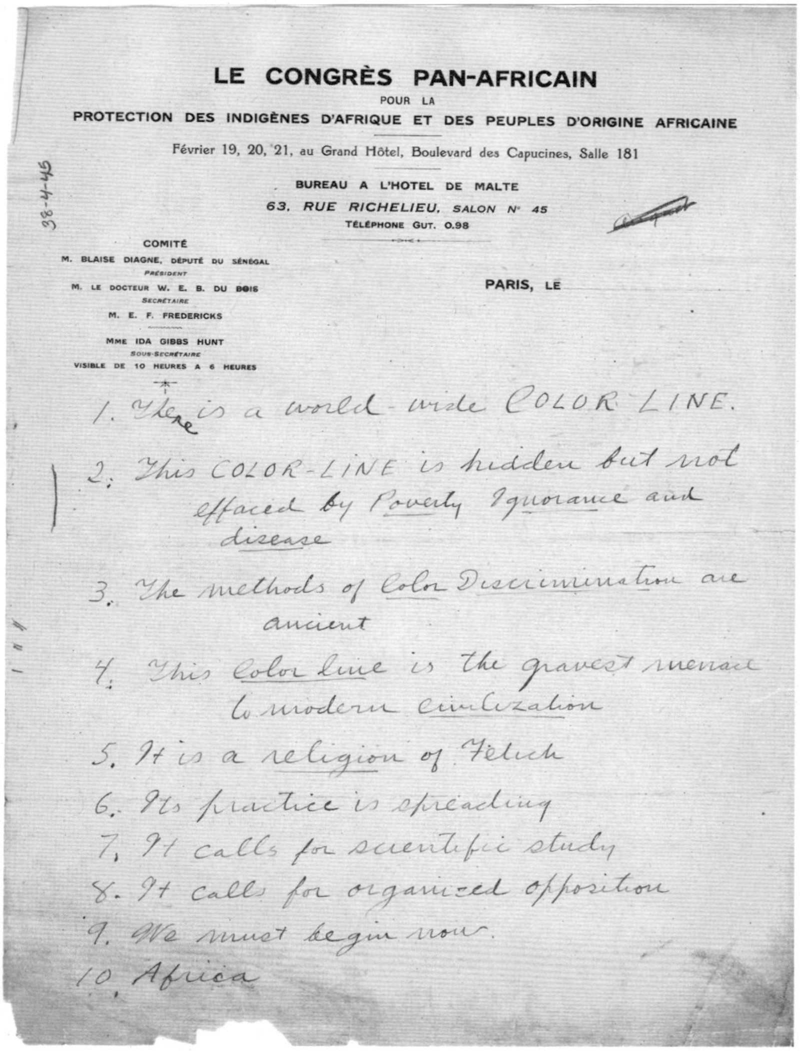
LE CONGRÈS PAN-AFRICAIN
POUR LA
PROTECTION DES INDIGÈNES D'AFRIQUE ET DES PEUPLES D'ORIGINE AFRICAINE
Février 19, 20, 21, au Grand Hôtel, Boulevard des Capucines, Salle 181

BUREAU A L'HOTEL DE MALTE
63, RUE RICHELIEU, SALON N° 45
TÉLÉPHONE GUT. 0.98

COMITÉ
M. BLAISE DIAGNE, DÉPUTÉ DU SÉNÉGAL
PRÉSIDENT
M. LE DOCTEUR W. E. B. DU BOIS
SECRÉTAIRE
M. E. F. FREDERICKS
MME IDA GIBBS HUNT
SOUS-SECRÉTAIRE
VISIBLE DE 10 HEURES A 6 HEURES

PARIS, LE

1. There is a world-wide COLOR LINE.
2. This COLOR-LINE is hidden but not effaced by Poverty Ignorance and disease
3. The methods of Color Discrimination are ancient
4. This Color line is the gravest menace to modern civilization
5. It is a religion of Fetich
6. Its practice is spreading
7. It calls for scientific study
8. It calls for organized opposition
9. We must begin now.
10. Africa

Outline of W. E. B. Du Bois's talk delivered at the Pan-African Congress held in Paris, 1919. Image courtesy of the University of Massachusetts Amherst.

After loyally serving the PCF and the UIC throughout the Rif campaign, by early 1926 Lamine Senghor had gradually come to resent the limited space devoted by the communist movement to black questions in general as well as to his own marginalized status in particular. Many historians of French communism have signaled "the imperial patriotism which coloured the colonial policies of the French Communist Party".[23] Although seeking to situate themselves as the natural allies of the colonized, the communists often saw themselves as culturally superior to those they were purporting to help. In March 1925, Lamine Senghor had already expressed his frustration when asked by the PCF to stand in the local elections in the 13th *arrondissement* in Paris, a bourgeois district in which he had little chance of winning (a tactic not unfamiliar to French political parties today when "promoting" minority candidates). As Dewitte argues, he was increasingly aware that he served as a "faire-valoir" and "caution nègre" for the PCF.[24] The final straw came when the PCF was invited to send two representatives to the Congress of Black Workers in Chicago in October 1925. The PCF selected Senghor and Bloncourt but, at the last minute, informed them that they would have to pay for the journey out of their own pockets. When Senghor objected, it was suggested that he either work his passage to America or travel as a stowaway: he refused. From that moment on, Senghor realized that in order to promote the interests of black people, it was necessary to create independent black organizations, and in March 1926 with the creation of the Comité de Défense de la race nègre (CDRN), he did just that.

Defending the Negro Race

On March 26, 1926, Lamine Senghor officially registered his new association and embarked on a tour of France's port cities (Toulon, Marseille, Bordeaux, Le Havre) in order to encounter the small working-class black community and attempt to convince them of the utility of joining the

23 J.D. Hargreaves, "The Comintern and Anti-Colonialism: New Research Opportunities", *African Affairs* 92 (1993): 255–61.

24 Philippe Dewitte, *Les Mouvements nègres*, 109.

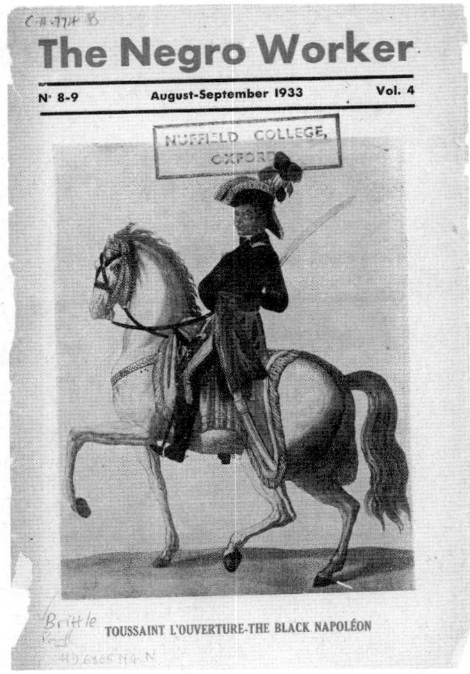

Cover of *The Negro Worker* 4, no. 8–9, August–September, 1933. Image courtesy of the Nuffield College Library, Oxford.

CDRN: his skills as a public speaker, honed during the Rif campaign, served him well and by the summer of 1926 it was estimated by the secret agents of the Ministère des Colonies' CAI[25] that he had recruited over 500 members (in a black population numbered at less than 20,000). Throughout the rest of the year, it appeared that he had broken entirely with the PCF and had decided to devote himself to defending the black community, deploying the reformist language of the Ligue des Droits de l'Homme and parts of the SFIO. The respectable CDRN fired off letters to the President and the Minister for the Colonies proclaiming their loyalty and devotion to France, and requesting financial and logistical support (the CAI archives reveal that these requests were met with silence by distrustful French authorities). In early CDRN documentation, there was no mention of capitalist imperialism; instead, the group diplomatically positioned itself within the lineage of France's great humanitarians and philanthropists:

> *For centuries, philosophers have spoken out to defend us. Setting aside religious and political issues, they have united to make heard their protests against slavery. Above all, they have promoted the supreme cause of Humanity. However, the task to which these Great Men have devoted their fortunes, their intelligence and their very lives is not yet complete.*[26]

Like many contemporary groups seeking equality for black people in France, the CDRN posited slavery and racism towards black people as a betrayal of the ideals and values of Republican France (rather than a paradox inherent in the alleged universalism of the postrevolutionary nation). It is thus unsurprising that one of the first acts of the Comité was to organize a procession in July 1926 to lay a wreath on the grave of Victor Schœlcher (a procession to the abolitionist's grave was the default gesture on which almost all black associations fell back upon at some point during this period). Far from the scathing attacks on imperialism found in *Le Paria*, the CDRN evoked the notion of "la Grande famille humaine". Senghor's self-presentation was as a "war-wounded veteran", thereby underlining his service to "the homeland". Almost pleadingly, the CDRN claimed that all they wanted was that "the Negro to be treated with a bit more humanitý" and they proposed a set of concrete proposals for black community institutions: a museum, a library, a bar-restaurant, and a hostel.

An agenda of this sort would appear to situate the CDRN less within the frame of an emerging black internationalism than within the type of reformist assimilationism that critics have seen as the hallmark of black politics in France, especially in the 1920s. However, Republican politics in the interwar period were inherently bound up in a complex set of trans-

25 The full title of the CAI was the Service de Contrôle et d'Assistance aux Indigènes. Its files are available for consultation in the SLOTFOM section of the colonial archives in Aix-en-Provence, now officially entitled the Archives Nationales d'Outre-Mer (ANOM).

26 Senghor, "La Violation d'un pays," 44.

national allegiances that simultaneously acknowledged and sought to challenge the universality of the Republic, as Gary Wilder has argued:

> *...in an imperial nation-state—containing a multinational population spread across disjunctive territories and subject to diverse regimes of governance—nation-centred politics may themselves be transnational. And transnational forms of identification become a modality through which to participate in the national politics of an imperial power. Within this system, Panafricanism and republicanism often entailed one another.*[27]

Moreover, as, both Miller (1998) and Edwards (2003) have shown in their meticulous analysis of CDRN writings, what is most original about the movement is its critical reflection on the language of race and its exploration of the modes of self-definition available to black people. The CAI records indicate that there had been much internal discussion within the CDRN about whether to use the term "noir" or "nègre" in their title, and Lamine Senghor appears to have played a central role in pushing the committee towards the latter term.

The two key newspaper articles in which Senghor articulates his ideas on the language of race are: "Le Réveil des nègres", published in *Le Paria* in April 1926, which constituted an intellectual "manifesto" announcing the creation of his new movement; and "Le Mot Nègre" from the first issue of *La Voix des Nègres*, the newspaper of the CDRN, published in January 1927. The latter article has received by far the greater critical attention but, in fact, the two pieces are almost identical, the latter essentially a minor reworking of the former. This complicates the notion of the "racial" turn in Senghor's thinking as evidence of his complete disillusionment with communism: the publication of such an article in the columns of *Le Paria* makes it clear that in many respects the break with his former communist allies was only partial (and alongside him in the CDRN were stalwarts of the UIC—Max Bloncourt, Camille Saint-Jacques and Stéphane Rosso).

In "Le Réveil des nègres", Senghor articulates a racial identity that is based not on shared racial characteristics but (like the Islamic identity outlined in his article on the Rif war) on a shared sense of oppression:

> *One of the great questions of our age is that of the awakening of the Negro.*
>
> *[...] The imperialists who dominate the peoples of the negro race, acting in fear of an explosion of anger by this latter group whose hearts bear the daily burden of their mistreatment, seek to exploit the divisions between castes and tribes that exist within our race by dividing negroes into three species: "Men of Colour", "Blacks" and "Negroes".*
>
> *[...] To be a Negro is to be exploited until one's last drop of blood has been spilt or to be transformed into a soldier defending the interests of capitalism against those who would dare try to stop its advance.*[28]

27 G. Wilder, "Panafricanism and the republican political sphere," in *The Color of Liberty: Histories of Race in France*, eds. S. Peabody and T. Stovall (Durham NC: Duke University Press, 2003), 237–58.

28 Senghor, "La Violation d'un pays," 41–2.

In 1926, to call for a "réveil des nègres" was immediately to evoke a set of ideas and a vocabulary that had been rendered popular by Marcus Garvey. In the course of his seemingly inexorable rise as a major leader of black America (until his conviction for mail fraud in 1925), Garvey had consistently called for the black world to wake from its long sleep, and his calls for black people to take pride in themselves had resonated around the world. Indeed, although not directly acknowledging his influence, the CDRN clearly owed a lot to Garvey—in terms of iconography (the shooting star in the naive and romanticized image of Africa featured on the association's headed paper, and the black star of its official stamp) and of language, especially the repeated appeals to black pride and solidarity. Equally, Senghor and the CDRN rejected the elitism of the Jamaican's African American rival W. E. B. Du Bois who argued that racial progress should be led by a "talented tenth" of black people. The influence of Garvey on black politics in interwar France has commonly been underplayed, as the general assimilationism that marks these French groups seems in many ways to be the antithesis of Garvey's identitarian discourse, and the Jamaican's anticommunist stance meant that it would have been difficult for Senghor and other militants to embrace him openly (Garvey did meet black groups including the LDRN when he visited Paris late in 1928). However, from Kojo Tovalou Houénou to Lamine Senghor and later Aimé Césaire, Léon-Gontran Damas and Léopold Sédar Senghor, these black French activists are operating (consciously or not) within a discursive space opened up by Garvey when they argue for the dignity of "le Nègre" and call for the rejection of the white world's stereotypical and racist vision of the black world. This dialogue between Garvey and the militants of the CDRN should not come as a surprise, for as Edwards[29] has so convincingly argued, the black movement of the interwar years is a resolutely transnational phenomenon in which translation (both literal and metaphorical) of ideas from one context to another plays a central role. Such translation can often appear as *mistranslation*, but, for Edwards, the translational and transnational nature of black diasporic practice inevitably highlights differences across black communities in the very process of seeking to imagine unity.

The most striking aspect of this transnational process of translation of Garvey's ideas is the CDRN's use of the term "nègre" as a proud badge of self-identification, just as Garvey had proclaimed himself a "Negro" (always with a capital "N"). In an era when the term "noir" was widely gaining prominence as a more dignified replacement for "nègre", which was seen as derogatory and demeaning, Senghor and the CDRN deliberately chose "Nègre" as the term that encompasses all black people:

> *[W]e pick up this name [negro] in the mud where it has been thrown.*
> *We will make it our symbol!*
> *This name is that of our race! [...]*
> *It is our honour and our glory to call ourselves Negroes with a capital N. It is our negro race that we wish to guide along the path towards its total liberation from the yoke of slavery. We want to*

29 Edwards, *The Practice of Diaspora*, 2003.

> *impose the respect due to our race, as well as its equality with all of the other races of the earth; which is our right and our duty.*[30]

The "nègre" is an individual who has been downtrodden and oppressed through slavery, colonialism and segregation: the terms "noir" and "homme de couleur" are seen merely as escape routes for educated blacks seeking a place in a dominant white society. The first step towards liberation is to embrace one's identity as a "nègre", for that allows one to see the true nature of Western oppression of the black world. The transnational black identity evoked here is, in sociological terms, "thin", that is, a strategic identity designed to create a coalition against empire: it was not until Négritude a decade later that a "thick" black identity, based on culture and philosophy, would begin to be articulated.

As Senghor believes that only the independence of the colonies and liberation from the white man can bring freedom and equality for "les nègres", this means that there can be no liberty within the Western colonial system. His articles for *Le Paria* envisage a color-blind community bound together by communist ideals, and the revolutionary conclusion to his most sustained piece of writing, the anticolonial allegory *La Violation d'un pays* published in June 1927, might be deemed an attempt to imagine a multiracial future post-empire. However, as he writes in an article in the first issue of *La Voix des Nègres*: "Negroes are not of any European nationality and do not wish to serve the interests of any imperialist power against its enemies."[31] Under empire, black people cannot and will not be French.

Even as the first issue of *La Voix des Nègres* proudly and insistently proclaimed the unity of "les nègres", the CDRN was in fact in the middle of a long and protracted schism that would several months later lead to the break-up of the organization, with Senghor and his fellow radicals deserting en masse to create the Ligue de Défense de la Race Nègre (LDRN). The split in the organization was the result of complex personal, political and cultural issues but appears primarily to have played out along ideological lines with the more assimilationist members remaining within a rump CDRN and the more radical, communist-leaning members departing for the LDRN.

In the midst of the CDRN in-fighting, Lamine Senghor enjoyed one final moment of glory, which sealed his reputation as the leading black anticolonialist of his day, when he was invited to speak at the inaugural meeting of the League against Imperialism (LAI) in Brussels (February 10–14, 1927). The LAI was largely a communist initiative, but in its initial phase it sought to rally all anticolonial forces together (a realization of the Comintern's 1924 call for alliances between communist and nationalists that would within a year be superseded by a shift to the promotion of class-versus-class struggle). In his speech at the Congress, Lamine Senghor, liberated from the moderation that had marked most of his contributions to the CDRN, launched into a vehement attack on imperialism as a renewed form of slavery. Imperialism cannot hope to bring civilization to the colonies for it is an inherently unjust system of domination. Senghor denounced the cruel treatment of the colonized, the violence, forced labor

30 Senghor, "La Violation d'un pays," 36.
31 Ibid., 47

and, yet again, the iniquity and double standards of the pensions paid to colonial veterans of the First World War:

> *The Negro youth can now see clearly. We know and are very conscious that, when we are needed, to get ourselves killed or to work, then we are French; but when it's a question of giving us our rights, then we are no longer French, we are Negroes.*[32]

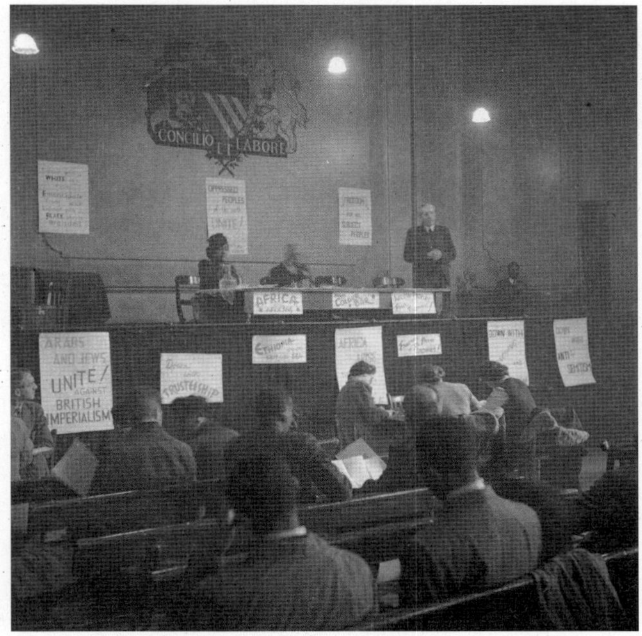

The Fifth Pan-African Congress held in Manchester in 1945. Reproduced by permission of John Deakin/Picture Post/Getty Images.

The speech was a huge success not solely in the Congress hall but around the world: it was immediately translated into English and reproduced in journals in the U.S.[33] In a fascinating article published just a few months after the Congress (1927), Roger Baldwin,[34] the director of the American Civil Liberties Union, cited Senghor as one of the most eminent of the "hommes sans patrie", those political exiles who had made Paris their home. In the final stages of the Congress, the LAI placed Senghor at the head of the working party asked to draft the "Résolution sur la question nègre" and the finished document bore all the hallmarks of his fiery stance. The situations of blacks in Africa, the Caribbean and the Americas were brought together within a history of oppression dating back five centuries: "For almost five centuries, the Negro peoples of the world have been victimized and cruelly oppressed."[35] The unity of all "nègres" and all colonized people would finally bring such oppression to an end. Little more than two years after his first public appearance, this young man from Senegal had managed to carve out a position as a radical spokesman for black people not only in France but also internationally. In parallel, Senghor had been pulling together similar ideas on slavery and colonialism in *La Violation d'un pays.* The text marked a desire to take the anticolonial struggle into the cultural sphere, however, at that very moment, his health faltered. Senghor retreated to the south of France in the hope that its drier air would give him some respite from the tuberculosis that was ravaging his lungs, but on November 25, 1927, he succumbed to the illness, almost exactly three years to the day after his appearance at the Diagne—*Les Continents* trial. The black community in France would not see a more effective political leader until after the Second World War.

In February 2010, yet another "affaire du foulard" controversy broke out when Ilham Moussaïd, a young female candidate for Olivier Besancenot's Nouveau Parti Anti-Capitaliste stood in the regional elections in the Vaucluse, and campaigned wearing a Muslim headscarf. The controversy arose in the middle of the public debate on the law that would

32 Ibid., 63.
33 B.H. Edwards, "The Shadow of Shadows," *East Asia Cultures Critique* 11, no. 1 (2003): 11–49.
34 R.N. Baldwin, "The capital of the men without a country", *The Survey* 1 (August 1927): 460–68.
35 Senghor, "La Violation d'un pays," 63.

eventually be introduced early in 2011 by the Sarkozy government, banning women from wearing the *burqa or niqab* in public places. The affair was essentially cast as the homogeneous, secular Republic attempting to deal with the arrival of a new religious and racial diversity. Critics called on Besancenot to reread Marx and Trotsky, as though it were unthinkable that Marxism might ever find common cause with Islam.

As this article has attempted to demonstrate, such attitudes reveal a lack of awareness of an earlier period in modern French politics in which a more diverse vision of left-wing politics had been possible, one in which issues of religion and race were (potentially) less divisive than they have become in the contemporary period. As Frederick Cooper has argued in relation to the complex constitutional arrangements of the Fourth Republic and its attempts to reconcile the Republic with its religious and ethnically diverse populations in the colonies:

> *...historical analysis ... can show that the spectrum of political possibility in the past was wider than people in the present—projecting backward their own positions—allow it to be. Perhaps a less closed past could help us at least to recognize the possibility of a more open future.*[36]

The past does not offer the present an easily digestible lesson on diversity and tolerance, and we must be wary of turning to the past solely in order to bolster our contemporary visions of race, religion and the public sphere. This points to a potential problem with certain ways in which the past has been revisited in some of the cultural artifacts discussed at the outset of this article: for a recurring feature is their (understandable) desire—in a contemporary period in which racist and anti-Islamic discourse have returned to the mainstream of public debate—to promote inclusive notions of Frenchness, in which the longstanding black presence (particularly, but not exclusively) in metropolitan France can be integrated into a more inclusive historical narrative of the Republic. The status within this revised historical narrative of a figure such as Lamine Senghor appears especially thorny, for he was far less concerned with carving out a space for blackness within French society than with forging an alliance between different black communities and the "darker nations" more generally in order to create a radical break with France.[37] In contrast, the black activists of the 1930s were generally more moderate than the radicals of the 1920s: direct confrontation with the imperial nation-state appeared undesirable for a wide variety of reasons. Aimé Césaire, Léopold Sédar Senghor and Léon-Gontran Damas did not shy away from politics (far from it) but they saw culture as a key area in which they could both prise open a space for blackness within French culture and create strong bonds between diverse black groups: "These colonial moderates were never as organised or activist as their radical counterparts, but they were perhaps more successful at maintaining

36 Cooper, "From Imperial Inclusion," 93.

37 Witness, for example, the almost unanimously positive response to Rachid Bouchareb's film *Indigènes* (2006) which deals with colonized Algerians participating in the liberation of France in the Second World War and the far more muted and in some cases hostile reaction to its follow-up *Hors-la-loi* (2010), which traced the way in which these same troops later formed the heart of the FLN rebellion against France in Algeria.

Pan-African cultural alliances without exploding from internal and external pressures".[38]

Négritude was both a celebration of blackness and an appeal for *le droit à la différence* within French Republican identity: it was a discourse that engaged simultaneously with national and transnational politics as well as national and transnational forms of identification, just as Lamine Senghor had sought to do by means of the (trans)national politics of communism and Pan-Africanism. This, in turn, belies the view that contemporary debates on race, religion and minority rights in France are the result of a shift from national to transnational concerns in a globalized world. For if there is one thing that the inter-war period can definitively teach us, it is that the Republic has been engaging with racial and religious diversity for far longer, and in far more complex ways, than is usually imagined.

38 Wilder, "Panafricanism and the republican political sphere," 244.

On *Souffles*: Geographies of Solidarity[1]

Clare Davies

"The duty of every revolutionary is to make the revolution", or "El deber de todo revolucionario es hacer la revolución"—a celebrated call to action borrowed from the 1962 Second Declaration of Havana—appeared in calligraphic form in a 1968 issue of the Francophone Moroccan literary journal *Souffles* (1966–1972).[2] Artist Mohammed Melehi's rendition of the phrase in what might be termed a square-Kufic style, reinscribed the legacy of the Cuban revolution and the nascent Third World liberation movement within a genre increasingly associated at the time (and subsequently canonized) as exemplary of Arab art (*fann 'arabi*). Melehi's work was reminiscent of the distinctive titular emblem he had designed for the cover of *Souffles*. It was described on the journal's title page as an example of *calligraphie* [calligraphy] and an *affiche congrès* [conference poster], ostensibly in reference to the Havana Cultural Congress (January 4–11, 1968); a topic addressed in depth over the course of the issue. Contributions centered around the relationship of culture to the revolutionary struggle and the role of the Third World intellectual in view of landmark political and cultural events, and anticolonial ideologies.[3]

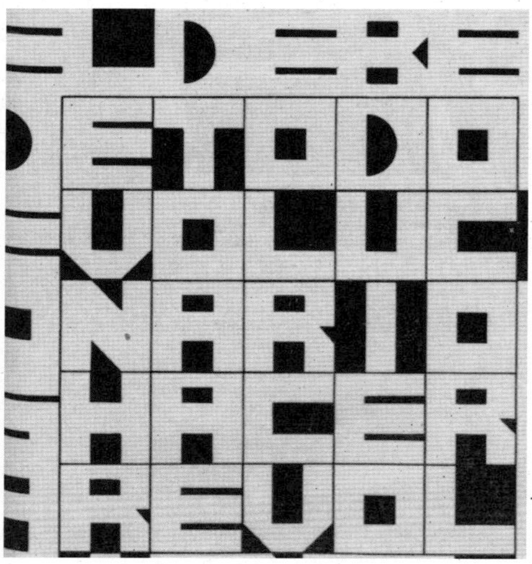

Mohammed Melehi, Untitled (Caligraphie/affiche congrès). As it appeared in *Souffles*, no. 9, 1968. Reproduced by permission of Abdellatif Laâbi.

Souffles was founded by three francophone Moroccan poets in 1966.[4] Violent crackdowns on demonstrations and the declaration of a "state of exception" the year prior inaugurated the so-called Years of Lead [*années de plomb*] associated with the reign of Hassan II (1962–1999). In 1965, Moroccan politician Mehdi Ben Barka, head of the left-wing National Union of Popular Forces and an organizer of the first Tricontinental Congress, disappeared in Paris under mysterious circumstances. The journal cultivated an explicitly Marxist-Leninist perspective and offered an interdisciplinary and international platform dedicated to "*la decolonisation cultur-*

1 This research was generously supported by the Irmgard Coninx Prize for Transregional Studies and the Forum Transregionale Studien, Berlin, and was originally delivered as a lecture at the Forum in October 2014. I am grateful for feedback offered by the 2014–2015 EUME fellows and audience members in attendance, which was useful in further developing the work. The text was first published as part of the Forum's *Essays* series in collaboration with *perspectivia.net*, and benefited from editorial review by Jenny Meurer, Stefanie Rentsch, and Georges Khalil. Fellow members of the Shatana study group (Saleem al-Bahloly, Samah Hijawi, Kristine Khouri, and Anneka Lenssen) shared documents pertaining to the founding of the institutions of Arab art. Translations are credited to the author, unless otherwise noted.

2 *Souffles* 9 (1968): n.pag. 29. *Souffles/Anfas* were banned in Morocco, and subsequently revived for a period in Paris. See Kenza Sefrioui, *La revue Souffles, 1966–1973: Espoirs de révolution culturelle au Maroc* (Casablanca: Éditions du Sirocco, 2012), 126–29.

3 The issue included a French-language translation of "The Manifesto of June 5, 1967" by Syrian poet Adonis [the pseudonym of 'Ali Ahmad al-Said], documents related to the "Havana Cultural Congress", discussions of Léopold Sédar Senghor's concept of "Négritude", and a text by Mário de Andrade (1893–1945) entitled "Culture and Armed Struggle".

4 Founders of *Souffles* included Abdellatif Laâbi, Mostafa Nissaboury, and Mohammed Khaïr-Eddine. See Jacques Alessandra and Richard Bjornson, "Abdellatif Laâbi: A Writing of Dissidence", *Research in African Literatures* 23, no. 2 (Summer, 1992): 153. For an in-depth account of the publication see Kenza Sefrioui, *La revue Souffles, 1966–1973*. I thank Suzanne Kassab for bringing this book to my attention.

elle" [cultural decolonization].[5] This goal would be achieved, writes literary historian Olivia C. Harrison, by means of, "the elaboration of literary and artistic forms that would break with French canons without seeking a return to tradition [...] identified as a colonial construct".[6]

Mohammed Melehi (b. 1936) and fellow artist Mohammed Chebaa (1935–2013) formed part of the core "working group" that headed the journal in the late 1960s.[7] By 1966, they had begun delineating the contours of a distinct project defined, in part, through their opposition to the terms of an artistic and cultural status quo.[8] An exhibition held in Rabat in 1966, helped establish Melehi, Chebaa, and Farid Belkahia (1934–2014) as the so-called Casablanca group.[9] All three belonged to a generation of artists that had grown up in Morocco under the French and Spanish Protectorates (both through 1956) and had undertaken similar educational trajectories, consistent with the broader contours of twentieth-century artistic pedagogy in the Arab world.[10] After pursuing parceled educational opportunities in the arts available to them in Morocco, they took up advanced studies in the beaux-arts academies of one or more of Europe's postwar-era metropoles. A grant from the Rockefeller Foundation brought Melehi to the United States; in 1963, he participated in an exhibition of "Hard Edge and Geometric Painting and Sculpture" at the Museum of Modern Art in New York.

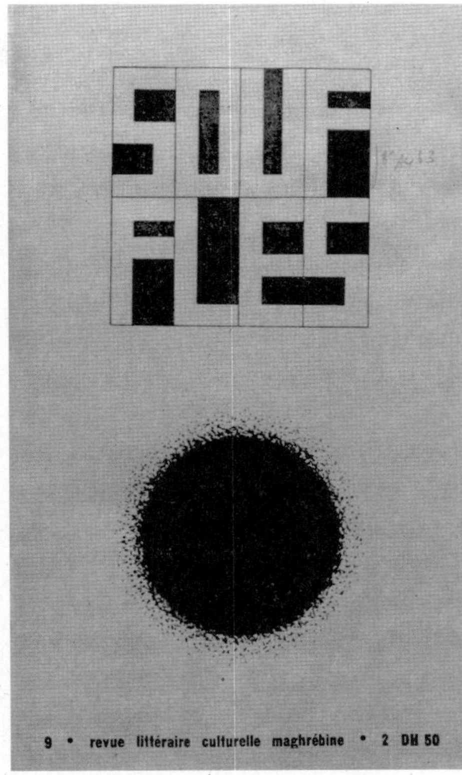

Emblem of *Souffles* designed by Mohammed Melehi. Reproduced by permission of Abdellatif Laâbi.

5 Abdellatif Laâbi, "La culture nationale, donée et exigence historique" *Souffles* 4 (1966): 4–12. The journal commonly featured work by "non-Moroccan" contributors including Toni Maraini, Afif Bahnassi, Adonis, Etel Adnan, Malek Alloula, and Rene Dépestre.

6 "Founded as a venue for experimental francophone poetry, from the second issue onwards *Souffles* published articles on popular theater, film, and art, and it quickly became a platform for debates ranging from national culture and language to the continued effects of what is founders called 'la science coloniale' [colonial science] on artistic and scholarly endeavors in postcolonial Morocco". Olivia C. Harrison, "Cross-Colonial Poetics: *Souffles-Anfas* and the Figure of Palestine", *PMLA* (March 2013): 127–28. The essay offers an especially rich account of the journal's "cross-colonial" perspective, and discusses contributors' engagement with contemporary political developments including the May 1968 protests in Paris.

7 Laâbi, Nissaboury, Melehi, Chebaa, and Abdelaziz Mansouri were joined by Abraham Serfaty after April 1968. See Alessandra and Bjornson, "Abdellatif Laâbi," 153.

8 Farid Belkahia, Mohammed Chebaa, and Mohamed Melehi, "Des peintres protestent", *Souffles* 4 (1968): 36–37.

9 "Belkahia Chebaa Melehi", Muhammad V Theatre Gallery, Rabat. January 19–February 17, 1966.

10 I retain the spellings of names that seem to have been preferred by the artists themselves in the context of *Souffles*. Melehi was born in Asilah in northern Morocco. He attended the École des Beaux Arts in Tetouan for two years, before receiving a fellowship to study sculpture at the Academie des Beaux Arts in Seville (1955) and Madrid (1956–57). He studied painting, mosaic-making and sculpture in Rome (1957–60) and resided in Paris (1960–61), before traveling to the U.S. (1962–64). He worked as a teaching assistant in painting at the Minneapolis School of Art (1962) and lived in New York. Mohamed Chebaa studied in Italy from 1962 to 1964, before returning to Morocco, where he taught architectural decoration and calligraphy at the École des Beaux Arts in Casablanca. As a young man in Marrakech and al-Jadida, Belkahia studied in the atelier of a resident artist (Teslar), before teaching primary school at Ouarzazate. He studied at the École des Beaux Arts in Paris from 1954 to 1959, and went on to pursue courses in scenography and theater decoration in Prague (1959–62). He traveled to Syria, Jordan and Egypt between 1956 and 1957. Belkahia served as the director of the École des Beaux-Arts de Casablanca from 1964 to 1972. Bibliographic information on all three is available in Mohamed Sijelmassi, *La peinture marocaine* (Paris: Arthaud), 1972, and "Situation arts plastiques Maroc", special issue, *Souffles* 7–8 (1967). See also *Melehi*, Exh. cat. Institut du Monde Arabe, Paris, June 27–August 27, 1995 and Mustapha El Kasri, *Farid Belkahia* (Rabat: Imframar, 1963).

In the mid-1960s all three artists returned to Morocco and joined the faculty of the École des Beaux-Arts de Casablanca (est. 1919). The school's curriculum was radically reconfigured to serve the goal of "visual regeneration", much in line with the goals pronounced by the editors of *Souffles*.[11] "Man requires re-adaptation to the world of today, to his ambient environment, which has undergone enormous changes", claimed Belkahia in 1967. "*The essential problem can be identified as an anachronism in man's perception.* It is not the artist who is ahead of his age, as they say, but society that is behind its age. It's a question, therefore, of undertaking an education of the visual sense [emphasis original]".[12] The school sought to disassemble hierarchies of visual production, and students were trained to draw on Moroccan craft, or "plastic tradition" in the production of new work.[13]

The following pages trace the contours of an aesthetic of decolonization as it manifested in works and writings produced by these artists for *Souffles* between 1966 and 1969. In this period, artistic contributions to the journal were presented in various guises, including, as we have seen, that of calligraphy and the conference poster. In other instances, they were described as a form of *action plastique*. The choice of terms was not accidental. Artists affiliated with the journal, I argue, understood each as central to the achievement of cultural decolonization, and they guide my own reading.[14]

The journal developed an increasingly strident critique of the Moroccan state after 1969. Meanwhile, support for *Souffles* amongst the Casablanca group artists fractured. Following the appearance of the special edition dedicated to the arts in Morocco, Belkahia distanced himself from the review. Mounting tensions lead to his dismissal of Chebaa and Melehi from the faculty of the École des Beaux-Arts in Casablanca in 1969, claims Kenza Sefrioui.[15] Two of the journal's editors were imprisoned on January 27, 1972, and tortured.[16] More key figures, including Chebaa, were arrested in May; others went into exile.[17] Subsequently, Melehi, Belkahia, Chebaa, among others, represented Morocco at the first large-scale regional biennales of art, where their works contributed to wider debates around the nature of "Arab plastic art". *Intégral*—a monthly francophone "review of plastic and literary creation" founded by Melehi in 1971—helped nudge the terms of debate, at least initially, closer to this frame of reference. This migration towards a Pan-Arab context has tend-

11 Hamid Irbouh, "Art in the Service of Colonialism: French Art Education in Morocco, 1912–1956", (PhD diss., Theory of Art and Architecture Department, Binghamton University, 2000), 337.

12 Farid Belkahia, "Questionnaire", in "Situation arts plastiques Maroc", special issue, *Souffles* 7–8 (1967): 29.

13 Irbouh, "Art in the Service of Colonialism," 13–14; 336–38. While explicitly opposed to the precedent of French arts education in Morocco, Irbouh argues convincingly that the approach cultivated in Casablanca retained some important consistencies with the latter.

14 In focusing primarily on the terms this discourse offered for its own self-explication, I reproduce some of its blind spots. A number of scholars address the ways in which the emancipatory discourse of *Souffles* and the Casablanca group artists tended to elide various axes of inequality structuring cultural life in Morocco in that period. See Katarzyna Pieprzak, *Imagined Museums: Art and Modernity in Postcolonial Morocco* (Minneapolis: University of Minnesota Press, 2010), and Cynthia J. Becker, *Amazigh Arts in Morocco: Women Shaping Berber Identity* (Austin: University of Texas Press, 2006).

15 Sefrioui, *La revue Souffles,* 29. See also Mohammed Melehi, "Entretiens-M. Melehi", 350, in the same volume.

16 Sefrioui, *La revue Souffles*, 123.

17 Ibid., 122–25.

ed to obscure an original commitment to a Third World framework, and vice versa.[18] Against this backdrop, I am interested in shifting the focus to the ways in which understandings of Third World and Arab art constituted one another. Returning to the terms set out for the work of art on the pages of *Souffles* reveals the extent to which debates around "Arab art" in the 1970s were informed by engagements with a transregional solidarity movement committed to decolonization and class struggle. At the same time, it becomes possible to make sense of the way in which artists such as Melehi, Belkahia, Chebaa, and others moved from a platform advocating radical political and cultural transformation to institutions of Arab art often supported by increasingly reactionary and repressive postcolonial regimes.

Background

In the wake of the Second World War, the political and cultural leadership of newly-minted states across Africa, Asia and the Arab world negotiated for positions within the horizon of a Cold War order that divided the globe into First, Second and Third Worlds, respectively. The term "Third World" originally gained currency in the early 1950s to refer to those nations that were not party to the North Atlantic Treaty Organization (est. 1949), or the First World, and not affiliated with the USSR, or the Second World.[19] Use of the term accelerated following the first Conference of the Organization of Solidarity of the Peoples of Africa, Asia and Latin America (commonly referred to as the Tricontinental) in Havana in January 1966.[20] At this event, the representatives of seventy participating states declared their "solidarity with all those peoples fighting imperialism", as well as the workers of capitalist countries.[21] They defined imperialism as operating simultaneously across multiple fields: "the political, military, economic, racial, ideological, and cultural" and identified decolonization as a goal to be

18 Critics of the term "Third World" rightly point out some of the disadvantages of its use, and suggest alternatives, including "Tricontinental". Its application in this text is intended to conjure the terms of its original appearance in the context I address. "Third World", or "Tiers Monde" was the term adopted within *Souffles*.

19 In 1952, the term "Third World" appeared on the pages of the French newspaper *L'Observateur* in an article by Alfred Sauvy. Sauvy intended to evoke parallels with the role of the Third Estate (or bourgeoisie) in the French Revolution, and the article concluded: "In the end, this Third World, ignored, exploited, and scorned like the Third Estate, wants, too, to be something". Alfred Sauvy, "Trois mondes, une planète", *L'Observateur*, no. 118, August 14, 1952. Also see Vijay Prashad's account of the history of the term in *The Darker Nations: A People's History of the Third World* (New York: The New Press, 2008), 6.

20 Robert Young frames the Third World platform established in Havana as both the culmination of the Non-Aligned Movement and its substitute: "The Bandung Conference of 1955, which is better known today, as the first major conference of independent African and Asian states, represented a coming together of recently decolonized nations and a strategic decision of non-alignment with respect to the major two powers of the Cold War. The difference of the Tricontinental of 1966 was in the first place that it gathered together representatives from the entire non-western world, the three continents, and secondly that it aligned itself with a radical anti-imperialism located firmly in the socialist camp, through emphatically independent from any direction from the Soviet Union or China". Robert J. C. Young, *Postcolonialism: An Historical Introduction* (Oxford: Blackwell Publishing, 2001), 213. The same period marked a shift, argues Dipesh Chakrabarty following Arjun Appadurai and others, from a model of decolonization that aspired towards the "Europeanization of the earth" to a contemporary form of globalization in which the West is no longer considered "as the most important agentive force in the world". Dipesh Chakrabarty, "Legacies of Bandung: Decolonisation and the Politics of Culture", *Economic and Political Weekly* (November 12–18, 2005), 4815.

21 Portions of the General Declaration were reprinted in the first issue of *Tricontinental*, published by the General Secretariat of the Tricontinental Conference. "Déclaration Générale de la Tricontinentale," *Bulletin Tricontinental* (April 1, 1966), 18–22.

pursued on each of these fronts.[22] Meanwhile, many leading theorists of colonialism and postcolonialism insisted (despite striking differences in other regards) on the centrality of culture to the project of national liberation and nation-building. In this context, many artists dedicated themselves to what art historian Iftikhar Dadi has referred to as an "aesthetic of decolonization: one that would remain in dialogue with metropolitan developments but would also account for regional and nationalist specificities".[23]

In the same period, an internationalist framework for the arts emerged with the establishment of institutions such as the United Nations Educational, Scientific and Cultural Organization, or Unesco (est. 1945), just as a new generation of initiatives based on principles of solidarity and identity coalesced outside of a Euro-American context. Often, the principles of Asian-African (non-aligned) solidarity or the promotion of Négritude, Pan-Africanism, and Pan-Arabism served to further the political clout of specific regimes, heightening competition amongst postcolonial nations seeking to establish regional spheres of influence.[24] On the other hand, the same initiatives served, at times, to facilitate a critique of postcolonial statehood.

The 1940s through to the 1960s (a period generally designated within Euro-American art history as "postwar") were marked by great violence, and, indeed, war. As Hannah Feldman points out, art produced in these decades, "was created within, shaped by, and fully legible only in the historical context of ongoing war—or wars, as the case may be".[25] By the mid-1960s, many anticolonialist leaders and thinkers deemed the legitimacy of armed struggle an unfortunate yet necessary step towards independence. Portuguese colonial rule in Africa faced armed resistance, while victories in Cuba and Vietnam appeared to vindicate the efficacy of guerrilla warfare.[26] The 1966 Tricontinental helped enshrine armed struggle as a guiding principle of the Third World liberation movement.[27] The

22 "Appèl de la Havane", republished in *Souffles* 9 (1968): 32–33.

23 Iftikhar Dadi, "Ibrahim El Salahi and Calligraphic Modernism in a Comparative Perspective", *South Atlantic Quarterly* 109, no. 3 (2010): 561.

24 Political scientist Robert Vitalis argues that the assertion of Asian-African solidarity identified with the Bandung Conference of 1955 is productively understood as masking the political tensions animating relations between the leaders of major postcolonial states in the Cold War period. See Robert Vitalis, "The Midnight Ride of Kwame Nkrumah and Other Fables of Bandung", *Humanity: An International Journal of Human Rights, Humanitarianism and Development* 4, no. 2 (Summer, 2013): 266–88. Vitalis writes: "Those who hold up the banner of Bandung today prefer to imagine that these sometimes rival, sometimes simply orthogonal convocations track the evolution of a 'movement': the meeting of Afro-Asian, including Russian, peoples, not states, at Cairo in 1957, which led to the creation of the Afro-Asian Peoples Solidarity Organization with backing by the Soviets; the meeting of Independent African States in 1958 and of Pan-Africanists in Accra in 1959; [and] of Non-Aligned Heads of States or Governments in 1961". Ibid., 267–68. I am grateful to Timothy Mitchell for bringing this text to my attention.

25 Hannah Feldman, *From a Nation Torn: Decolonizing Art and Representation in France, 1945–1962* (Durham: Duke University Press, 2014), 2. While Feldman focuses on France, the observation applies, of course, to art produced outside of Europe.

26 See Young, "From 'Positive Action'", 248–52. "In 1961 the CONCP, a united front to co-ordinate the armed struggle against the Portuguese colonies in Africa, was formed, and at the Khartoum Conference of 1968 this alliance developed links with other freedom organizations that had moved to armed struggle, notably the ANC, ZAPU and SWAPO of South Africa, Zimbabwe and Namibia". Ibid., 250.

27 "The General Declaration" authored at the Tricontinental echoed the opening sentence of Frantz Fanon's influential work *Les damnés de la terre*, first published in 1961, in which he stated: "decolonization is always a violent phenomenon". See Tricontinental, "Déclaration Générale", 22.

militarization of the Palestinian liberation movement followed the humiliating defeat of Arab armies to Israel in June 1967.[28]

A 1968 poster commemorating the third anniversary of the Tricontinental made explicit the significance of the guerrilla fighter as an emblem of Third World identity. The image, designed by the Cuban artist and graphic designer Alfredo Rostgaard (1943–2004), points to the figure's dual nature as a universal symbol of anticolonial resistance and a figurehead of struggles taking place in specific locales around the world. Rostgaard juxtaposed the image of the fighter with an index of racial typologies: each standing in for one of the three continents.[29] This racialist classification of world "peoples", which drew on a tradition of nineteenth-century social-scientific discourse and had so recently played an important role in justifying and furthering repressive colonial regimes around the world, returned here under the banner of Third World solidarity and militant anticolonialism.

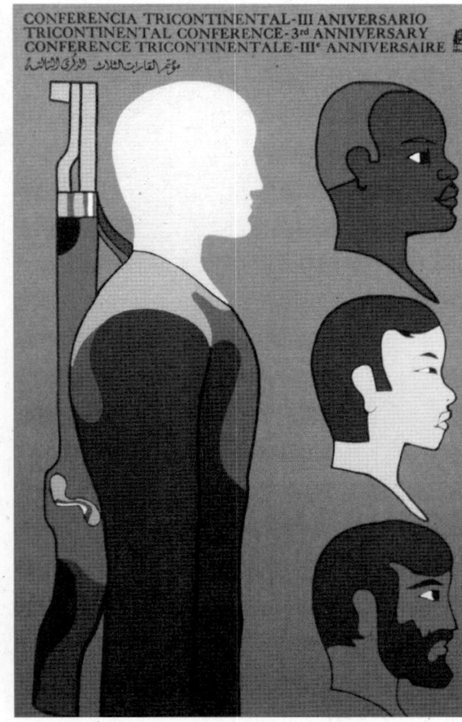

Alfredo Rostgaard, *Poster commemorating the third anniversary of the Tricontinental Conference*, 1968. Reproduced by permission of OSPAAL Archive.

Within both Arab and Third World frames of reference, the Palestinian revolution was understood as emblematic of global struggles against political and economic oppression. It provided a crucial point of reference in mediating Third World, Moroccan and Arab identities on the pages of *Souffles*, argues Harrison, in the guise of "a literary interlocutor that was neither European nor Maghrebi, yet offered a model for political and aesthetic revolution in the postcolonial Maghreb".[30] By 1969, the image of the Palestinian guerrilla fighter, or "*fida'i*" [literally, martyr], a "secular saint" equipped with gun and grenade, circulated as a cipher for the Palestinian liberation movement, as well as the broader transnational cause of popular resistance against surviving colonial outposts and the devastating effects of colonialism in newly established states.[31]

28 A new visual identity was developed for the Palestinian liberation movement following the humiliating defeat of Arab armies by Israel during the so-called *Naksa*, or Setback of June 1967: a six day war that led to Israel's annexation of the Gaza Strip, as well as territories in Syria, Egypt, and Jordan, and the flight of thousands of Palestinian refugees to neighboring countries. In 1968, the wing of armed resistance within the Palestinian Liberation Organization (Fatah) took over leadership of the organization. In the same moment, the PLO's original charter, authored in 1964, was rewritten to reflect a new emphasis on an "Arab" identity for Palestine, Palestinians, and the organized resistance to occupation. Nadine Picaudou, *Le mouvement national palestinien: Genèse et structures* (Paris: Éditions Hartmann, 1989), 126. As historian Nadine Picaudou points out, Article 1 of the 1968 charter begins with the assertion that, "Palestine, the homeland of the Palestinian Arab people, is an inseparable part of the greater Arab homeland, and the Palestinian people are an integral part of the Arab Nation". See ibid., 126. The "Palestine National Charter" was adopted on July 17, 1968 in Cairo at the fourth session of the Palestine National Assembly. Reproduced in Edmund Jan Osmańczyk, *Encyclopedia of the United Nations and International Agreements*, ed. Anthony Mango, 3rd ed., vol. 3 (New York: Routledge, 2003), 1744.

29 David Kunzle, "Cuba's Art of Solidarity", in *Decade of Protest: Political Posters from the United States, Viet Nam, Cuba, 1965–1975*, ed. Susan Martin (Santa Monica: Smart Art Press), 72.

30 Harrison, "Cross-colonial Poetics", 354.

31 The appearance of the fida'i on the pages of *Souffles-Anfas*, Harrison has argued, manifested as "a vector of protest" against many of the autocratic governments that paid lip service to ideals of Pan-Arab solidarity and anticolonialism. Harrison, "Cross-Colonial Poetics", 356; 360.

The guerrilla fighter merged with the artist (and the writer) on the pages of *Souffles*.[32] Meanwhile, within the fida'i nestled a series of other figures: the scientist, the technocrat, the lexicographer, and the archon. Artists were armed with the visual and technical "expertise" capable of effecting an epistemic break with colonialism, and regarded as specialists of a revolutionary vision or as educators and technicians of the collective; a function well-served by the expansion of the arts into various fields of graphic, industrial, decorative, and architectural design.[33] Third World works of art served simultaneously as a vehicles of destruction and construction. The tension implicit in this dual function seems at times to manifest as a latent, if barely-repressed energy that threatens to detonate within the pages of the journal and its associated networks of cultural decolonization/armed struggle.

These developments linking cultural production and guerrilla warfare took place on the cusp of a decade that witnessed the creation of the first major transnational institutions of Arab art. In 1969, Kuwait inaugurated a modestly scaled biennale of Arab art.[34] In 1970, the Arab League established an organization focused, specifically, on coordinating regional cultural policies at the state level.[35] The Arab League Educational, Cultural and Scientific Organization (ALESCO) hosted, for example, the First Conference of Arab Ministers of Culture in Amman in 1976.[36] However, it was a series of parallel initiatives that took on the mantle of Arab art in this period and were funded primarily by individual Arab states.[37] The General Union of Arab Plastic Artists [*al-Ittihad al-'amm li-l-fannanin at-tashkiliyin al-'arab*] was founded in Damascus in December 1971 at the First Arab Conference of Fine Arts [*al-Mu'tammar al-'arabi al-'awwal li-l-funun al-jamila*]. The Union required the participation of an "Association of Artists" representing each state.[38] In April 1972, the Iraqi Ministry of Information hosted the "Yahya al-Wassity Festival" [*Mahrajan al-Wassity*] in Baghdad, while, later the same

32 The same relationship was posited by writers contributing to *Souffles*. "[Khaïr-Eddine] refers to his poetics of textual violence as a form of 'linguistic guerrilla' whose primary aim is to prevent the birth of a plot or any sense of character development". Hédi Abdel Jaouad, "Mohammed Khaïr-Eddine: The Poet as Iconoclast", *Research in African Literatures* 23, no. 2 (Summer, 1992): 147.

33 In doing so, they drew on the writings of Frantz Fanon among other influential theorists of the time. "For Fanon", notes Harrison, "this did not signify a return to tradition or what he called 'coutume' (custom [...]), the reified, fossilized product of a stultified culture that was the fruit of colonial, orientalist fantasies. To the contrary, he called on the formerly colonized world to cease imitating its old masters and develop 'une pensée neuve' ('a new way of thinking' [...])". Harrison, "Cross-cultural", 353.

34 Toni Maraini, "Baghdad 1974. Première Biennale Arabe des Arts Plastiques: Un compte-rendu", *Intégral* 9 (December 1974): 16.

35 The Arab Cultural Unity Pact and the Statutes of the Arab League's Educational, Cultural and Scientific Organization were approved by the Congress of Arab Ministers of Education convened in Baghdad in February 1964, and adopted by the Arab League Council in May. In 1970, the cultural services of the General Secretariat of the Arab League were transferred to a dedicated organization: the Arab League Educational, Cultural and Scientific Organization (ALESCO). M. J. Menou, "The Department of Documentation and Information of the Arab League Educational, Cultural, and Scientific Organization (ALESCO), November 28–December 27, 1972" (Paris: Unesco, May 1973).

36 "Final Report: Meeting of Experts Preparatory to the Intergovernmental Conference on Cultural Policies in the Arab States, Hammamet, Tunisia 18–21 September, 1978" (Paris, Unesco, February 16, 1979), 2.

37 More research needs to be done on this topic. However, according to Ismail Shammout, the Iraqi state contributed 25,000 dinars (100,000 USD) to support the "First Two-Year Exhibition." The Arab League also contributed funds, as did a number of other Arab states not mentioned by name. Ismail Shammout, interview with Mostafa Nissaboury. "Entretien avec Ismail Shammout", special issue, "Biennale arabe de Baghdade", *Intégral* 9 (December 1974): 34.

38 Union of Arab Artists, "al-Nitham al-Assasi/Constitution Statuts", 1973.

year in Damascus, the Syrian Syndicate of Fine Arts [*Niqabat al-Funun al-Jamila*] hosted the First Arab Festival of National Plastic Art [*al-Mahrajan al-'arabi al-'awwal li-l-fann al-qawmi al-tashkili*].[39] The Union convened in Baghdad in April 1973, and the "The First Two-Year Arab Exhibition" (*[Mar'id al-sanatayn al-'arabi al-awwal]* the Arabic-language phrase was intended to replace the French loanword "biennale") was inaugurated, again in Baghdad, in March 1974.[40]

These developments helped embed the Arab plastic arts movement in an intergovernmental platform, while further centralizing resources, professional networks, and arts institutions at the national level. A number of participating nations achieved independence from colonial rule in the same period; others were fighting for autonomy and asserting claims to a national existence.[41] The *Naksa*, or Setback of the 1967 Arab-Israeli War appeared to discredit sitting Arab regimes and to effect a shift towards an extra-national site of action, while also acting as a catalyst for self-organization amongst artists in the region.[42] "[W]hat had been a state-sponsored battle for Palestine between armies had become a dispersed choreography of paramilitary actions with multiple heads and myriad headquarters", notes art historian Anneka Lenssen: a development that carried with it implications for art patronage and practice in the region.[43] In the wake of 1967, the consolidation of state control over various domestic sectors, including artistic production, corresponded with the reassertion of state power at a regional level.

In this context, statehood and its consolidation were not to be taken for granted. Neither was it clear, however, that the institutional framework coalescing around the project of Arab plastic arts was capable of

39 Syndicate of Fine Arts, *al-Mahrajan al-'Arabi al-'Awwal li-l-Fann al-Qawmi al-Tashkili* (Damascus: Mataba' al-'Idara al-Siyasiyya li-l-Jaysh wa-l-Quwat al-Musallaha, 1973). The publication cites conflicting months for the date of the event, or both October and November 23–28, 1972.

40 General Union of Arab Plastic Artists, *Manhaj f'aliyat Ma'rid al-sanatayn al-'arabi al-awwal/Programme and Activities of the First Arab Biennal [sic] Baghdad 1974* (Baghdad: Ministry of Information, Directorate General of Art, 1974). The exhibition ran from March 15 to April 15, 1974. A second "two-year exhibition" was held in Rabat (December 27, 1976 to January 27, 1977) and third (and final) exhibition in Tripoli, Libya (March 1980). See Alia Nakhli's account of the three events in "Les grands messes panarabes: festivals et biennales d'art arabe dans les années 1970", *Revue des mondes musulmans et de la Méditerranée*, published online May 23, 2014, http://remmm.revues.org/8577. A print version of the article is due to appear in *Revue des mondes musulmans et de la Méditerranée*, no.138 (Fall, 2015). I thank Sama Waly for sharing this reference.

41 At the first Two-Year Exhibition in Baghdad, the Palestine Liberation Organization was granted its own pavilion and participated in the biennale on an equal basis with other states, a development that mirrored its recognition as the sole legal representative of the Palestinian people by the Arab League and its observer status at the United Nations.

42 See, for example, Ghazi al-Khalidi's account of the prehistory of the General Union of Arab Plastic Artists, which he traces to a meeting called in Damascus "in the first days of the June 1967 war" to discuss the creation of a union of plastic artists. Ghazi al-Khalidi, "Harakat al-funun al-tashkliyya fi-l-qutr al-'arabi al-suri", *al-Ma'rifa* (July 1, 1975): 170–71.

43 Anneka Lenssen, "The Plasticity of the Syrian Avant-Garde, 1964–1970", *ARTMargins* 2, no. 2 (June 2013): 43. The PLO drew primarily on a "foco" theory of revolution, inspired by Guevara's successful 1959 insurrection in Cuba. The latter prescribed small-scale, targeted offensives undertaken by guerrilla resistance groups, popular uprising and, ultimately, revolution. Picaudou, *Le mouvement national*, 115–116. French philosopher and sometime associate of Guevara, Régis Debray (b. 1940) articulated a *foco* theory of armed struggle with reference to Cuban and Vietnamese precedents. "By restricting itself to the task of protecting civilians or passive self-defense, the guerrilla unit ceases to be the vanguard of the people as a whole and deprives itself of a national perspective. By going over to the counter-attack, on the other hand, it catalyzes the people's energy and transforms the *foco* [the guerrilla group] into a pole of attraction for the whole country". See Régis Debray, *Revolution in the Revolution? Armed Struggle and Political Struggle in Latin America*, trans. Bobbye Ortiz (New York: Monthly Review Press, 1967), 44–5. Compare with Abraham Serfaty's comments on *foco* theory in "Entretiens-A. Serfaty", in Sefrioui, *La revue Souffles*, 330–31.

serving the cause of "national culture" and realizing the aim of cultural decolonization, despite the ready embrace of both within Union discourse. As was the case with similar initiatives elsewhere, many artists associated the new institutions of Arab art with state-sponsored agendas; a relationship that seem to have elicited as much anxiety and resentment as expressions of gratitude and support.[44] Meanwhile, these regional institutions of art founded within an intergovernmental framework continued to draw on the terms established in the 1960s for the mobility of the work of art and its relationship to national, regional and international publics.

Mobile Works of Art: Art Print/Conference Poster

In the 1960s, the poster, print, and other reproducible media emerged as a privileged site for the elaboration of a new self-identified Third World aesthetic.[45] High-profile initiatives aimed at refounding culture on an international footing in the wake of the Second World War presented the color print as a vehicle for the dissemination of a new global canon of art. Meanwhile, the rise of new solidarity initiatives embraced graphic arts, printmaking, and poster design as effective tools of anticolonial pedagogy and propaganda. An internationalist model of art and emerging postcolonial networks of contestation intersected in these mobile media. In focusing on graphic art and poster design, artists could claim an international purview for their practices without compromising the status of the work of art: "The poster", claimed Chebaa, "is a painting that is accessible to all".[46] As early as 1973, prominent Iraqi artist Dia al-Azzawi published an account of the development of the "artistic poster" [*al-mulsaq al-fanni*] in Iraq, positioning this history within the scope of international developments.[47] In the 1960s and '70s, regular international exhibitions of posters helped claim the medium for the self-identified "Third World" artist.[48]

During the First World War, French propaganda campaigns made use of new reproductive technologies to organize exhibitions of color prints of works of art with the aim of modeling French cultural and civilizational prowess. Subsequently, the French state played an important role in disseminating this approach within the framework of a model of international intellectual, cultural and artistic exchange developed under the auspices of the League of Nations (est. 1919). The League's Institute

44 Interview with Youssef Abdelke, October 5, 2014. See also Nancy Adajania's discussion of the inaugural Triennale of Contemporary World Art held in New Delhi in 1968. Nancy Adajania, "Globalism Before Globalization: The Ambivalent Fate of Triennale India", in *Western Artists and India: Creative Inspirations in Art and Design*, ed. Shanay Jhaveri (London: Thames and Hudson, 2013), 168. I thank Nida Ghouse for bringing this text to my attention.

45 It seems worth noting that many of the posters referred to in this section and the networks they originally inhabited have acquired a second life today via the internet with initiatives such as the Modern Art Iraq Archive http://artiraq.org/maia/; the website of the Organization of Solidarity of the People of Asia, Africa & Latin America http://www.ospaaal.com; and the Palestine Poster Project Archives http:// www.palestineposterproject.org. Last accessed February 5, 2015.

46 Mohamed Chebaa, "Questionnaire", in "Situation", 41.

47 Dia al-Azzawi, *Fann al-mulsaqat fi-l-Iraq: Dirasat fi-bidayatihi wi-tatwirihi, 1938–1973* (Baghdad: Ministry of Information, 1973).

48 The first "Biennale Internationale de l'Affiche Varsovie" in Poland took place in 1966. Towards the end of the 1970s, Iraq was especially active in organizing poster exhibitions. Notable examples include: Iraqi Cultural Centre, "Ma'rid Baghdad al-'alami li-l-mulsaqat/The Baghdad International Poster Exhibition '79", London, March 28–April 17, 1979 and Baghdad, May 9–30, 1979 and "Ma'rid al-mulsaqat al-jidariyya/Exhibition of Iraqi Posters", National Gallery of Modern Art Gulbenkian, Baghdad, April 1–8, 1979.

for International Intellectual Cooperation (IIIC) was inaugurated in Paris on January 16, 1926, with Julien Luchaire (1876–1962), Inspector General of the French Ministry of Education, as its president.[49] Its predecessor, the International Committee for Intellectual Cooperation (est. 1922), had identified international intellectual cooperation with the moral authority of individual thinkers working in the arts and sciences. In contrast, the IIIC sought out an intergovernmental framework for exchange focused on the creation and dissemination of reproductions of books and works of art, the development of international agreements regarding intellectual property and copyright law, as well as the establishment of networks of museums and other cultural institutions.

After the Second World War, Unesco built upon the foundations laid by the IIIC in assembling a collection of "fine color reproductions of the world's greatest works of art".[50] This collection was subsequently exhibited in various countries across the Arab world.[51] An article published in the *Unesco Courier* on the occasion of the first traveling exhibition of the prints made explicit the resonances of this approach with the concept of the *musée imaginaire* (most consistently translated into English as "museum without walls") famously elaborated by novelist, art theorist, and France's first minister of cultural affairs (1959–1969), André Malraux.[52]

Unesco's collection of reproductions appeared to inaugurate a new, global model of museum that relied on reproductions to facilitate ease of travel and ensure the inclusion of non-Western cultures, while continuing to rely on a trope of universal culture and the assertion of an international "superoeuvre" grounded in a European (and predominantly French) artistic tradition. Malraux's "erasure of the contextual in favor of a universal abstraction grounded in the photographic optic", writes Feldman, "is the prerequisite for a colonial project that rests precisely, and especially in Malraux's case, on the authority inherent in surveying and ordering the world and its history from the totalizing vantage point of the museum".[53] In contrast, the Third World artist relied on new technologies of reproduction to displace Eurocentric models of internationalism and the museum. The Cuban revolution (1953–1959) brought poster design to the fore of artistic practice as a vehicle of political and cultural agitation. Subsequently, the inauguration of the Third World liberation

49 On the French role in the founding of the IIIC see Jean-Jacques Renoliet, *L'UNESCO oubliée: La Societé des Nations et la cooperation intellectuelle: 1919–1946* (Paris: Publication de la Sorbonne, 1999), 73; 203–05. See also "Section d'Information, Secretariat de la Societé des Nations," in *La Societé des Nations et la Cooperation Intellectuelle Nancy*, Paris, 3rd ed. (Strasbourg: Imprimerie Berger-Levrault, 1927), 46.

50 "Colour Reproduction: Unesco's First Traveling Exhibition", *Unesco Courier* 2, no. 7 (August 1949): 12. I am grateful to Kristine Khouri for generously sharing with me her collection of documents related to this initiative.

51 "Traveling Exhibition. Country numbers 60/66" (Paris: Unesco Archives), file 7A145.02.

52 "Art Treasures to Be Put Within Reach of All", *Unesco Courier* 1, no. 8 (September 1948): 6. The relevant resolution is numbered 6.1331, and was adopted at the General Conference of Unesco (Beirut, 1948).

53 Feldman, *From a Nation Torn*, 23–24. Douglas Crimp has described the universalism of Malraux's museum in the following terms: "All of the works that we call art, or at least all of them that can be submitted to the process of photographic reproduction, can take their place in the great superoeuvre, art as ontology, created not by men and women in their historical contingencies but by Man in his very being. This is the comforting 'knowledge' to which the *Museum without Walls* gives testimony. And concomitantly, it is the deception to which art history is most deeply, if often unconsciously, committed". Douglas Crimp, *On the Museum's Ruins*, with photographs by Louise Lawler (Cambridge, Mass: MIT Press, 1993), 56.

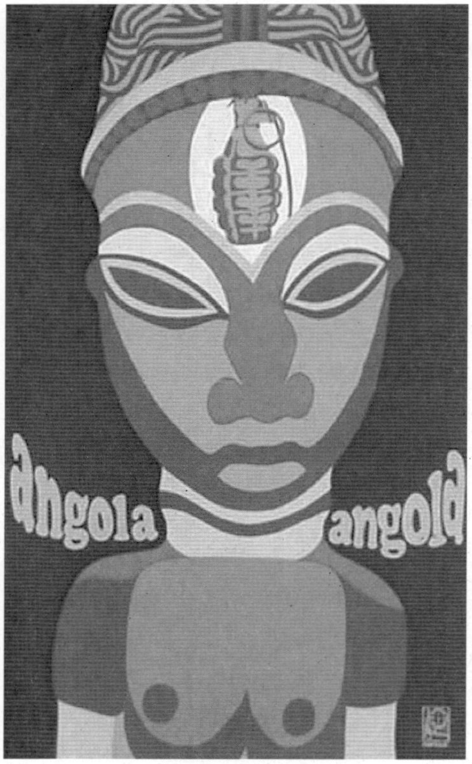

Daysi Garcia, *Angola*, 1969. Offset print, 33×56 cm. Reproduced by permission of OSPAAL archive.

movement in Havana in 1966 helped establish the relevance of the conference poster, or *affiche congrès*, to postcolonial configurations of the international, and defined parameters for its success or failure.

A Third World aesthetic aimed to disrupt established habits of vision (and of being) within occupied territories and the postcolonial state. One tactic involved artists in "correcting" colonial-era tropes that dominated the representations of the non-Western world. Unesco publications and ephemera tended to draw on ancient artifacts and monuments as stand-ins for non-Western societies, predicating their "authenticity" on their reification as artifacts and images. Notably, Unesco's adoption of these terms for the representation of Third World nations reflected the latter's rising influence within the organization, as former colonies turned nation-states joined its ranks. Nevertheless, this effort to valorize non-Western cultures tended to reinscribe a logic of representation that consigned Asia, Africa and the Arab world to "history", while Europe raced ahead into "modernity".[54] At this stage in the decolonization process, reflected the poet and co-founder of *Souffles*, Abdellatif Laâbi, "[c]ulture is an exhibition object".[55]

Artists associated with the Organization of Solidarity of the Peoples of Africa, Asia and Latin America (OSPAAAL) in Cuba, and its quarterly journal, *Tricontinental*, took up familiar emblems of Third World cultural heritage—i.e., the statue of Buddha, the African "tribal" sculpture, the Pharaonic wall relief—and wedded them to symbols of armed struggle. In the catalogue of a 1971 exhibition dedicated to Cuban posters of the period, novelist and one-time editor of *Casa de Las Americas*, Edmundo Desnoes, describes OSPAAAL's *détournement* of this visual trope in the following terms:

> *Combining the traditional cultural symbols of each country with those of armed struggle (rifles, grenades, bullets), numerous [OSPAAAL] posters developed merging armed struggle with those national values imperialism tries to destroy: from the bas-reliefs of ancient Egypt in which the hieroglyphs become bullets and grenades to African sculptures carrying rifles in their arms and grenades in their thoughts, and the symbolic winged figures of pre-Colombian culture turned into guerrillos.*[56]

54 Chloé Maurel, *Histoire de l'UNESCO: Les trentes premières années. 1945–1974* (Paris: L'Harmattan, 2010), 141.

55 Laâbi, "La culture nationale", 6. He is describing Frantz Fanon's schema of cultural decolonization.

56 Edmundo Desnoes, "From Consumerism to Social Conscience: The Poster in the Cuban Revolution, 1959–1970", *Cubaanse Affiches* (Amsterdam: Stadsdrukkerij, 1971), 18–20. Published in coordination with the eponymous exhibition held at the Stedelijk Museum Amsterdam, May 7–June 6, 1971. *Souffles* and *Cases de las Americas* were known to each other. See Sefrioui, *La revue Souffles*, 78.

In this manner, the familiar proxies of non-Western peoples were literally armed and sent back into the field to destroy those who would produce them as the static symbols of dead civilizations. This approach brought into relief the context within which these artifact-symbols circulated historically, while the addition of "rifles, grenades, bullets" annexed them to the cause of the Third World liberation movement. These rectified images of Third World heritage circulated as a form of revolutionary political and cultural education. At the same time, they suggested the conflation of the figure of the guerrilla fighter with the ancient artifact, as well as the contemporary artist.

It was not only the quality of mobility associated with the poster and print, or the movement of images from one site, frame, and medium to another that helped define Third World art, but the nature of the networks they traversed as a result. The possibility of mobility implied in the model of the Third World work of art as print could hardly be made to rely on the channels facilitated by a global market system associated with capitalism and dominated by former European colonial powers. It was the situated nature of artistic practice and its relationship to existing modes of production that determined the nature of the work of art as revolutionary in this regard.

Contributors to *Souffles* accused the former French colonial arts administration of reducing Moroccan art to tourist-trade trinkets produced for sale abroad and in local resorts.[57] Counter to this, it was claimed, the postcolonial-era artist operated in the absence of a market: a condition that helped guarantee their status as "militant".[58] That is, the Third World work of art was to circulate within a network that shielded it from market forces, which threatened to transform works of art into commodities, thereby assimilating them to First World conditions and neutralizing their critical charge.[59] Similarly, the model of international intellectual exchange promoted by Unesco positioned its peripatetic, global museum of reproductions within a coordinated effort to establish and enforce international copyright laws. Within this postwar framework, both works of art and artifacts and their reproductions were to be increasingly assimilated to a global system of exchange subject to regulation from the metropole.

On the other hand, Third World artists relied on what Kodwo Eshun and Ros Gray have subsequently termed, "the new modes of production, exhibition, distribution, pedagogy and training made possible by forms of political organisation and affiliation".[60] This was to be an "art of

57 Various discussions of arts policies in the period help contextualize this claim. See Roger Benjamin, *Orientalist Aesthetics: Art, Colonialism, and French North Africa, 1880–1930* (Berkeley: University of California Press, 2003); Hamid Irbouh, "Art in the Service of Colonialism: French Art Education in Morocco, 1912–1956", (PhD diss., Theory of Art and Architecture Department, Binghamton University, 2000); and Katarzyna Pieprzak, *Imagined Museums: Art and Modernity in Postcolonial Morocco* (Minneapolis: University of Minnesota Press, 2010).

58 Melehi, "Questionnaire", in "Situation", 68.

59 Ibid., 70.

60 "Ciné-geography designates situated cinecultural practices in an expanded sense, and the connections—individual, institutional, aesthetic and political—that link them transnationally to other situations of urgent struggle. It refers not just to individual films but also to the new modes of production, exhibition, distribution, pedagogy and training made possible by forms of political organisation and affiliation". Kodwo Eshun and Ros Gray, "Editor's introduction", special issue, "The Militant Image: A Ciné-Geography", *Third Text* 25, no. 1 (January 2011): 1.

combat" [*art de combat*], wrote Tahar Ben Jelloun in an essay published in *Souffles*, explicitly positioning the works featured on the pages of the journal in relation to guerrilla-cinema and guerrilla-theater, and distinguishing them from the "art of the salon and of mystification".[61] Ultimately, artistic production was to be inscribed within an international horizon of critical engagement rather than a species of colonial and postcolonial coercion that was at once cultural, political, and economic in nature.

Beginning in 1968, artistic contributions to *Souffles* were consistently identified as a form of *action plastique*. One term recalls another: The phrase *arts plastiques* [plastic arts] was associated at the time, notes Lenssen, with internationalist initiatives in the arts spearheaded in the postwar period by Unesco; in the 1950s, official arts institutions in the Arab world increasingly adopted the Arabic-language translation of the French-language term, or *funun tashkiliyya*.[62] In Morocco, as elsewhere in the Arab world, the "plastic" artist exercised control over not only artistic material, but the material of the social and political life of a nation. A special issue of *Souffles* titled "Situation arts plastiques en Maroc" sought to clarify and make explicit this relationship of art to a national public, and the centrality of the artist within it.[63]

It was not necessarily the introduction of the term that sparked this approach. Indeed, elsewhere in the region, a similar logic of art-making far preceded the widespread use of *funun tashkiliyya*. In early twentieth-century Egypt, for example, the artist adopted a role predicated upon that assigned to an anticolonialist cultural and political elite within Nahda-era discourse: As "sculptors of the nation", the artist bestowed form upon the otherwise "formless" (and, hence, potentially threatening) masses.[64] Similarly, at the height of the Iraqi state's prowess as primary patron of Arab plastic arts in the 1970s, the artist and the intellectual were to play an important role in remaking the population in the image of the regime, albeit perhaps in a more explicitly coercive or baldly "utilitarian" manner.[65] In this period, writes historian Eric Davis, "[s]tate-sponsored

61 T.B. [Tahar Ben Jelloun], "*Souffles* 18 (January–February 1970): 46. Contributors to *Souffles* believed that the threat of mystification was not confined to the salon, but also could imply a critique of identity-based solidarity initiatives such as "Négritude". See Abdallah Stouky, "Le Festival Mondial des Arts Négres, où les nostalgies de la négritude", *Souffles* 2 (1966): 41–45.

62 Anneka Lenssen, "The Shape of Support: Painting and Politics in Syria's Twentieth Century", (PhD diss., MIT, September 2014), 285–86.. Addressing the transfer of the French term into Arabic within the context of a discussion of the work of Syrian "plastic abstractionists" at the College of Fine Arts in the 1960s, she remarks: "[T]he concept of art's formal malleability that lies within the Arabic word for plastic formation—*tashk l*—is a particularly appropriate term. Literally describing the quality of having been formed (rather than the possibility of continual reformation, as in the English term plastic), the idea of plastic art would, after 1967, accrue a heroic quality. Where once the forward-looking arts had been abstract, they became, by their reclamation by new liberation movements, plastic examples of total creative mastery". Ibid, 285–286. On the application of the term in Egypt, Patrick Kane writes: "In early twentieth century Egypt, the notion of the 'modern' was averred through an emphasis on form, hence the prevalence of the term *al-funun al-jamila* [the fine arts], for the pre-revolutionary period, and the term *al-funun at-tashkiliyya* [the plastic arts], for the post-revolution period." Patrick Kane, *The Politics of Art in Modern Egypt: Aesthetics, Ideology and Nation-Building* (London: I.B.Tauris, 2012), 12.

63 "Situation arts plastiques Maroc", special issue, *Souffles* (1967): 7–8.

64 See Clare Davies, "Modern Egyptian Art: Site, Commodity, Archive, 1891–1948" (PhD diss., NYU, 2014), 59–60.

65 Silvia Naéf, *À la recherche d'une modernité arabe: L'évolution des arts plastiques en Égypte, au Liban et en Irak* (Geneva: Éditions Slatkine, 1996), 278.

cultural production sought to create a new definition of the citizen as subject, based on corporatist ties to the Iraqi nation-state".[66]

However, within the terms of the critique presented by *Souffles*, the constructive role of the artist in the processes of modernization and nation-building coincided with the destructive potential of the work of art; the decolonization of culture required the development of a "new way of thinking". Asked on the pages of *Souffles* to identify how painting might contribute to the "elaboration of a national culture", artists adopted military terminology. "We must fight a battle in the arena of visual education", Chebaa declared.[67] The French verb *plastiquer* translates as "to blow up, to carry out a bomb attack", while the nouns *plastique* and *plastiqueur/euse* denote "explosive/bomb" and "bomber", respectively. The identification of works published in *Souffles* as examples of an *action plastique* identified them as explosives capable of destroying the distortions within Moroccan culture and society degraded by decades of colonial rule. As a play on "arts plastiques", the term simultaneously situated artistic contributions to the journal within the institutional frameworks established for the arts within individual Arab states, as well as an expanded field of Third World struggle and resistance to the "false independences" headed by postcolonial regimes around the world.

Katarzyna Pieprzak describes *Souffles* and related publications as "discursive museums". The journal, she argues, offered Moroccan artists a way out in the face of "constant marginalization at home and abroad", while affirming their commitment to "being a transformative force in Moroccan society, providing a critique of the restrictions of a nationalism that was fixated with the past, and arguing against a superficial modernity that attracted those in power".[68] Meanwhile, textual contributions to the journal served to frame works of art, helping readers/viewers to understand the latter's intended terms of reception. According to Pieprzak: "The critical frame of the journals functioned as did the critical practice of valorization in a museum. It staged modern Moroccan culture and ultimately educated and disciplined its visitors".[69]

At the same time, I would argue, this approach offered a way of repositioning the work of art in Morocco in relation to a viewership or public, or outside of the otherwise dominant binary of the autonomous object encountered within the discreet space of the gallery (a luxury commodity circulating within a Western market system) and the tourist trinket produced under the supervision of colonial arts administration for sale in the "Arab bazaar".[70] In this sense, *Souffles* is perhaps best understood as reconfiguring the relationship of the work of art to existing conditions of display. Rather than "simulating" a visit to an art museum or extending the parameters of the gallery and bazaar to print media,

66 Eric Davis, *Memories of State: Politics, History, and Collective Identity in Modern Iraq* (Berkeley: University of California Press, 2005), 170. I am grateful to Sonja Mejcher-Atassi for bringing this source to my attention.

67 Chebaa, "Questionnaire", in "Situation", 42.

68 Pieprzak, *Imagined Museums*, 125.

69 Ibid., 97.

70 Ibid., 113.

Souffles appeared to encourage the opposite: substituting the network of contestation for the market.[71]

Moreover, as the significance of the journal and the poster became increasingly salient, artists were testing new approaches to the display of work, and, especially, its relationship to the gallery. Members of the Casablanca group continued to exhibit in galleries in Morocco and Europe, but declared in 1969 that they would no longer agree to display their works in foreign cultural centers, which represented some of the few formal exhibition spaces available in Morocco.[72] The same year (during May 9–19, 1969), they famously set up an exhibition of their work in Marrakech's main square, or Jami' al-Fina, doing away with the gallery space entirely in favor of "direct" engagement with the public—an account published in *Souffles* identified the event as *action plastique*.[73]

This interest in the circulation of the work of art outside of the gallery and bazaar (and its identification as a potentially disruptive encounter rather than an object) carried over into some of the first events dedicated to "Arab plastic arts". Writing for *Intégral* in 1972, art historian Houcine Tlili recognized this approach at the Yahya al-Wassity Festival in Baghdad in a text dedicated to the posters that "paper[ed] the walls of Baghdad by the hundreds" rather than the works of art on view inside those walls. The posters possessed a rare "artistic" quality and a "*caractère engagé*", he claimed, pointing to the poster's place with public thoroughfares and centers as a form of address to "the people".[74] A book published five years later, in 1977, or on the anniversary of the foundation of the Ba'ath Party in Iraq and dedicated to the topic of "*art engagé*" described the poster as, "one of the major accomplishments of the 1970s", while at the same time, arguing that it, "must evolve in its contents and, too, its essence towards the universe of mural painting".[75] Nevertheless, in arguing for the necessity of this shift, the author appears primarily to monumentalize the poster, or rather, to translate its "direct effect on the masses" to the scale of the public monument and statue.[76] In the 1960s, the poster offered artists expanded possibilities of

71 Ibid., 96. I draw the term "contestation" from Ilham Khuri-Makdisi's history of the rise of a global "culture of contestation" linking the Eastern Mediterranean with other areas of the Ottoman Empire and with diasporic populations in South and North America. Ilham Khuri-Makdisi, *The Eastern Mediterranean and the Making of Global Radicalism, 1860–1914* (Berkeley: University of California Press, 2010).

72 Irbouh, "Art in the Service of Colonialism", 337.

73 The text described the artists as ridding themselves of the mediating role of the gallery and boasted of the novelty of the approach: "Cette manifestation constitue la première exposition en dehors des galeries dans l'histoire de la peinture moderne au Maroc". See "Action Plastique", *Souffles* 13 and 14 (1969): 45. The terms of this institutional critique supported participating artists' identification with an international "avant-garde" and their self-stylization as an alternative to the Moroccan arts establishment. At the same time, their complaint allowed for seemingly contradictory positions. For example, while developing a critique of the museum and gallery space *per se*, Chebaa and Belkahia suggested retrospectively that they were interested in protesting the exclusionary, provisional, and makeshift nature of exhibition sites available to them in Morocco at the time, and, in fact, sought the allocation of energy and resources towards the transformation of these spaces rather than their dissolution. These positions could be understood in 1969 as situated in opposition to a multifaceted cultural status quo that demanded consistent negotiation. "Entretiens-F. Belkahia", 341–42 and "Entretiens-M. Chebâa", 365–66, in Sefrioui, *La revue Souffles*.

74 Houcine Tlili, "Le Poster en Irak", *Intégral* (January 1973): 30. In a telling that may have been intended to recall the 1969 *action plastique* of Jami' al-Fina, Tlili quoted al-Azzawi's assertion that the posters advertising the festival "*sont* [...] *'confronté' aux masses*." Ibid., 31.

75 Muhammad al-Jaza'iri, *"al-Fann wa-l-qadiya,"* in *À la recherche*, ed. Naéf (Baghdad, 1977), 107; 281.

76 Ibid.

circulation and implicated artistic production within far-flung networks of political and cultural affinity and solidarity. However, as governments sought to institutionalize the terms of various cultural agendas, they tended to translate the logic and aesthetic of the poster into more permanent forms.

Figuration and Abstraction: Defining Didactic Form

The work of art's mobility and relationship to the market played a key role in determining its ability to realize the goal of cultural decolonization within both "Third World" and "Arab" framings. At the same time, the stylistic coordinates assigned to both were often explicitly left open to debate. Artists appeared free to engage with the same visual idioms as their peers in the United States and in Europe, while the circulation of their works within alternative networks necessarily injected them with a critical faculty otherwise missing from forms destined for commodification by the art market.

Art historian David Craven identifies visual idioms of Western consumer culture and the high-art forms that engaged them as such as Pop art and Op-art as important influences on the development of OSPAAAL design in Cuba. A Third World aesthetic invested in a definition of visual experience as a form of political and cultural reeducation responded to the use of bright colors, the repetition of geometric motifs or of text, and the application of bold graphic effects evident in so-called Western advertising and mass culture. At the same time, Craven argues, Third World artists turned Western mass culture and advertising strategies to their own ends: "[E]ven when the genuine popular culture of a Third World country recycles Western mass cultural forms, the result is necessarily generated from below by the most exploited sectors and in marked opposition to the above mentioned values of corporate capital."[77] Nevertheless, Third World artists remained susceptible to the threatening embrace of the Western gallery system. Their works were perfectly capable of passing through the formalist readings and art historical filters applied by the latter, he argues; and, once commodified, the Third World work of art was not necessarily distinguishable from those "First World" works of art traversing the same market system.[78]

In a glossary of terms produced for the special issue of *Souffles* devoted to the plastic arts in Morocco, contributors embraced a "function-

77 "Populist images of Western mass culture (Coca-Cola billboards, Walt Disney Comics, Las Vegas architecture, TV soap operas and the like) are largely engineered from above by multinational corporations in order to sell products, inculcate hierarchical values, and even promote Western ethnocentrism," he writes. The American and European art forms that transferred mass culture into the gallery context were uncritical because they were implicated in the same market system. David Craven, *Art and Revolution in Latin America, 1910–1990* (New Haven: Yale University Press, 2002), 92.

78 In this vein, Craven offered the negative model of the six-member *Groupe de Récherche d'Art Visuel* (GRAV), which included Julio LeParc and Francisco Sobrino, who met at the Escuela de Bellas Artes in Buenos Aires in the 1950s. The group's 1966 manifesto called for a dematerialization of the art object as a means of resisting its potential for commodification, to facilitate new forms of spectator participation, and serve the cause of "social incitement." See Groupe de Rechèrche d'Art Visuel (GRAV), "Manifesto," 1966. Republished in Kristine Stiles and Peter Selz ed., *Theories and Documents of Contemporary Art: A Sourcebook of Artists' Writings* (Berkeley: University of California Press, 1996), 411. Here, Craven echoes a criticism of the group articulated in a 1969 article by Jean Clay titled "Art Tamed and Wild," in Alexander Alberro and Blake Stimson ed., *Conceptual Art: A Critical Anthology* (Cambridge, MA: MIT Press, 1999), 137. Originally published in *Studio International* (June 1969).

alist" Bauhaus approach, and defended abstraction as an investigation into the "atemporal, intrinsic, essential, and permanent" qualities of things.[79] At the same time, they identified socialist realism with Marxist theories of art elaborated in Latin America and Europe, rather than with the normative optic enforced as official policy in the Soviet Union.[80] In principle, abstraction and figuration inhabited a continuum of practices available to the Third World artist, while the principles of creative freedom and the significance of the artist's role in guiding popular taste were affirmed. In practice, laying claim to one or the other might require the artist to elucidate their choice within the broader terms of their practice and to elaborate its implications for the art work's relationship to a Third World frame of reference.

Figuration ensured a clarity of communication. As a result, works burdened with an especially urgent political message were often expected to avoid excesses of abstraction and forego all but the most symbolic imagery and allegory. Belkahia forthrightly rejected the binary of figuration-abstraction: a testament perhaps to the pressures the latter could impose on an artist. At the same time, the artist's description of his own development aligned figuration with political or humanist concerns, i.e., his preoccupation with histories of horrendous violence he witnessed in Morocco in 1950–52 and encountered on a trip to Auschwitz.[81] On the other hand, abstraction appeared better suited to his more recent exploration of "sensuality" as a productive rubric for artistic production.

The opposition of figuration and abstraction and the disavowal of this binary carried over from discussions of the Third World work into discussions around Arab plastic art. An account of the Palestinian pavilion at the First Two-Year Exhibition in Baghdad published in *Intégral* was adamant regarding the proper application of figuration. The author contrasts the "descriptive realism" of Ismail Shammout (1930–2006) with the "obscure and surrealist" allegories of Mustafa al-Hallaj (1938–2002).[82] By this account, Shammout's painting, "evokes a heroic image of the Palestinian people and places the accent on 'iconic' effects, that is ennobled and composed situations and figures whose classical nature is accentuated by the fixity of their gaze." In contrast, works by al-Hallaj are condemned as "too obscure and surrealist"; his allegories, "too obscure, too pessimistic, too erotic and over intellectualized. In short, too difficult to comprehend for the correct assessment of the struggle of his people, even if this struggle, in one manner or another, is the sole and obsessive theme of the work." Notably, both artists were working in a figurative vein. It was not figuration, per se, that was at stake, but, rather its proper nature as "didactic and explicative" that determined the work's success.

79 "Lexique," in "Situation," 72.

80 Ibid. It is perhaps useful to compare this approach with the way in which developments in the arts in Cuba have been defined in opposition to a Soviet model. "In Cuba, as contrasted with Russia, there has been no attempt to create a simple art that can be immediately understood by the people; rather there has been an education of the people to the point where they understand the complexity of art. I was told that this has been the official policy of the Cuban Revolution." Ernesto Cardenal, "En Cuba," in Craven, *Art and Revolution*, 94.

81 Belkahia, "Questionnaire," in "Situation," 27.

82 Maraini, "Baghdad 1974," 12. All quotes in this paragraph refer to this source. See also Mohammed Chebaa, "Révolution palestinienne et peinture révolutionnaire," *Intégral* 9 (December 1974): 41.

A special issue of *Souffles* and its Arabic-language companion *Anfas* (c. 1969/1971–1972)[83] published in Morocco in 1969 celebrated the Palestinian revolution with an image of the fida'i.[84] Adapted from a poster designed by Mohamed Chebaa, the figure is seen from below and at close range; a perspective that monumentalized the fighter, while also forcing an uncomfortable proximity. Chebaa's fida'i appeared as an article header inside the journal's issue of March-April 1970.[85] It surfaced again in the same issue on a placard held aloft in a photograph of Moroccan workers commemorating the centenary of Lenin's birth and celebrating International Labor Day.[86] Later, details annexed from the image appear on the cover of the journal's November-December 1971 issue. In this instance, elements of the figure's machine gun are confined to two square frames, while a third contains what appears to be a detail of the distinctive Palestinian scarf, or *kufiya* covering the lower part of the fida'i's neck and face. The original image, now almost entirely dissimulated, is reconstituted again inside the issue: one of a series of otherwise nonfigurative emblems introducing journal articles.[87] The migration of Chebaa's guerrilla fighter across pages and posters highlighted the quality of mobility and insisted on the image's inscription with the framework of solidarity offered by the Palestinian revolution. At the same time, it pointed to some of the ways in which a didactic and explicative art might manifest along a continuum of figurative and abstract approaches.

Inside the "Palestinian Revolution" issue of 1969, the reader encountered a series of six graphic works dedicated to the same cause and interspersed between texts.[88] Each modeled a distinct solution to the

83 The special issue of *Anfas* dates to 1969. Information provided on the title page lists the issue as "Special issue, no. 15/Year 4, volume 3". To my knowledge, however, this specific enumeration pertains exclusively to *Souffles*, and no previous issues of *Anfas* exist. Evidence speaking to the logic of this conflation can be found in the use of a calligraphic rendering of the Arabic-language title "Anfas" (a translation of the French *souffles*, or breaths) before 1969 on the pages of the French-language journal. This gesture suggests that the editors always considered the French and Arabic language publications as coexistent, with the Arabic always (already) present in the French. The next issue of the Arabic-language publication did not appear until May 1, 1971, and is listed as year two/issue one. It was published in Rabat by Matba't al-Tumi. Sefrioui cites this as the first issue of *Anfas*. See Sefrioui, *La revue Souffles*, 101.

84 The journal's engagement with the Palestinian revolution in 1969 seemed to herald a new "Arab" identity for *Souffles*. Various scholars have identified the significance of this issue in marking a shift in the direction of the journal. See, for example, Harrison, "Cross-colonial Poetics", 362; Sefrioui, *La revue Souffles*, 92; and Mary Ellen Wolf, "Textual Politics in Contemporary Moroccan Francophone Literature", *The Journal of the Midwest Modern Language Association* 25, no. 1 (Spring, 1992): 36. In the double issue of January–February 1970, the journal's tagline was changed from "Souffles: A Moroccan Literary and Cultural Review" [*Revue littéraire culturelle maghrébienne*] to "Souffles: An Arab Cultural Review of Morocco" [*Revue culturelle arabe du Maghreb*]. The journal had originated as a "revue poétique et littéraire" (issue no. 1, 1966) or, simply, as a "revue trimestrielle" (issue no. 2, 1966). In practice, however, this shift towards a more explicit alignment with an Arab frame of reference tended to extend the terms of an inclusive, Third World identification debuted in the first year of the journal's existence. Dedicated to African cinema, the Pan-African Cultural Festival in Algeria (1969), and "the Arab Nation", the first issue to describe the journal as "An Arab Cultural Review of Morocco" also featured on its cover a photograph of a performer at the festival, and, to the right, the by-now familiar figure of the fida'i.

85 Abdelkarim Dhofari, "Nation Arabe: *La lutte des classes en Égypte de 1945 à 1968* de Mahmoud Hussein", *Souffles* 18 (March–April 1970): 9.

86 In this instance, the image of the fida'i is sandwiched between two phrases: the French above states, "*Palestine vaincra*" [Palestine shall overcome], while, below, the Arabic reads, simply, "*Filistin*" [Palestine]. The photograph accompanies a text by Abraham Serfaty, "1er Mai et centennaire de Lenin", ibid., 7.

87 See for example, *Souffles* 22 (November–December, 1970).

88 Artistic contributors to the issue included Melehi, Tahar Ben Jelloun, Mohammed Hamidi (b. 1941), Abdallah Hariri (b. 1949), Ali Noury, and Saâd Benseffaj (b. 1939). Ben Jelloun is better known today as a Francophone novelist. Hamidi attended the École des Beaux Arts in Casablanca (1955–1958),

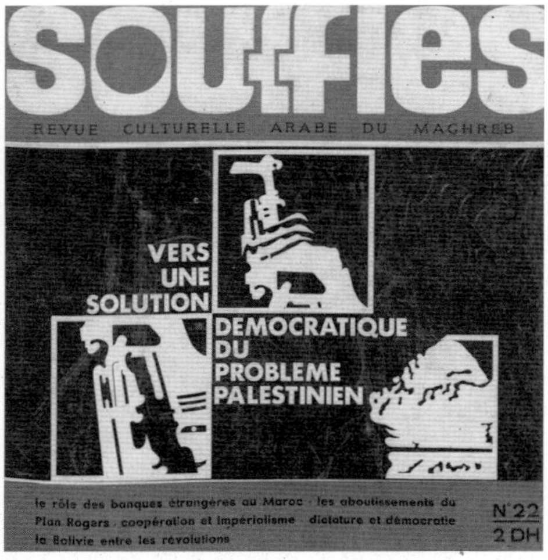

Mohammed Chebaa, Cover design for *Souffles*, No. 22, November–December, 1971. Reproduced by permission of Abdellatif Laâbi.

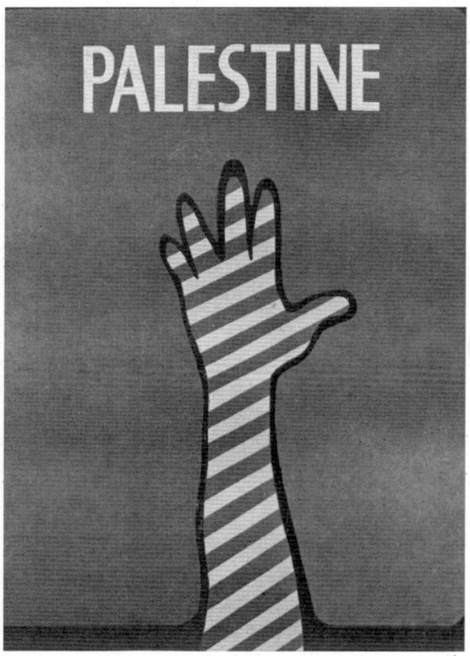

Action plastique, affiche by Mohammed Hamidi as it appeared in "Special issue for the Palestinian Revolution," *Souffles*, no. 15, 1969. Reproduced by permission of Abdellatif Laâbi.

problematic posed by the Third World work of art. A work produced by Melehi featured stark black and white "waves" [*ondes*] topped by the French-language proper noun "Palestine" in capital letters. The meticulously undulating lines dissolve into a flame-like movement.[89] In 1967, he identified the enigmatic quality of the abstract work of art as the site of "visual education":

Our [Arab] artist offers contemplation rather than a frozen reality. Our [Arab] art, which appears static and artificial is an art of the transcendental, of mobility and vibration. This mobility and vibration remain the sole points of intrigue for the spectator, wherein manifests a visual message and education.[90]

Moreover, Melehi went on to link the ahistorical nature of abstraction, as developed within a tradition of Islamic art upon which the Arab artist relied, to its expanded terms of address. Notably, he associated the universal nature of a work of art with the terms required of the viewer for its consumption:

When the occidental artist paints a scene, the spectator must be familiar with the event so as to better consume the work. On the contrary, our art is permanent, present and accessible to every individual, independent of their education or culture. An art unlimited, necessarily, to a dynasty of styles or periods. Our culture thus elaborates a universal art at the level of consumption.[91]

According to Melehi, figurative art (associated with a Western tradition) relies on the cultivation of taste through a bourgeois education. The terms of its reception further propagates class difference and unequal terms of access. In contrast, what he described as the "functionality" of art in the Islamic world circumscribes this requirement of social and cultural privilege, opening the work up to a broader spectrum of potential interlocutors.[92] The flame, or wave-like motif that had appeared under the banner of "Palestine" in 1969, reappeared on the cover of the inaugural issue of *Intégral* (October 1971). Inside, texts approach Melehi's ongoing work in the terms he had set out for them in 1967.

Ultimately, I have argued, a carefully constructed logic of cultural decolonization engaged by the Third World work of art relied as much on

the École des Beaux Arts in Paris, and the École des Metiers d'Art. He received a degree in the "teaching of monumental art", and served on the faculty of the École des Beaux Arts in Casablanca. Hariri attended the École des Beaux Arts in Casablanca between 1965 and 1969 and the Institut Européen d'Architecture et de Design in Rome in 1973. Benseffaj graduated from the Institut National des Beaux Arts Tetouan. He attended the École Superieur des Beaux-Arts in Seville and took courses in art history at the École du Louvre, Paris. He served as a professor of art history, painting and drawing at the École Nationale des Beaux-Arts in Tetouan.

89 Sefrioui describes the piece as symbolizing "the re-awakening of the Arab world". It's not clear what her basis is for this analysis. See also her discussion of Ben Jelloun's contribution as a reworking of the journal's cover design. See Sefrioui, *La revue Souffles*, 91.

90 Melehi, "Questionnaire", "Situation", 62.

91 Ibid.

92 Ibid., 61.

a consideration of form as on the possibilities it posed for its own mobility; indeed, the interrelation of form and mobility offered the necessary conditions for the mutual constitution of the work of art and its public. Melehi's *Palestine* appeals to an expanded public through the terms of a synchronic reading: an immersive act of contemplation capable of dissolving convention and intellect within presence.[93] At the same time, Melehi identified the universal quality of the work of art with the act of consumption; a gesture reminiscent of OSPAAAL's engagement with Western advertising and popular culture. The following section considers the status of script and sign within the terms posited for them in this manner on the pages of *Souffles*, later, at the first biennale of Arab plastic arts.

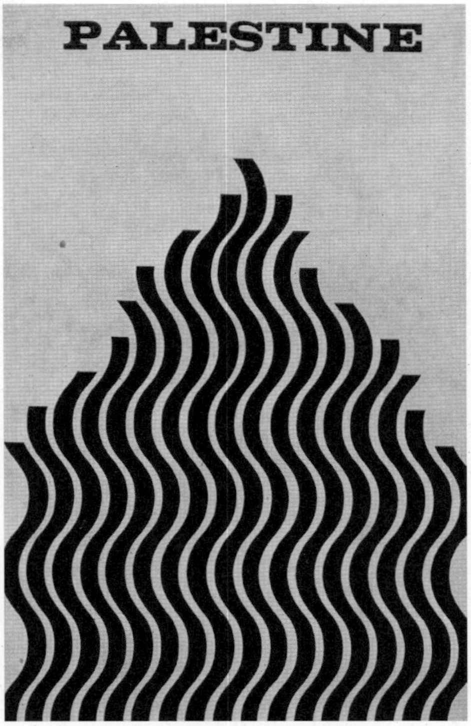

Mohammed Melehi, Untitled (action plastique, affiche), as is appeared in *Souffles*, no. 15, 1969. Reproduced by permission of Abdellatif Laâbi.

Script and Sign: Calligraphy in Plastic Art

Calligraphy represented an increasingly significant point of reference for artists affiliated with regional institutions of Arab plastic art. In part, this salience stemmed from the open-ended relationship of script and sign to the poles of figuration and abstraction. Exhibitions of Arab plastic arts in the 1970s pushed various approaches into the same frame; works presented by Moroccan artists figured prominently in this context.

Melehi began experimenting with the wave motif in 1964 and drew on it consistently thereafter.[94] In the same 1967 questionnaire, the artist described the primarily visual quality of Op art as offering an alternative to established Western art forms.[95] Moreover, in flattening perspectival space, Op art lent itself to architectural and design applications,[96] and served as an instance of the convergence of "modern" artistic concerns and a popular "Moroccan plastic tradition" sought by the artist.[97]

Once again, the significance of this specific conjunction for the self-identified Arab and Third World artist could be traced, in part, to the legacy of the French colonial art administration in Morocco. The latter had invested in the production of an urban artisanal class rather than investing in industrialization and related "modernization" projects.[98] In contrast, the arts movement in Morocco after 1956 often identified the artist as scientist, educator, and administrator, and made participation in the development of the industrial sector central to an understanding of artistic practices. As noted, the Casablanca group described Moroccan architectural monuments, archaeological artifacts, and vernacular, or folk arts as a "plastic tradition" that shared affinities with Western art while offering an appropriate point of departure for the development of modern

93 Melehi relies on his understanding of "Zen" in articulating the terms of this encounter. Ibid., 58–59.
94 Toni Maraini, "Chroniques: Expositions M. Chebaa, M. Melehi", *Souffles* (1967): 45.
95 Melehi, "Questionnaire", in "Situation", 63.
96 Elsewhere in the issue, Farid Belkahia promoted Op art as "a striking example" of the way in which artists could collaborate with technicians to revitalize various arenas of industrial design. Belkahia, "Questionnaire", in "Situation", 30.
97 Melehi, "Questionnaire", in "Situation", 63.
98 Pieprzak, *Imagined Museums*, 15.

Moroccan painting capable of shattering patterns of vision and thought established under colonial rule.

Similarly, the salience of artistic motifs and genres specifically associated with Arab or Islamic art on the pages of *Souffles* constituted a response to a local history of arts discourse and institutional practices. According to Laâbi, the French regime in Morocco had imposed its own hierarchy of cultural reference with the aim of "pacification" and "colonization".[99] Morocco's Arab identity had been disavowed in favor of a Berber lineage.[100] Colonial-era "berberophilia", as Laâbi termed it, framed the Arab presence in Morocco as a "failure".[101] In contrast, Moroccan artists would henceforth claim an explicitly Arab identity as one strand among others comprising the fabric of Moroccan identity. Here, as well as elsewhere, the local application of colonial policy helped mediate the terms by which artists related to a Pan-Arab identity.

Melehi singled out Arabic-language calligraphy as offering a particularly significant point of reference for the development of Moroccan art. "Calligraphy is a pure form of painting", he wrote in 1967.[102] At the same time, the absence of trained calligraphers represented not only a formal, visual, or aesthetic problem; Latin letters crowded out Arabic script along Moroccan city streets.[103] Courses led by Chebaa at the École des Beaux-Arts in Casablanca introduced students to calligraphy "not as a linguistic system", writes Hamid Irbouh, "but as pictorial signs to extract their visual and gestural dynamism".[104] Likewise, the application of "calligraphy" to the pages of *Souffles* and the surface of canvases produced by Melehi and others tended to emphasize the status of the letter or the word as sign rather than signifier.

In part, this approach spoke to a politics of language specific to Morocco and to which the editors of *Souffles* were highly sensitized. Speakers of French, Arabic, and/or Berber could assert competing claims to national identity. Contributors to the journal insisted on the legitimacy of each, while asserting their right to speak from within an Arab frame of reference: "no matter what language we use, in this precise phase of decolonization our literature is part and parcel of Arab(ic) literature, to which its destiny is in any case linked".[105] The equivalence of distinct languages, in this sense, may have contributed to their interest in the application of script as sign. Indeed, it is in these terms that Amazigh script enters the so-called abstract paintings of Moroccan artist Ahmed Cherkaoui (1934–1967). Cherkaoui offered the Casablanca group a significant example of an artist capable of situating himself within both an international framework and a "healthy" popular tradition.[106] He is described in early biographies as entertaining a passion for Arabic calligraphy from a young age.[107] Before his premature death in 1967, a grant from Unesco allowed him to

99 Abdellatif Laâbi, "Le gachis", *Souffles* 7–8 (1967): 11–12.
100 Pieprzak, *Imagined Museums*, 9.
101 Laâbi, "Le gachis", 11–12.
102 Melehi, "Questionnaire", in "Situation", 67.
103 Ibid.
104 Irbouh, "Art in the Service of Colonialism", 337.
105 "Appèl aux écrivains maghrebiens", *Souffles* 15 (1969): 100. On the editors' relationship to language see also Wolf, "Textual Politics".
106 Georges Boudaille, *Ahmed Cherkaoui* (Rabat: Imframar, 1964), n.p.
107 Sijelmassi, *La peinture marocaine*, 58; Boudaille, *Cherkaoui*, n.p.

study "the Berber sign and Arabic calligraphy".[108] His vividly colored oil paintings produced in Warsaw, Paris, and Morocco in the 1960s incorporated Tifinagh script: a choice that reinforced the identification of script and sign. Cynthia Becker describes the significance of Tifinagh in this period in Morocco in the following terms:

> *The Tifinagh script is an Amazigh writing form believed to be related to the ancient Punic script and used primarily by Tuareg women and blacksmiths to write short, intimate messages on household objects and jewelry [...] Although the script has not been used for hundreds of years in North Africa, Amazigh activists in Morocco and Algeria adopted Tifinagh to write poetry, songs, and political slogans promoting their Amazigh heritage. Until recently, the public display of Tifinagh was considered to be a political charged act of aggression against the Moroccan government.*[109]

Approached from this perspective, it is possible to see how the word "Palestine" in Melehi's work could be understood to draw on the expanded legibility of the sign, inviting the viewer to "see" rather than "read". In this sense, word and wave proved interchangeable.

Conversely, the illegibility of script did not diminish its centrality to the work. A painting located in the collection of the National Gallery of Fine Arts in Amman offers another iteration of Melehi's wave motif underscored by an unintelligible script.[110] Wijdan Ali's landmark 1997 survey *Modern Islamic Art* classifies this painting as an example of "marginal calligraphy". As a result, it has entered the canon (of what she calls, at this later date, "Islamic art") as an example of those paintings in which, "writing, whether clear or obscure, is no more than part of the background of the main theme, although it might occupy a sizable part of the composition. Its purpose is to provide a setting for the principal characters and figures rather than to be the content, as in the central calligraphic branch".[111] While eschewing semantic content, the calligraphic script that resists reading nevertheless continues to fulfill its role as sign within the terms established for it by Melehi and others; a role on par with other elements of the composition, and not marginal in the sense Ali suggests.

Indeed, one of the effects of this approach of script-as-sign was to destabilize the (hierarchical) relationship of figure to ground, producing a tense equivalence between elements of the composition. A work by Chebaa, which appeared under the title *Géométrie palestinienne* inside a special issue of *Intégral* (March 1978) dedicated to the second Two-Year Exhibition (here, *La Biennale panarabe*) in Rabat, combined another celebrated symbol of the Palestinian resistance with motifs associated with the Casablanca group. The following month, *Géométrie palestinienne* was featured in color on the cover of the quarterly *Shu'un Filastiniyya*

108 Sijelmassi, *La peinture marocaine*, n.p.

109 Becker, *Amazigh Arts in Morocco*, 179. See also Becker's discussion of the varied reception of works of art incorporating Tifinagh script. For a discussion on the gender politics surrounding the use of the script, see Becker and Pierprzak, 103–05.

110 Distinct letters (but not words) are legible. Mohammed Melehi, *Untitled*, 1981. Enamel on wood, 120 x 100 cm, Collection of the Jordan National Gallery of Fine Arts, Amman. See Wijdan Ali, *al-Mathaf al-Watani al-Urduni li-l-Funun al-Jamila/Jordan National Gallery of Fine Arts*, (n.p., 2005), 110.

111 Wijdan Ali, *Modern Islamic Art: Development and Continuity* (Gainesville: University of Florida Press, 1997), 177.

[*Palestinian Affairs*] (April 1978): a magazine issued by the Palestine Research Center of the PLO (1971–1993). Here, the black-and-white *kufiya* was juxtaposed with a brightly hued composition in a way that makes it impossible to determine spatial precedence: Does the kufiya provide the ground against which we view the rest of the image or vice versa?

A poster titled *The ABCs of Palestine* [*Alfiba'iyat Filistin*] composed by Egyptian illustrator and caricaturist Mohie Eldin El Labbad (1940–2010) and produced circa 1985, offers something of a summation of the many approaches I have traced thus far in the context of Melehi's work, contributions to *Souffles*, and a Third World aesthetic of decolonization. Here, El Labbad adapted the familiar schoolroom format of the illustrated alphabet poster to the Palestinian cause. The design acknowledges the elevation of a series of symbols and motifs to the status of a "national" or "revolutionary" visual language.[112] At the same time, it asserts a relationship between language and image that affirms the viewer's ability to "see" language and "read" image.

The markers of identity institutionalized within a postcolonial imaginary of the international make their appearance with the flag [*'alam*], the map [used here to denote the *watan*, or nation], and the postage stamp [*adh-dharf*, or the envelope].[113] Symbols of organic life proliferate, e.g., the olive [*zaytun*], the fig [*tin*], the orange [*burtuqal*]. At the same time, colorful flowers form the flagpole holding aloft the Palestinian flag, burst forth from the borders of the map and the cactus, decorate the dress of the little girl [*sughayara*], and cozy up to the figures of the armed "youth" [*shabab*] and the fida'i—hinting at the irrepressible vitality of both nature and a grammar of ornament rooted in a tradition of Arab, or Islamic art and in the vibrant graphics of the Third World poster. Finally, the motif of "armed" cultural symbols explored by OSPAAAL returns with the inclusion of various hand-held weapons.

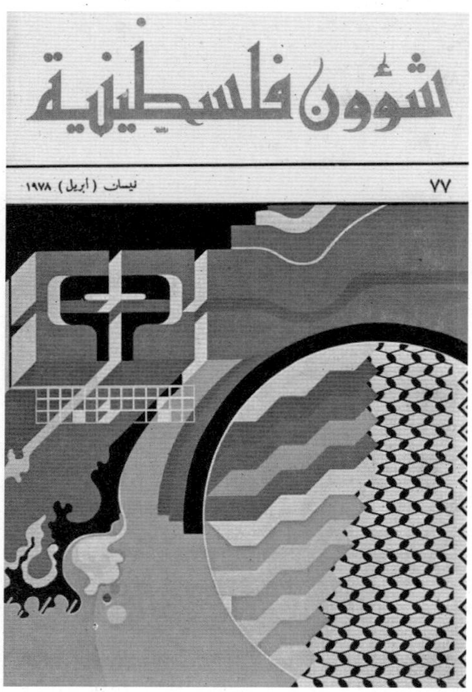

Mohammed Chebaa, cover design of *Shu'un Filastiniyya*, April, 1978.

El Labbad's figure of the fida'i/the letter "fa" combine the national symbol, the organic motif, and the weapon in a single frame. Content and style help blur the lines between innocence and menace: burly arms and paw-like hands cupping a cartoonish machine gun are topped by the almost mask-like facial features of a clown. The row of flowers foregrounding the figure are sweet in their child-like simplicity, while their thick stalks belie any sense of fragility and their heavy leaves taper to sharp, thorny

112 "One of the important aspects of the Nakba was the dispersion of the Palestinian people and the loss of their land. The trend in Arab countries, at the time, was to wipe out Palestinian identity. So it became the most important thing in Palestinian painting, to emphasize this identity and to make it into a major issue. To recreate Palestinian identity, painters started to use symbols such as scenes from Palestinian villages, dabke dancing, as well as the color of the flag, the flag itself, barbed wire, prison bars, etc. So much so that in 1981, the Israeli authorities passed a law forbidding the use of the Palestinian flag in all contexts. I was once summoned to the military governor in Ramallah, and was told by the officer that we were not allowed to use the colors red, white, green and black in our works". Suleiman Mansur, interview, "The Nakba and Palestinian Painting", *Palestine-Israel Journal of Politics, Economics and Culture* 5, no. 2 (1998).

113 On the relevance of the "*thob*" in this context, see Nada M. Shabout, *Modern Arab Art: Formation of Arab Aesthetics* (Gainesville: University Press of Florida, 2007), 51.

points.[114] Here, the constructive and destructive tendencies of the project of cultural decolonization (of an action plastique negotiated at the intersection of armed struggle and artistic production) return at the hand of the artist to the guerrilla fighter, and the guerrilla fighter is revealed as both figure and script, or as sign.

Third World Artists and the First Arab Exhibition

The nationalization of oil industries in the 1970s contributed to the development of new circuits of intellectual artistic exchange in the Arab world. Davis describes a boom in events of this kind across various fields following the nationalization of Iraqi oil in June 1972. Designed to position Iraq as a regional leader, these events were also intended to shore up domestic support for the ruling Ba'ath party:

> *State-sponsored conferences, professional associations, and journals invariably included intellectuals from other Arab countries, ostensibly demonstrating Iraq's commitment to Pan-Arabism, while the state's focus on its Mesopotamian and Arab-Islamic heritages underscored Iraq's cultural superiority over its main rivals, Egypt and Syria, for Pan-Arab leadership. Until the late 1980s, Iraq's oil wealth allowed it to bring numbers of Arab and foreign intellectuals to the country, where they were lavishly treated, highlighting its status as arriviste leader of the Arab world.*[115]

In the same period, Baghdad acquired a leading role vis-à-vis the emerging institutions of Arab plastic arts, and poured funds into developing national arts infrastructure and art collections. As in other arenas of cultural production, the contours of a so-called Arab frame of reference for the arts were never predetermined. Rather, they were to be painstakingly negotiated at each turn, thereby reflecting the intricacies of a situation brokered amongst multiple actors working simultaneously at both the level of the national and the transnational.

Nevertheless, the significance of the Palestinian struggle within regional politics guaranteed its centrality to the negotiation of the terms of a Pan-Arab cultural identity, and helped inscribe a Third World politics at the center of the project of Arab plastic art as it emerged in the early 1970s. Both Palestinian and Moroccan artists who participated in the new institutions of Arab art referenced the Palestinian liberation movement as a constitutive point of Third World solidarity. In late 1974, Ismail Shammout, Secretary General of the General Union of Arab Plastic Artists, granted an interview to *Intégral* in which he asserted the mutual production of the Palestinian revolution, the Third World liberation movement, and Pan-Arabism.[116] Asked to expand upon the aims of the General Union of Arab Plastic Artists, he emphasized the centrality of "engagement" and stressed Arab art's simultaneous investment in concepts of Arab identity

114 In this regard, they are reminiscent of Cuban artist, Alfredo Rostgaard's silkscreen poster *Cancion protesta* [Protest Song], 1967.

115 Davis, *Memories of State*, 158.

116 Almost immediately following the 1974 biennale, Shammout and his wife, the artist Tamam al-Akhal, exhibited their work at the Galerie Municpale de Rabat at the invitation of the Association Marocaine des Arts Plastiques (May 17–25, 1974). The interview was likely conducted at the time of Shammout's visit on this occasion.

and the Third World liberation movement: "We want to define our concept of engagement: firstly as Arabs, and secondly as part of the Third World".[117]

By the date of this interview, Shammout was well-established as one of the most powerful figures in the arts administration of the Palestine Liberation Organization (PLO) in a period marked by the organization's accelerated attempts at self-institutionalization.[118] Initiatives dedicated to the production and promotion of the visual arts were included in an elaborate bureaucracy erected to support the organization. In 1965, the PLO founded an Arts Education Department headed by Shammout.[119] In the late-1960s, Shammout, then a resident of Beirut, helped found Dar al-Karameh, reports artist and art historian Kamal Boullata, "as a gallery and meeting place hosting seasonal exhibitions of young talents emerging from the [refugee] camps".[120] Shammout also served as a cofounder of the Union of Palestinian Artists (est. in 1971), as well as Secretary General of the Union, and would play a central role in the organization of the First Two-Year Exhibition in 1974.

In the same interview, Shammout pointed out that the 1974 pavilions of Palestinian and Moroccan art shared an important attribute missing from many of the other pavilions: Both enjoyed a certain internal consistency, he argued, as defined by their own "characteristics" or "artistic tendency".[121] However, beyond the quality of internal cohesion as observed by Shammout, Moroccan and Palestinian schools of art, at first

117 Shammout and Nissaboury, "Entretien", 33.

118 Born in Lydda in 1930, he was displaced alongside thousands of Palestinians by the Nakba of 1948, grew up in the Gaza refugee camp of Khan Yunis (at the time under Egyptian administration) and studied painting at the College of Fine Arts [*Kuliyat al-Funun al-Jamila*] Cairo between 1950 and 1954: a period bridging the Free Officers' coup of 1952. He held his first solo exhibition in Gaza City in 1953. His first exhibition in Cairo the following year (July 21, 1954) was attended by Haj Amin al-Hussayni and Yasir 'Arafat, and inaugurated by Egyptian president Gamal 'Abdel Nasser. See Kamal Boullata, "Artists Re-Member Palestine in Beirut", *Journal of Palestine Studies* 32, no. 4 (Summer, 2003): 27. He studied at Academie des Beaux Arts in Rome between 1954 and 1956. Shammout and Nissaboury, "Entretien", 32.

119 "Established in 1965, the Department of Information and Culture did not receive official PLO sanction and support until 1978. A strong Palestinian national identity and culture are part of the PLO's program of national liberation, thus this Department is systematically collecting, preserving, creating and transmitting Palestinian culture". Cheryl A. Rubenberg, "The Civilian Infrastructure of the Palestine Liberation Organization: An Analysis of the PLO in Lebanon Until June 1982", *Journal of Palestine Studies* 12, no. 3 (Spring, 1983): 70. Rubenberg records the existence of separate Plastic Arts and Graphic Arts divisions within the department and provides a brief overview of each: "The Plastic Arts division of the Department of Information and Culture supports Palestinian painters by providing supplies and funding for international exhibitions. In return for such support, the artists contribute five percent of their earnings to the General Union of Palestinian Artists. This division also runs two art galleries in Beirut, one housing a permanent collection and the other for temporary exhibits. The Plastic Arts division provides 25 scholarships each year for Palestinian artists to further their education. The Graphic Arts division of the Department of Information and Culture produces posters, placards, post cards, greeting cards, book covers, etc., for mass consumption. Graphic art is an important medium for the Palestinians to communicate their political ideas and cultural themes to their people and to the rest of the world". Ibid. Her primary source for information on this department is an interview with Michel Najjar, whom she describes as: "artist, and Director of the Graphic Arts Section of the Department of Art and Culture. May–June 1982, Beirut, Lebanon". See ibid., 69, no. 26. The PLO founded a High Committee for Education, Science and Culture in 1972. See Picaudou, *Le mouvement national*, 137.

120 Boullata, "Artists Re-Member", 27. Boullata offers further insight into the mission of the Art Department: "Art from the camps never made it into Beirut's art market or commercial galleries. When it was publicly viewed, it was usually at group exhibitions in improvised public spaces under the sponsorship of the Art Education Department of the Palestine Liberation Organization (PLO). Such exhibitions were generally organized to commemorate a national event or as part of a solidarity rally in Beirut or elsewhere in the Arab world or abroad". Ibid., 25. See also Isma'il Shammout, *al-Fann al-Tashkili fi-Filastin* (Kuwait: al-Qabas Printing Press, 1989), 67–68. I thank Kirsten Scheid for sharing this reference.

121 Shammout and Nissaboury, "Entretien", 34.

glance, appeared to have very little in common. As representatives of a colonized and embattled people, Palestinian artists were often considered beholden to an idiom that presented the Palestinian cause in (to borrow Shammout's terms) the "clearest" and most "efficient" manner. At the same time, enforcing the existence of a certain internal consistency amongst Palestinian artists, many of whom were scattered across the diaspora, helped support the idea of a spiritual and political unity of a Palestinian identity. In contrast, the Moroccan artists exhibiting at the biennale drew on a primarily (but not exclusively) abstract idiom of the sign, as discussed.

If, in attempting to qualify a category of Arab art, writers consistently relied on a binary opposition of figurative and abstract work, the aesthetics associated with the "national" schools of Moroccan and Palestinian art could be understood to represent opposing poles of an emerging continuum of Arab artistic expression. At the same time, the so-called abstract works of artists associated with *Souffles*, on the one hand, and the figurative visual language of Palestinian resistance, on the other, were understood not only as aesthetically and politically compatible in this period, but also as examples of the same kind of creation. The latter were defined by their simultaneous adherence to an Arab and Third World identity, while the positions developed by the artists themselves tended to undermine the usefulness of the neat division of figurative and abstract.

In leveraging the term "Third World" as a means of defining the role of the Union and its biennale, Shammout was able to validate the broadest possible parameters of stylistic diversity within the category of Arab art, on the condition that artists adhere to a specific concept of engagement that rested on the centrality of the Palestinian struggle and referenced the logic of a Third World art elaborated, as I have argued, on the pages of *Souffles*, and elsewhere. These qualities provided the necessary grounds upon which to assert the possibility of similarity-in-difference, or the existence of affinities between works that were essentially highly diverse in the formal choices they embraced.

"Arab art" has been defined consistently as a search for Arab identity in the visual arts undertaken by artists across the region, as well as a felicitous expression of that identity. Both the art and the identity are consistently understood today in essentialist terms. By this account, Arab art is, by definition, not African, Asian, European or American. The anachronism of this approach lies in its failure to acknowledge the many and various ways in which self-identified producers of Arab art deliberately positioned their practices within a variety of frameworks of artistic collaboration and exchange available to them at the time. This paper endeavors to trace one thread in a very rich and complex history of artistic debates and practices of the 1960s and '70s, which engaged in significant ways with various models of postcolonial solidarity, while claiming a place for itself within an emerging canon of Arab art.

Lotus Notes[1]

Nida Ghouse

1

Tashkent 1958. I try and imagine it for a moment. The first conference of the Afro-Asian Writers is in session. Faiz Ahmed Faiz, the poet representing Pakistan, is there. I find archival images on the internet: W. E. B. Du Bois lecturing into a bunch of microphones, meeting with the Nigerian delegation, chatting with the Chinese, raising his arms in affirmation with others. Non-alignment is in the air. In a unanimous motion a Permanent Bureau is declared. They must have thought the future as theirs. Headsets in hand, or pressed to the ear, translation devices hanging around their necks. Afro-Asian Writers. Tashkent 1958.

* * *

I am in Cairo. History is impossible. The year is 2012.
A friend and I are walking in midsummer heat against midday traffic along Qasr al-Aini—the road on which I came to live in early 2007. We've both been away a while and don't quite know what to make of the man climbing, somewhat impishly, over to the graffitied side of the army wall on the corner of Sheikh Rehan Street. We're looking for Dar al-Odaba. Number 104. If we were to be approaching the other way, with the cars, from Mounira or Garden City, coming toward Tahrir, we'd find it on our left, right after Barclays, or so I've been told. That is to say I used to pass the place, oblivious of it, back and forth, on my route, almost every other day.

In 1962, the second conference of the Afro-Asian Writers Association was held in Cairo, and a decision to transfer the headquarters from Colombo to here was made. Dar al-Odaba, or Writers House, was designated in all its palatial glory as the address of the Permanent Bureau, and the Egyptian writer Youssef El Sebai was elected, for his pinkish popularity, as its general-secretary.

The reasons for the relocation, I've come to learn, were not insignificant. They hint at a checkered history that played out in the name of Afro-Asian militant solidarity on a map of the Non-Aligned Movement against the backdrop of the Cold War. They tell a tale of ideological affinities and strategic aversions indicative of the political aspirations endowed on literary production in the wake of anti-imperialist struggles for national liberation. They chart an unusual geography of how, for instance, Somalis in the 1960s could have come to "Sing the Praise of Chairman Mao," in their own language no less, and then also songs in Chinese, such as "The East is Red."

The motivation behind the move was an aggressive one. In 1962, India was at war with China, and allied with Egypt. The Sino-Soviet communists had started to split. The conference in Cairo effectively removed the organization from under China's influence by ousting its pro-Chinese Ceylonese secretary-general, R.D. Senanayake, and repositioning the

1 "Lotus Notes" began in 2014 as a monthly series commissioned and edited by Jenifer Evans for the online platform Mada Masr. It is part of a writing project by Nida Ghouse called Inner States.

Peking-controlled Colombo-based headquarters into more Soviet-compliant territory.
In 1966, a so-called Emergency Meeting of Afro-Asian Writers was summoned in Peking. It was arranged under the auspices of the Chinese Committee of Afro-Asian Solidarity, which, as the host organization, probably paid all the expenses. Having proclaimed the resolution to shift the Afro-Asian Writers Bureau from Colombo to Cairo as illicit, the conveners pronounced the Soviet revisionists as the "chief culprits," who they thought ought to consider themselves excluded from the rank of Afro-Asian Writers affiliates. That four years later the Chinese, led by Kuo Mo-jo, still felt compelled to retaliate suggests that they were more than just upset. All the Afro-Asian Writers Association did back then was meet and take minutes, and so to think that the entity was seen as something to vie for is curious.

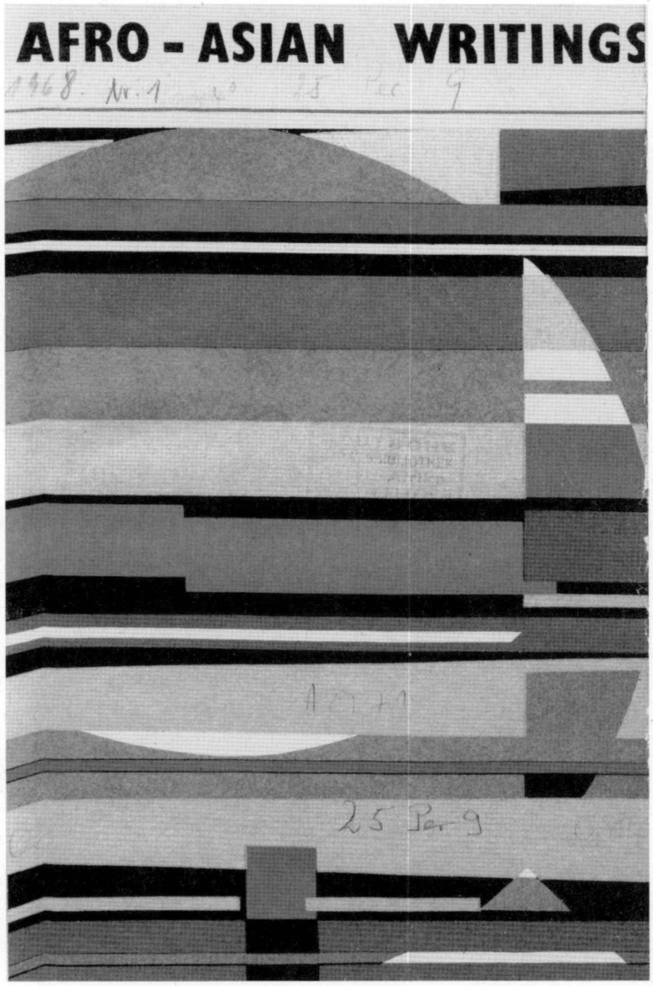

Afro-Asian Writings, no.1, Cairo, March 1968.

The gathering in Peking, attended only by China's geographical neighbors and the odd émigré, blatantly used its home court advantage to arouse anti-Soviet sentiment and claim leadership over Third World cultural consciousness. Speeches were made to disavow Soviet modern revisionist literature for serving American imperialism by virtue of being too bourgeois. But the language of all thirty-eight resolutions considered, the event was effectively a failure. The Vietnamese contingent refused to condemn modern revisionism and overtly sided with the USSR absentees. It was a gesture of historical significance that tread a measure between what would and did not happen.

* * *

We ask a man who happens to be at the gate if this is the Afro-Asian Writers Bureau, and whether it was from here that a periodical called *Lotus* had once been published. There is a big board right above us for Dar al-Obada, it's printed in white on blue, in an angular/kufic font of Arabic. On the side of the building that faces the road, there is also a relief of block letters that says "WRITERS HOUSE" in English. But this seems to have exceeded itself as a sign: though the structure is still intact, the color is nondescript, and one has to really look to notice it.

We've brought along with us this old book my friend grew up with, a compilation of short stories translated from various languages into Arabic. We turn to the colophon and point to what is the same address, as if to legitimize our quest. We do this even though the man has already offered us a yes. Our demeanor toward him is casual and courteous, but I notice we are hesitant as well. We have no sense of what goes on in here these days, nor can we be certain what attitude awaits. Are we welcome? He ushers us in, tells us to go down the corridor, across the hall, and up the stairs. And what does it even mean for this to be the right place? We're in search of a magazine that is defunct and an editor who is dead.

When we step inside the building, we leave the sun behind. Our eyes adjust to the difference in light, which, as we cover the length of the corridor, starts to feel more like a passage in time.

The conference hall is lined with chairs that have cushioned seats and metallic frames. They are all neatly arranged, save a stray few, which makes it seem as though people were just there—for a lecture from decades ago—before they got up and left. The room is dim as the shutters are barred, and it feels as though the world outside has not been let in. The ghosts are here; the conversations once had, trapped in an attempt to keep their vision of what they wanted intact.

We're now in the stairwell, dilapidated and grand, a billiards table, its cover covered with dust, stored under the slant. We're both looking up silently as we take our first steps; we spiral slowly and turn on ourselves. There are rays coming in through blue-green panes of broken glass that hit on particles of dust and make them burst into sparks.

The main room upstairs is flooded with light, and the reality of the streets outside enters inadvertently, making itself felt. On the wall across the doorway are two portraits and a nail: Gamal Abdel Nasser, Anwar Sadat—a suit, a uniform—and a conspicuously missing frame. At first I don't notice, but I am pointed to it, with the raising of an eyebrow and a tilt of the head.

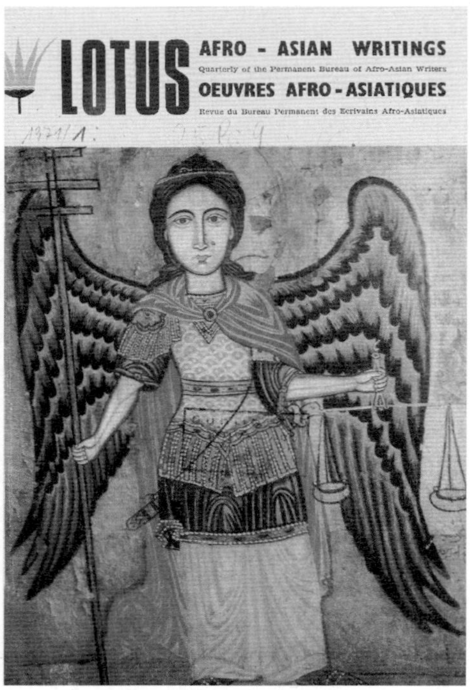

Lotus, Afro-Asian Writings, no.1, Cairo, January 1971.

There are two adjoining offices that seem to be the only ones occupied at the far left end. We walk over, peer in, and announce ourselves.

A few minutes later, I've been offered a chair. I sit down and to my right I notice a glass cabinet, in which all I can see is piles and piles of *Lotus*. My friend takes on the talking, introduces what I do, where I'm from, why I've come, while I can't seem to get my eyes off them. Most of the magazines are lying flat, stacked one on top of the other at the back. But the front row is on display, covers with images of art facing out. All these volumes, all these years, this is what I have come looking for.

I turn my attention to the conversation that is taking place between the three men and across the two generations present in the room. I find myself assembling some of the Arabic. We are being told that we are sitting at the desk that was the desk of Youssef El Sebai. This was his office, and the one out front his assistant's ... or maybe the other way round. Either they're not sure, or now I'm not sure. The confusion is contagious, it passes on from what is said to the language in my head, becomes mine. In any case, this was definitely his desk. We are sitting at the desk that was the desk of Youssef El Sebai. In a tone that has been weighed down and washed over by the time that has gone longing for everything he (was thought to have) stood for, this is said again.

* * *

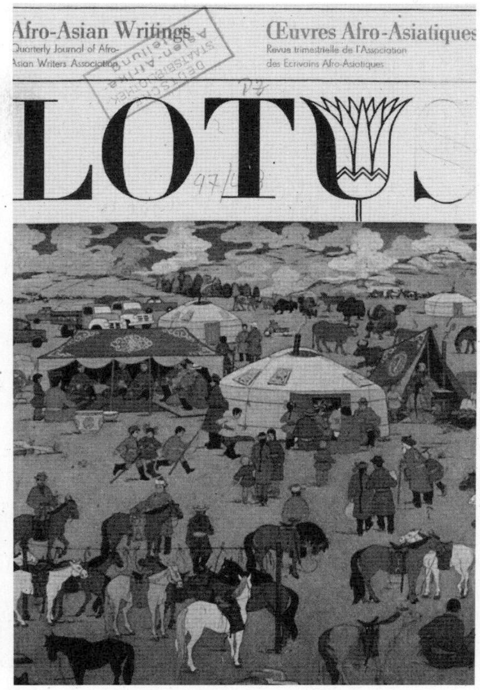

Lotus, Afro-Asian Writings, no. 47/48, Beirut, January-February, 1981.

By the end of 1978, the Afro-Asian Writers Bureau in Dar al-Odaba was disbanded. When President Anwar Sadat eventually defected to the U.S. and signed the Camp David Accords, the Arabs insisted that *Lotus* could no longer be the charge of Egypt. Besides, earlier that year, Youssef El Sebai, its editor-in-chief, had been assassinated in Cyprus. He had travelled to Nicosia to preside at a conference of the Afro-Asian People's Solidarity Organisation (AAPSO), but had been targeted on account of having accompanied Sadat, as his friend and confidant, on his infamous visit to Israel. At the time, Sebai was not just the minister of culture, but also the chairman of the state's flagship daily *Al-Ahram* and the head of the Egyptian Journalists Syndicate. He had been warned that his name had appeared at the top of some underground hit list. But he had proceeded with his plans nonchalantly, refusing to be fazed by this.

On the morning of February 18, the AAPSO meeting was called into session on the fifth floor of the Hilton. But then at around 11 am, Sebai was seen, off on his own, loitering in the lobby. Had he been waiting for someone? For someone who was in fact never going to come? As one account goes, he stepped out of the hotel and walked over to a nearby newsstand. Two cars drove up, three bullets went off, papers that had scattered in the air, lay strewn on the ground. Sebai was shot in the head in cold blood and broad daylight, by a pair of Palestinian gunmen belonging to what was reported to be "a tiny renegade movement."

2

The second time I met Michael C. Vazquez was the first time I heard that *Lotus*, the Journal of Afro-Asian Writings, had been published out of Cairo.

It was the summer of 2011. We were at a café called Downtown 34, sitting beside a wall of windows that looked out onto the fortified synagogue on Adly Street. To put it plainly, our talk was like a time warp. What I recall is being hurled into a universe in which the island of Cyprus, that said haven for hijackers, had transformed itself into a portal for an unpredicted past.

Mike remembers more. "We came to the same place with different magazines in our heads that were the same magazine," is how he puts it. What he means to say is that while he had known *Lotus* as a Cairo-based publication, I had thought it to be of Beirut. There was a reason why this was not trivial. His coherence complements my cause, which is that of dizziness.

Mike was chronologically correct. The periodical did start off in Cairo, and was edited here for a good ten years. Initially titled *Afro-Asian Writings*, its inaugural edition ostensibly appeared in March 1968, in Arabic and English, followed by the French version. By its sixth issue, which came out in October 1970, the trilingual quarterly had acquired the name *Lotus*. The Afro-Asian Writers Association (AAWA), and its over-arching affiliate, the Afro-Asian People's Solidarity Organisation (AAPSO), both had headquarters that hailed from this interface of Africa and Asia, the capital of Egypt. During those heydays, these institutions had been granted mansions that still operate to date, through some sort of leftover mandate, in their names. As it turns out, the prudence of Mike's account stood firmly on the floor.

Then one day *Lotus* moved. It went from Cairo to Beirut.

* * *

In the wake of Youssef El Sebai's death, the streets of Cairo swelled up in protest.

On February 19, 1978, as his body arrived from Cyprus to be wrapped in a flag and readied for a state-sponsored service, the newspapers had spread a rumor—that the Palestinian Liberation Organisation (PLO) was responsible—and this in turn had spurred hate. The crowds were in a frenzy as the procession took place, and ceremonious sorrow—with its customary incantation, "There is no god but God!"—gave way to more passionate and perverse political refrains: "No more Palestine, no more Palestine! Arafat, round up your dogs!"

Prime Minster Mostafa Riyad stood up and declared: "No more Palestine after today!"

The bullet that had killed the minister of culture was seen as having hit all of Egypt. Aggrieved as he was, Anwar Sadat did not attend his dear friend's funeral, and sent Vice-President Hosni Mubarak to show face instead. Sadat was six months from secretly signing Camp David, and he had already gone across to talk peace at the Knesset, which was, after all, why Sebai had been targeted in the first place.

In the week that followed: a man was thrown off the metro by a mob gone mad; children at school were harassed and attacked; the police carried out a spate of unwarranted interrogations and arbitrary arrests; a shopkeeper turned up to work one morning to find that his storefront window had been smashed. Many have marked this as the moment when public opinion in Egypt swerved. For whatever Pan-Arabism may or may not have meant, citizens were now incited to feel that—four wars later—they had sacrificed too much of their bread in standing up against Israel, and the media took it upon itself to fuel the brazen anti-Palestinian sentiment that surged forth.

On February 28, the official daily *Al-Ahram* announced that the government would reassess the privileges granted to Palestinians as nationals in Egypt, and then later in the year, two decrees were put into effect—administrative regulations 47 and 48—to deny them rights they had thus far availed.

* * *

Back in Nicosia, Sebai's murder had wreaked havoc in the lobby of the Hilton on that morning of February 18. As per most reports, he was shot inside and not outside the hotel, as mentioned above. The meeting of the Afro-Asian People's Solidarity Organisation (AAPSO) had been disrupted, and the two assassins had rounded up the delegates in the hotel cafeteria and held them captive. They threatened to kill them with hand grenades as they bargained with the Cypriot authorities, demanding to speak directly with the minister of interior, Christodoulos Veniamin, for safe passage to the Larnaca International Airport, as well as for an airplane—both of which they were granted. They singled out the Arab men in the room, instructed them to undo their ties from their necks, then to use them to rope each other's hands behind their backs, as the assassins escorted them with their guns onto a bus, while releasing all the women as well as the non-Arab rest.

Sadat was furious. Not only had Sebai been killed—in direct retaliation to his diplomatic doings—but four of the eleven hostages were Egyptian. He went as far as to accuse Cyprus of colluding with the militants and if not that then of abetting them by having insufficient security stationed. There was even a round of suspicion as to why Nicosia had been chosen as the venue for the AAPSO conference, when safer locations such as Moscow and Berlin had been proposed during the planning and preparation stages.

Sadat was quick to level allegations against Yasser Arafat as well; that this was an operation ordered by him. But the leader of the PLO had at least one of his own representatives caught in the crisis and was the first to call Spyros Kyprianou, the Cypriot president, to extend armed assistance—an experienced twelve or maybe sixteen man squad equipped with Soviet AK-47 assault rifles—were it needed. The offer was accepted in good faith and a plane was sent to Beirut to collect them.

At some point the assailants identified themselves. They belonged to a militant faction whose leader Sabri Al Banna had broken off from Arafat's political party Fatah back in 1974, which had then in turn issued a death warrant on him. The splinter group, which was first called the Fatah Revolutionary Council (FRC), was also known as the Abu Nidal Organisation (ANO). Its politics were aggressively rejectionist, and as a radical outfit its primary objective was to eliminate key figures seen to be enemies of the Palestinian people, especially Arabs who held too moderate a stance toward Israel.

Aboard a Cyprus Airways DC-8, the assassins-turned-hijackers commanded the civil aviation crew to head toward Tripoli, but to their surprise, and despite the hostage situation, they were not allowed to land. They possibly tried Damascus and then Aden, but at both locations they were told the same thing. In a final attempt they managed to touch down in Djibouti—it was about 4 or 5 am. While one of the hostages—it was Veniamin, who had offered himself as an emissary—was able to step off the aircraft and eventually get onto a telex line with Cyprus, the rest were not sanctioned to disembark. They spent the day there appealing to various governments for assistance, and eventually refueled the aircraft and headed right back to Larnaca—it was early evening on February 19 by then.

In the meantime, Sadat had grown really restless. Despite the assurance Kyprianou had given him—that he was handling the matter himself—the Egyptian president was scarcely comforted, thinking that Cyprus had long harbored Palestinian militants. He was determined to get involved in the rescue attempt and decided to order his special commando unit Task Force 777 to interfere. He dispatched them to Larnaca in a C-130H military transport plane without informing the Cypriot president what he intended—this by itself was already a disregard for the sovereignty of the other state, a violation of international norms even. Led by General Nabil Shukry, the assault team included around seventy personnel, most of whom were in combat gear, although some were disguised as if for an undercover expedition, wearing bellbottom denims and platform shoes, or sportswear.

The aviation authorities were led to believe that Egypt's minister of information was arriving to observe the negotiations, and thus although the aircraft raised some eyebrows it landed at around 6:40 pm without any hassle, parking itself within a kilometer of the DC-8. When Cypriot officials went over to greet a member of cabinet, they were stunned to find a full-fledged Special Forces unit as well. When this was conveyed to Kyprianou in the control tower, the Egyptian ambassador was summoned from the plane. It was made clear to him that there was no permission for a commando raid. Failure to comply and the Cypriot National Guard would not hesitate to attack them.

Meanwhile, a series of exchanges with the hijackers had been underway—a push, pull and wait game on the tarmac was being played. Vassos Lyssarides, the vice president of the AAPSO committee, had taken charge, reaching an agreement at around 7:30 p.m. or so to hand over passports to the militants that had their photos—to be taken onsite with a Polaroid camera being called in from the city—so that they could exit easily. The Cypriot armed forces and plain-clothes police snipers were concealed so as not to provoke anything, but this made Shukry, who had overheard something on the radio communication, assume that the hijackers were going to get away. He did not know that Kyprianou's plan was to arrest them once the hostages—who had started brushing their teeth and combing their hair—were released.

At around 8:30 p.m., the Egyptian minister of information returned to the C-130H. He informed the commanding officer in English, and in the presence of the Cypriot chief of police, what had been discussed—that they were not authorized to intervene. But then the Egyptians started to speak with each other in Arabic. And it was soon after this that the tail of the Egyptian aircraft dropped, and a jeep charged out with four men firing blindly into the dark. It headed for the DC-8, which didn't retaliate. Following suit, down the ramp, the rest of the troops marched on, but at an almost leisurely pace. Was this a decoy? A deliberate diversion, so that the actual killer team could get its act underway? At least one Western military observer seemed to ask this question.

A fifty-minute gun battle ensued on the runway between the Egyptian Task Force 777 and the Cypriot National Guard and what had started as murder ended in massacre. The jeep blew up with the four men in it. The plane too was badly damaged by a shell and eleven other Egyptian commandos were slain. At one point, the so-called crack anti-terrorist unit were shooting at the tower in which Cyprus' president was sitting and his soldiers had no choice but to ambush them. By the end of it, the Egyptian forces surrendered, having taken cover under an empty airliner, another sixteen injured. Astonished at the outbreak of violence, the hijackers too were persuaded by the DC-8's civilian pilots to turn themselves in.

It was an episode of diplomatic idiocy at best, and yet Sadat claimed credit for having solved the hostage crisis. As soon as his surviving commandos were deported, he cut official ties with Cyprus—later calling Kyprianou "a political dwarf," and saying, "Cyprus must explain to me the treachery that was committed against my sons," while almost in tears. He also remained convinced that Arafat had colluded against his fighters when in fact the PLO squad from Beirut had not even fired a bullet. When the ANO assassins were put on trial, he demanded they be given capital punishment. They were sent to death row at first, but then when Cyprus commuted the sentence to life imprisonment—on procedural grounds as well as for not wanting to alienate certain Palestinian factions—Sadat tried to insist that as Sebai's murderers they should be transferred to Egypt to be properly dealt with.

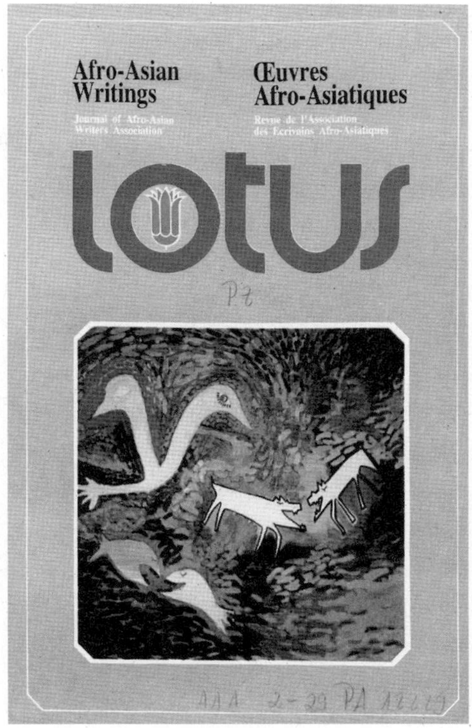

Lotus, Afro-Asian Writings, no. 59, Beirut, 1988.

He welcomed his surviving men home as national heroes, and the fifteen who died were honored at a grand funeral as having sacrificed their lives for the eleven hostages. But besides the U.S. and Israel, who were willing to praise his bravado regardless, all other nations saw this for what it was: The Egyptian soldiers were victims of the irresponsible behavior of their government, is how a Soviet newspaper put it.

* * *

In the summer that followed, the fault lines of a complex web of relations between Cyprus, Egypt and the PLO were reorganized and reimposed, and repercussions of this would be felt at the magazine called *Lotus*.

It's hard to tell whether Youssef El Sebai's last editorial, which only appeared in print after he had passed away, was specifically intended for the thematic issue on "Africa" in which it was included. Titled "The Historic Cultural Task of the Afro-Asian Intelligentsia," it covered more or less the same ground as what he had produced for the launch of the journal a decade prior—that article had been called "The Role of AFRO-ASIAN Literature and the National Liberation Movements." Marked for the months of April-September 1978, the posthumous volume was co-edited by South African writer Alex La Guma who had probably stepped up as deputy secretary-general from his position as assistant editor at the last minute. And it was this issue no. 36/37 that also concluded Cairo's term: Dar al-Odaba was no longer the Permanent Bureau of the Afro-Asian Writers Association.

* * *

Soon after the Permanent Bureau of the Afro-Asian Writers Association in Cairo folded, a poet from Pakistan by the name of Faiz Ahmed Faiz arrived in Beirut to take over the chief editorship of *Lotus*. Both the man and the magazine had relocated from different places to be granted home and hospitality by the Union of Palestinian Writers, many of whose members were probably there as exiles themselves. Mahmoud Darwish was responsible for the Arabic edition, and Yasser Arafat also became involved in an occasional advisory capacity. Curious then is this: Why were the PLO so invested in *Lotus*, extending in-house resources to revive it? And what made Faiz leave Lahore—at the age of 67 no less—to set up base in the midst of it? Though the worst may not have happened yet, the Lebanese Civil War was well underway by then. The year was 1978.

* * *

When Mike mentioned his fascination with the assassination of Youssef El Sebai, I had had a faint sensation that I knew about this already, like I'd come across it elsewhere. But up until then, as far as my fixation with the magazine went, there was no reason for *Lotus* to have even been before Beirut. It was the idea of this Urdu poet moving to that city which was soon to be sacked that had been my hook. Clearly I was there more on a whim, asserting my own angle of incidence onto things, as if it were that of Faiz.

We were the only two customers in the café that morning, and had taken the liberty of asking the waiters to turn off the disco-pop—the one thing reminding us of the present. The high ceilings and the hardwood floors, the placemats with images of long ago, had all probably contributed in some subconscious measure to the air of our exchange, and as we whirled our way into Cyprus, time curved around us from another direction and I was left with no indication of when we were anymore.

It was in fact as he spoke of Cyprus that some sort of undefined awareness had surfaced. "What was this Egyptian editor guy called again?" I imagine myself having asked. And while I can still hear Mike's voice in my head pronounce "youssefalsebai" just as he always does—like a word that I would never have been able to spell—in that moment the name itself had drawn a blank. In any case, it had felt far too early in the morning to be making notes, so I had carried on listening, and let the whole thing pass.

All of which is to say, I was sure I had no sense of Sebai, and thus no cause to dwell on my unlikely knowledge of this piece of the puzzle that was his demise. It was only over time and on its own terms, as my research expanded and I started to put more of it together, that I too found myself perplexed by the pivotal role his death had played in a certain unraveling of the not-so Non-Aligned/Pan-Arab nexus—it was after all the event around which so much had turned. But a trace of a vague familiarity lingered... somewhere at the back of things.

Recently, when I walked past the place where Mike and I had first encountered each other's affinity for *Lotus*, I found that it was all boarded up. The café had only been open a couple of years and now it was soon to be like it had never occurred.

Pan-Asianism and the Question: "What is Asia?"

James T. Hong

The story of Pan-Asianism is indelibly linked to the actions of Japan from the late nineteenth century until its defeat in the Second World War. It was Imperial Japan that gave Pan-Asianism a prescriptive political meaning by employing the idea as a government-sanctioned, holy mission. Without Japan's championing of a "New Order in East Asia," Pan-Asianism as a reactionary ideology is naive at best and incoherent at worst. The fundamental weakness of the early, inchoate Pan-Asianist dream is precisely the vagueness of the concept of "Asia." The second and fatal Pan-Asianist flaw is the inscription of Japanese superiority into the very fabric of Pan-Asianist dogma, which resulted in the murder and unnecessary deaths of millions.

What is Asia?

"Asia" as a geographical term purportedly comes from the Ancient Greeks; it was later adapted by the Romans, and then eventually defined as a continental landmass conceptually detached from the European continent. The geographical borders of continents such as Antarctica or Australia are clear even to primary school students, but the border between Europe and Asia has shifted throughout time and continues to be contentious, with a number of scholars denying any meaningful geographical break between Europe and Asia at all. Since the notion of a unitary and distinct entity called "Asia" is of European origin, its widespread acceptance is just one example of what Martin Heidegger deemed "the complete Europeanization of the earth and man."[1]

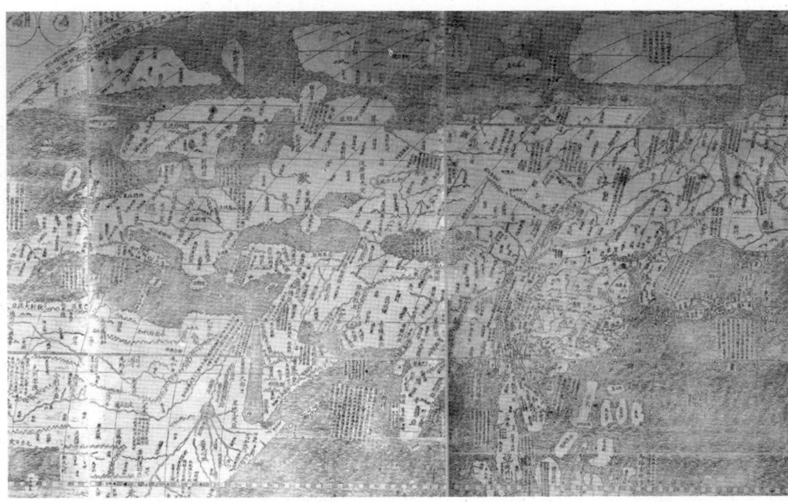

"Asia" in Matteo Ricci's 1602 world map.

Jesuit scholars first introduced the concept of "Asia" to China in the late sixteenth century. In 1602, Matteo Ricci, one of the first Jesuits to seriously take up the study of classical Chinese, printed a map in the Chinese language that introduced the term "亞細亞" (Asia). What is now East Asia was then culturally dominated by China in a "premodern" system of tributary relations. Hierarchical, this tributary system placed China (or specifically a dynasty within China) at the politico-cultural center and can be called the "Sinocentric Order." Educated Chinese during dynastic rule did not see themselves as just one part of a regional bloc. For them, the most basic differentiation between peoples was that which existed between civilization and barbarism.

1 Martin Heidegger, *On the Way to Language*, trans. Peter D. Hertz (New York: Harper & Row, 1982), 15.

It took centuries before "Asia" became an identity, and even now it competes with ethnic, racial, and most frequently nationalist identity formations. In other words, the idea of a distinctive "Asian identity" is elusive and still unsettled. India, for instance, was once identified with Asia, with the natives in the Americas still being called "Indians" today. But after the debates concerning "Asian values," India no longer came to be associated with Asia, or at least with the Asian economic successes of the 1990s. And the Russians, ostensibly located on the continent of Asia, have, for the most part, seen themselves as European.

Moreover, those at the center of the Sinocentric Order had no reason to question their cultural identities, and it was only on the periphery of Asia, such as Japan, where the question of Asian identity arose as a conceptual problem and as a means of displacing the stagnating Sinocentric Order. Even today, many Japanese consider themselves "Westerners" as opposed to "Asians," with some of them even identifying themselves as "white."

Since the precise geographical, cultural, and ethnic borders of Asia have never been duly established, even to Europeans, the concept of Asia made more sense as a term signifying "non-European." "Asia" represented a terrestrial black hole that was beyond the comprehension and therefore the control of Europeans. If a singular Europe exists, within which people can say, "we are European," then there needs to be a discursive "Other," and one of these "Others" was posited as "Asia." Or to put it in Karl Jaspers' words: "Asia is turned into a mythical principle, that falls apart when it is analyzed objectively as an historical reality."[2]

What is Pan-Asianism?

A series of historical events during the Age of Imperialism would begin to remap Asia. The British had subdued India and invaded Qing Dynasty China during the first and second Opium Wars; Commodore Perry's "black ships" had forced Japan open to trade, while the French and Dutch colonized Southeast Asia. Intellectuals in India, China, and Japan were forced to accept the technological superiority of the Europeans and/or the U.S., and seeking a way to allay their own national vulnerabilities, began to speak of Asian solidarity and regional cooperation.

"Asia is One"

The concept of Asian solidarity known as "Asianism" evolved and mutated through the late nineteenth century, but did not come to be what is now known as "Pan-Asianism" until the 1930s. In her detailed *Pan-Asianism and Japan's War, 1931–1945,* Eri Hotta distinguishes between three types of Pan-Asianism: Teaist, Sinic, and *Meishuron* (Japan as leader).[3] The first, what she calls "Teaist Pan-Asianism," is exemplified by Okakura Kakuzo (1862–1913), who famously wrote in his *Ideals of the East* (1903):

> *Asia is one. The Himalayas divide, only to accentuate, two mighty civilizations, the Chinese with its communism of Confucius, and*

2 Karl Jaspers, *The Origin and Goal of History*, trans. Michael Bullock (New Haven Connecticut: Yale University Press, 1953), 70. See also Wang Hui, *The Politics of Imagining Asia*, ed. Theodore Huters (Cambridge: Harvard University Press, 2011), 13–14.

3 Eri Hotta, *Pan-Asianism and Japan's War 1931–1945* (New York: Palgrave Macmillan, 2007).

> *the Indian with its individualism of the Vedas. But not even the snowy barriers can interrupt for one moment that broad expanse of love for the Ultimate and Universal, which is the common thought-inheritance of every Asiatic race, enabling them to produce all the great religions of the world, and distinguishing them from those maritime peoples of the Mediterranean and the Baltic, who love to dwell on the Particular, and to search out the means, not the end, of life.*[4]

Okakura, better known as the author of *The Book of Tea,* wrote in English for a Western and Indian audience. His aim was to establish the inimitable spirituality of an imagined Asia of which Japan was the custodian. He travelled to India, and as an associate of Rabindranath Tagore (1861–1941)[5], promoted the idea of a comprehensive Asia, which not only included India, but also much of the Middle East. Within his nascent Pan-Asianist conception, Japan had a special role to play:

> *It has been, however, the great privilege of Japan to realize this unity-in-complexity with a special clearness. The Indo-Tartaric blood of this race was in itself a heritage which qualified it to imbibe from the two sources, and so mirror the whole of Asiatic consciousness. The unique blessing of unbroken sovereignty, the proud self-reliance of an unconquered race, and the insular isolation which protected ancestral ideas and instincts at the cost of expansion, made Japan the real repository of the trust of Asiatic thought and culture.*[6]

Reformulating Okakara's Pan-Asianism into a coherent argument is difficult, as much of what he claims is unsubstantiated, vague, or simply wrong. Moreover, Okakura would most likely be opposed to using Western logic to interpret his philosophical, Asiatic sermon. However, despite his metaphysical posturing, Okakura is presenting an argument to his readers:

1. *There exists a singular, geographical, and spiritual entity called Asia, which includes a number of different ethnicities, cultures, and religions.*
2. *These ethnicities, cultures and religions are exclusive to Asia and can be called "Asianness."*
3. *Asianness eventually traveled to Japan and other Asian nations.*
4. *All of these other Asian nations are politically unstable and/or have been conquered by the West.*
5. *Conquered and/or unstable nations cannot adequately express their inherent Asianness.*
6. *Japan is stable and has not been conquered.*
7. *Therefore, only Japan can express inherent Asianness, or, in his own words, "Japan is the museum of Asiatic civilization."*[7]

4 Okakura Kakuzo, *Ideals of the East: The Spirit of Japanese Art* (New York: Dover Publications, 2005), 1.

5 Unlike a duped W. E. B. Du Bois, Tagore would become a fierce critic of Japanese nationalism and atrocities in China. See Z. Cipris, "Seduced by Nationalism: Yone Noguchi's 'Terrible Mistake'", 2007, http://www.japanfocus.org.

6 Kakuzo, *Ideals of the East,* 2.

7 Ibid., 3.

Put in this way, we can see how Okakura's seemingly benign and uplifting Asianism is actually an unsubtle claim to Japanese metaphysical preeminence vis-à-vis Asia's helplessness. However, Okakura's "Asia" is never clearly defined and most of his descriptions of Asiatic religions such as Buddhism never elevate themselves above hackneyed Orientalist conceptions of the East, which of course he himself popularized. Furthermore, Okakura's admittedly "aesthetic" Pan-Asianist agenda never promotes a prescriptive plan of action. We may only assume that if Japan is the museum of Asia *par excellence*, then as a museum, it should be preserved but not necessarily recreated in other less fortunate Asian nations. Okakura's claim of Japanese superiority would become more explicit and prescriptive in later formulations of Pan-Asianism.

"The Same Letters, The Same Race"

In the late nineteenth century, Japanese intellectuals were presenting the idea of a Sino-Japanese alliance exemplified in the slogan "the same letters, the same race." During the Sinocentric Order, Japan as a nominal tributary state absorbed much of Chinese culture almost wholesale, including written language, customs, cuisine, and architecture. Hence many educated Chinese saw Japan as a less creative and inferior culture. This is one of the reasons why the Japanese invasions of China were considered (and still are considered by some) particularly offensive.

As a subversion of the Sinocentric Order, this Asianist vision for Sino-Japanese cooperation, what Hotta terms "Sinic Pan-Asianism," imagines a superior Japan manipulating and safeguarding a primitive China. However, if we consider this state of affairs to be a version of Pan-Asianism, then surely the historical Sinocentric Order is also a type of Pan-Asianism. For Japanese Pan-Asianists such as Inukai Tsuyoshi (1855–1932) and Sawayanagi Masataro (1865–1927), so-called "Sinic Pan-Asianism" is just the initial phase of a total Pan-Asianist project: the domination of all of Asia.[8]

While in exile in Japan, Sun Yat-sen (1866–1925) befriended a number of Pan-Asianists, and like any other, Sun had his own nationalist agenda, namely overthrowing the Qing Dynasty and founding a republic in China. To this end, he was a practiced political opportunist and courted rich and powerful people around the world including the Japanese. In 1924, thirteen years after the fall of the Qing Dynasty, Sun delivered a speech on Pan-Asianism in Kobe, Japan.

> *At present Asia has only two independent countries, Japan in the East and Turkey in the West. In other words, Japan and Turkey are the Eastern and Western barricades of Asia. Now Persia, Afghanistan, and Arabia are also following the European example in arming themselves, with the result that the Western peoples dare not look down on them. China at present also possesses considerable armaments, and when her unification is accomplished she too will*

8 "The future history of Greater Asianism will be divided into four stages. In the first stage, the Yellow race—the strongest country of Mongol ethnicity, Japan, and the largest country, China—must be united under the banner of Greater Asianism." Sawayanagi Masataro, "Asianism," (1919) in *Pan-Asianism: A Documentary History, Volume 1: 1850–1920*, ed. Sven Saaler and Christopher W. Spilman (Maryland: Rowman & Littlefield, 2011), 262.

become a great Power. We advocate Pan-Asianism in order to restore the status of Asia. Only by the unification of all the peoples in Asia on the foundation of benevolence and virtue can they become strong and powerful.[9]

Elaborating upon Okakura's comprehensive notion of Asia, Sun's Pan-Asianism explicitly delineated the far-flung borders of his Pan-Asianist conception of the continent. And like Okakura's, Sun's concept of Asia relies upon the vague European conception—a mystical realm of "benevolent" cultures and "virtuous" civilizations that originated to the east of Europe. Sun's criterion for Asianness can be reduced to the trivial notion that any ethnic nation on the entire Asian landmass is Asian, except of course Russia.

A frequent guest of Japan, Sun was well aware of Japanese designs on Manchuria and cognizant of the ultimate path Pan-Asianism might take. By 1924, China had descended into warlordism, and Sun wouldn't live to see a China at least nominally united under the republicans. While acknowledging the military superiority of Japan, Sun calls on the empire to uphold the values of Asian cooperation, rather than dominating Asia for herself:

Japan today has become acquainted with the Western civilization of the rule of Might, but retains the characteristics of the Oriental civilization of the rule of Right. Now the question remains whether Japan will be the hawk of the Western civilization of the rule of Might, or the tower of strength of the Orient. This is the choice which lies before the people of Japan.[10]

What Happened to Korea?

For Korean nationalists such as Ahn Jung-geun (1879–1910), Japan's actions after the Russo-Japanese War (1904–1905) betrayed Chinese and Korean trust in Japan's purported Asianist mission. Asianists and many intellectuals of color around the world had celebrated Japan's victory over a European empire, whereas white supremacists saw it as a bad sign of things to come. Despite the Japanese Emperor's claim that the Russo-Japanese War was fought to defend Korea, by 1905 Japan had forced Korea into becoming a Japanese protectorate and would later annex it completely into the Japanese empire in 1910. As Ahn puts it in his unfinished treatise:

If Japan fails to change its political strategy and if oppression continues to increase daily, then the Chinese and Koreans will no longer endure the humiliations inflicted upon them by the people of the same race, but will prefer defeat at the hands of another race. The consequences are clear. The oppressed inhabitants of China and Korea will jointly and voluntarily collaborate with the white people.[11]

9 Sun Yat-sen, "Speech on Pan-Asianism (1941)," *wikisource*, last modified June 12, 2011, http://en.wikisource.org/wiki/Sun_Yat-sen%27s_speech_on_Pan-Asianism.

10 Ibid.

11 Ahn Jung-geun, "A Discourse on Peace in East Asia," in *Pan-Asianism: A Documentary History, Volume 1: 1850–1920*, ed. Sven Saaler and Christopher W.A. Szpilman (Maryland: Rowman & Littlefield Publishers, 2011), 209.

Ahn's frustration with Japan led to his most famous act: assassinating the Resident-General of Korea and Japan's first Prime Minister, Ito Hirobumi, in 1909. To Korean and Chinese nationalists, including Sun Yat-sen, Ahn was lionized as a hero. Memorials and monuments in his honor have since been erected in Korea and China, the most recent in Harbin where Ito was assassinated. In 2014, the Japanese government protested China's newly opened Ahn Jung-geun Memorial Hall and called Ahn a "terrorist."[12]

Pan-Asianism as "Greater Japanism"

What Hotta dubs "*Meishuron* Pan-Asianism" is closest to the postwar Tokyo Trial interpretation of ideological Pan-Asianism. The term "Meishuron" is the romanization of the Japanese pronunciation of the Chinese characters 盟主論 which mean something like "leader theory." Whereas, Sun Yat-sen and Ahn Jung-geun's Asianist visions presented an equitable collaboration between multiple powers—Chinese and Japanese or Chinese, Korean, and Japanese—Pan-Asianism at its most mature concretizes Japanese supremacy.

Before the 1930s, Asianist ideologies had little bearing on Japan's internationalist foreign policy. Underground Japanese ultranationalist groups and intellectuals had been calling for Japanese expansionism for decades.[13] Ever since the Meiji Restoration (1868–1912), Japanese leaders had striven to make the Empire of Japan a great power within the emerging internationalist order. Changing world conditions and the League of Nations' 1933 refusal to accept Japan's puppet state in Manchuria led Japanese leaders back to Pan-Asianist ideology. It made perfect sense to use Pan-Asianism as a vehicle for legitimizing the Empire's expansionist policies as a moral and honorable mission of Asian liberation. Once the government began officially endorsing a Pan-Asianist doctrine, intellectuals and politicians went to work codifying the vague and sometimes incoherent Pan-Asianist themes that had been circulating since the nineteenth century.

Pan-Asianism as tangible foreign policy would be most famously articulated in 1940 as the "Greater East Asia Co-Prosperity Sphere." Looking back on the origins of the policy, the indicted war criminal Tojo Hideki (1884–1948) would claim:

> *The key point of the Greater East Asia policy was the establishment of a Greater East Asia. Regarding the formulation of this policy, the Japanese Government at the time held the following fundamental views. The underlying prerequisite for the lasting peace of the world is that each and every nation in the world should be placed in its*

12 Emily Rouhana, "104 Years Later, a Chinese Train Station Platform is Still the Site of Anti-Japanese Rancor," *Time*, January 30, 2014, http://time.com/2609/104-years-later-a-chinese-train-station-platform-is-still-the-site-of-anti-japanese-rancor/.

13 In 1887, the Japanese secret society, Genyosha or "Black Ocean Society," claimed: "As a colored race, it is imperative for us to have military facilities and equipment to counter the Europeans and the Americans. Especially, for our country, as a prosperous new up-and-coming nation in Asia, and with our hope to one day become the leader of Asia, this is the right time for state militarism." Takeuchi Yoshimi, "Nihon no Ajia shugi" [Japan and Asianism], quoted in and translated by Faye Yuan Kleeman, "Pan-Asian Romantic Nationalism: Revolutionary, Literati, and Popular Oral Tradition and the Case of Miyazaki Tōten," in *Sino-Japanese Transculturation: From the Late Nineteenth Century to the End of the Pacific War*, ed. Richard King et al. (Maryland: Lexington Books, 2012), 50.

proper place, and that it should enjoy happiness and prosperity by depending on and cooperating with every other nation.[14]

The crucial phrase is "proper place." The Japanese conception of a "New Order in East Asia" was hierarchical by design. The propaganda surrounding the puppet state of Manchukuo was dominated by familial, particularly patriarchal, images and metaphors, in which a benevolent and advanced Japan would guide and protect its vulnerable and backward Asian children. For Japanese Pan-Asianists, Japan was tasked with a civilizing mission not unlike that of the "white man's burden." As Sawayanagi Masataro put it in 1916:

One can say that the Japanese state and the Chinese state are the twin sons of one and the same nation. In accordance with this special relationship, Japan has a special duty to promote peace in the Far East and to protect China—but it also has the right to claim a special position....[15]

Implicitly or explicitly, Pan-Asianism, as a Japanese construct, always maintained the superiority of Japan. In its most benign expressions, the Japanese were dominant in Asia only because they had modernized first. But Japan's initial successes would become essentialized. Rapid industrialization, a growing colonial empire, and victories against the Sinocentric Order and then Russia would go to their heads. It wasn't modernization that made Japan superior to other Asian nations; Japan already was superior, so it was destined to modernize before any other competing Asian nation could. Foundation myths leave no room for accident.

Okakura's mystical Pan-Asianism never claimed that each and every Asian nation was equal to the other. Japan had nurtured a unique "custodial" function in Asia. This function, as realized by the Imperial Japanese government, would come to be expressed as political terror, oppression, exploitation, and mass rape and murder—not so different from the imperialism practiced by the Europeans. Victims of Japanese expansionism would learn very quickly that liberation looked a lot like invasion. Li Dazhao (1888–1927), considered a co-founder of the Chinese Communist Party, put it very clearly in 1919:

First, one should know that the term "Greater Asianism" conceals the doctrine of China's annexation.... Second, one should be aware that "Greater Asianism" is just another name for Greater Japanism.... All the Asian nations listen to orders from Japan; the problems of Asia are all being solved by the Japanese; Japan is the leading power in Asia, and Asia has become a stage for the Japanese. So Asia is not the Asia of the Europeans or Americans, and neither is it the Asia of the Asians—it is simply the Asia of the Japanese.[16]

Li was not the first to equate Pan-Asianism with "Greater Japanism." Just two years earlier Kita Reikichi (1885–1961), a prominent Japanese nationalist intellectual and politician, made the same equation: "So,

14 Tojo Hideki, "Affidavit to the International Military Tribunal for the Far East," 6.

15 Masataro, *Pan-Asianism: A Documentary History,* 262.

16 Li Dazhao, "Greater Asianism and New Asianism," in *Pan-Asianism: A Documentary History, Volume 1: 1850–1920,* ed. Sven Saaler and Christopher W.A. Szpilman (Maryland: Rowman & Littlefield Publishers, 2011), 220–21.

if the so-called Asianism with its slogan of "Asia for the Asians" has any significance, it must essentially be Greater Japanism."[17]

Japanese nationalism, Emperor worship, militant State Shinto, and ethnic and racial chauvinism would renovate Pan-Asianism into a consistent political argument. Since Asian nations were not and would not be equal "under one roof" of the Japanese empire, promoting and believing in Pan-Asianism did not necessarily entail any type of cognitive dissonance. Furthermore, the program of strong Pan-Asianism would also answer one relevant question: what is Asia?

1 *Any territory that is determined by Japan to be Asian is thus Asian.*
2 *With the exception of Japan, every Asian nation is weak and/or colonized by European powers.*
3 *A weak Asian nation or one colonized by non-Asian powers cannot liberate all Asian nations, i.e., Asia.*
4 *Japan is a strong Asian nation.*
5 *Only a strong Asian nation can liberate Asia.*
6 *Therefore, only Japan can liberate Asia.*

So what is Asia, and how is it one? Asia is, to put it in Pan-Asian terms, a real or potential Japanese empire. It admittedly sounds strange to claim that a territory is Asian, if the Japanese decide that it is.[18] But consider the example of Southeast Asia, which the Japanese invaded in 1941. Before the war, the area was known colloquially as the "South Seas," "the Tropics," or the "East Indies." Japan's actions placed Southeast Asia firmly within the realm of Asia or specifically in "Greater East Asia." The Empire of Japan was not only disrupting European colonial possessions, it was also reshaping the dominant spatial imagination. Europeans had long enjoyed the power of cataloging and naming various parts of the Earth, and the Japanese "New Order" aimed to usurp that power. Had the Japanese been able to penetrate more deeply into Asia, especially India, the notion of "East Asia" would have expanded as well. A secret Japanese document from 1943 outlines the stages of Japanese expansion:

> *Stage 1. Japan, Manchuria, Mongolia, North China, major islands of the China coast, Central and South China under the Wang Ching-wei regime.*
>
> *Stage 2. Remaining areas of China, French Indochina, Thailand, British Malaya, Burma, Dutch East Indies, New Guinea, British Borneo, New Caledonia, Australia, New Zealand, South Sea Islands with the exception of the Philippines.*
>
> *Stage 3. Soviet territory east of Lake Baikal, peripheral regions of China, the Philippines, India and its coastal islands.*

17 Ibid., 301.
18 Consider the determination of Pan-Islamic territory. An Islamic territory is any territory that happens to have a sufficient number of Muslims or is deemed to be Islamic by the Caliphate.

Stage 4. Assyria, Turkey, Iran, Iraq, Afghanistan and other central Asian countries, West Asia, Southwest Asia.[19]

The Failure of Pan-Asianism

Japan's defeat in the Second World War ended the Greater East Asia Co-Prosperity Sphere and Pan-Asianism as a political mission. Japan's Pan-Asianist agenda had resulted in the deaths of millions, with tens of millions in China alone. In the last weeks of the "Greater East Asia War" an estimated 10,000 people per day were murdered or died as a direct result of Imperial Japanese policies.[20] After Hirohito's surrender, former Japanese Pan-Asianists of all stripes renounced the aims of Pan-Asianism, with some claiming that only in defeat did the Japanese really "return to Asia."[21] Mimicking its denazification efforts in postwar Germany, the U.S. government made concerted efforts to transform a defeated Japan into a model puppet state. Japanese politicians and ideologues of the strong Pan-Asianist persuasion were purged from any official capacities (at least temporarily) or arrested for war crimes.

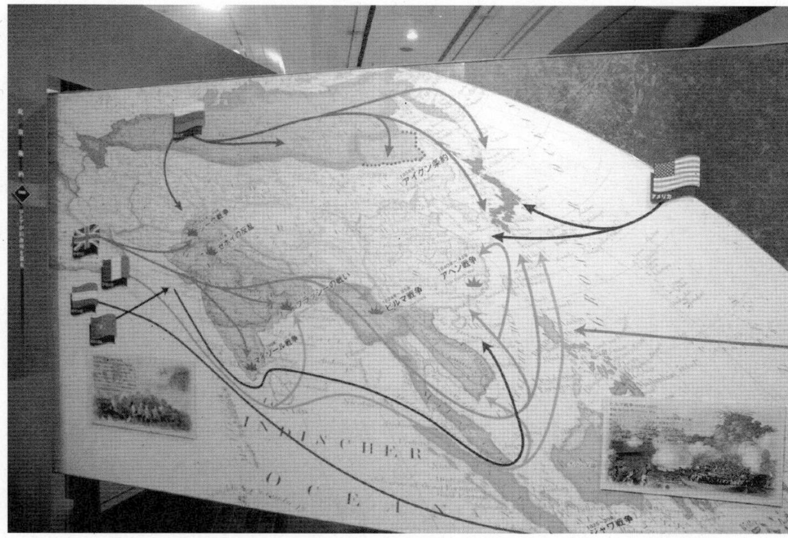

A display showing the encroaching European powers at the Yushukan Museum on the grounds of Yasukuni Shrine.

However, unrepentant Pan-Asianists would take heart in the postwar events of Southeast Asia and India, where anticolonial nationalist movements that had been supported by Japan during the war, began fighting for their own independence. Japanese revisionists, ultranationalists, and Pan-Asianists point to these independence movements as evidence that the Pan-Asianist mission was not entirely self-serving and that it actually did give rise to the liberation of various subjugated Asian nations. This is the view that is enshrined at the Yushukan War Museum on the grounds of the ultranationalist Yasukuni Shrine in Tokyo.

While it is true that some Japanese intellectuals and military officers supported Asian liberation movements, it is not always clear what their motivations were.[22] As Japan had declared war on a number of European powers, it made perfect sense for the Japanese government to support cobelligerents fighting common enemies. Most governments, if

19 "An Investigation of Global Policy with the Yamato Race as Nucleus," quoted in John Dower, *War Without Mercy* (New York: Pantheon Books, 1986), 273.

20 See Werner Gruhl, *Imperial Japan's World War Two: 1931–1945* (New Jersey: Transaction Publishers, 2007).

21 Sven Saaler and Christopher W.A. Szpilman, eds., *Pan-Asianism: A Documentary History, Volume 1: 1850–1920* (Maryland: Rowman & Littlefield Publishers, 2011), 209.
See also Oguma Eiji, "The postwar intellectuals' view of 'Asia'," in *Pan-Asianism in Modern Japanese History,* eds. Sven Saaler and J. Victor Koschmann (London: Routledge, 2002), 200.

22 Japan hosted a number of exiled nationalists and independence leaders from China, India, and other nations in the decades leading up to and during the Second World War. See Cemil Aydin, "The Politics of Anti-Westernism in Asia: Visions of World Order in Pan-Islamic and Pan-Asian Thought" (New York: Columbia University Press, 2007).

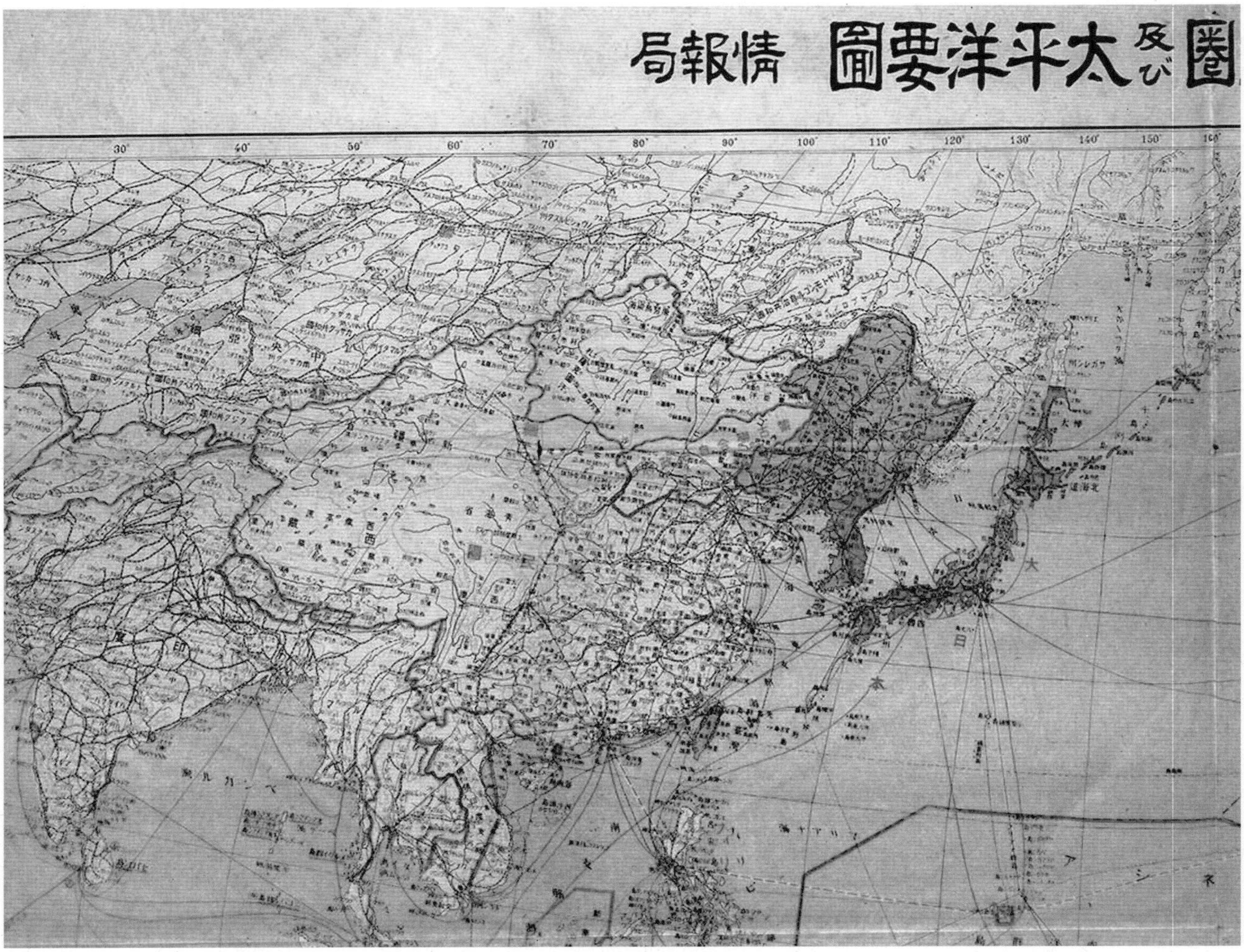

The rising Greater East Asia Co-Prosperity Sphere according to a 1941 Japanese map.

not all of the Allied and Axis powers, adhered to the proverb "the enemy of my enemy is my friend."

The Yasukuni Shrine/Yushukan War Museum version of history omits the massacres, rapes, indiscriminate torture, biological warfare, enslavement, and beheadings that accompanied the Pan-Asianist mission. Most of the victims of the Empire of Japan remain anonymous and forgotten to history, and it is reasonable to conclude that none of them wanted to be killed, raped, or tortured to further the Japanese Pan-Asianist cause of Asian liberation.

The Japanese answer to the question "What is Asia?" proved to be homicidal and intolerable, but the possibilities for regional cooperation were not totally dashed. Asiatic organizations, such as ASEAN, the still dominant U.S. World Order, and rising states such as China and India will attempt to answer that question in the future.

Performing Solidarity: The Bandung Conference 1955

Shirin M. Rai

The despised, the insulted, the hurt, the dispossessed—in short, the underdogs of the human race were meeting. Here were class and racial and religious consciousness on a global scale. Who had thought of organizing such a meeting? And what had these nations in common? Nothing, it seemed to me, but what their past relationship to the Western world had made them feel. This meeting of the rejected was in itself a kind of judgment upon the Western world!— Richard Wright (civil rights journalist who attended the Bandung Conference in 1955)

The countries that met in Bandung, were many things but not "the despised, the insulted, the hurt, the dispossessed". The representatives that gathered in Bandung were looking forward—they were emergent—and what they had to say had an audience ready to receive their messages in their countries and more broadly. Independent India's first Prime Minister, Jawaharlal Nehru bemoaned the status of Asian-African nations with remembering a glorious past that, as Edward Said reminds us, becomes a leitmotif for harnessing the dreams of the future:

Has it come to this, that the leaders of thought who have given religions and all kinds of things to the world have to tag on to this kind of group or that and be hangers-on of this party or the other carrying out their wishes and occasionally giving an idea? It is most degrading and humiliating to any self-respecting people or nation. It is an intolerable thought to me that the great countries of Asia and Africa should come out of bondage into freedom only to degrade themselves or humiliate themselves in this way...[1]

As Itty Abraham has pointed out, "The reversal of familiar racial hierarchies, especially around the trope of civilisation, recurred in the opening speeches of delegates from across Asia."[2]

The host countries were Burma, Ceylon, India, Indonesia and Pakistan, who cohosted twenty-four other Asian African countries at the Bandung Conference April 18–24, 1955. Twenty-nine countries representing more than half the world's population sent representatives to Bandung. Opening the conference, President Sukarno said: "This is the first intercontinental conference of the coloured people, the so-called coloured peoples, in mankind"[3]—the move from "coloured" to the "so-called coloured" was as much due to the reproduction of categories of race that the peoples of Asia had grown up with as a conscious attempt to rephrase and reframe these.

1 Prime Minister Nehru, "Speech to Bandung Conference Political Committee," 1955, *Modern History Sourcebook*, http://www.legacy.fordham.edu/.

2 Itty Abraham, "From Bandung to NAM: Non-alignment and Indian Foreign Policy, 1947–65", *Commonwealth & Comparative Politics* 46, no. 2 (April 2008): 200.

3 President Sukarno of Indonesia, "Speech at the Opening of the Bandung Conference," April 18, 1955, *Modern History Sourcebook*, http://www.legacy.fordham.edu.

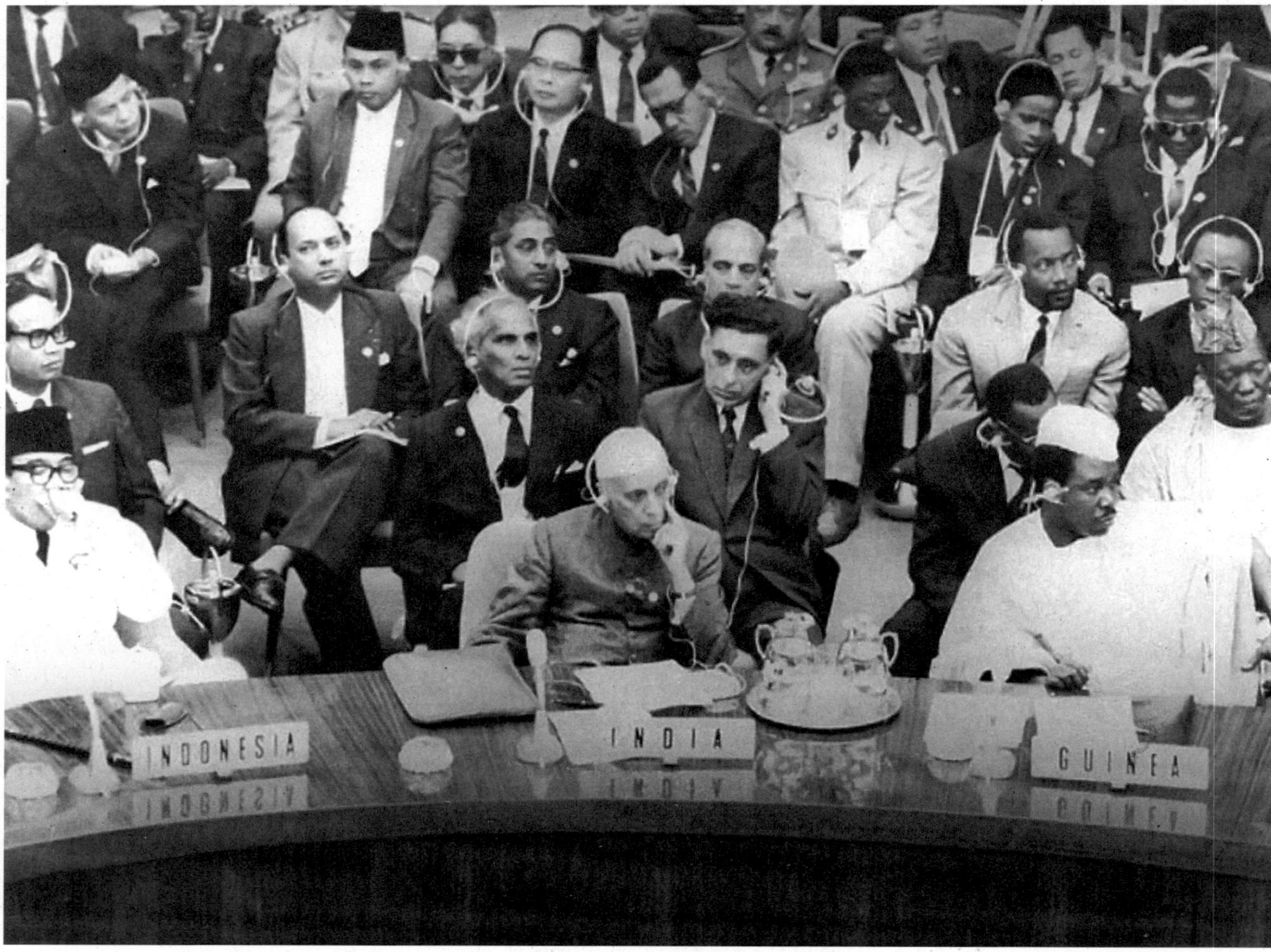

Bandung Conference, April 18–24, 1955. Reproduced by permission of indonesia-digest.net.

This conference was a bid by the newly independent nation-states to perform on a world stage—to create a space between the two superpowers that were crowding out the voices of those who spoke differently. The conference was a successful performance—one that had a strong script, actors, stage and backdrop. It was also a conference that was framed by power relations that it could challenge, but not necessarily shift.

While the Soviet Union, with its socialist alternative model of development, attracted many—including Nehru and Nasser—among the nations represented in the conference hall, others were openly hostile to both the Soviet Union and socialist politics. Major debate centered upon the question of whether Soviet policies in Eastern Europe and Central Asia should be censured along with Western colonialism—freedom was lacking in both spheres of old colonialism and newer manifestations of inequality among nations. A consensus was reached in which "colonialism in all of its manifestations" was condemned, implicitly censuring the Soviet Union, as well as the West. A new political space was discursively created—a space which tried to erase privilege wherever it manifested itself.

Another aspiration expressed at the conference was for peace: "We can demonstrate to the minority of the world that we the majority are for peace, not war, and that whatever strength we have will always be thrown on to the side of peace... mobilizing 'the Moral Violence of Nations in favour of peace'" (President Sukarno). If peace was at stake vis-à-vis the superpowers, then it was also at stake among the attendee nations—India and Pakistan, for example, had emerged out of a most brutal period through which one country became two; in the moment of independence were sown the seeds of conflict and war. Similarly, the People's Republic of China saw the importance of building bridges with Asian and African nations as it sought to negotiate U.S. support for Taiwan, and China's increasingly fractious relations with the Soviet Union. Aware that increasing U.S./China tensions might lead to a new major war in the region inspired the decision to invite the People's Republic.

India supported this move and the inclusion of communist China in the conference. These were the days of *Hindi-Chini bhai bhai* (Indians and Chinese are brothers)! India had recognized Tibet to be part of China in 1954—the first country to do so. This was a marker of postcolonial solidarity—that the divisions created by colonial Britain would not find recognition in a new period of cooperation. As Kahin noted, Bandung thus played a "significant ... if relatively minor" role in the first, brief post-Stalin "détente between the Communist and non-Communist worlds".[4]

Racism was what united all the countries and nations represented at the conference. Throughout that week, delegates had condemned apartheid in South Africa on these grounds. Twenty-five attendees also agreed that those among them still excluded from the UN—Cambodia, Ceylon, Japan, Jordan, Libya, Nepal, and a "unified Vietnam"—were entitled to membership. While they also affirmed the legitimacy of the UN, they wanted a greater voice in the Security Council. They collectively endorsed the UN Universal Declaration of Human Rights, pressed for general disarmament, and called for greater economic cooperation and cultural exchanges among their countries and regions.

We might add that they also reaffirmed the right, specified in Article 51 of the UN Charter, of a state to defend itself, "singly or collectively". President Nasser of Egypt, who made his debut on the international stage at Bandung, spoke of the complicity of the UN and the West in the displacement of the Palestinians: "under the eyes of the United Nations and with its help and sanction the people of Palestine were uprooted and expelled from their fatherland to be replaced by a completely imported populace." He said that "never before in history has there been such a brutal and immoral violation of human practices," adding: "It is almost impossible to believe that such injustice could exist in the 20th century, the age of world order, and under the eyes of the United Nations, the guardian of international law and justice", reported *JTA*, a Jewish newspaper.[5]

A ten-point "declaration on the promotion of world peace and cooperation," incorporating the principles of the United Nations Charter and Indian Prime Minister Jawaharlal Nehru's Five Principles ("mutual respect" for other nations' "territorial integrity and sovereignty," nonaggression, noninterference in "internal affairs," equality and mutual benefit, and "peaceful coexistence"), was adopted unanimously:

4 George McTurnan Kahin, *The Asian-African Conference: Bandung, Indonesia, April 1955* (Ithaca: Cornell University Press, 1956).

5 *Egyptian Premier Attacks Israel Violently at Bandung Conference, JTA*, April 19, 1955, http://www.jta.org.

The Ten Principles of Bandung, which came to encapsulate the "Bandung Spirit" were:

1 *Respect for fundamental human rights and for the purposes and principles of the Charter of the United Nations.*
2 *Respect for the sovereignty and territorial integrity of all nations.*
3 *Recognition of the equality of all races and of the equality of all nations large and small.*
4 *Abstention from intervention or interference in the internal affairs of another country.*
5 *Respect for the right of each nation to defend itself singly or collectively, in conformity with the Charter of the United Nations.*
6 *(a) Abstention from the use of arrangements of collective defense to serve the particular interests of any of the big powers.*
(b) Abstention by any country from exerting pressures on other countries.
7 *Refraining from acts or threats of aggression or the use of force against the territorial integrity or political independence of any country.*
8 Settlement of all international disputes by peaceful means, such as negotiation, conciliation, arbitration or judicial settlement as well as other peaceful means of the parties' own choice, in conformity with the Charter of the United Nations.
9 Promotion of mutual interests and co-operation.
10 Respect for justice and international obligations.

The response of the U.S. to the conference and its declarations was hostile. "This meeting of the rejected was in itself a kind of judgement upon the Western world", wrote Richard Wright. The U.S. expressed concern that the meeting was a sign of a leftward shift in the ideological leanings of the newly independent nations of Africa and Asia. U.S. leaders worried that the anticolonialism of Bandung and the discussion of global racial politics taking place there could turn anti-U.S. or anti-Western. W. E. B. Du Bois and Paul Robeson were invited to Bandung as was Malcolm X—none made it there, the latter because of refusal of the U.S. to let him out of the country.

The questions that tend to get asked when we think about the legacy of the Bandung conference are about its long term effects and about the romanticization of the Bandung Spirit.

Robert Vitalis, for example, points to the fact that

Nkrumah, leader of the Gold Coast, not Sudan, and anxious not to do anything to upset the timetable for independence, sent his friend Kojo Botsio as an "observer" rather than a full-fledged delegate, with instructions to keep his head down. Kenyatta wasn't invited. Nor was Tito.[6]

The implication here is that Bandung had come to be seen as the precursor of the Non-Aligned Movement and therefore much is bundled into its analysis that is patently not true. Vitalis also suggests that, "Nehru

6 Robert Vitalis, "The Midnight Ride of Kwame Nkrumah and Other Fables of Bandung (Ban-doong)", *Humanity* 4, no. 2 (Summer, 2013).

and others acted instead to prevent the creation of any kind of permanent structure or organization, and various would-be conveners of a follow-up meeting—Nasser, Sukarno, Pakistan's Zulfikar Ali Bhutto, Algeria's Ben Bella—failed repeatedly over the next ten years to bring Asian and African states together once more..."

The question for us here is what matters? The exact attendance and absences? The direct or indirect linkage between Bandung and the Non Aligned Movement? The fact remains that in the minds of the audience of this conference then and now, Bandung became the space where Asian-African solidarity first found institutional form. The power of the images is such that the two are often aligned—photographs from the NAM meeting are often catalogued under Bandung and include Tito and Nkrumah, both of whom were absent in 1955.

Jacques Rancière points out that the spectator or the audience

> *...observes, selects, compares, interprets. She links what she sees to a host of other things that she has seen on other stages, in other kinds of place. She composes her own poem with elements of the poem before her. She participates in the performance by refashioning it in her own way.*[7]

Such an audience saw, and continues to think of the Bandung conference as a moment in time that recognized the elements of the nationalist poem that had been sung successfully in the countries that came together as the Third World—but also as an imaginary of a universalist, peaceful world independent of the dualities of the Cold War.

In this sense, the Bandung Conference and its final resolution laid the foundation for the Non-Aligned Movement during the Cold War. However, Bandung was itself always part of Cold War games and strategies. Major schisms among the sponsors of the original conference emerged in 1961 and again in 1964–65, when China and Indonesia pressed for a second Asian-African conference. In both instances India, together with Yugoslavia and the United Arab Republic (Egypt), succeeded in organizing rival conferences of Non-Aligned states that refused to take the strong anti-Western positions urged by China and, in 1964–65, by Indonesia. In November 1965 the second Asian-African conference (to have been held in Algiers, Algeria) was indefinitely postponed.

On April 24, 2005, the leaders of countries attending the Asia-Africa Summit arrived at Bandung from Jakarta, commemorating the 50th anniversary of the Bandung Conference. The Chinese press reported the event:

> *The banners welcoming Asian and African leaders are hung in the main streets and the flowers in the parterres are blooming... the leaders from Asia, Africa and other regions walked to the old site of the Bandung Conference... This is a historic walk. When the Bandung Conference was held 50 years ago, the Asian and African leaders walked to the Independence High-rise to attend the conference from the Savoy Homann hotel. Today all leaders attending the Asia-Africa Summit walked along the same route again to review the history and carry forward the Bandung spirit of solidarity,*

7 Jacques Rancière, *The Emancipated Spectator* (London: Verson, 2009).

> *friendship and cooperation.... The Bandung spirit of solidarity, friendship and cooperation advocated by the summit has become the powerful impetus to encourage most developing countries to unswervingly strive for realizing the national rejuvenation and promoting the [sic] human's progress for half century [sic]. It has advanced the joint self-empowerment of the Asian and African countries and promoted the peace and development of the entire world.*[8]

Despite such hyperbolic rhetoric, the event passed almost unnoticed. Books commemorated the event—"Bandung Revisited" was the theme in most cases[9]; mostly critical but with some reminders of its importance as a postcolonial moment.

Whatever our views on Bandung—then and now—it does posit a question for us. What would our world look like if we were standing in the global South? At one level this is an impossible question to answer. Colonial histories stand in the way of any alternative visions of life or a different world. Folded into the power of global capitalism, today's postcolonial states position themselves to survive, to make the best of or to make inroads into a world not of their making. Solidarity among the postcolonial nations was performed well in Bandung, but was ephemeral. So, can today's rejected and insulted find a new voice? The Arab Spring seemed to suggest that they could—but the autumn came all too soon. So, worldist approaches[10] building on postcolonial ethics and focusing on syncretic engagements and border crossings that build new communities can have a great intellectual pull. At the same time, as Bandung's history shows, we need to be cautious about the promise of agential strategies of historical border crossings. Structures of power tether struggles against dominant relations, and limit our visions of change. Bandung then remains only a marker of possibilities—but can that be such a bad thing? Imaginaries of change are made up of such possibilities—grasped as well as unrealized.

8 Ministry of Foreign Affairs, PRC, http://www.fmprc.gov.cn/eng/topics/hjtfw/t193910.htm.

9 Seng Tan and Amitav Acharya, *Bandung Revisited: The Legacy of the 1955 Asian-African Conference for International Order* (Singapore: NUS Press, 2008).

10 Anna Agathangelou and L.H.M. Ling, *Transforming World Politics: From Empire to Multiple Worlds* (London: Routledge, 2009).

Travelling Communiqué Reading a Photo Archive (1948–80), Presidential Press Service, Yugoslavia

The *Travelling Communiqué* project undertakes a durational investigation into the photographic archive of the Presidential Photo Service of the Yugoslav partisan leader and statesman Josip Broz Tito, through a range of contemporary practices, from art, through theory, history, architecture, typography, to cinema and education. Its point of entry into the archive of approximately 300,000 photographic records, permanently housed at the Museum of Yugoslav History in Belgrade, is the collection of 1,200 photographs taken during the first Conference of the Non-Aligned Movement (NAM), held in Belgrade from September 1–6, 1961.

For the first time, those who were fighting against imperialism and colonialism in Africa, Asia, Europe and Latin America announced the global necessity of anticolonial thinking in the form of a collective message by the twenty-five delegates of the first Conference of the NAM to the world. At that moment, the world faced an acute crisis exemplified by the nuclear threat of the Cold War "that lead towards a world conflict in the transition from an old order based on domination to a new order based on cooperation." The NAM can be understood as a third space of emancipation that sought to unsettle the bipolar world without calling for a third power but through insisting on the need to "eradicate colonialism in all its manifestations."[1]

What does this archive provide us with and how can we relate, today, to the politics of universalism beyond existing dominant political and ideological concepts?

We propose to inquire into the possibilities of "prolonging" the formation of the NAM into the social conditions of the present. Instead of exposing the photographs and documents as historical artifacts, we approach the archival textures as a set of nonhistorized diagrams for the conception of contemporary means to analyze the continuities and discontinuities of entangled geographies in conflicts of global scale.

We speculate about a *Communiqué* (public declaration) that was published in an early moment of the Non-Aligned Movement, but continues to travel. The idea of the *Communiqué* forces us to rethink the Movement's basic concepts in relation to today's paradoxical forms of the politics of exclusion—perpetuated by globalization—that are entangled with the politics of inclusion legitimized by a state of permanent war. The *Travelling Communiqué* project is an attempt to understand the processes of becoming a political subject, initiated by those without names whose voices exist despite efforts to silence them.

Who is the addressee of the Communiqué today?

1 Both quotes from the Declaration of the Heads of State or Government of Non-Aligned Countries, Belgrade, September 6, of 1961. English in original.

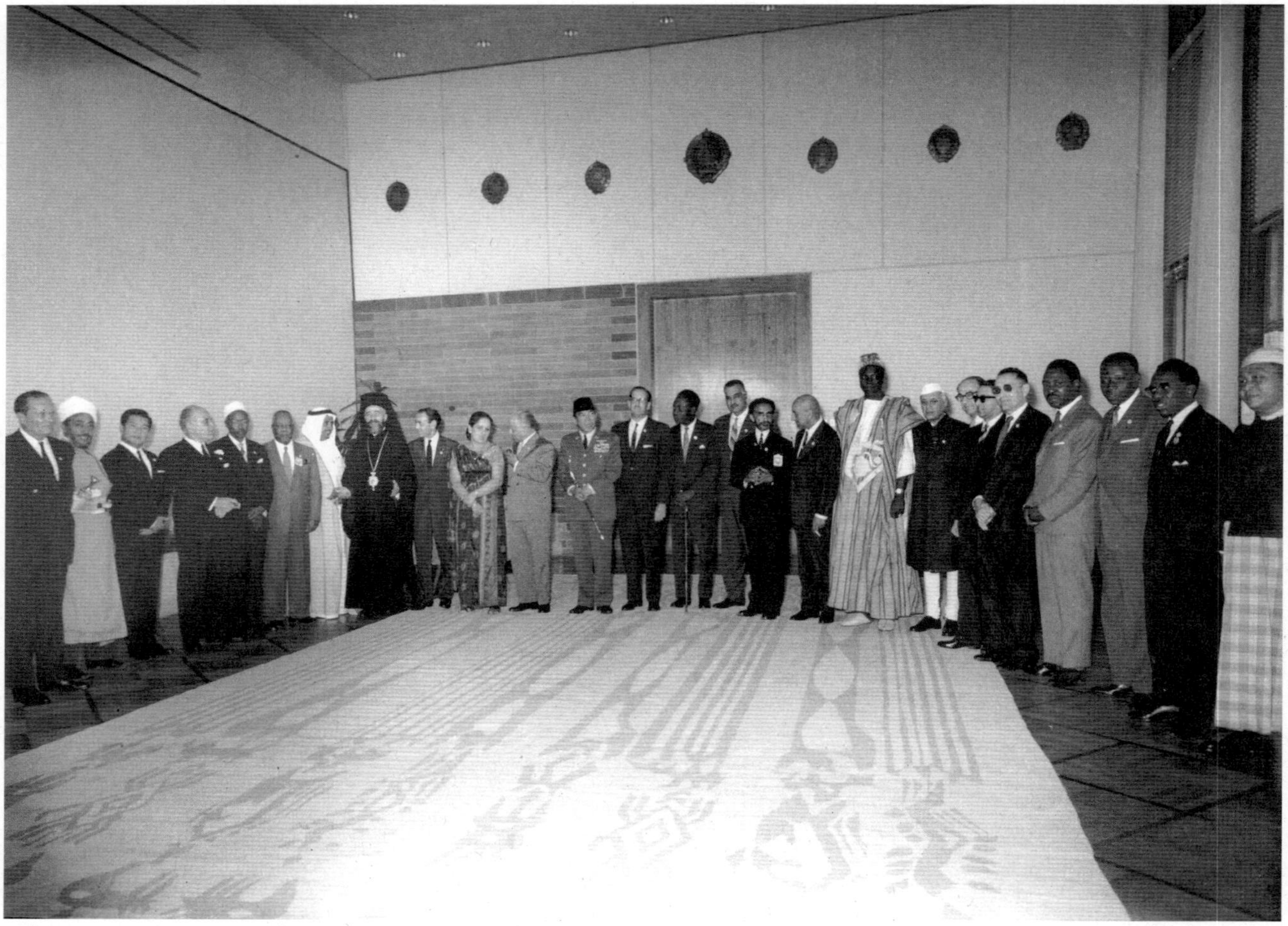

MYH 1961_179_97: All the Heads of Delegations on the first Conference of the Non-Aligned Movement, Belgrade, September 5, 1961 (from left): President of FPRY Josip Broz Tito, Prince Saiful Islam Al-Hassan of Yemen, Prime Minister of Cambodia Prince Norodom Sihanouk, Prime Minister of Lebanon Saeb Salam, President of Somalia Adem Abdullah Osman, Chairman of the Supreme Military Council of Sudan Ibrahim Aboud, Minister of Foreign Affairs of Saudi Arabia Sheikh Ibrahim Soweil, President of Cyprus Archbishop Makarios, The King of Morocco Hassan II, Prime Minister of Ceylon (Sri Lanka) Sirimavo Bandaranaike, President of Tunisia Habib Bourguiba, President of Indonesia Ahmed Soekarno, President of Cuba Dr Osvaldo Dorticós Torrado, President of Ghana Kwame Nkrumah, President of the United Arab Republic Gamal Abdel Nasser, Emperor of Ethiopia Haile Selassie, Prime Minister of Afghanistan Sardar Mohammed Daud Khan, President of Mali Modibo Keita, Prime Minister of India Jawaharlal Nehru, Minister of Foreign Affairs of Iraq Hashim Jawad, The King of Nepal Mahendra Bir Bikram Shah Dev, President of the Provisional Government of Algeria Benyoucef Benkhedda, Minister of Foreign Affairs of Guinea Louis Lansana Beavogui, Premier of the Republic of Congo Cyrille Adoula, Vice-premier of the Republic of Congo Antoine Gizenga, Prime Minister of Burma U Nu; The photograph was taken in the building of the Federal Executive Council (SIV) in New Belgrade during the first summit of the Non-Aligned Movement, at the conference on September 5, 1961. From the Photo Collection of the Museum of Yugoslav History, Belgrade.

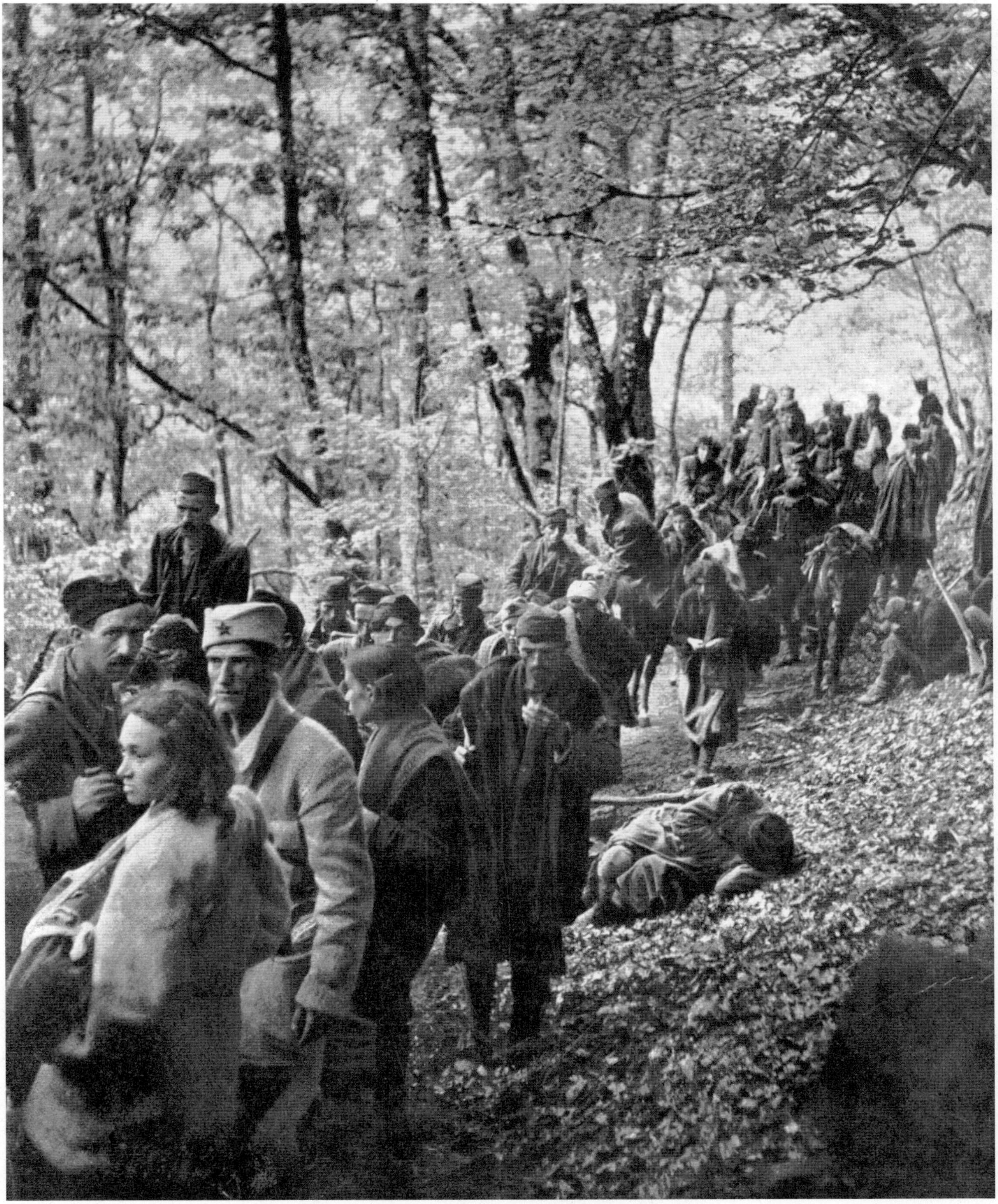

Photo: Žorž Skrigin. During the 5th Enemy offensive, Zelengora, Bosnia and Herzegovina, 1943.

Vitrine 7: Travelling Communiqué was specified for the exhibition "AfterYear Zero" at Haus der Kulturen derWelt in an interview session with Branimir Stojanović, and byTheo Eshetu, Armin Linke, Doreen Mende and MilicaTomić in discussion with Fabian Bechtle, Mirjana Dragosavljević, The Museum ofYugoslav History (Radovan Cukić, Ivan Manojlović, Mirjana Slavkonić) and Olga Manojlović Pintar in Belgrade in September 2013. Display design by Laure Giletti, Brussels. It is the first public exposure of the *Travelling Communiqué* project-at-large, conceived by Armin Linke, Doreen Mende and MilicaTomić.

At work since 2012, the *Travelling Communiqué* project-at-large has been initiating its own conditions of production within current globalizing forces by contemporary investigations into the foundational conditions of the Non-Aligned Movement. It fosters a transdisciplinary way of working together towards the idea of political friendship. The project relies on fragile vocabularies, educational sessions, students' work, group constellations and means of articulation still to arrive.

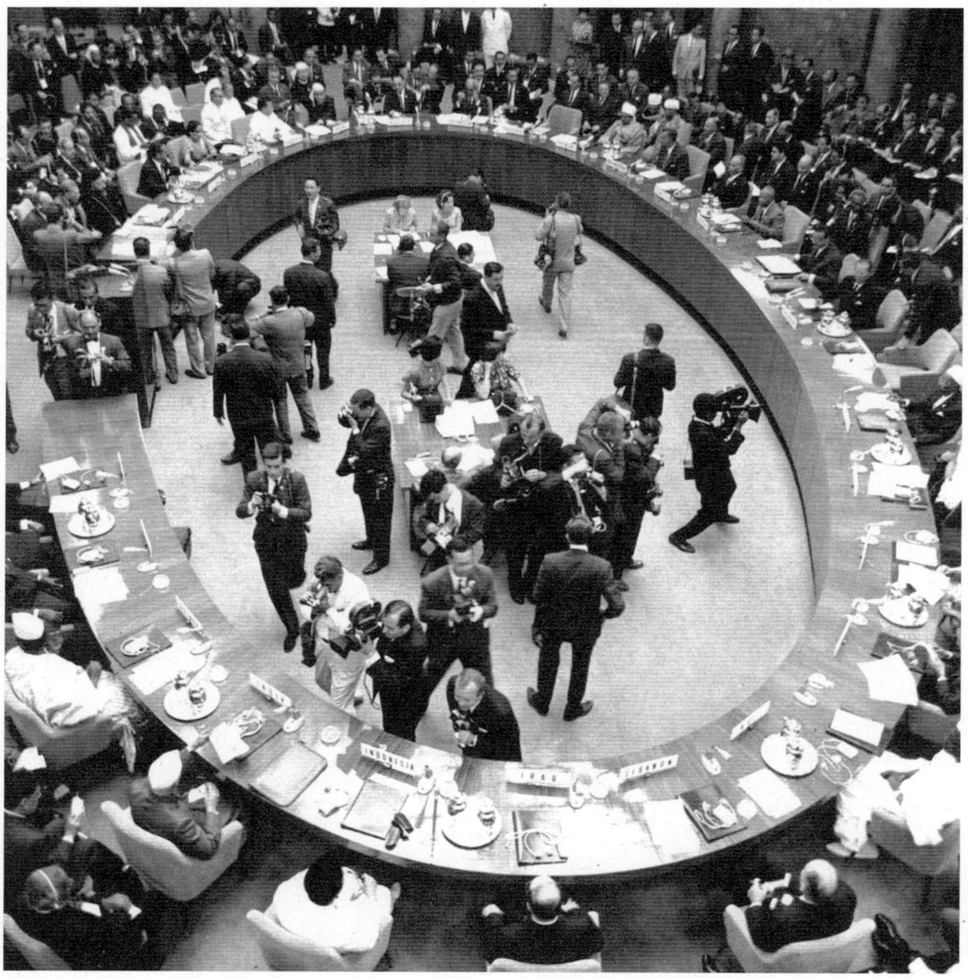

MYH 1961_179_0030: Hall for plenary sessions, on the opening day of the Conference of Non-Aligned Movement, Belgrade, September 1, 1961. Photographers of the Presidential Photo Service of Josip Broz Tito during the first Conference of the Non-Aligned Movement in Belgrade in 1961 were Dragutin Grbić, Miloš Rašeta and Aleksandar Stojanović. From the Photo Collection of the Museum of Yugoslav History, Belgrade.

Statecraft: An Incomplete Timeline of Independence Determined by Digital Auction

Kodwo Eshun

Do the colour sequences of the long sets perhaps refract the light of a strange sun? Walter Benjamin[1]

The Logics of Postal Politics

On October 15, 2013, the coalition government of the United Kingdom finally succeeded in floating the state-owned Royal Mail on the London Stock Exchange at a value of £3.3 billion. By March 2015, the Royal Mail, now owned by investors such as GIC Private, formerly known as Government of Singapore Investment Corporation, Kuwait Investment, Abu Dhabi Investment Authority and UBS (Luxembourg) SA, was seeking ways to renege upon its Universal Service Obligation to deliver postage to twenty-nine million homes across the United Kingdom for six days a week at the same price. The partially privatized Royal Mail clearly resents the USO as a relic of its role as a former government department and is searching for ways to restructure the postal system. Under the current economic regime, the postage stamp, which certifies that postage has been prepaid on a letter, appears as the antiquated ornament of a superannuated infrastructure and the visible face of a backward looking British state. These critical attitudes characterize the privatized corporation's hostility to postal communication: if the letter is redundant and unprofitable, then the postage stamp, according to this logic, must be the apotheosis of unprofitability. The specialist collector, by contrast, exemplifies an antiquarian rather than a critical attitude to the future of the postage stamp. The specialist market prizes the stamp for its rarity. It values the exception and devalues the rule. It excludes the uniformity that characterizes the industrial production process of the postage stamp that was engraved and printed in factories such as Royal Joh. Enschedé in Haarlem, Holland, Hélio Courvoisier SA in La Chaux-de-Fonds, Switzerland, Harrison & Sons in High Wycombe outside London and E.A. Wright Bank Note Co in Philadelphia.

Between these two positions of economic antiquarianism and privatized critique, is it possible to formulate a third position that evaluates the future of the postage stamp according to its powers of standardization and centralization rather than its rarity and value? What if the stamp is understood as an industrial design process whose integral role in the new state's fashioning of nation, territory, and peoples, makes it useful for producing an analysis of the arts of statecraft? To encounter the stamp as the vehicle of postal politics entails taking seriously its powers of replication. It means constructing a figurative project capable of

1 Walter Benjamin, "Stamp Shop," in *One-Way Street and Other Writings*, trans. Edmund Jephcott and Kingsley Shorter (London: Verson, 1979), 92.

drawing attention to the stamp whose monumentalism appears in the form of mass manufactured miniaturism. Such a project would direct spectatorial attention towards an artifact whose ubiquity condemns it to customary condescension. It would find itself face to face with the reductionism of the postage stamp which, upon close examination, reveals itself to be a medium capable of compressing colossal forces. It would find itself forced to reckon with whatThomas Pynchon presciently characterized as "temporal bandwith."[2] It would be obliged to register the methods by which the stamp mobilizes the forces of iconography, indexicality and iconoclasm upon a scale that is never less than planetary.

The Promethean Politics of Pan-Africanism

The capacities of iconography and indexicality are common to all stamps. The postage stamp assumes a renewed relevance when it provides insights into the forms of inattention consistently bestowed upon the nation building projects of newly independent states. When postal politics is harnessed to the Promethean politics of Pan-Africanism, a work such as *Statecraft* allows one to perceive the stamp as a medium with specific designs upon its users. As an industrially produced artifact whose uniformity insists upon its machine-made manufacture, the form of the stamp cannot help but draw attention to Pan-Africanism's industrial ambitions to engineer new citizens for a new Africa. From the perspective of *Statecraft*, Pan-Africanism becomes understandable as a grandiose political project of continental proportions assembled by and for the new governments of new states. In *Africa Must Unite*, Kwame Nkrumah, first President of Ghana, envisaged a Union Government of African States:

> *Under a major political union of Africa there could emerge a United Africa, great and powerful, in which the territorial boundaries which are the relics of colonialism will become obsolete and superfluous, working for the complete and total mobilization of the economic planning organization under a unified political direction.*[3]

If *Statecraft* appears as a model of the political unification of the continent, then its scale also allows the spectator to grasp the fissiparous proliferation of newly independent nations whose appearance seemed to confirm Nkrumah's mistrust of the "gift of fictitious independence"[4] offered by France to its former colonies in Equatorial Africa now renamed *Republique Centrafricaine, Republique du Tchad, Republique du Gabon, Republique du Congo-Brazzaville* and *Republique Federale du Cameroun.* Frantz Fanon recognized the panic disguised as benevolence in France's "gift of independence" when he mimicked the words of a French colonial governor: "...quick, quick, let's decolonize. Decolonize the Congo before it turns into another Algeria. Vote the constitutional framework for

2 "Temporal bandwidth is the width of your present, your now...The more you dwell in the past and in the future, the thicker your bandwidth, the more solid your persona. But the narrower your sense of Now, the more tenuous you are." Thomas Pynchon, *Gravity's Rainbow* (London: Penguin Books, 2006), 517.

3 *Africa Must Unite* was published to coincide with the first meeting of the Organisation of African Unity at Africa Hall in Addis Ababa in 1963. Kwame Nkrumah, *Africa Must Unite* (London: Heinemann, 1963), 221.

4 Ibid., 193.

all Africa, create the French Communauté, renovate that same Communauté, but for God's sake let's decolonize quick...And they decolonize at such a rate that they impose independence on Houphouet-Boigny."[5] Nkrumah and Fanon suspected that leaders such as President Felix Houphouet-Boigny of the Republic of Côte d'Ivoire and President Leon M'Ba of the Gabonese Republic ran their countries as "client states, independent in name but in point of fact pawns of the very colonial power which is supposed to have given them independence."[6] Nkrumah drew on Lenin's understanding of the "diverse forms of dependent countries which, politically, are formally independent, but in fact are enmeshed in the net of financial and diplomatic dependence."[7] Pan-Africanism oscillated between the euphoric prospect of a dawning unity, dismay at the sight of Eurafrican economic conferences in Yaoundé and Brazzaville and paranoia at the prospect of regional, tribal, communalist and sectionalist "fissions in the national front."[8] The profound uncertainties, instabilities, reversals and betrayals initiated by Pan-Africanism's confrontation with Europe's empires become uniquely evident in the operational collusion and integral complicity of postal politics.

More than a witness to the aspirations of the newly independent nations, the postage stamp presupposed an imperial infrastructure that could be reverse engineered by those intimate with its logics of colonial centralization. In *The Political Thought of Patrice Lumumba*, Jean-Paul Sartre elucidated Patrice Lumumba's ministerial ambition to unify the Republic of Congo in terms of postal politics. According to Sartre, Lumumba's work as a postman:

> *integrated him into the colonial Administration and enabled him to discover its principal characteristic: centralization. This discovery was all the more easy for him because chance made him a cog in the centralized communication system. The Post Office network extended into all the provinces and even into the bush; through it, the government's orders were relayed to the local gendarmeries and the Force Publique. If one day the Congolese Nation were to exist, it would owe its unity to a similar centralism. Patrice dreamed of a general uniting power which would apply everywhere, impose harmony and a community of action everywhere, would receive information from remote villages, concentrate it, base the directions of its policies on it and send back orders by the same route to its representatives in every little hamlet. The Government atomized the colonized and unified them from outside as subjects of the King. Independence would be just an empty word unless this cohesion from without were to be replaced by unification from within.*[9]

5 Frantz Fanon, *The Wretched of the Earth*, trans. Constance Farrington (London: Penguin Books, 1974), 55.

6 Nkrumah, *Africa Must Unite*, 174.

7 Lenin, *Imperialism: The Highest Stage of Capitalism*, quoted in ibid., 174.

8 Ibid., 173.

9 Jean-Paul Sartre, "The Political Thought of Patrice Lumumba (1964)" in *Colonialism and Neocolonialism*, trans. Azzedine Haddour, Steve Brewer and Terry McWilliams (London and New York: Routledge, 2006), 190–91.

The "African political imaginary"[10] envisioned by Lumumba took on its specific form through the "general uniting power" of the postal network. As the ambiguous expression of oppression by centralization and emancipation through unification, the postage stamp participated in the processes of monopolization within and beyond the unstable borders of the new states. *Statecraft* emulates the postal procedures of epic reductionism and monumental miniaturism in order to produce an immanent enactment of the logics of unification deployed by ruling political parties throughout the continent.

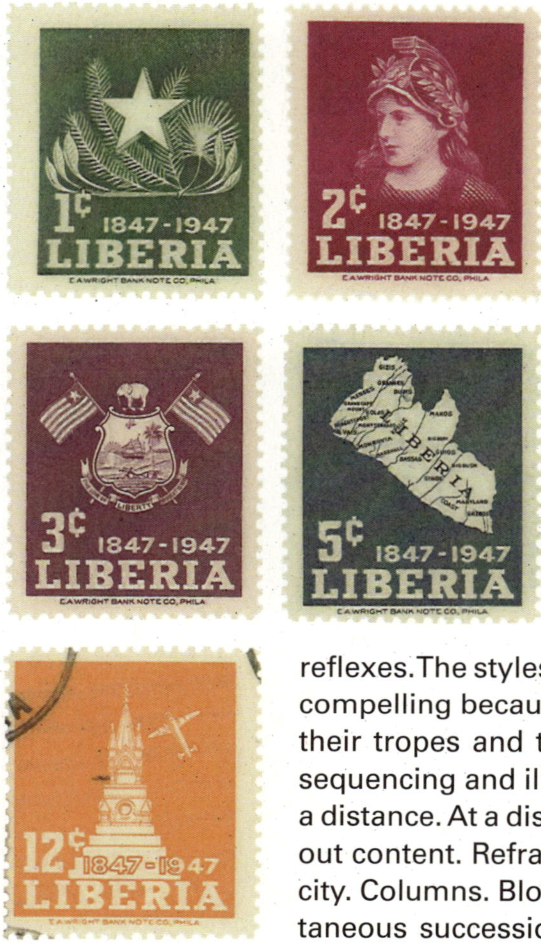

Republic of Liberia, 1947—a detail from The Otolith Group's *Statecraft*, 2014. Lightbox display system, encapsulated stamps. Dimensions variable.

An Immanent Analysis of Iconography

As a visual study that assembles a figurative project in order to study images by way of images,[11] *Statecraft* makes visible the vocabulary invented by designers for visualizing Pan-Africanist polity. *Statecraft* is not informed by the imperative to appropriate found objects nor by an archival impulse. It is an enquiry into the capacities and incapacities of the philatelic image. To respond to its visual language through a recourse to terms such as "propaganda" or "cult of personality" is to fall back upon critical reflexes. The styles of Pan-Africanist Pop Art encountered in *Statecraft* are compelling because of, not in spite of, their clichés and their archetypes, their tropes and their metonyms. In *Statecraft*, forms of arrangement, sequencing and illumination converge in an architecture perceived from a distance. At a distance of two to three metres, one observes colors without content. Refractions from a strange sun. Elements from a chromatic city. Columns. Blocks. Squares. Sequences suspended in series of simultaneous succession. *Statecraft's* philatelic skyline is determined by an economy that is not perceptible and whose causation must be reconstructed. The online auction that determines the availability and sets the price for the stamps assembled in *Statecraft* plays the role of the hidden hand that crafts its ultimate form. eBay and delcampe.net are used as digital platforms for auctions organized by collectors from cities in the former colonial states of U.K., Germany, France, Spain, Italy, Belgium, Holland and Portugal as well as U.S., Canada, India and Argentina.

Face to face with the stamps at thirty centimeters, a timeline begins to make itself apparent. A timeline that begins with five blocks of twenty-five stamps each dated 1847–1947 and captioned by the engraver E.A. Wright Bank Note Co, Philadelphia. The dark green 1c depicts the white five-pointed Lone Star of Liberia surrounded by ferns. The violet 2c personifies Liberty as the Goddess of the Republic. The purple 3c depicts the

10 John Akomfrah introduced the term in the lecture that he delivered at the conference "Geographies of Collaboration 1: Writing of History" on October 5, 2013 at Haus der Kulturen der Welt.

11 Nicole Brenez, "Harun Farocki and the Romantic Genesis of the Principle of Visual Critique," in *Harun Farocki: Against What? Against Whom?* ed. Antje Ehmann and Kodwo Eshun (London: Raven Row, 2009), 128.

heraldic shield of Liberia that recounts the allegory of a ship at sea, the sun, a dove carrying a charter in its beak, land, furrowed, a plough standing idle, a palm tree. Beneath the escutcheon, a motto reads: "The Love of Liberty brought us here". On either side can be seen the national flags of Liberia flanking an elephant. In the dark blue 5c is a map of Liberia indicating its eight counties. The orange 12c portrays the Monument to Joseph Jenkins Roberts, the first President of the Republic of Liberia; at its right circles an aeroplane.

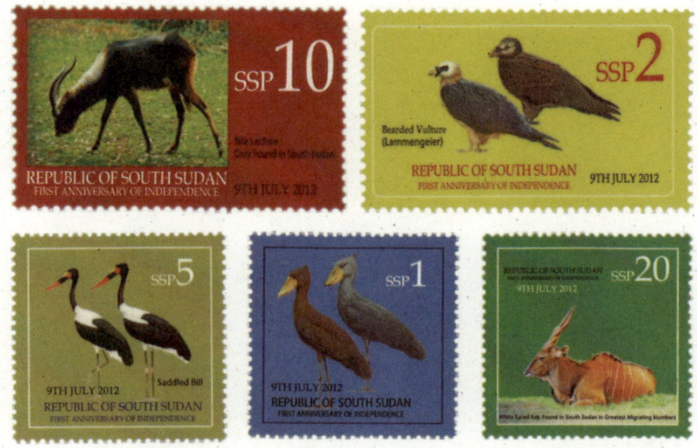

Republic of South Sudan, 2012—a detail from The Otolith Group's *Statecraft*, 2014. Lightbox display system, encapsulated stamps. Dimensions variable.

The timeline concludes with the incomplete issue of the First Anniversary of Independence of the Republic of South Sudan dated July 9, 2012. The red SSP10 integrates a photograph of a Nile Lechwe grazing. The blue SSP1 features male and female Shoe-billed Storks. In the yellow SSP2 can be seen male and female Bearded Vultures. The gold SSP5 depicts an identical pair of Saddle-bill Storks, the left one with its right leg crossed over its left. The green SSP20 displays the "White-eared Kob found in South Sudan in Greatest Migrating Numbers", its legs are folded under its bulk. At no point do the Liberia stamps explain that July 26th 1847 was the date when the freemen of the American Colonization Society declared Liberia a Republic. Nor do the stamps that memorialize the First Anniversary of Independence of the Republic of South Sudan mention the civil war from which the new Republic emerged. What is critical is to note that these elisions are not explained or clarified by *Statecraft. Statecraft* neither elucidates nor celebrates the ways in which the newly independent governments celebrated the ceremony of independence. Instead, *Statecraft* visualizes Pan-Africanism in the same ways as the states themselves. It sees like a state by restricting itself to the "internal construction of image" produced by the state.[12]

The Emotional Values of the Political Calendar

A political sequence gradually begins to emerge from the interrupted political calendars instituted by each nation state. In her essay on the posters produced during the Cuban Revolution, Susan Sontag observed how Tricontinentalist posters connected the "days commemorating the martyrdoms in Cuba's own history" to the "days of solidarity with other peoples", instilling an internationalist consciousness in daily life by cultivating a "sense of obligation" and a "willingness to renounce pri-

12 "Just as the architectural drawing, the model and the map are ways of dealing with a larger reality that is not easily grasped or manageable in its entirety, the miniaturization of high-modernist development offers a visually complete example of what the future looks like," James C. Scott, *Seeing like a State: How Certain Schemes to Improve the Human Condition Have Failed* (New Haven and London: Yale University Press, 1998), 258.
See also Simeon Allen on his work *Stamp Collection*: "Stamp Collection presented an image of South Africa that was and is constructed by the official voice of government and was therefore, for me, an internal construction of image" in "The Image of South Africa," *Newspapers: A Project* by Simeon Allen (Anderson Gallery: Duke University, 2004), 21.

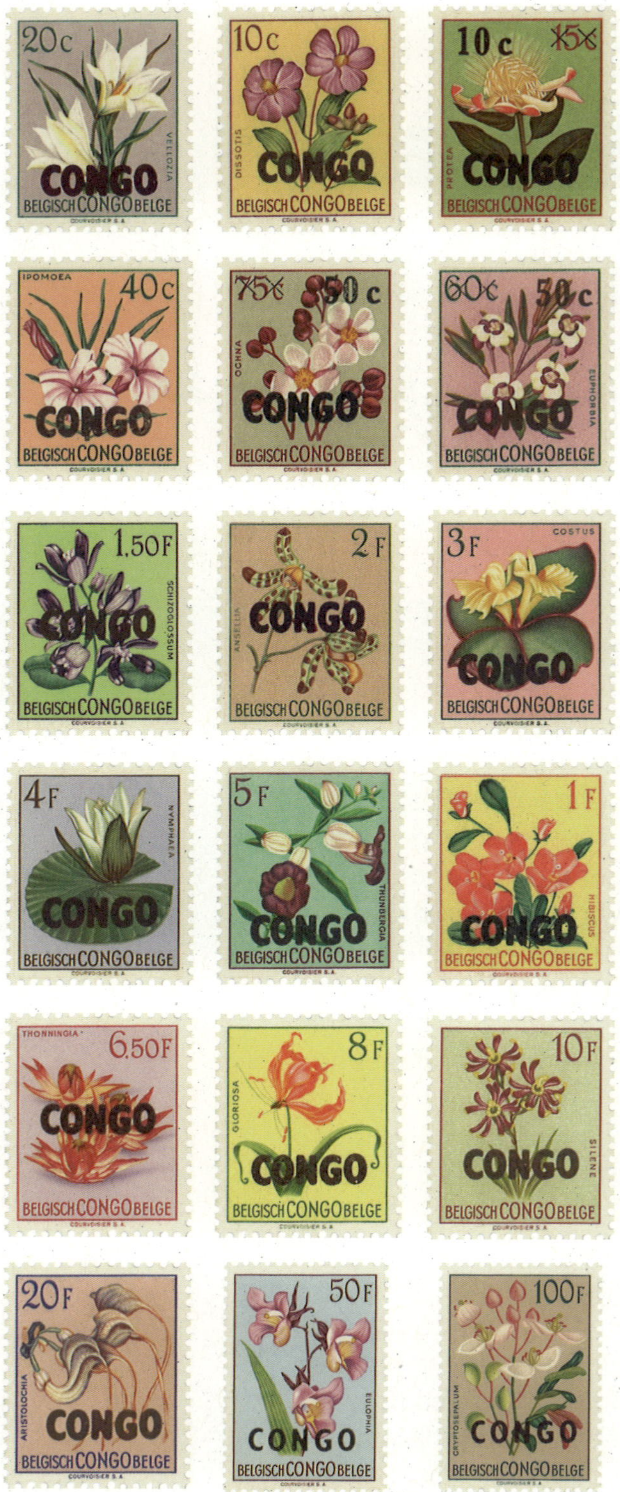

Republic of Congo, 1960—a detail from The Otolith Group's *Statecraft*, 2014. Lightbox display system, encapsulated stamps. Dimensions variable.

vate desires and liberties."[13] Pan-Africanist stamps promoted their own version of the political calendar by sustaining forms of attachment to the future memory of events linked to specific dates: The Anniversary of Independence; The Anniversary of the Republic; The birthday of the Founder; The signing of the Charter of African Unity; African Freedom Day; The Conference of Independence African States of April 1958.

Each of these dates was visualized as an allegory that formed a pictorial pageant that popularized the progress of the nation towards the liberation of the continent. If the intracontinental unity of Pan-Africanism was envisioned as the outline of the continent, then its emblem was the five-pointed Black Star radiating from Accra. In Pan-Africanist Pop Art, policy was pictured: a conference charter became a laurel wreath, a declaration, a curved scroll with a quill, decolonization, a chain broken in two. Peace became Picasso's *Dove with Olive Branch* (1961), its wings outstretched. In this combination of neo-Garveyite, French Republican and Communist pacifist imagery, policy appeared in the form of objects while the new state often appeared in the form of a Pop Art of indigenous species. In the 1960 independence air mail stamps of the Federation du Mali, the Federation is an aviary that hosts native birds like the 100F violet backed merle amethyste, the 200F bateleur eagle and the 500F yellow-crowned gonolek. How surprising it is to see all these birds! How unexpectedly exuberant are their colors!

The Republic of Congo did not issue any stamps featuring Prime Minister Patrice Lumumba during his tenure in 1960. Instead, it reprinted the colonial Congo Belge floral stamps of 1952 with new printed values and the word "CONGO". At a moment of extreme political crisis in 1960, the new government expressed its vision of the nation in a compendium whose yellows and pinks and purples shocked with their inappropriately excessive enthusiasm: the 10c yellow dissotis, the 10c green protea, the 20c grey vellosia, the 40c salmon pink ipomoea, the 50c pale green ochna, the 50c pink euphorbia; the 1F yellow hibiscus, the 1.50 F mint green schizzoglossum, the 2F pale orange ansellia, the 3F

13 Susan Sontag, "Posters: Advertisement, Art, Political Artefact, Commodity," in *The Art of Revolution: 96 Posters from Cuba 1959–1970* ed. Dugald Stermer (London: Pall Mall Press, 1970), viii.

pink costus, the 4F pale blue nymphaea, the 5F mint green thunbergia, the 8F yellow gloriosa, the 10F pale green silene, the 20F pink aristolochia, the 50F blue eulophia, the 100F grey pink cryptosepalum. Perhaps the euphoria generated by these stamps was audible enough to cloak the crimes committed by the new government of the Congo against its Prime Minister. Could the annual blooms of the protea provide a clock capable of counting the years in which the soil presses down upon the graves that hold the corpses that fertilized the floriography of the state?

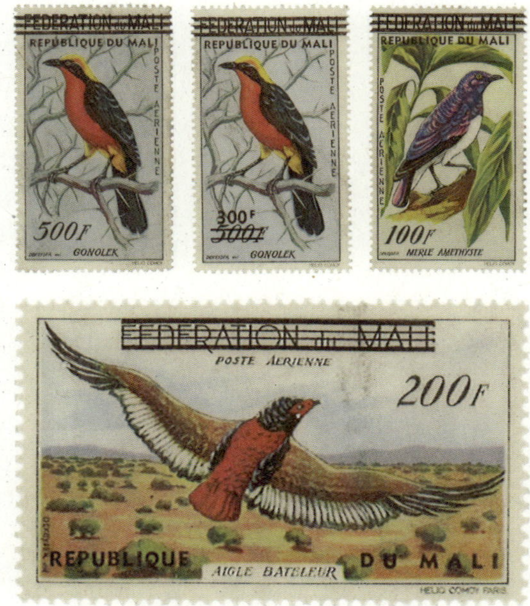

Republic of Mali, 1960—a detail from The Otolith Group's *Statecraft*, 2014. Lightbox display system, encapsulated stamps. Dimensions variable.

In *Statecraft*, independence does not appear as a singular date devoted to a ceremony organized according to diplomatic protocols and coordinated with press agencies. Instead, it approaches independence as the public phase of an extended process by which the ruling party seeks to determine the external and internal directions of the nation by unifying the state with the territory and the peoples with classes and with minorities. The stamp operates in the temporality of prospective commemoration. It looks forward to the future of the date it honours. It confers a prospective authority upon the face whose history it memorializes. It does not represent the heads of state as much as it plays a vital role in crafting the social body of the state whose head it represents. It is complicit in the crimes carried out by governments in the name of its nations and its peoples.

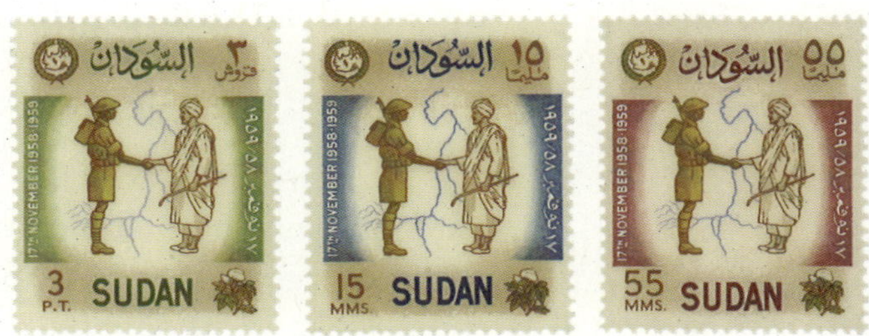

Republic of Sudan, 1959—a detail from The Otolith Group's *Statecraft*, 2014. Lightbox display system, encapsulated stamps. Dimensions variable.

The despotic figure of Francisco Macias Nguema, President for Life of the Republic of Equatorial Guinea is replicated in the issue of the red 0.50Pta Guineanas, the purple 1Pta Guineanas, the green 1.50 Pta Guineanas, the grey 2Pta Guineanas, the blue 2.50Pta Guineanas, the brown 10Pta Guineanas and the pale brown 25Pta Guineanas that marks October 12, 1969 as the first anniversary of his government. The halo that cradles the seven profiles of President Nguema do not dignify the head of state. Instead, the colors of the seven identical heads impress themselves upon their subjects. It is as if the powers of unification, legitimation, multiplication and centralization have captured the tendencies of the future and the past in order to decrease the temporal bandwidth of the present. Is this why stamps find it difficult to depict the rupture of the military coup, or the novelty of independence? It is not just a matter of the delay inherent in postal commemoration. It is rather that the imagery of the coup d'état is indistinguishable from the legend of independence.

In the 1959 blue 15mms, the pink 55mms and the green 3P.T, the khaki-clad soldier shakes hands with the peasant in white robes while the map of the Republic of the Sudan glows behind them. The date of November 17, 1958–1959 is not explained but is described on its first day cover as the commemorative stamp for the first anniversary of the Sudanese ar-

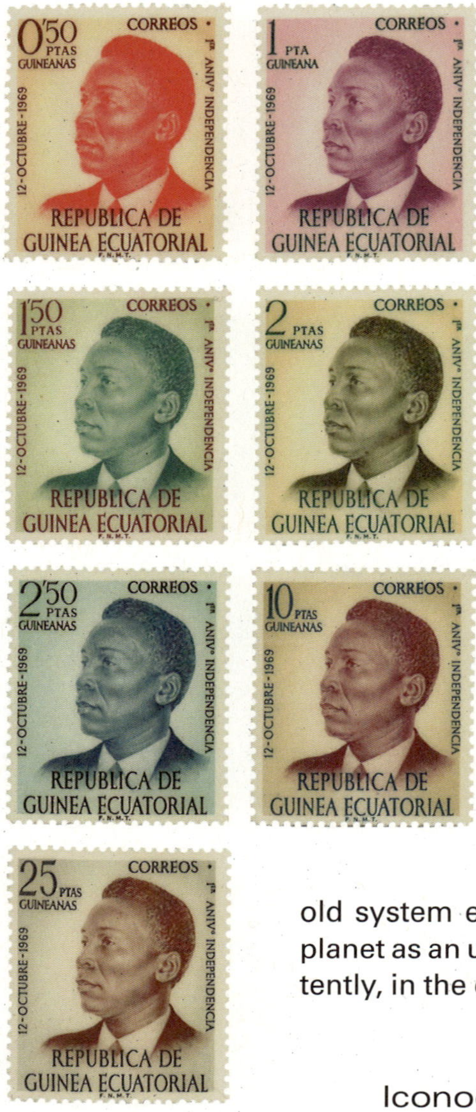

Republic of Equatorial Guinea, 1969—a detail from The Otolith Group's *Statecraft*, 2014. Lightbox display system, encapsulated stamps Dimensions variable.

my's coup d'état. The euphemistic imagination of the military coup of 1959 renders the stamp an unreliable witness to history. The 1967 1Np blue, the 4Np brown, the green 12 1/2Np and the 25Np stamp describe the military coup that deposed the government of President Nkrumah as "1st Anniversary 1967 Ghana's Revolution of 24th February 1966". General Afrifa, the leader of the so-called National Liberation Council is nowhere to be seen. Instead, the generals are zoomorphized in the shape of an eagle, a haloed, hallowed bird, Ghana's flag supported between its wings, broken chains dropping from its claws. Postal politics emerges in the inability of the stamp to distinguish between the coup d'état and the day of independence.

Statecraft is careful neither to clarify nor to correct this indistinction. Instead it emphasizes the formal continuities which indicate that the non-party state of the military dictatorship adopts the centralized postal system of the unitary state. The former adopts the infrastructure of the latter even as it topples its statues, burns its photographs and its paintings, torches its files, its publications and its newspapers, proscribes its cadres and its unions and privatizes its corporations and its industries on pain of detention without trial. Only the stamps issued by the old system escape the fires set by the new system. They circulate the planet as an unplanned, unaccountable anarchive that emerges, intermittently, in the digital aggregates of the online auction.

Iconoclasm Inadvertent and Intentional

At a distance of fifteen centimeters and armed with a magnifying glass, it becomes apparent that the principle of prepayment that organizes the postal system effectively exposes the stamp to the ignominity of the postmark. By registering its date and location upon its face, the anonymous postal worker carries out inordinate acts of inadvertent iconoclasm. She routinely disfigures the image of the President for Life. Fangs emerge from the dictator's lips. A broken circle bisects his nose. Welts and weals mark his cheeks. The postmark renders its verdict upon the head of the state. It is a judgment that issues from the nameless hand of the worker. It pronounces sentence upon despots and freedom fighters alike, both of whom are revealed as monsters of history that personify the "occult part of the stamp."[14]

Such unintentional iconoclasm cannot, however, be compared with the calculated indignity of the overprint. To overprint means to redact the name and print value of a stamp with the new name and print value. This definition cannot account for the graphic mortification visited upon the newly deposed head of the state. By impressing its rule upon the face of the stamp, the overprint publicizes and participates in the forces of humil-

14 Walter Benjamin, *Stamp Shop*, 92.

iation unleashed by the military coup, the popular uprising and the civil war.

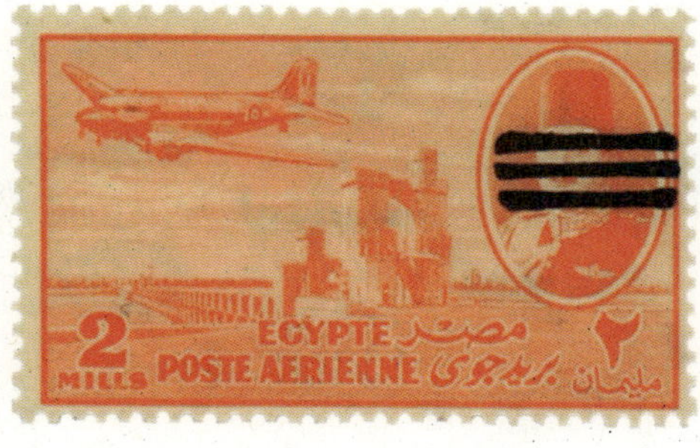

Republic of Egypt, 1953—a detail from The Otolith Group's *Statecraft*, 2014. Lightbox display system, encapsulated stamps Dimensions variable.

In 1953, the new government founded by the self-proclaimed Free Officers Movement that led the military coup of July 23, 1952 against the ruling monarchy of Egypt recycled sixteen stamps issued in 1948. Across the brown 1mill, the red 2mills, the pale brown 3mills, the dark green 4mills, the pale green 6mills, the purple 10mills, the red 13mills, the light purple 15mills, the mid green 17mills, the grey 20mills, the bright blue 22mills, the pale green 30mills, the pale brown 40mills, the pale blue 50mills, the pale black 100mills and the light purple 200mills, are printed three black horizontal lines, evenly spaced across the face of His Majesty Farouk 1 of Egypt and the Sudan. The first line starts at the eyes, the second, below the fez and the final line concludes at the chin. With this triple redaction, the Republic cancels the face of King Farouk and draws Egypt's royalty to its conclusion.

On January 12, 1964, His Highness the Sultan Seyyid Sir Abdullah bin Khalifa of Zanzibar fled the murderous uprising of the Zanzibar Revolution in his yacht, the Seyyid Khalifa. Between January 12, and April 1964, the new government of the People's Republic of Zanzibar reissued thirteen stamps from 1961. Each set of four, in pink, black, green and blue, featured the head of the Sultan floating above the interior of his palace, the palace exterior, fishing boats and a map depicting the coastline of Zanzibar. In 1964, the new Republic overprinted the words "JAMHURI 1964" on the eyes of the exiled Sultan. This single uppercase word, which means "Republic" in Swahili, terminated the Sultanate by pronouncing the final word on its last Sultan. In the dishonoured face of King Farouk and the discredited gaze of the Sultan, the new regime installs its principles by demeaning the public images of its enemy's value system. Severed from the progress of its calendrical march, each stamp lives on as a date that no longer commemorates an event nobody recollects ever celebrating.

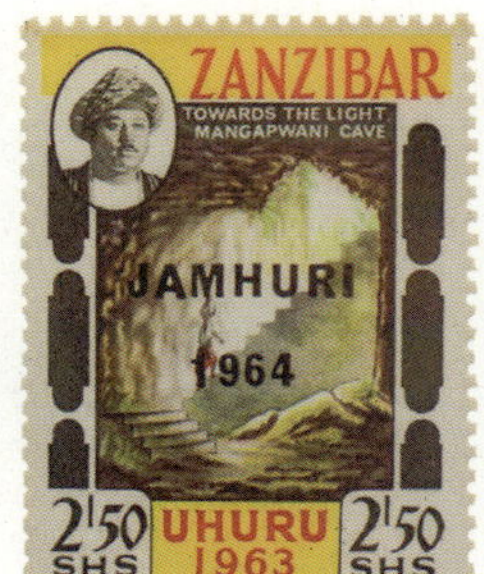

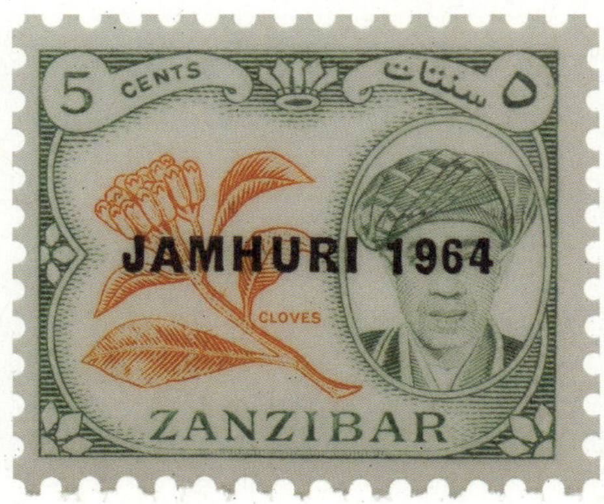

The People's Republic of Zanzibar, 1964—a detail from The Otolith Group's *Statecraft*, 2014. Lightbox display system, encapsulated stamps Dimensions variable.

In November 1965, the government of the First Republic of Nigeria issued six stamps that depicted birds against indigenous habitats set against an abstracted background. The color of the latter deliberately clashed with the former even as both, in turn, jarred with the chromatic exuberance of the birds that perched on branches that joined dissimilar scenery. The crowded designs of the 1/ blue-breasted Kingfisher in a yellow habitat on a grey background with red leaves, the 1/3d Crowned Crane on a pale blue sky on a dark blue sky, the 9d Grey Parrot in a pink habitat on a dark blue background, the 6d Saddle-bill Stork in a pale purple habitat against a dark purple background, the 1/ and 1/2d Splendid Songbird in a grey habitat on a violet backdrop and the 2d Village Weaver and Red-headed Malimbe on a pale orange habitat on a dark orange backdrop offered an allusive portrait of the nation's ability to embrace its mismatched birds, peoples, places, customs and habits.

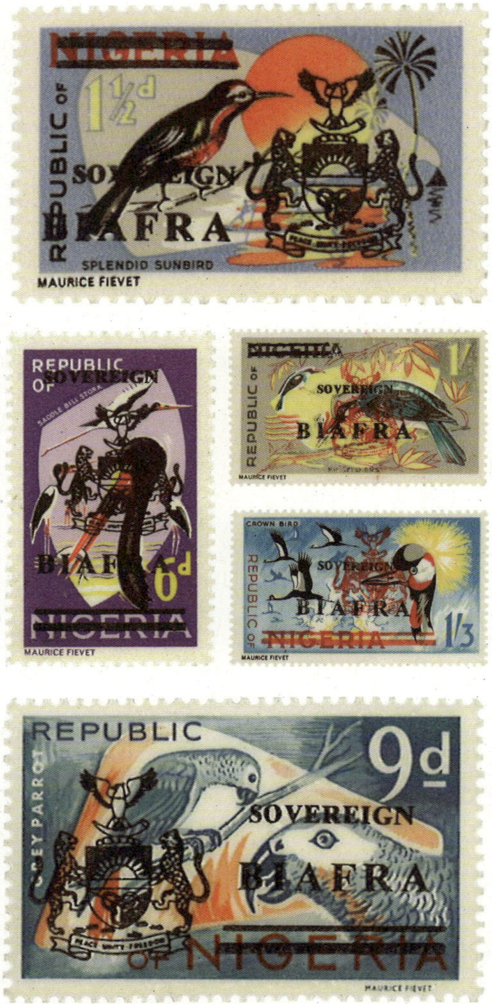

Sovereign Republic of Biafra 1968—a detail from The Otolith Group's *Statecraft*, 2014. Lightbox display system, encapsulated stamps Dimensions variable.

The military coups of January 1966 and July 1966 triggered ethnocidal violence throughout Northern Nigeria. On May 30, 1967, Lieutenant Colonel Ojukwu declared the Eastern Region of Nigeria an independent sovereign state with the name and title of The Republic of Biafra. In July 1967, the central government of Nigeria declared war on the breakaway Republic of Biafra. It was in the context of the civil war that supplies of Nigerian stamps ran low. The Biafran postal service overprinted the stamps of November 1965 with the coat of arms of the new Republic and reissued them on April 1, 1968.[15] Postal politics participated in and contributed to civil conflict on multiple levels. In the clash between the overprint of 1968 and the jarring designs of 1965 could be read the antipathies that fractured Pan-Nigerianism along regional and ethnic lines. The coat of arms of the new Republic was printed in black and sometimes red in the center of the stamps of 1965. It impressed itself upon the crowded images of the Blue-breasted kingfishers and Crowned Cranes. Biafra's postal system overruled the word "Nigeria" with two black lines and retained the word Republic so as to combine it with the new words "Sovereign Biafra". Imprinting the heraldic shield of the Sovereign Republic of Biafra upon the sophisticated graphics of the 1965 issue seemed to overload both designs until they created partial superimpositions that inadvertently evoked Sigmar Polke's *Mao* (1972). Identical leopards, partially legible in obscured details, could be glimpsed supporting the shield. Their left paws rested on land linked by the unreadable motto of "Peace. Unity. Freedom." Some of the eleven points of the divided sun could be discerned but not the lower sections divided into three and linked by what looked like chains. Most identifiable was the crest in the shape of an eagle, its wings stretched, claws resting upon a tusk above a wreath rope that heraldic specialists call a torse.

The pictorial antagonism conducted in the compressed space of the stamp seemed to concentrate the agonies of the Civil War. Maurice Fievet's excessively stylized designs appeared to resist the incursion by the official shield of Biafra. It was as if the clashing colors of November 1965 and the beleaguered overprint of April 1968 were fighting each other for the foreground. In many ways, the Biafra overprints of 1968 epitomize the entirety of *Statecraft*. They indicate the ways in which *Statecraft* functions as an experiment in immanent method.

Instead of emulating the museological collection or instituting a critique of the museum or celebrating independence struggles or correcting contemporary misreadings of Pan-Africanism, *Statecraft*'s epic incompletion speaks of the antipathies and enthusiasms generated by the

15 The overprints were printed at the engravers known as the Government Printer at Enugu, Biafra's capital city. See *Stanley Gibbons Stamp Catalogue Commonwealth & British Empire Stamps 1840–1970*, 11th ed. (2008; repr., London: Stanley Gibbons ltd., 2009), 460.

ambition to assemble a new Africa on an intracontinental basis. To encounter Pan-Africanism as the scale model of a political sequence is to reveal the extent to which it flourished under the refracted light of a black star at odds with the sleepless light of the digital economy. Such a meeting brings one face to face with the assertions, adjustments, antinomies, aspirations, accommodations, accusations, arrangements and antagonisms adopted by newly independent states forced to craft new forms of encumbered dependence from the inherited infrastructures of European imperialism. In its totality, *Statecraft* suggests that the postage stamp, like its close relative, paper currency, is less an emissary of history than its apologist. An ornament whose official optimism rewards ever closer inspection.

The Otolith Group, Statecraft: *An Incomplete Timeline of Independence Determined by Digital Auction*, 2014. Lightbox display system, stamps, dimensions variable. Photograph: Thor Brødreskift.

Accra, an Urban Promise

Łukasz Stanek

"Nine miles of street have been constructed, complete with street lights. Coconut trees and royal palms have been planted, not to mention the acres of green grass that is being planted. There is also a car park to take about 2,500 cars at a time. Over a thousand people have been employed on the site."[1] This is how the Ghanaian journal *Daily Graphic* reported on the International Trade Fair in Accra, two weeks before its opening in February 1967: as an essentially urban project. The sense of an urban everyday was at the center of the Fair and its programs, including restaurants and snack bars, a post office and a cinema, an exhibition gallery, a newspaper, and a drive-in banking window, the first in Ghana. Dance events, drumming performances, football matches, an open air cinema and jazz concerts unfolded, night and day, on the backdrop of the radical modernity of the Fair's architecture: smooth walls, sharp edges, large spans, levitating volumes, rhythmic patterns, were shown in the Ghanaian press on a daily basis.[2]

The Fair was launched in 1962 as a prestige project of Kwame Nkrumah, the first leader of independent Ghana, but the project was opened in 1967 by Joseph Arthur Ankrah, who led the putsch which toppled Nkrumah one year before. The design architects of the Fair arrived from Warsaw: Jacek Chyrosz and Stanisław Rymaszewski. They were employed by the Ghanaian state planning office, the Ghana National Construction Corporation (GNCC) with the Ghanaian Vik Agebite as the head architect. Chyrosz and Rymaszewski travelled to Ghana on the contract of Polservice, the central agency of foreign trade which mediated the export of labor from socialist Poland. With a dozen other Polish architects at the GNCC, they worked together with architects and draftsmen from Ghana and from the U.K., but also with professionals from other European socialist countries, including Bulgaria, Yugoslavia, and Hungary.[3] All these states were represented at the pavilions of the Fair, where the newest fashion from the GDR mixed with U.S. household equipment, British machines, and goods from other West African countries.

The daily press not only circulated the photographs of the Fair's architectures, but also informed the readers how to speak about them, how to look at them, how to use them, and how to find one's place in these buildings which promised a more fundamental spatio-temporal re-distribution of the new Ghanaian society. This promise was embedded in competing visions for Accra's urban future. Located between Accra and Tema New Town, at the time planned by Doxiadis Associates within the

1 "Ghana's First International Trade Fair," *Daily Graphic,* January 13, 1967. This text is a development of my article "Accra, Warsaw, and Socialist Globalization," in *Africa. Big Change, Big Chance,* ed. B. Albrecht (Bologna: Editrice Compositori, 2014), 162–64.

2 "Some Facts You Must Know", *Daily Graphic,* January 17, 1967.

3 Łukasz Stanek, "PRL™ Export Architecture and Urbanism from Socialist Poland", *Piktogram. Talking Pictures Magazine* 15 (2011): 1–54; Łukasz Stanek, *Postmodernism Is Almost All Right. Polish Architecture after Socialist Globalization* (Warsaw: Fundacja Bęc-Zmiana, 2012); Łukasz Stanek, "Architects from Socialist Countries in Ghana (1957–1967): Modernism and Mondialisation", *Journal of the Society of Architectural Historians* (forthcoming in December 2015).

overarching metropolitan master plan, the Fair was a part a larger urban reconstruction of the Ghanaian capital. This reconstruction concerned, above all, its immediate neighbor, Labadi, a major settlement of the Ga people. Labadi was assessed by the government as congested and without adequate services and roads, and hence earmarked for partial demolition. In the mid-1960s, the Town and Country Planning Department developed a new proposal for the site, linking it to the new plan of the Trade Fair. Designed by Polish planners Grażyna Luba, her husband Jerzy under the supervision of the Ghanaian planner Peter Turkson (1965), the plan integrated the water, sewage, and electricity networks of Labadi into the infrastructure of the Fair, and laid out a new road network. The latter was prepared by the mapping of the area, which allowed for the preservation of spaces of traditional culture and resulted in the irregularities of the realized road network. At the same time, the design of Labadi reflected the designers' previous experience of the planning of Powiśle, a nineteenth-century workers' district of Warsaw, on which they worked as members of the master planning team of Warsaw's reconstruction after the Second World War.

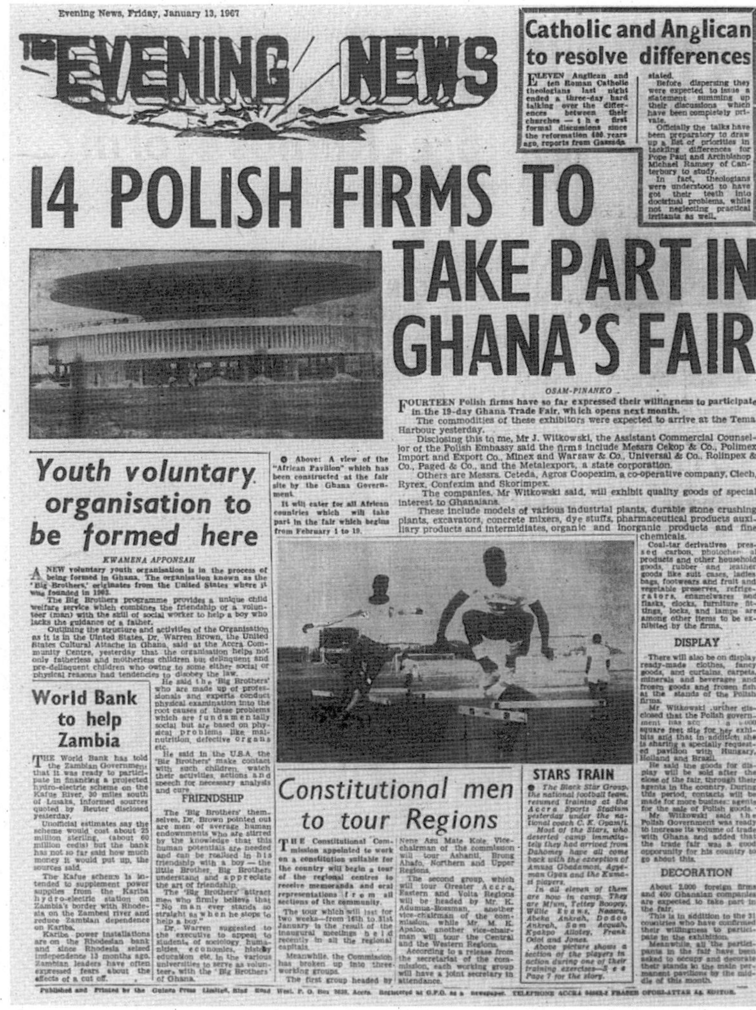
Evening News, Friday, January 13, 1967

THE EVENING NEWS

14 POLISH FIRMS TO TAKE PART IN GHANA'S FAIR

OSAM-PINANKO

FOURTEEN Polish firms have so far expressed their willingness to participate in the 19-day Ghana Trade Fair, which opens next month.

The commodities of these exhibitors were expected to arrive at the Tema Harbour yesterday.

Disclosing this to me, Mr J. Witkowski, the Assistant Commercial Counsellor of the Polish Embassy said the firms include Messrs Cekop & Co., Polimex Import and Export Co., Minex and Warsaw & Co., Universal & Co., Rolinpex & Co., Paged & Co., and the Metalexport, a state corporation.

Others are Messrs. Ceteda, Agros Coopexim, a co-operative company, Ciech, Ryrex, Confexim and Skorimpex.

The companies, Mr Witkowski said, will exhibit quality goods of special interest to Ghanaians.

These include models of various industrial plants, durable stone crushing plants, excavators, concrete mixers, dye stuffs, pharmaceutical products auxiliary products and intermidiates, organic and inorganic products and fine chemicals.

Coal-tar derivatives pressed carbon, photochem[unclear] al products and other household goods, rubber and leather goods like suit cases, ladies bags, footwears and fruit and vegetable preserves, refrigerators, enamelwares and flasks, clocks, furniture fittings, locks, and lamps are among other items to be exhibited by the firms.

DISPLAY

There will also be on display ready-made clothes, fancy goods, and curtains, carpets, minerals and beverages and frozen goods and frozen fish at the stands of the Polish firms.

Mr Witkowski further disclosed that the Polish government has acq[illegible] square feet site for her exhibits and that in addition she is sharing a specially requested pavilion with Hungary, Holland and Brazil.

He said the goods for display will be sold after the close of the fair, through their agents in the country. During this period, contacts will be made for more business agents for the sale of Polish goods.

Mr Witkowski said the Polish Government was ready to increase its volume of trade with Ghana and added that the trade fair was a good opporunity for his country to go about this.

DECORATION

About 2,000 foreign firms and 400 Ghanaian companies are expected to take part in the fair.

This is in addition to the 31 countries who have confirmed their willingness to participate in the exhibition.

Meanwhile, all the participants in the fair have been asked to occupy and decorate their stands in the main permanent pavilions by the middle of this month.

Catholic and Anglican to resolve differences

ELEVEN Anglican and ten Roman Catholic theologians last night ended a three-day hard talking over the differences between their churches — the first formal discussions since the reformation 400 years ago, reports from Gassada stated.

Before dispersing they were expected to issue a statement summing up their discussions which have been completely private.

Officially the talks have been preparatory to draw up a list of priorities in tackling differences for Pope Paul and Archbishop Michael Ramsey of Canterbury to study.

In fact, theologians were understood to have got their teeth into doctrinal problems, while not neglecting practical irritants as well.

Youth voluntary organisation to be formed here

KWAMENA APPONSAH

A NEW voluntary youth organisation is in the process of being formed in Ghana. The organisation known as the 'Big Brothers,' originates from the United States where it was founded in 1903.

The Big Brothers programme provides a unique child welfare service which combines the friendship of a volunteer (man) with the skill of social worker to help a boy who lacks the guidance of a father.

Outlining the structure and activities of the Organisation as it is in the United States, Dr. Warren Brown, the United States Cultural Attache in Ghana, said at the Accra Community Centre, yesterday that the organisation helps not only fatherless and motherless children but delinquent and pre-delinquent children who owing to some either social or physical reasons had tendencies to disobey the law.

He said the 'Big Brothers' who are made up of professionals and experts conduct physical examination into the root causes of these problems which are fundamentally social but are based on physical problems like malnutrition, defective organs etc.

He said in the U.S.A. the 'Big Brothers' make contact with such children, watch their activities, actions and speech for necessary analysis and cure.

FRIENDSHIP

World Bank to help Zambia

THE World Bank has told the Zambian Government that it was ready to participate in financing a projected hydro-electric scheme on the Kafue River, 30 miles south of Lusaka, informed sources quoted by Reuter disclosed

Constitutional men to tour Regions

STARS TRAIN

Evening News (Accra), January 13, 1967.

Considered on a larger scale, the Trade Fair was part of the seashore development of Accra, designed as one continuous landscape. This approach was introduced already in the 1958 masterplan of Accra, prepared by British planners working at the Town and Country Planning Division, which paid particular attention to the coastal strip from Manprobi to Labadi, envisaged as the "forecourt", or "front garden", of Accra.[4] Such vision was continued in the first designs for the Labadi Beach neighboring the Trade Fair, which included leisure, cultural, sport facilities and a high rise hotel free-floating between roads and vegetation: an "ultramodern structure" as a journalist exclaimed.[5] Yet together with the blueprint of a 300 foot revolving tower, and the artificial lake in the form of Africa, these plans were deemed extravagant and unnecessary by the Ankrah government, and abandoned. Only a modest restaurant was realized which allowed the parties to move to the beach, after the Fair grounds closed at 10pm.[6]

4 "Accra, a Plan For The Town. The Report for the Minister of Housing," 1958, 113.
5 "Ghana Plans for a Trade Fair", *Daily Graphic*, December 14, 2013.
6 "Fair Viewers Stranded," *Daily Graphic*, February 6, 1967.

Today, these beach facilities have been long taken over by upscale hotels overlooking Labadi Beach, as well as a new speculative housing development. By contrast, the Fair is still a focal place in Accra, even if it suffered from insufficient maintenance. Most structures, those built as permanent, those intended to be temporary, and those added ad hoc in recent years, are still in use, rented for exhibitions taking place every few months, political rallies, and religious festivities. The Fair has currently no less than 200 tenants, and the majority of its structures are rented by Ghanaian and West African firms. On the spot, melancholy is mixed with grand ambitions for a new beginning, and in the office of the director of the Fair one can admire the bird's-eye view delivered by a Dublin-based architectural office which shows a spectacular vision to replace the original buildings. Yet a major impediment to the development of the Fair is the contested ownership of the land on which it was built. The Ga leadership claims that the land was transferred to the government of Nkrumah without sufficient compensation; an assessment which the lawyers of the Fair dispute. This controversy brings to the fore, once again, the unlikely relationship with Warsaw and its post-socialist urbanism, marked by land disputes stemming from the nationalization of land by the socialist government after the Second World War.

Where to Begin, Where to Belong: The Many Returns of *Come Back Africa*

A Patchwork by Marie-Hélène Gutberlet & Tobias Hering

> *—The problem with the liberals is the vote. Wins the best; while they are laying the country that we owned. They should give back the country and we give them the vote.*
> *—Beautiful. I'll remember that!*

U.S. director Lionel Rogosin's *Come Back Africa* (USA/SA, 1958) is famed today as having been the first film in the collection of Arsenal – Institute for Film and Video Art in Berlin and also the first film to be distributed by its founders, Erika and Ulrich Gregor.

In the beginning then, there was *Come Back Africa*. What kind of a beginning is this for an institution, if it begins with a comeback? And what with Africa? If the beginning was *Come Back Africa,* it sounds like the beginning was already delayed, that something had already begun elsewhere, and that what had begun had then disappeared so that now, upon reappearance, it could be asked to *come back*. It makes me think of Serge Daney's observation that films, the cinema, "only exist to bring back what had already been seen once before, well seen, badly seen, unseen",[1] and that therefore in the cinema every first time is already a second time, and every beginning is inevitably delayed. Every discovery is a rediscovery—as it was in the case of *Come Back Africa*. The first time I heard that this had been the very first film in the Arsenal's collection was when it was "rediscovered" once again in 2012 by Darryl Els, a curator from Johannesburg who took interest in the film in the context of his contribution to the Arsenal's *Living Archive* project. Along with the film's re-appreciation came its canonization as the "beginning".

> *Shortly after the film was made [i.e. in 1959 or 1960] the founders of the Freunde der Deutschen Kinemathek [i.e. the forerunner of what was later renamed Arsenal—Institute for Film and Video Art] Erika and Ulrich Gregor came into contact with Jimmy Vaughn, an associate of Lionel Rogosin. Vaughn [...] arrived in Berlin with the reels of* Come back Africa, *which had just won the Italian Film Critics award at the Venice Film Festival. Despite this acclaim, Vaughn and Rogosin had little success in finding a European distributor, pleading to the Gregors to "Please do something for the film" [a quote picked up from conversations with the Gregors]. They replied that they would keep the film for him if he could "lift and fit the film reels into the tiny storage space above the front door of their Berlin apartment." As the international public interest in* Come Back Africa *grew, no doubt influenced by major political events occurring in South Africa such as the Sharpeville massacre in 1960, the Gregors would subsequently receive numerous requests to screen the film*

1 Serge Daney, "Serge Daney in Conversation with Serge Toubiana" in *Postcards from the Cinema,* trans. Paul Grant (New York, 2007), 90.

> *and so both archival and distribution aspects of the institution came into being.*[2]

Here the German story begins. The film's own story begins in South Africa in 1958, or even earlier, in the U.S., when Rogosin decided to make a film in South Africa about a regime with structures relating to the national socialist ideology, and the racial segregation in the U.S. Since I had seen *Come Back Africa* for the first time in the early '90s, I was astonished when I heard that of all things this film was somehow the starting point of the Arsenal film collection, which today appears to be one of the most important archives of films made in the context of liberation movements, documentaries and artists films and videos throughout the world. A friend of ours loves to emphasize the fact that there is not a single Nazi-film in this archive, which in Germany sounds oddly rare. (Actually it is not entirely true.)

> *I want to resist the idea that the Holocaust is merely another instance of genocide. I accept arguments for its uniqueness. However, I do not want the recognition of that uniqueness to be an obstacle to better understanding of the complicity of rationality and ethnocidal terror to which this book is dedicated. This is a difficult line on which to balance, but it should be possible, and enriching, to discuss these histories together.*[3]

As for *Come Back Africa*, Nazism comes into play with respect to the time that we talk about and the obtrusion with which it contaminated all dimensions of thinking in that specific period in the 1950s and later on. It is not by accident that *Come Back Africa* relates to it. Not only do we know that Hendrik Verwoerd, the architect and ideologist of apartheid, studied in Germany in the 1920s where he was in touch with nationalist ideas. Lionel Rogosin, son of Israel Eliezer (later Rogosin), whose family migrated from Belarus to the U.S. in 1890, resonates in the character of the hotel manager Levi in *Come Back Africa*, who helps Zachariah, the main character, to get a job and a pass, but has no power to protect him from the defamations of a guest and has to fire him. Rogosin's comprehension of the hotel manager's difficult position—the friction between his privileges as a white person, but not being South African enough as a Jewish migrant—is mirrored by the manager's understanding of Zachariah's difficult standing in being right, but powerless. The scene is short, but shows a hidden relationship between the filmmaker, a person he met during the filmmaking process, possibly a real hotel manager, and a fictional character who share a knowledge about forced migration and labor.

The dimensions of forced migration, inherent to South Africa's politics of space and work, correlates with another beginning, which the film implicates: a short scene showing Miriam Makeba sing a few songs in a shebeen. She was invited to participate in *Come Back Africa's* world première in Venice in 1959, which turned out to be a context in which the

2 Darryi Els, *Shifting Grounds: Reflections on National Identity in the Archive, Living Archive: Archive Work as Contemporary Curatorial and Artistic Practice* (Berlin: Arsenal—Institut für Film und Videokunst, 2013), 74.

3 Paul Gilroy, *The Black Atlantic: Modernity and Double Consciousness* (Cambridge: Harvard University Press, 1933), 213.

apartheid regime was heavily denounced. After Venice she couldn't return to South Africa and was banned. Her whole career happened outside her country. She was an internationally recognized woman in politics and music. *Come Back Africa* marks multilayered and multiple beginnings, the beginning of Makeba's exile till 1991, her political activism, and her remarkable international career.

> *— I'd like to get people to..., get people at each other to talk to each other. If I could get my worst enemy over a bottle of beer, maybe we could get at each other.*
> *— It's not just a question of talking to each other, but a question of understanding each other living in the same world.*

> *Come Back Africa addressed a public that was outlawed, and therefore could not be, and in so doing, constituted a public in the conditions of its absence. Projected to a public that significantly includes local Africans, its failure to circulate in South Africa meant that its actual publics were exclusively transnational. Consequently, the absence of black publics underwrote its publicness.*[4]

How do we come forward with questions about audiences, specific audiences, or audiences that films fail to reach? About shifts and disruptions in time and space related to films, their production and perception? What do transnational parameters create? If *Come Back Africa* failed to have a South African audience in the first place, it had an international audience, a black or partly black audience elsewhere, 1959 in Venice, 1960 in Berlin, London and Edinburgh, as early as 1988 in South Africa,[5] and since then the film has been screened all over the world: in 2011 at the Bioscope in Johannesburg, and 2013 in Berlin. The film has been restored by Cineteca di Bologna and released on DVD in France and the U.S. in 2013. All these details illustrate the role major interest festivals, archives, cinemas, educational and artistic institutions have had in this particular film and the value that is attributed to it.

Litheko Modisane seems to recognize that the film was seen by "black audiences" when he says that the film's public "significantly includes local Africans". However, these local publics immediately disappear again from the argument in the next sentence, when he concludes speaking of an "absence of black publics". Scattered localized audiences, it seems, are not sufficient to constitute what he calls a "black public". The appearance and disappearance of a missing but desired audience, this search for an audience, somehow recalls a remark which Paul Klee made in his often-quoted Jena lecture in 1924. Speaking of his role as an artist and particularly of the collaborative context of the Bauhaus academy, Klee describes himself and his peers as working for a future audience. Of "the artwork which the art of our times is working on", he says, "there only exist pieces. It still needs to grow. We must still look for it. We do not have the necessary power yet, because there is no people carrying us. But we

4 Litheko Modisane, "'Suddenly the Film Scene is Becoming our Scene!' The Making and Public Lives of Black-Centered Films in South Africa (1959–2001)." (PhD diss., Wits University, 2010), 107.

5 Ntongela Masilela, "*Come Back Africa* and South African film history", *Jump Cut* 36 (May 1991): 61–5.

are in search of a people."[6] If Paul Klee appears to be speaking here about a particular loneliness experienced by the avant-garde artist (similar to the loneliness of a prophet), he is not describing a solipsist project but a group effort. The work of a small group in the name of a future people. And the image he evokes is not one of an already achieved, yet unrecognized masterpiece awaiting its future audience, but the work as much as its audience are still in the making. Bits and pieces are there, glimpses and fragments, but neither artwork, nor people are complete yet, and their completion seems to be mutually conditioned: the artwork will only be completed once a people is ready (or free) to carry it. This inextricable vis-à-vis of an artwork-anticipating-a-people-anticipating-an-artwork is almost a paradox. Almost. A thin line of possibility is what saves one occasionally from madness, and what makes it likely, for example, that in a film addressing "a public that was outlawed, and therefore could not be" an actual group of intellectual outlaws (the members of *Drum* magazine), discussing the apartheid system which divides them up, can evoke the idea of the unity of a people speaking in many voices.

In 1959, in search of a space, the film print landed accidentally in Berlin. It is a clandestinely made movie which addresses freedom of movement within deeply restricted spaces in South Africa and in the U.S.; the Civil Rights Movement in the U.S. has set an example for protest and resistance against racist political orders, while in South Africa the Black Consciousness Movement emerges in the mid 1960s; Angela Davis studies sociology in Frankfurt in 1965, shortly before the 1968 students protests reached all levels of society, be it in Germany, Japan, France or Senegal, and in South Africa around Steve Biko.

Come Back Africa is actually a line from the ANC anthem, *Mayibuye Afrika* and goal and motto of the ANC, launched in the 1910s. Jabulani Buthelezi's comment reads like a blueprint of the shebeen scene with Miriam Makeba singing, and the previous discussion about black-to-black violence and white liberalism. Buthelezi writes:

> Mayibuye I-Afrika *is not translatable. Much is lost when "Let Africa come back" or "Bring back Africa" is imposed on* Mayibuye i-Afrika. *Baba Mandela joined the ANC well aware of what it stood for. He also vowed that he would uphold the* Mayibuye I-Afrika *goal of the ANC. The founders of the ANC hoped and desired that* ibuye i-Afrika. *They wanted Africa to regain itself in its totality, the African dignity, the land, the values, and the wealth and above all, the Africanity and Africanness of South Africa. The founders had seen all forms of wanton decentering, dismembering and dispossession of the African peoples. Their cultures, their knowledge, their languages and their names were mocked, marginalized, and mutilated. Their histories, and their voices were distorted, decentered and devaluated. The African was de-voiced, divorced from meaningful activities and castigated in a Gehenna of nothingness whose effusion of anomy, alienation, ennui and nihilism bred the so-called Black-to-Black violence which was fathered by White greed, nursed by racial*

6 Quoted from Thomas Kain ed., *Paul Klee in Jena 1924: Der Vertrag* (Jena, 1999), 69.

discriminatory laws, and choreographed by White intellectual cannibalism.[7]

Buthelezi's arguments are remarkable for their clarity and focus on language. The untranslatability or opacity of the African expression for example, and the sense that the main significance is lost, when it comes to the translation of an experience which we can understand, as a line of continuous misunderstanding of the film's title and direction of critique. Trying to understand what *Come Back Africa* wants to tell us, we may lose a main part of the story: the part which tells us that we can't come to terms with what apartheid meant for people in the late 1950s in South Africa.

But we can sense that the apartheid system affected peoples' entire life and thinking, and that it created violence and destruction, which the author tries to name through (again, another) translation practice: he translates the experiences into an endless alphabet of mortifications. Each scene of *Come Back Africa* can be related to a specific type of abasement and violation mentioned by Buthelezi. Even the scenes showing the masses alighting from the trains and running to work in their artificiality, rhythm and beauty condemn people to the highly regulated and unequal work in the mining industries and services.[8] With the exception of the unique scene already mentioned, which unfolds as an interval of relief, peace and talking within an unrelenting set-up.

—This guy here doesn't understand this intellectual mumbo jumbo.
— No, no. Let them talk. I don't understand, but I like it.
— He likes this.

In this improvised scene in the shebeen, Bloke Modisane, Can Themba and Lewis Nkosi—key figures and writers at *Drum magazine* in Johannesburg and involved in the making of this film—are having a conversation. Zachariah joins them; the main fiction character has been attacked shortly before by a Tsotsi and he doesn't understand what had happened. Can Themba then tells the story of Lamunu, the offender, which turns out to be an example of the type of black-to-black violence Buthelezi might have had in mind. Interestingly, Themba's friends strive not to judge hastily Lamunu's abuse of power; they take their time to negotiate and understand the situation while the conversation continues about matters of racialization and inequality related to color, about negotiation and mutual understanding. The character played by literary critic Lewis Nkosi, who was involved in the film's script-writing, argues that one should not expect to change relations over a cup of tea with white liberals.

—The liberals again, what liberals? Do you know who is the liberal in this country?

7 Jabulani Buthelezi, *Rolihlahla Dalibhunga Nelson Mandela—an ecological study* (2002), 46–47.

8 A comparison of Premesh Lalu's contribution *The Trojan Horse and the Becoming Technical of the Human* (2014) published online on future-memories.org and the film *Enthusiasm* (1931) by Dziga Vertov in relation to *Come Back Africa* would highlight the context of the mining industry as white capital and the becoming-tool of black labor as a key moment in South African history, set in a dramaturgy of space and movement.

The scene ends abruptly with a pass control. The interval of voicing and exchange is over. But for both contexts, Buthelezi's sketch of a vision for the future of South Africa being part of the Pan-African continent as much as for the discussion in the Shebeen, we can sense a moment of a practice anticipating an alternative, a way which is not yet fully measured but marks a process by which the film enables the group of the *drum* avant-garde to articulate itself against the backdrop of the rigid and racist apartheid system. Sitting together, trying to understand each other, drinking and smoking and being masters of their fates.

— *Hello Miriam, good to see you!*
— *Hi!*
— *Hey, just a song, one song.*
— *Where do you come from?*
— *I just came from a party.*
— *Look who is here...*
— *OK.*
— *Give me a tune.*

It is no accident that the film has been removed from the context of its emergence, being part of marginalized reality, and in consequence having no fixed geography, but different paths of negotiated meanings unfolding a complex heritage.

A Parallel Story

In a film made in Cologne in 1984 by Senegalese director Pape Seck for German television channel Westdeutscher Rundfunk (WDR), a young man, Góor, reclaims a ritual mask which, acting out of necessity, he had once sold to a German tourist in Senegal. Utterly lost in an indifferent German city full of looming remnants of history, Góor meets and befriends another African emigré, the South African Abraham Tiro. In a particularly intriguing scene, Abraham visits Góor in the cellar where he lives under the bar where he works. It is Christmas Eve and their togetherness helps them to ward off the isolation they are both suffering in Cologne. The damp brick walls of the cellar remind Abraham of the "mines and prisons" of South Africa in which he spent most of his life. The haunting impression of the cellar makes Abraham tell Góor his whole life story, beginning with his birth in 1934, the killing of his father, the rape of his mother, the slave labor in the gold mines, and his frequent arrests and brutalization by the South African police. "Apartheid is the disgrace," he says to Góor who has never heard the word before but identifies it with the same evil power which had allowed a woman in a white Porsche to snatch away his mask and refuse to return it to him. Abraham fled the racialized violence of his country, crossed the Mediterranean and followed the Rhine from the Alps northwards to "a country divided by an iron curtain, by a disgraceful wall." He came to Cologne. It was 1964, the "Wirtschaftswunder" (economical miracle). After living on the streets or seeking shelter in brothels, illegalized for several years (like Góor now), he was finally granted asylum as a political refugee and given work again in the mines, this time those of Germany, in the "Kohlenpott." Having reached the end of his solemn tale in the cellar, Abraham dies in Góor's arms, who then goes on to incinerate his friend's body the "Zulu way" in some copse by the Rhine.

Góor is played by Pape Oumar Diop, an actor, musician and poet who also contributed to the film's musical soundtrack and who later, as Abdourahmane Gilbert Diop, became a widely known griot in the musical scene of Berlin, where he died in 2012. The role of Abraham Tiro is taken by South-African actor Ronald Mkwanazi who went on to play in numerous German fiction films and is probably best known for his role in the popular television series *Lindenstraße* where in 1991 and 1992 for some 40 episodes he impersonated David Motibe, the first African character to appear in the series. The character was clearly designed to reflect on the rampant post-reunification racism in Germany. Apparently Mkwanazi himself had proposed this plotline to the *Lindenstraße* authors and was then cast in the role himself.

Among the many things that struck me in this altogether unforgettable (yet largely forgotten) film, was the strange dating in Abraham Tiro's story. Born in 1934, as he says, he must have been fifty when he died in that cellar in Cologne (assuming that the film's present is the real time of its production, i.e. 1984). The actor Ronald Mkwanazi however was actually born in South Africa in 1959 and even if makeup makes him look a bit older in the film than he actually is, he doesn't look like a fifty-year-old man ready to die. This means that when the real Ronald Mkwanazi was born, in 1959, his fictional twin Abraham was just about to start his exile. 1959 also marks the beginning of Miriam Makeba's long exile, and 1959 is also the year when the 35mm print of *Come Back Africa* came to Berlin. In retrospect all this dating and predating circuits the traumatizing mark of the Sharpeville massacre of 1960, which, as Darryl Els assumes in the quote above, created an impact strong enough to arouse awareness of apartheid violence among German publics and thereby interest in Lionel Rogosin's film. The parallels between Abraham's account of the mines and the violations against his family and Zachariah's story in *Come Back Africa* are obvious and hardly surprising. The fictional chronologies of both films create further connections, for example when reckoning that Zachariah, coming to Johannesburg as a young and able worker from the countryside in 1958 (i.e. in *Come Back Africa*'s "real time"), must have been in his early twenties, i.e. very near the same age as his fictional peer Abraham. Spinning this yarn a bit further, Zachariah's untold story after finding his wife murdered in their Sophiatown home could continue in the vein of Abraham's: he would flee the disgraceful conditions of apartheid in South Africa and would arrive in Germany a little bit later than *Come Back Africa*, the fictionalized account of his story captured on film. While Abraham meets death in a damp cellar under a bar in Cologne, *Come Back Africa* is said to have found refuge in the storage space in the hallway of an apartment in Berlin, where it became the founding film of a collection holding some 8,000 titles today. Such mixing of fiction and truth and messing with linear time-lines is also taking place in *Afrika am Rhein*, where not only real time and dream time are regularly blurred, but where at one point a Turkish newspaper seller is heard crying out the day's headline: "The Berlin wall has disappeared!" This is in 1984.

The cellar and the storage space: two spaces not made for the purposes they were to serve. Two nooks in Germany in which political histories and film histories, histories of violence, exile and refuge intertwine. Two refuges which, notwithstanding the fact that they were shelters, also tell of homelessness, of the fact that itineraries that originate in Africa and tell of the violence forced on African people did not easily find receptive ground in Germany. In both stories, Germany figures as a wavering and distanced host. Thinking on these two nooks, the cellar in Cologne and the storage space in Berlin, I remembered a third one, the room in a bungalow in an asylum seekers' camp in Zerbst in Sachsen-Anhalt in which Moïse Merlin Mabouna, a refugee from Cameroon, spent his first year in Germany, and about which, in a video he co-authored with Brigitta Kuster (*2006–1892 = 114 years*), he says the following: "This is the root, even the source of reflection. Here you exhaust all your energy, because you are sitting in this room collecting all your strength thinking about how to get out of this situation. Why is it such a mess of shit, so absurd!" This was 2002.

> *—It doesn't matter, if you are Indian or a Jew or a German or an Afrikaaner. If people can label you, they label you easily.*
> *—Now you are really going over border.*
> *—I know I am. But I am trying to explain the bigger things. The reason why we are labelled is because it is just easy to label us racially.*
> *—Why that?*
> *—Because it is easy to distinguish one colour from another. Because people think they can get away by playing one colour against another. Because physically they have—a person of one colour and a person of another colour—they do what they like.*

In May 2013, caught by a note I had found on some television history website, I started to trace *Afrika am Rhein* which I had never heard of before. The breakthrough in my initially unsuccessful search happened when by sheer coincidence I met Pape Seck's brother in December 2014 in Dakar. Amadou Saalum Seck, a filmmaker himself, had studied at the academy for film and television in Munich in the late 1970s and he kindly put me in touch with his brother Pape Seck, the director of *Afrika am Rhein*. Pape Seck provided me with all the names and information that made it possible to trace a digital copy of the film to the WDR archives. The television producer under whose supporting patronage the film had come into being (now in his late seventies) remembered the utter indifference with which the German press and public received this as well as a number of other films by African directors that he coproduced. He summarized how he remembered *Afrika am Rhein* as "the story of an African sitting in a cellar in Cologne who tries to come to grips with Africa". It is not really "Africa" he is trying to come to grips with, I think, but rather the Rhine and the many bridges crossing it and the many trains crossing those bridges, the buildings and the richness of Cologne, the trams circling the squares and the objects adorning streets and apartments, the cold and the indifference and the many words people have for telling him that he does not belong.

Come Back Africa has recently been screened in the context of the "Visionary Archive" project in Berlin, in the framework of a series of projections and discussions titled "It all depends". The series is curated by Marie-Hélène Gutberlet and Tobias Hering. By critically experimenting with various formats and engaging the public in the translocal work with and on aspects of African cinema, the series serves to accompany the five Visionary Archive sub-projects conducted in Berlin, Bissau, Cairo, Khartoum and Johannesburg. The title, "It all depends", places the focus on hegemonies, mutual references and dependencies between Africa and Europe into which cinema, curatorial work and the project's participants are interwoven as well as on the different lines of connection emerging between the subprojects as the "visionary archive" gradually takes shape.

Black Consciousness, Black Holes, Black Suns, and Black Collectivity

Stacy Hardy

Staffriding was a platform, a performance, a defiance. A dangerous and informal practice that developed in urban areas in South Africa during apartheid, it entailed boarding or disembarking a fast moving train or riding on the exterior of a train travelling at high speed. On one level staffriding was a practical solution to overcrowding on trains and unaffordable fares but more than that it was an act of bravado and liberation in defiance of oppression.

Conceived in reaction to the brutal constraints placed on black male bodies by the apartheid system's policies of racial segregation, separate development, and economic, social and psychological repression, staffriding was a way of moving when movement was contained, a way of free riding when nothing was free, and a way of subverting the official system by using the establishment toward one's own ends. As poet Lesego Rampolokeng writes:

> *To staff-ride means taking or shaking the train, on the hoof... back-front-sideways, death-dance down the years wrapped in romance, here... mutilation, there... amputated limbs. Staffriders hip-hopped before the fact while their heads got lobbed off....*
>
> *Those whistles were Mission Station Identification crackling thru past the clanging metal on shrieking skull... isiparapara... sound of takkies flapping across concrete. Slip, fall, get mashed up & watch the audience get tickled to cackling. And banana peels sought to turn the sick humour on. & keep the revolution green.*
>
> *And then... speak to someone out the side of your mouth & you'll be warned not to staffride. So there we go, sliding down this platform.*[1]

True to its name, the literary journal, *Staffrider*, sought to provide space where the challenging and turbulent energy that erupted in everyday practices like staffriding could find a voice. Started by Mike Kirkwood in March 1978, and later edited by Andries Walter Oliphant, the journal had two main objectives: to provide publishing opportunities for community-based organizations and young writers, graphic artists and photographers; and to oppose officially sanctioned state and establishment culture by opening up a space for imagination, dreaming and subversion.

"We will have to *donder* conventional literature: old fashioned critic and reader alike," wrote Mothobi Mutloatse, in his daring introduction to *Forced Landing*,[2] a compilation of black writing, much of which first appeared in *Staffrider*, "We are going to pee, spit and shit on literary convention before we are through; we are going to kick and pull and push and drag literature into the form we prefer. We are going to experiment

1 Lesego Rampolokeng, "Staffriding the Frontline (2008)," *Chimurenga Library*, accessed February 4, 2015, http://www.chimurengalibrary.co.za/staffriding-thefrontline-an-essay-by-lesego-rampolokeng.

2 Mothobi Mutloatse, "Introduction," in *Forced Landing*, ed. Mothobi Mutloatse (Johannesburg: Raven Press, 1980), 5.

and probe and not give a damn what the critics have to say ..."

Staffrider's pages were thus fierce but also filled with love and generosity. Produced by the same Durban "moment" that saw black consciousness leader Steve Biko begin the South African Students Association, it had a view of literature with a small "l". Subverting the typical concept of the political and the literary, its base was popular rather than elitist, and it sought to provide an autobiography of experience in its witnessing of daily black life in South Africa.

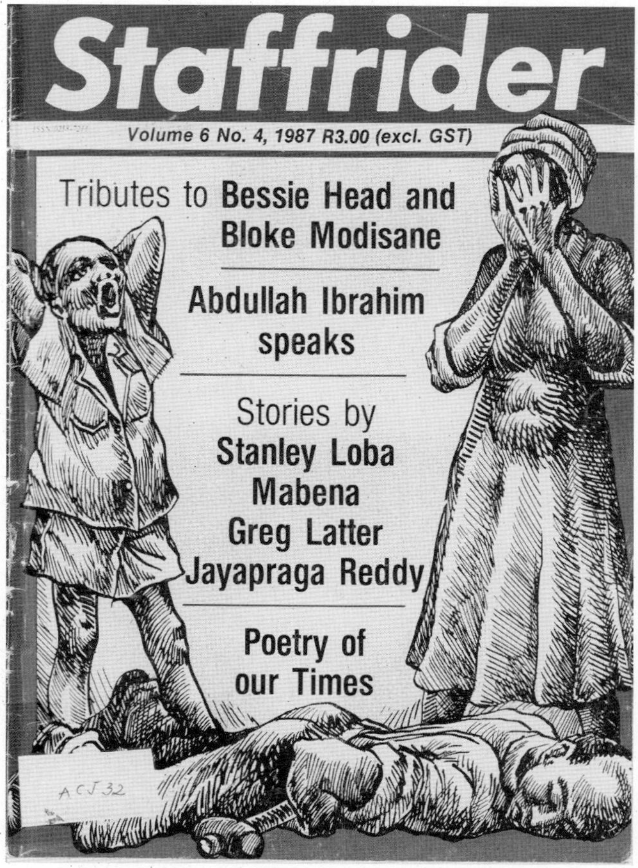

Cover of *Staffrider* 6, no. 4, 1987. Reproduced by permission of the Chimurenga Library.

In *Staffrider* the traditional binaries of writer/reader or artist/viewer were rejected so that established relationships between readers and writers were destabilized through various modes. It was not unusual for one person simultaneously to occupy the identities of writer, reader, critic and distributor. An unsigned note in the magazine published under the heading "Critics wanted" announced:

> *The phenomenon of art groups linked to particular township communities in present-day South Africa [allows for] the art group [to] put forward the work it wants to be published, and then assists in the distribution of the magazine to the community. In this way editorial control is vested in the writers as participants in a community based group.*[3]

Mike Abraham recalls, "I saw all the black suffering and I saw more black resistance and knew I was a staffrider too. That same year I became a *Staffrider* vendor at the bus rank. I even built up a small group of loyal readers ..."[4]

The magazine was an expression of its time in other ways. In an essay on the *Staffrider* years, writer and editor Ivan Vladislavić writes:

> *Chris van Wyk was editor, writing teacher, mentor and friend to more writers than I can remember, especially the beginners. He spent half his time at the kitchen table or on a rickety bench in the garden, drinking coffee and talking with some poet who had come all the way from Evaton or beyond, the handwritten work spread out between them. That was the hallmark of the submissions: written in longhand in ballpoint in a school exercise book. In the end, all this talking and advising was bad business: a commercial publishing house is not meant to be a writing school. But it was good in every other way.*[5]

3 "Critics wanted", *Staffrider* 2, no.3 (1979): 58.

4 Mike Abraham, "Of 'Brothers with Perfect Timing' (2008)," *Chimurenga Library,* accessed February 4, 2015, http://www.chimurengalibrary.co.za/of-brothers-with-perfect-timing-an-essay-by-mike-abraham.

5 Ivan Vladislavić, "Staffrider (2008)," *Chimurenga Library,* accessed January 4, 2015, http://www.chimurengalibrary.co.za/staffrider-an-essay-by-ivan-vladislavic.

I was not one of those writers lucky enough to have taken a seat at Van Wyk's kitchen table. By the time I started writing, *Staffrider*, like so many other apartheid-era platforms of dissent, had ceased publication. It was the mid 1990s, a turning point of our history, a time of rapid change and radical uncertainty, but also one of tremendous excitement and possibility. It was a moment of equilibrium between extremes, the moment of uncertainty from which the future emerges. Yes, everything was being questioned: education as well as social, political, religious, and cultural life. To my generation, the dream of a free South Africa provided a space for new audacities, transgressions and a new quest for collective identity.

When you write, you write both with and against literature. You write out of inspiration from writers and books, but you also write against mediocrity and the clichés the literary establishment promotes. Maybe it was unfair to some writers of the generation that preceded mine, but like many of my generation I was frustrated with much of the didactic political writing of the past and even more frustrated by the static, conservative Western view of literature still prescribed by the literary establishment. At the same time, I felt deeply for literature produced by collections of literary rogues operating on the fringes of culture, independent journals like *Staffrider*, innovative writers, dissonant poets, BC poets[6] and other outsiders. I was equally attracted to writing by radicals from elsewhere—speculative fiction, cyberpunk, postmodern fiction, alt lit, literature in translation.

My first prose embraced chance, play, bad taste and fragmentation to upend the authority of the author and the omniscient narrator. Sex and desire with their erotic drives had a great part in it. Part of what I was writing was consciously political, at least at the level of intention. Let's say that my questions started to flow about identity, imagination, history, and then more and more about language and the incredible fraud I was discovering in the accumulated layers of lies told through centuries of the white patriarchal ordering of reality.

I soon found myself amongst a small community of writers who published in the online literary journal *donga*. Like *Staffrider*, the journal took its name from everyday South African experience. *Dongas* are the deep-ridged gullies found in open veld or near new industrial developments in South Africa. In many ways it was a homecoming. When I was a child growing up in Limpopo, *dongas* were everywhere. They broke the flat, even bushveld and provided hidey-holes, places to hang out, to learn to smoke dagga, to play hide and seek and other more dangerous games.

It's difficult to articulate exactly what made *donga* so important at the time. Its short three-year lifespan, modest minimal design and seeming simplicity, masked an unexpected depth. As Alan Finlay, who together with Paul Wessels, edited *donga* explained, "I wanted to create an open, white space for the poems, where the poem could look comfortable."[7]

6 Black Consciousness (BC) philosophy in South Africa was born from the realization that "the most potent weapon in the hands of the oppressor is the mind of the oppressed." A. Mngxitama, A. Alexander, and N.C. Gibson, eds., *Biko Lives! Contesting the Legacies of Steve Biko* (London: Palgrave Macmillan, 2008).

7 Stacy Hardy, "Liberated Zones(1): Re:visionary Inter-textuality in South Africa (2003)," *ISEA International Newsletter*, accessed January 5, 2015, http://www.isea-web.org/_archives/newsletters/2003-2/091-feb-mar-2003.

The space *donga* created was certainly open but it was far from neutral. "*donga* itself has got something to say, over and above all the submissions, all the parts put together that make up the 'hole'," said Alan. "The submissions we get change and refine that space we call 'donga'. And you can't predict it... Maybe a donga's a place that collects things. Things we chuck away. Or others chuck away, the other publications."[8]

I was struck by Alan's use of the word hole, a word with so many connotations in South Africa. As Alan pointed out, "hole" is a homonym of whole. It rhymes with mole and sounds like hold. But what kind of hole? Is it a peephole? A body cavity? A crude sexual representation? A gaping maw in the physical earth? And caused by what—Mines? Bombs? Shovels? Erosion? Is it a grave? A wound? A hole in the wall? An escape hatch? An entrance? An exit?

A manhole covers a sewer, but is permeable, spewing gas and steam and sometimes liquid. A *donga* is open, but forbidden, a no-go area where unwanted rubbish collects. And as www.donga.co.za suggested back in the day, and my mother often warned me: "*dongas* are dangerous to people and animals. They undermine houses."

And, like *Staffrider* before it, *donga* did undermine the fixed walls and halls of the existing literary structures and conventions in South Africa. It captured the reality of a new generation and gave voice to its profound contradictions, its myriad cultural clashes and human frailties, its emergent political energies, as well as its hopes and dreams. With many common threads intertwining, doubling back, sometimes unraveling, donga created a matrix of poetic conversation.

On its pages I encountered the wisdom of Lionel Abrahams, the velocity and precision of Lesego Rampolokeng's word bombs, the roiling imagination of Ivan Vladislavić, Aryan Kaganof's political pulp, Graeme Feltham's sex-crazed anti-fiction and so much more. Who else would have had the sheer bravado, to run an interview with Arthur Mafokate on his riotous Kwaito re-claimer "Don't Call Me a Kaffir" along with Greg Latter's dark, unnerving short story "Piccanin (Born in the RSA)"? Where else could you learn "how to put together a book of poems" and "how to shoot a crime"? Rather than trying to build a bridge across the gap that existed between languages and cultures, between literary genres, *donga* simply descended a rope ladder into the chasm itself.

Paul Wessels always said, "The criterion for me is what I like." Whether or not someone agreed with his choice, he stuck to this principle, rigorously. Paul also said, "Good writing is never boring." It's a phrase that stuck with me over the years as a defiant challenge to the white South African literary establishment and the Western novel with its preordained order, its fixed meaning, its causality and noncontradiction.

Paul was a rigorous editor but also a subtle and generous one. He believed the best stories destabilize a reader's view of the world. His approach was always to identify the unsaid possibility within a piece of writing—the tipping point where the writing became unstable, where it faltered or tripped, lost its footing. Hence a sort of precariousness, a feeling

8 Ibid.

that nothing was ever certain, that if something was tried, it might work, or then again not. And more importantly, that that didn't matter.

He was less interested in any kind of experimental formalism than in writing from a place of immediacy, writing "fighting to remain alive and kicking,"[9] slapdash, one might say, texts written in the white heat of a South African summer or a collapsing star. This opened up an enormously exciting territory for a young writer—a space of freedom and of play where one could take risks, fuck up, or, as Graeme Feltham put it, "pluck in the middle of the fucked-upness."[10] Stepping into an antigravity chamber might be comparable, a sense of entering an enormously new context, where the minutest, previously taken-for-granted everyday thing, a swing of the foot, becomes adventurous.

donga was also always as much about reading as it was writing. A culture of critical reading was advanced through regular reviews, interviews and analyses of exciting contemporary writing from around the world. While *donga*'s focus was unashamedly South African, this was not the bunkered South Africa of the apartheid era, but a country in conversation with the larger global literary community. The active conversation that happened as I read and thought towards my own writing gave me a new sense not only of what was necessary, but also of what was possible. As Paul wrote, "to read is to recognise. If in luck one can recognise what one has never seen before. Aha! A new, or another thought. It is rare for all of us, I think. To read is also to be read."[11]

I soon found myself in conversation with other writers on *donga*. This was never forced. There were no prearranged social events or dinner parties. Rather it happened naturally over emails, telephone calls, conversations in bars and coffee bars—out of our shared excitement and our shared fear. Basically we all found ourselves together in a hole. Apart but a whole.

Maybe that (w)holeness is best viewed in retrospect, in the surprising affinities found in the writers' techniques and compositional methods, and also in their use of content. It's there in the interstices of Pravasan Pillay's texts; the shadows of Robert Berold's writing; the mistakes in Graeme Feltham's prose, the blip-outs and flip-outs that "morph good music into good-bumps";[12] the hiccup in Nadine Botha's poems; the buckshot that sprays Aryan Kaganof's novels; the corrigendas that Paul Wessels finds littering Ivan Vladislavi 's *Restless Supermarket*; the line breaks and shudders of Joan Metelerkamp's verse; in Lesego Rampolokeng's short circuits and blown fuses and "x-rayed burn"[13] and Arthur Mofokeng's zero budget music production model; and in Ike Mboneni Muila's stomach ulcer, and the typos that litter Lauren Beukes's short story 'Dear Mariana.'

donga eventually died. Isn't it, after all, the fate of all holes to eventually collapse, to cave in? Without *donga* there was a definite hole, a hole unfilled. Black holes are a complicated phenomenon. They aren't really

9 Ivan Vladislavi, "What Does He Need Me For? [instead of an Interview with Paul Wessels]," in *donga*, eds., P. Wessels and A. Finlay (Johannesburg: BleKSEM, 2012), 118.

10 Graeme Feltham, "Getting Squelchy, Naked and Yummy with Graeme Feltham and the Ordained Inevitable," in *donga*, eds., P. Wessels and A. Finlay (Johannesburg: BleKSEM, 2012), 69.

11 Ibid., 119.

12 Ibid., 75.

13 Lesego Rampolokeng, "Koshun In The Bog," in *donga*, eds., P. Wessels and A. Finlay (Johannesburg: BleKSEM, 2012), 75.

holes but objects that because of density and gravity look like emptiness. Their light is darkness. They do not reflect light but capture it and reflect the absence of light. Maybe then, in its absence, donga remains as significant as it was in its presence. Maybe in its death and its refusal to die, it allows us to ask what's next. How can we operate in the void of today's critical and political apathy? How can quantum mechanics work at the center of a black hole? How does an individual writer function and act in the center of a cultural void?

By the turn of the century, South Africa was in the grips of a rapid, rampant capitalism. For the older generation, it was becoming more and more difficult not to feel the cauterizing contradictions of the post-apartheid era. For old "staffriders" like Mike Abraham, it was impossible not to feel a very uncomfortable nostalgia for the good bad old days:

> *Now, as I wander the new South Africa, around Newtown, Berea, Yeoville, Melville and sometimes Rosebank I see young people chasing a recording deal, funding for one or another project, connections for a show or some publishing contact and I yearn for staffriders, for those who jumped off fast moving trains with the grace of dancers, who did not wait for handouts, dared, defied and took the leap.*[14]

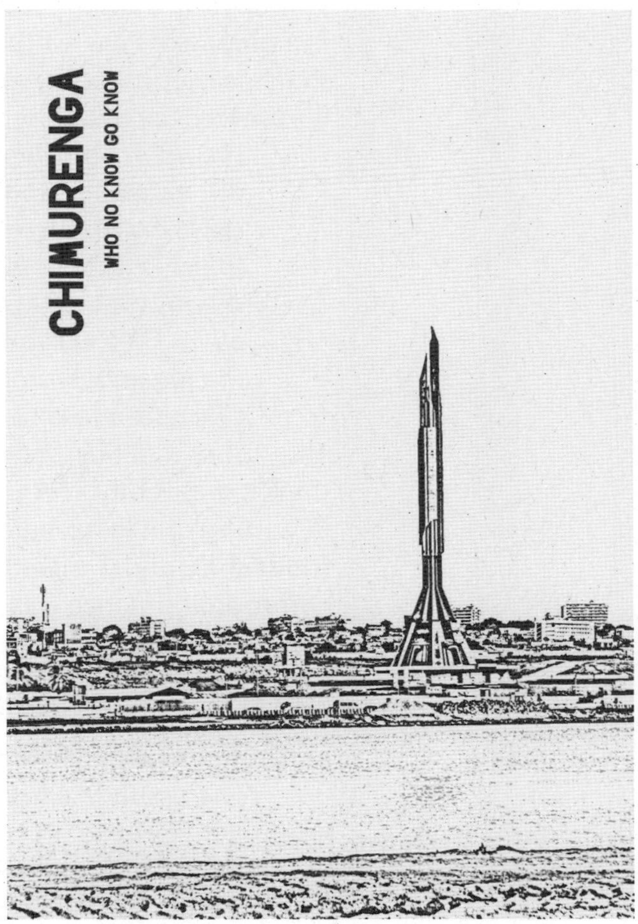

Chimurenga, 12/13, "Dr. Satan's Echo Chamber," March 2008. Reproduced by permission of the Chimurenga Library.

But there are also always holes within holes, and like a black hole, the energy that both *Staffrider* and *donga* created never entirely vanished. It was *donga* that led me inadvertently to the literary journal *Chimurenga*. My first encounter with its editor happened in a small bar in Cape Town. Ntone Edjabe, *Chimurenga*'s Cameroonian-born, Nigerian-educated editor, sidled up to me and in his characteristic low loping growl, said, "I like your 'Nigerian Drug Dealer'." He was referring to a story I wrote for *donga*. We started a conversation that ran from the verbal revolutions of Nigerian pidgin through to silence as a strategy of resistance. Before long I was contributing to *Chimurenga*, and by 2008 I was an editor.

Chimurenga works across a range of platforms, it's a literary journal, a quarterly Pan-African newspaper titled the *Chronic*, an annual reader on African cities, a regular series of pocket literature, and it hosts a Pan-African radio station. The initiative takes it title from Murenga, the name of a mythic Shona warrior. It came to mean the struggle for freedom during the Zimbabwean wars of liberation. It's also the name of the music made popular by political artists such as Thomas Mapfumo. The name is fitting. *Chimurenga* has a fiercely political agenda, but more than that it

14 "Of 'Brothers with Perfect Timing'", *Chimurenga Library*, 2008.

understands that politics is equally expressed through style as it is through content. How you write is as important as what you write.

Ntone isn't interested in writing that doesn't take risks, that doesn't propose something beautiful, new or dangerous. He has little interest in writing with boring structures, boring language. He is interested in publishing literature that is musical and visual and also explosive. Most of all he is interested in our capacity, through imagination and invention, to produce something radically new and original.

Here, like *Staffrider* before it, and in a different way *donga*, *Chimurenga* take its inspiration from everyday life on the continent, from the inexhaustible capacity for innovation that defines even the most apparently superficial instances of life here. It draws on the way we somehow manage to live our lives with joy and creativity and beauty, sometimes amidst upheaval, suffering and violence, and sometimes perpendicular to it. It invites us to imagine our lives and our futures differently.

What *Chimurenga* publishes then reflects what preoccupies us, here and elsewhere, or what preoccupies others we're close to. The project's byline in many ways lays out its agenda. "Who no know go know" is a phrase of Fela Kuti's, exemplifying his wit. In it we hear Fela signaling that knowledge is something that one makes (or takes) rather than merely receives; an active rather than passive process. As Ntone explains:

> *We do not always try to overexplain, overclarify and always justify our existence and say "Well, the reason why we do this is because we are trying to liberate the mind"—No! Not that this would a bad thing, but there is no absolute necessity for us to know why we are doing what we are doing. We are doing it primarily because we are alive. That was a very libratory idea for us and it kind of canalized the ideas behind the design and the writings we take on.*[15]

Chimurenga is made through a process of engaging a different reality, other realities; secretions and accretions of reality to help us see and think it differently. The journal is always produced through a comradeship in writing that is based on human contact, on passionate and committed friendship, and a meeting of minds and ideals. It is produced through a communal practice based in the informal Pan-African networks and circuits that span the globe. Most stories and commissions begin as conversations between friends, colleague, and comrades, in shebeens, urban nightclubs, business meetings, university hallways, taxi ranks, street corners and on skype, facebook, twitter and email.

The result is a language that features an extraordinary cosmopolitan inventiveness. Published work ranges from long form journalism, personal memoir, political analysis, journalism, fiction, historical narrative, polemic tracts. *Chimurenga* publishes primarily in English, but also in French, Xhosa, Arabic, and its pages are charged with pidgin phrases, multilingual neologisms and a sort of slangy insouciance that forces even the most experienced editor to reassess what they know, or think they know.

15 Moses März, "Embracing Opacity: Interview with Ntone Edjabe", *Africavenir* (2011).

Like *donga* then, *Chimurenga* is vividly aware of the link between reading and writing, aware that the best writing always happens in conversation. As Ntone confirms:

> *Generally one starts a publication because they want to add something to the publishing universe they inhabit, to transform it somehow. It's not always the case with commercial publications, but often with small magazines such as* Chimurenga. *I have always admired magazines that imagined a world as much as they reported it—publications such as* Transition, Black Orpheus, Staffrider. *These publications confronted their world but also mediated and shaped it. When I founded* Chimurenga *I wanted to create a space where we could speak with similar force and imagination in this time.*[16]

In 2008 *Chimurenga* started the Chimurenga Library to explore the publications that have influenced its ideas as a publisher; the little magazines, journals and periodicals which have been influential platforms for dissent and which have broadened the scope for print publishing on art, new writing, and ideas in and about Africa. Gathered in an online library, these selections, some dating back to the early 1970s and others appearing in print for the first time, provide an opportunity to trace the diverse networks, influences, dialogues, dialectics, and interventions that have and continue to challenge the official discourse on and from Africa, and the already written history.

Doing the research I was struck by the energy and innovation of many of the journals I encountered. What I seemed to be reading was a secret history of the continent, one that posed a virile challenge to what Achille Mbembe calls "a crisis of language"[17] in writing on Africa in the world and writing the world from Africa, which presents itself in the tendency to presents Africa as a pathological case, a figure of lack—and focuses on what Africa is not (yet) rather than what it is.

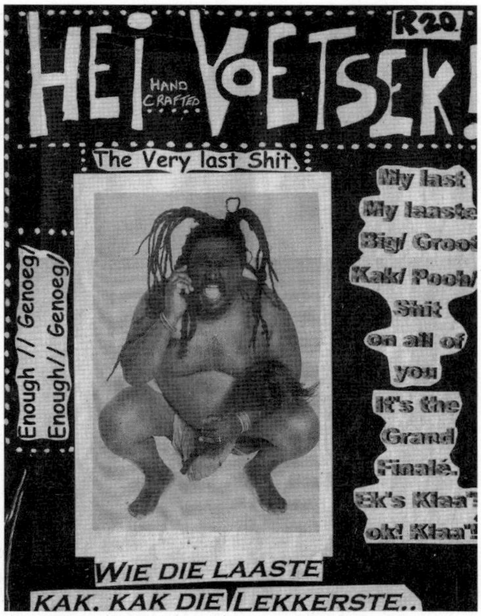

Cover of *Hei Voetsek!* 1, 1997. Reproduced by permission of the Chimurenga Library.

Through page after page of poetry, prose, critique, art and photography—often filled with luminous and fugitive experiences—I learned of the richness or complexity of African social and creative experience. Not only are these journals an astonishing reflection on the past, but they also show how the past resurfaces in the present, lending a new dimension for which we have no name, where the here and now is framed by what was, where memory is transposed by imagination, and where experience through the spell of art is alchemized into eternal moments.

Mostly I was drawn to journals that, like *Staffrider, donga* and *Chimurenga*, seemed to work in and against accepted language, journals that recognized language as inherently problematic and a perpetual sub-

16 D. MacViban, "An Interview with Ntone Edjabe: Breaking Divides (2013)," *The Ann Arbor Review of Books*, accessed on Janurary 10, 2015, http://www.a2review.net/tag/prince-claus-award.

17 Annalisa Oboe, "Africa and the Night of Language: An Interview with Achille Mbembe (2010)," *Johannesburg Salon*, accessed on January 10, 2015, http://www.jwtc.org.za/the_salon/volume_2.html.

ject of inquiry. Journals that featured writing that demands a heightened level of attentiveness and attunement to what language can do on the page and in the social worlds of its making.

My favorites included *Mfumu'Eto*, a Cameroonian comic, self-produced by the one-man guerrilla empire of Mfumu'Eto Nkou-Ntoula, printed using stencils and photocopying machines, and distributed informally in Kinshasa in the early 1990s. Like other comics produced in Kinshasa at the time, it was heavily influenced by urban culture, and smeared with local indiscretions known as "kinoiseries." *Mfumu'Eto* however also drew inspiration from local traditions, combining black magic and religion, pulp fiction and politics, irony and attitude in a wild display of interdisciplinary bravado that directly contested dominant colonial systems of knowledge.

I was similarly inspired by *Hei Votsek!*, (loosely translated: Hey! Get lost!), a diatribe of a publication, that burst upon the Cape Town writing and peddling scenes in 1997, at a time when the South African cultural journals happily basked under the rainbow. Written, designed, drawn, photoshopped and photocopied by self-proclaimed culture terrorist Elliot Josephs aka Zebulon Dread, *Hei Voetsek!* dissected South African politics, culture, society and sex. Using Cape Flats taal, a street-smart mixture of English, Afrikaans and slang, Dread railed against the establishment. As the editorial of the first issue read: "This magazine is just to say we're out there and we don't buy your shit. It's freedom of expression and the means by which a long-suffering artist becomes an entrepreneur, taking destiny into his own hands and out of the devious honkies who so love control."[18]

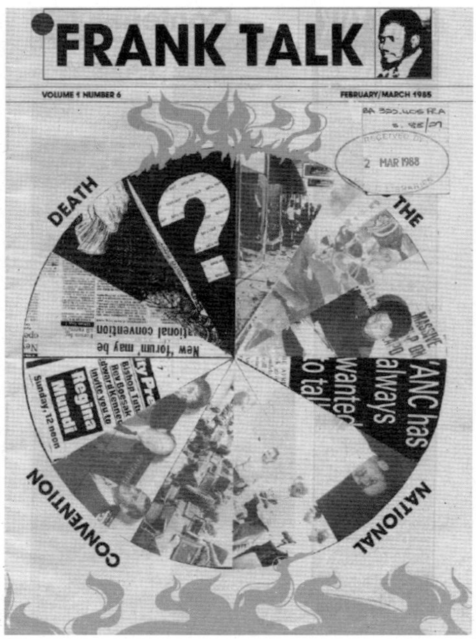

Cover of *Frank Talk* 1, no.6, February–March, 1985. Reproduced by permission of the Chimurenga Library.

Nigerian musician Fela Kuti's "Chief Priest Say" was born of a similar defiance. Bypassing editorial censorship in Nigeria's predominantly state controlled press in the 1970s and 1980s, Kuti began buying advertising space in daily and weekly newspapers such as *The Daily Times* and *The Punch* in order to run outspoken political columns. Published under the title, "Chief Priest Say," these columns were essentially extensions of Fela's famous "Yabi Sessions", consciousness-raising word-sound rituals, with himself as "chief priest", conducted at his Lagos nightclub, the African Shrine. Employing genre malleability, a trickster's penchant for play and language games, withering social satire, incantations and invocations, Fela's writing constituted a literary symphony of dissent and resistance.

Moroccan quarterly magazine, *Souffles* was an equally provocative platform. Founded by leftist intellectual Abdellatif Laâbi in 1966, as a reaction against imperialist and colonial cultural domination, the journal used language as the starting point for revolution. From its first issue, *Souffles* posed an aggressive challenge to the traditional Francophone and Arabophone literary divides by encouraging experimentation, translations and collaborations. This approach birthed a new generation of young subversive writers whose "guerilla linguistique" combined French and Arabic to

18 "Hei Voetsek!", *Chimurenga Library*, 2008.

challenge the hegemony of the French language in Morocco and topple traditional literary models, whose respect for chronology, accuracy, and punctuation they regarded with disdain. Writer Issandr El Amrani recalls, "It was not a magazine that one bought and read in one's living room or at the café; it was a manifesto for a young and diffuse political movement."[19]

There are so many others I could name: *Lamalif*, another Mococcan publication from the 1960s that believed, "the goal in this tragic situation was not to lose hope, to build an alternative"; *FrankTalk*, published in South Africa in the 1980s byThe Azanian People's Organization (AZAPO), a nationalist group committed to Steve Biko's ideas of Black Consciousness; London-based artist and cultural theorist Rasheed Araeen's *Third Text*, a bimonthly international scholarly journal that set out to challenge the West's position as the ultimate arbiter within arts and culture; *Tsotso*, "a magazine of new writing in Zimbabwe," published in the '90s, whose mandate was to undermine the continued colonial domination of literature; *Amkenah* [Places], founded in Egypt in 1999, in direct response to elitism, parochialism and conservatism in the literally scene in Egypt, as well as its Cairo's centralism.

Many of these journals no longer exist. This does not matter. What matters is that they did exist and that their energies, ideologies and imagination lives on in work that is published in other journals on the continent today.

Chimurenga, for its part, continues to reimagine its world. The Chimurenga Library has expanded into a series of exhibitions in libraries around the world. The next of *Chimurenga*'s literary journal is a collaborative novel, while the forthcoming issue of the *Chronic* asks: what if the maps were made by Africans for our own use, to understand and make visible our realities and imaginaries? The issue uses texts and testimonies as data (including fiction, where it provides a deeper truth) to produce beautiful representations of the new that is emerging or reemerging across the continent geopolitically and otherwise. Expect to encounter "secret countries"; Qaddafi's financial and military network; soft power (foreign cultural agencies; the entertainment complex and its relationship with the trendy "Africa Rising"); new trade routes (scrap cities, soccer cities, religious and market cities, drug and prostitution ports and more); water conflicts (tied to land and water grabs); neopats and repats (new and returnees migrants from the West and Asia); pidgins (meeting points of major language groups, spoken and written); transnational armies (that explode the fiction of national armies and various players in armed conflicts). And more.

Chimurenga also just started work on an Arabic edition of the *Chronic*. In the prologue to the inaugural issue of *Souffles*, Laâbi wrote: "Something is afoot in Africa and in other Third-World countries. Exoticism and folklore are falling by the wayside... the day will come when the real spokespersons of these collectives make their voices heard, and it will be like dynamite exploding the rotten arcana of the old humanisms."[20] Almost fifty years later, I can't help wonder, could *Chimurenga* be one of the spokespersons he foresaw?

19 Issandr El Amrani, "In the Beginning There was Souffles (2008)," *Bidoun* 13, accessed January 10, 2015, http://www.bidoun.org/magazine/13-glory/in-the-beginning-there-was-souffles-by-issandr-el-amrani.

20 Ibid.

New Culture[1]

Bisi Silva

One of the lingering consequences of the failure of the postcolonial state is inadequate investment in the development of education. With the rise of authoritarian and dictatorial regimes from the late 1970s to the late 1990s, a frontal attack was made on academia and any form of intellectual life. The plethora of journals, magazines and reviews that followed the euphoria of the independence period were soon to be consigned to obsolescence. Nonetheless, a few have been able to reinvent themselves, outside of the continent. Some of the best known Pan-African titles, which focused on art, culture, politics and society, included *Drum Magazine*, *Black Orpheus* and *Transition*,[2] and they complemented the scholarship that was coming out of the dynamic university presses across the continent at the time.

My discovery of *New Culture: A Review of Contemporary African Arts* highlights the informational vacuum that exists with regards to past critical endeavors. Until Janet Stanley, Chief Librarian at the National Museum of African Art, Smithsonian Institute, offered to provide the library of the CCA, Lagos[3] with copies of the publication, I was not aware of the existence of the review. Only eleven issues underline its brief existence over a fifteen-month period in the late 1970s. During this period in Nigeria, a handful of defunct magazines stood out for their focus on the arts, such as *Nigeria Magazine4* and *Uso: Nigerian Journal of Art*.[5] *New Culture: A Review of Contemporary African Art* placed a particularly strong emphasis on the visual arts. It started with an illustrious editorial team that consisted of important artists based both on the continent and elsewhere, as part of the diaspora, such as the American sculptor Melvin Edwards, the London-based artist Taiwo Jegede, and Nigerian artists such as Demas Nwoko (founder) and Uche Okeke, who were subsequently joined by Ola Oloidi, an art historian and professor at the University of Nigeria.

The review delved into many issues such as identity, colonialism, postcolonialism, as well as history and tradition as they came to highlighting the new African reality, and the way these were engaged by the artists in their work. The key section of the review focused on the aesthetics of African art and culture, which propounded a return to the study of

1 This article was originally published as part of the *Manifesta Journal* #17 "Future(s) of cohabitation." The MJ is published by Manifesta Foundation and is available online and in print at manifestajournal.org.

2 *Drum Magazine* (initially called *African Drum*) was started in South Africa in 1951 by Bob Crisp and Jim Bailey. It was a lifestyle magazine that targeted the black population. However it became popular for its coverage of township life under apartheid in the 1950s and 1960s. *Black Orpheus* was founded in 1957 in Nigeria by German expatriate Ulli Beier as a journal of African and Afro-American literature. *Transition: A Journal of Arts, Culture and Society* was started in Kampala, Uganda in 1961 by Rajat Neogy as a platform for East African intellectuals.

3 Full disclosure: the writer is the director of CCA, Lagos, http://www.ccalagos.org.

4 *Nigeria Magazine* may be the longest running arts and culture magazine in Africa. It was founded in the 1930s and the final volume was published in 1990.

5 *USO: Nigerian Journal of Art* came out sporadically, only managing to release three publications in three volumes (one edition per year) between December 1995 and December 2001.

traditional art, which the founder, artist, architecture, poet and writer, Demas Nwoko (b. 1935) considered to be the "only one art stylistic idiom... valid to the African and the Blacks of African descent the world over, its origin being the well-known form of traditional African arts, a form that was created and nurtured to maturity by African people themselves, with a history that dates beyond 2000 years." In espousing a return to the past he also acknowledged the need for "a new aesthetic position relevant to our time."[6] To achieve these objectives, the reviewers covered the arts across the continent. The drawings by Sudanese artist Ibrahim El Salahi (b. 1930) that were featured in the May 1979 issue are a good example, as they reached out to the diaspora. The eleven editions are filled with reviews and essays, in addition to containing a vibrant children's section that makes palpable the dynamism of the cultural and creative sector of the period. The exhibition review I found to be the most illuminating was that of Theresa Luck-Akinwale (b. 1934),[7] one of the few trained female artists in Nigeria who still remains inadequately represented in the history of Nigerian Art. As such, the eleven editions constitute an indispensable archive of our cultural life in a context where such information remains difficult to find.

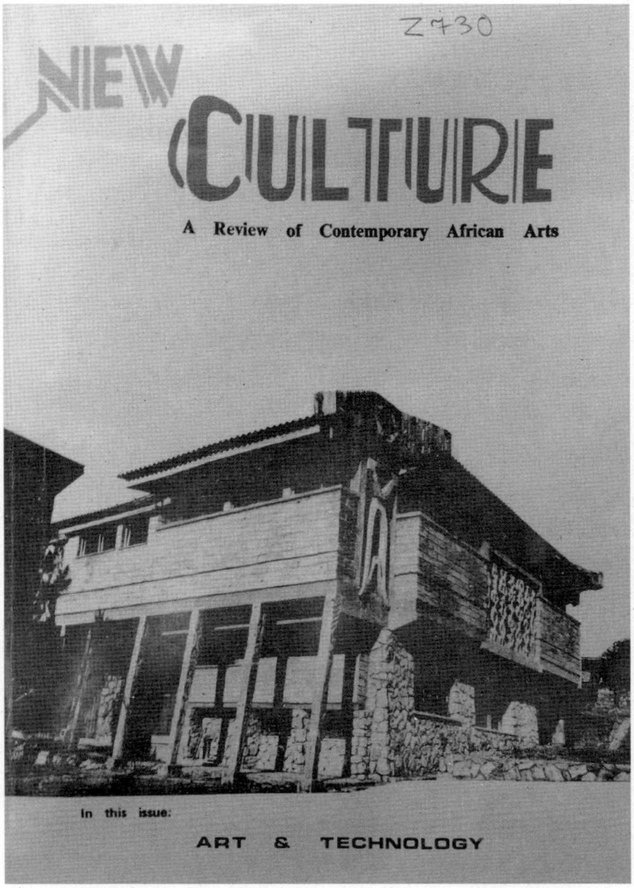

Cover of *New Culture: Art and Technology* 1, no. 7, June 1979. Image courtesy of New Culture Studios, Ore-Meji Heights, Ibadan.

6 *New Culture Magazine* (November 1978): 1.
7 Pat Oyelola, "The Art of Theresa Luck-Akinwale", *New Culture Magazine* (1979): 29.

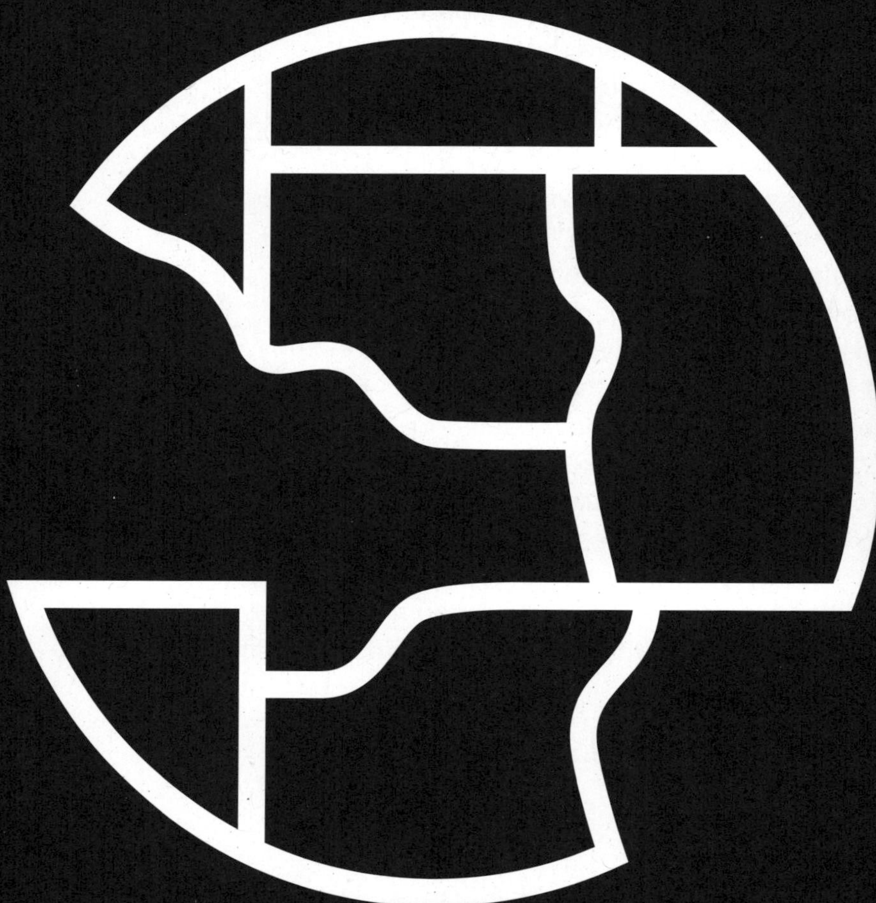

Diggin' or (Yes, Mr. Neogy, Magazines Do Culture... Sometimes)

Bongani Madondo

I

Although when I came around to it a wee-bit later, Rajat Neogy's essay *Do Magazines Culture*? published in *Transition* (Issue 24, 1966), the periodical he founded aged twenty-two in Uganda, has stamped its literary footprints on my mind in ways I have yet to shake off. Can't say I'm exactly in a hurry to.

To this day, I cannot say *fosho* if it was his rhetorical manner of posing the question, or the substance with which he wove, threaded and anchored the argument on the role of magazines in *our*—black and brown folks'—multi-cultural entertainments and psychic self-perceptions, how we look at ourselves and invite the gaze from others, that kept me awake all these years.

Sure you can relate? D'y'know that feeling that strikes you that someone could be on to something, though what exactly needs a bit of sweating hard on the small stuff, paying a bit more attention or just kicking back and waiting with a hunch in your belly that the essence of what's being hinted at, will, somehow reveal itself?

That's how I felt, *listening* to Neogy's question, for it indeed sounded like music to me. What genre, we'd soon found out.

Or not.

Neogy's *song* done gone hooked me on that specific essay and the magazine itself. Coming off age in several spaces—honey, told you my momma was a rolling stone; a single woman in perennial search of a convenient home to raise a bunch of kids—in this village here, that village there, an unforgiving, hard township at some point, and then over there across the main road just beyond the green patch of fertile veld the size of a gigantic soccer field, where the village's cattle graze you will arrive at an Old Money freehold settlement, in Leboneng, northwest of Pretoria, I grew up curious and restless.

Other than my mother's own built book and magazine collection the broader culture was barren, that's if literary entertainment was your kind of thing as it was mine.

I was only introduced to Neogy's cool, if a bit something of an intellectual gladiatorial journal long after my contemporaries elsewhere in the world had heard of, read...nah, worshipped at its alter. Long after it had de-

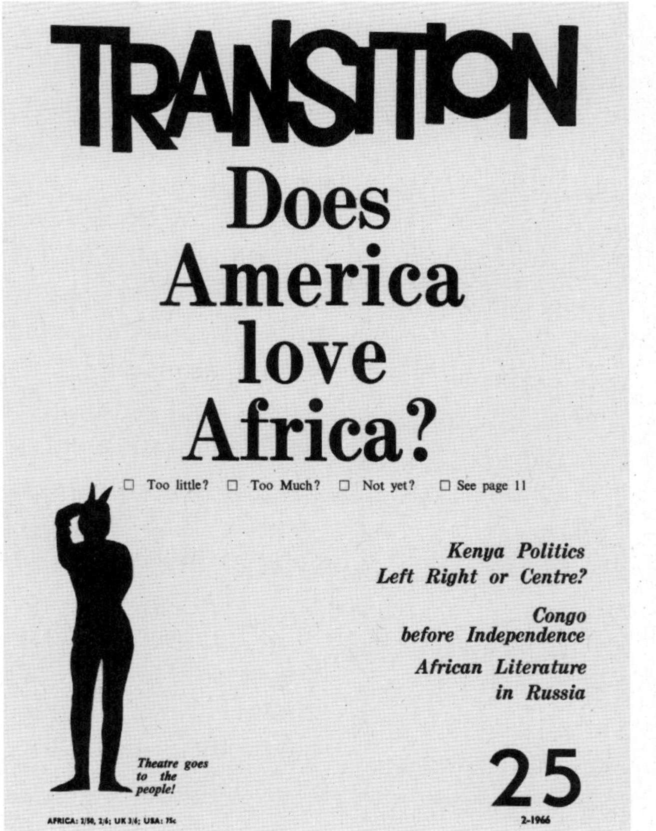

Cover of *Transition*, no. 25, February 1966. Image courtesy of Peter Bonsey and copyrighted by Transition, Ltd., 1966. Reproduced by permission of Indiana University Press.

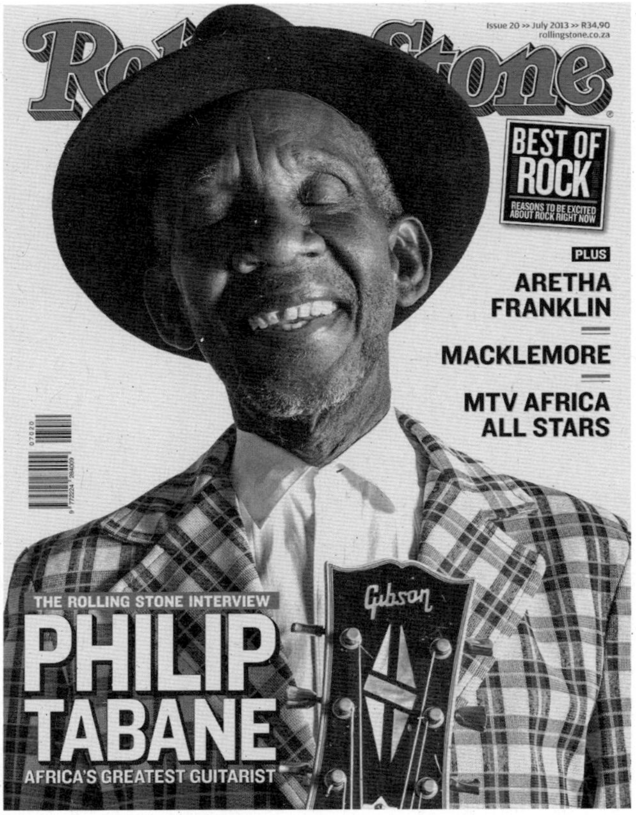

Cover of *Rolling Stone* South Africa, Issue 20, July 2013.

camped from Kampala to Accra and from Accra to Harvard.

The lucky ones among my generation overseas went on to contribute to it, under its magical revolving door of editors from Anthony Kwame Appiah and Henry Louis Gates Jr, Michael Vasquez, Kelefa Sanneh, Tommie Shelby, Vincent Brown and so on.

I first got acquainted with *Transition* much later in 1999 by then, a resident of Johannesburg, by a mutual friend, the England-raised Nigerian writer Ken Wiwa, scion of the famous poet famously slain by the man known as "The Butcher of Abuja," General Sani Abacha.

Wiwa junior, a gifted storyteller with a singular writer's voice distinct from his father's, arrived in Johannesburg to work on a chapter for his then in-the-works memoir *In the Shadow of a Saint*.[1]

He was here to interview the children of South Africa's "Struggle Royalty"—Nelson Mandela's and Steve Biko's—in between paying courtesy calls to Archbishop Tutu and saying hello to "Aunty" Nadine Gordimer.

1999 it was.

His fellow Bri-Gerian (I jokingly refer to cosmopolitan Nigerian children born to first, second or third generation middle class parents in Britain...or is it England?), anyhow, a fellow Bri-Gerian friend of Wiwa's Emeka Nwandiko, then based in Johannesburg, brought him to my digs in Yeoville, the once Jewish bohemian village and now African metropolis slap-bang on the east wing of the city, for dinner.

Two weeks later Wiwa and I were still there. Discussing everything, and everyone there was to discuss; harmlessly gossiped a bit about other writers, as is writers' nature, admired and quarreled with their ideas and shared a lot about literature and specifically magazines and journals in that fleeting moment he was there.

Just when he was about to leave, heading back to London, Naija or Canada, he pulled two books, dog-eared books, out of his rucksack and slapped them on the kitchen counter by way of settling his lodgings.

I felt already way over compensated just by his presence.

Spending time with another writer, especially one with a different background to yours is pure gold-dust for writers and I believe all sorts of artists. For me it was gold-stock in the transient cultural stock exchange that binds us all in this biz called journalism, or so-called "serious" literature, meaning fiction.

"Haba! Oga-o," he playfully shouted. Pretending to be outraged by the thought.

1 Ken Wiwa, *The Shadow of a Saint*, New York: Alfred A. Knopf, 2000.

"You mean you have not come across or read these?" He slapped a brand new copy of *ww* and Salman Rushdie's essay collection *Homelands* on the kitchen counter.

"There's just no way you have not come across this."

With that, swoosh!, he was gone.

He left a copy of what was once Neogy's "baby" which by then had found a home (at Harvard's Institute for African and African American Research) far away from *home* geographically although scarcely removed, I'd love to believe, from its founder's cultural and literary ambitions.

It is fifteen years since Wiwa left and the question he, inadvertently came bearing—like a tweeting bird flip-flapping over the vast African borders, across the Atlantic—even on behalf of Neogy, haunts me to this day: *Do Magazines Culture*?

II

Late last year, at the time the editors (of this publication) asked me to consider performing an essay on the subject "Magazines You Grew up Reading," part of my mind meandered back to Neogy, who, because I had never metremained a fictional character to me, but also for the great legacy he'd gifted the world with, felt like a mentor I never had.

I actually do not have a riposte as it is, although his question, rather an argument for the need for magazines and journals to commit and believe in an ideal, whatever the ideal; say African—and not traditional, nationalistic or consciouss indigenization merely as a bulwark against the colonial West's onslaught—has stirred something quite profound in me.

I never, for a moment, imagined magazines, by their nature possessed such powers. Here am I now stepping back to my youth, in present real time, to assess and romance with magazines that had radically shaped a greater part of my youth, by extension, the self I'm drawing from to critique a past then in formation.

I arrived in cold and unforgiving Hillbrow, Johannesburg's multicultural borough with only sixty cents; a homeless nomad, university drop-out, barely out of his teens. The only thing that mattered then was the inexplicable constant search for identity and something to put in the tummy.

Back then I was also nursing dreams of making it as a fiction writer. I had nothing at all, no friends, relatives and nothing to my name 'cept ambition. As it turned out, it was also the time I reacquainted myself with magazines, a journey that began around the age of five.

I was one of those weird types with no address at all always reading magazines freely in the magazine kiosks and corner café shelves in the city that never so much sleeps as throws you a wink.

Sometime I'd lurk around libraries, with no library card. Often, I'd sneak in and stay there until the librarian coughed twice; a signal to me, and some homeless old man who, like me, had made the library his home, that the library hours have long ticked-tocked, ticked-tocked and hey, tomorrow's another day, gentlemen. Until then, I had always confused *Rolling Stone* the magazine with the name of that band of wiggly-*waist*-ed geriatrics.

By the time I discovered the magazine *Rolling Stone*, its grand-sleazed-out, gonzo, literary, jazzy and psychedelic allure had long faded off.

Although still helmed by Jann S. Wenner, gone was its gonzo-spirit; as was its cinematic, immersion style of narrative later embalmed as *New Journalism* by one of the magazine's contributors, the white suited elf, Tom Wolfe.

Gone were the "Noise-boys": Bangs, Tosches, Meltzer, et al, and their descendants. Gone also was the alternative dream, gobbled up by the 1980s and Reaganomics and the bloated second arrival of harmless pop-culture since, well, the late 1950s postwar boom.

Gone also was Robert Palmer's mystic excursions into otherworlds. Early in the 1970s after a chance meeting with the magazine's editor-publisher Wenner at the author of *Dispatches*, Michael Heller's digs in Manhattan, Palmer copped an assignment to head out to then mystical Morocco, perhaps pursuing William Burroughs or his longtime pal Brion Gysin. Up there, he discovered, as now recounted in his posthumous collection *Blues & Chaos* (Scribner), the sacred Jajouka villages, Phoenician temple ruins, right deep into the ancient Afro-Islamic trance music of Gnawo. About these discoveries, he set out to pen a series of literary sonic testimonials delivered through vivid pieces such as, "Up the Mountain" ("We Fell through Each Other, Weightless, Into the Sky") excerpted in *RS* October, 1971.

Oi', by the time I got my hands on the magazine all that too was gone. What I now know of is way after the fact. Clearly, I arrived to read about the greatest party in the pop-cultural tent twenty years after the last, gloriously drunk guest had crawled home.

And yet, even in the graveyard of a once soul-altering magazine, I found my journalistic gold-dust. The 1990s version was the *Rolling Stone* of *my* and Kurt Cobain's generation and not my hero Nick Tosches' time.

It spoke to my age, my era, my dreams, anxieties, my sexy, my rock'n'roll, my punk, my funk, my politics, my bullshit, my uncertainty, more than any magazine on the shelves then.

Not only did it capture my soul, this "Rolling Stone" *cultured* me Mr. Neogy.

The writing was something I more than related to: It was me! Especially, back then the screeds of the single-named curiosity called Touré.

Touré's soul-quenched *Neo-Soul Journalism*; itself a combo of Nelson George's understated nuance, NAACP-era pull *ya*-self by the bootstraps, Jim Crow-era front-store religious sermonizing and the grittier, swingier, edgier, *New-Jack Journalism* happening just across town at *Vibe* Magazine, gifted us, children of those denied the right to dream with a right to do just that.

Although Touré could never ever be, say, as cerebral cineaste as Armond White was, as operatic as Hilton Als, nor as techno-genius as Kodwo Eshun was, he was something black writing at that time seemed in need of: for the 1990s, the sort of new blackness James Baldwin exhorted his little nephew to dream about, knowing too well the dream might soon become deferred in *The Fire Next Time.*

At his best he performed his *Gonzo-Soul* journalism in total mimicry of—better still, elevated—the very performances of those he reported about.

For a time, I felt a ball of fire and disgust, wondering, as they say in Anglo West Africa, *whycome* his series of biographical sketches of the pain of Lauryn Hill never scooped a Pulitzer?

But *soul brotha* was not the only one in the 1990s *Rolling Stone* tent of gifted testifiers.

When cats such as Neil Strauss went out to profile say, Courtney Love, or headed out on the road with the Mötley Crüe, survived and came back to tell the tales, a reader instinctively realized they were bewitched by nothing else but magic at its darkest genius.

Only in between *Rolling Stone's* sheets, even a defanged *Rolling Stone*, could you find as eclectic a variety as David Fricke, Greil Marcus, Anthony De Curtis, PJ O'Rourke, Lola Ogunnaike, and for me the prime example of a rock scribe as a shaman, Mikal Gilmore.

At Touré's *Rolling Stone* almost all of those smart-word slingers were white.

For a boy raised with a healthy diet of Steve Biko's *negritudinal* philosophy of blackness, the periodical's whiteness (that's before all American media latched on the black-originating, all-cannibalizing term, "Urban Culture") t'was always going to send me into an existentialist crisis all *heart-core* Afropunks had dealt with at some point of their moshing.

And so I kept on movin.'

Searchin.'

Diggin'...

III

Johannesburg: summer of 1992.

The new *Afropolis*: Defiant, show-offy, pouty, reckless, totally African in make up without managing that distinct Pan-Africanism that Lagos, Kinshasa, parts of Paris and New York City have.

Here was a Johannesburg at the cross roads. A city desperate to curate a new image, in a country gripped uncomfortably between a racist past and the scary future unknown. Mandela had just been out for a year. The stillborn revolution was indeed televised.

South Africa was thick with excitement, anticipation and tension.

Out of those streets issued forth a new musical expression forged out of a mélange of Detroit's "house", "mbaqanga," and of course nascent "rap" beamed through the telly from Gotham City's boroughs of the Bronx and Harlem, the uptown African republic in whose salons and dives black artists birthed a post-Depression (1920s) black-elegance, innovations and hustle—*The Renaissance*.

Johannesburg heat was unbeatable.

Down the local Nu Metro cinema on Pretorius, abutting corner Edith Cavell, the block I prowled night and day, Quentin Tarantino's *Reservoir Dogs* charted unchartered areas of gross, pastiche violence, especially the manner in which blood oozed from his victims as some kind of *avant-pop* art, or *avant-prop*.

In my country, then still gripped in the internecine wars between African hostel dwellers from the rural areas, and the over-politicized city's young and restless who foolishly, as per all youth, still itched for a *real* revolution, bloodletting was not as visually attractive.

Shit was real.

They shot to kill. To this day I will never forget the day a bunch of Zulu impis armed to the teeth cornered and shot at us, a group of youths.

In Johannesburg, baby, they hacked each other with real machetes, blades running deep into the ribcage of both father and son, leaving and scores of women howling at the African ancestors, when not singing dirges for their lost hubbies and sons.

Back then, we had no such fortune of listening to redemption songs. Instead of reflecting, as pop radio is faintly expected to, radio right across all channels was dead.

No innovative play-listing, no socially engaging talk-radio, the sound of nothing and aural death was deafening.

Sadly, despite the bells and cymbals of agitation and loud bangs of anxieties pervading the air, there was not a single magazine I felt captured either the city or the country's zeitgeist. Once again, I turned my sights across the black Atlantic.

Or maybe once receiving harbor in the black Atlantic, the African American pop story (for there, essentially is only *one* story, from which every other incarnation, narrative, chapter and testimonial issues from, the "Blues") found me, a man on the run from his physical past, in my restless city of Hillbrow, Johannesburg.

Could be said there was and there's still nothing revelatory about this: lost and found by America in our own country.

Going back to the late nineteenth century, my forbearers in literature and the arts, simply among the founding fathers of all of Africa's black modernity, had themselves been "lost", found, (mis)educated, rescued and influenced by the potent and accessible Negro culture, in post-Gold Rush Johannesburg and elsewhere: Sophiatown, District Six and Marabastad.

IV

The first issue of *Vibe* magazine—which I've archived to this day—reeked of an insubordinate don't-fuck with me air.

On the cover—a profile portrait penned by Kevin Powell—was a proto-nativist image of a fiercely fit, topless African man who could be anywhere in any period. Looking at him, 1920s images of missionaries and explorers resurfaced from the self-suppressed conscious: Africans in Sundiata's Bamako, tribal warriors in the Sudan, street boys, from the Paris *banlieue*s, hardened Bloods and Cripps cats out of L.A.'s "brothers" (black/latino) hoods, postcard snapshots of India's devout Hindus after purification ceremonies in the Ganges.

Dang! He could've been a teenage me and my friends after a swim in the treacherous local Tshwane river in Hammanskraal.

The cover star, Treach of Naughty, then the face, the body and the spiritual representative of Naughty by Nature, one of the popular and belligerent rap outfits of the time, looked as ungovernable, as Maasai-chic...princely, even.

Right there and then, something stirred in me.

The magazine spoke to the restless, angsty, searching soul in me as it would have, then, thousands of those black like me.

I felt both a sense of liberation and uplift.

It struck me there and then that here was a magazine that knew and spoke of my, and my generation's, inner secrets and dreams. Who we are, not what we desired as much as what we will claim.

There was the magazine that would feel, in its editorial pulse, our darkest and most erotic dances, a magazine that'd lay bare the rhythm of the voices in our heads, hold a key to our code-speak, slang, temper and report all that in a tempo and beat, inherently ours.

No doubt the magazine also pandered to the uneducated, unchallenged masculinities of the time in all subcultures, and marginalized communities dotting the globe.

It assumed a laddish spirit, though unlike the British laddish culture, with its twin tropes of football obsession and slacker culture.

It became, quite simply assumed the symbolism of a young defiant man: Latino toughie from Spanish Harlem, Pantsula stylist from Soweto, flossing brother from uptown New York or "rude" *bwoy* from Kingston, Jamaica.

In *his* company and era, we never as much looked back as dug deep into our yesterdays, if only to mine the reservoirs of nostalgic blackness. With him, we dreamt we could rule the world—imagine that.

Check: Black Renaissance style? We swagged and updated it. Proof? Janet Jackson's *Got Till It's Gone video. Vibe* Blues poetry? We re-imagined it as slam. Funk? We invested it into West Coast gangstah cultural stock-exchange, and cashed it out of the dense and "Dirty South" *stankonia* as per Mr. André Benjamin's futuristic sermons.

Did I, a semi-village boy in Africa even care or know what "stankonia" meant? Not an inch. Only that it carried the right dosage of putrid energy and almost hyper-physical pulchritude beats in one, if you can imagine it.

As for the general writing, the magazine created space for a new ways of expression without totally tossing the stylistic forbears, Chester Himes, Larry Neal, Amiri Baraka, Keorapetse Kgositsile, the "*sin*-thesis" curmudgeon spirit of Melvyn Van Peebles with the wild style of a Fab 5 Freddy and so on.

In *Vibe* journalism, though the slang and context was different to mine, I could hear the similar sounds of my folk's jazz attitudes, the raucous and merry chaos of never ending village weddings, and picture the pimp-roll shuffle of older township *tsotsis* I knew back home.

The story of me and *Vibe* is the story of my life, almost. It certainly is the story that best narrates how I got into this art-racket called journalism, or aspects of it: cultural, sociopolitical and profile writing.

Thus it is beyond mere memoir. It is a full-on, galloping, fat, raging, anecdotal autobiography and some more. Because of that I can afford to be at least honest, somewhat.

Unlike my forbearers' favorite periodical, *Drum* magazine, or my mother's beloved *Pace* (South Africa's township middle class glossy journal founded and funded by the apartheid government's Department of Information) I felt *Vibe* lacked ass-kicking cover visuals.

Sure, there was that black and blue-ish sepia October 1993 cover with Wesley Snipes. The image looks inspired, if not evocative of otherworldly sexy, on its own. Underneath the *Vibe* mast it, again, projected fantastic imageries of an African warrior, or sage or North West African groom (in cultures where men's looks are more valued than the opposite sex), ready for the taking.

How about that now famous June/July 1997 cover of Tony Braxton buck-naked bar a piece of white towel covering just the bare essentials?

Although not as racy as Ms. Braxton's cover the Mary J. Blige cover just three months earlier, as moody as any worthy heir of Dinah Washington, Letta Mbulu and 'Retha Franklin should be: Mary in a turquoise get-up, astride a chair, no smile, no bullshit, no cover lines at all 'cept "Hip Hop Soul Survivor", messed up my head, hormones and just about the way I proceeded to listen to her music in ways I can only describe as heart-snatched.

Overall though, the art of covers, I am afraid, were not the magazine's strength. Helmed by the sharp, philosophical style maven, the director of photography, *Vibe's* photo-desk was not quite visually blind.

The very restrictive frame of the cover page has never allowed much artistic transgression in traditional lifestyle magazines, and *Vibe* at heart was a lifestyle product. The inside pages offered a different visual gist altogether.

In between the *Vibe* sheets, photographers such as Marc Baptiste, Piotr Sikora, Lyle Ashton Harris, Mpozi Mshale Tolbert, Jonathan Mannion, Koto Bolofo, Catalina Gonzalez, Dana Lixenberg, David LaChapelle, Albert Watson and Norman Watson among others, conspired to tell a wide variety of wildly, urban, inspired, pop documentaries and portraits fit for both the Louvre and Harlem's Studio Museum, the boulevard and the the black boys *On the corner*.

I will echo James McBride, the writer who, by his own admission, "slept through the entire revolution" of his lifetime, hip hop.

In the 2007 essay "Hip Hop Planet" in *National Geographic* which took him from New York to corners as far as Dakar's medina, McBride speaks of hip hop as "dipped-deep in the boiling cauldron of race and chaos." You could have same about this magazine.

V

One of the reports from beyond America's frontiers I remember fondly, if not with shock (some of the photographed artists carried AK47s, live ammunition and made no apology for it) was a piece simply titled "Rebel Music" written by one of the culture's pioneers Fab 5 Freddy. He'd flown to the heart of Rio de Janeiro's shantytowns to report about Brazil's booming rap scene. I remember Fab 5's establishment shot-like opener as though it was yesterday.

"Think of Brazil and the first images that come to mind are the massive freak-fest of *carnival*, soccer, samba, and exotic women cavorting on booty-full beaches. But as I saw for myself when I visited for two weeks last January, Brazil is more like a ticking bomb, especially in its largest city, Sao Paolo and Rio…"

Boom!

You just had that feeling deep from your belly that what followed was indeed a "freak fest" you, dear reader, would've felt so blessed not to be part of, but even more elated for reading about its empathetic insights.

For a reader, it did feel like strange things happened wherever it was that *Vibe* was put together and it seeped through into the pages. Rare among magazine, in *Vibe* virtues such as empathy were expressed interchangeably and sometimes in the same story, with freewheeling gonzo. The two should not work but they did.

Take for example Kevin Powell's work, especially his first interview with Tupac or whenever he told stories of fatherlessness or the lack of black male role models.

The man spoke from the depth of his belly. His sentences and sub-texture issued from the traditions of gospel pastors even when he was reporting on the most debauched of stories.

In addition to, and beside Powell, I kept a *Dream-Team* list of writers the magazine was never the same without: B nz Malone, Joan Morgan, Scott-Paulson Bryant, Cheo Hodari Coker, Greg Tate, Charlie Braxton and Kris X.

In retrospect, I would've loved to read a wider diverse voices such as Paul Beatty, Barry Michael-Cooper, Kodwo Eshun, Chris Abani, Ben Okri, Yvonne Bynoe, Kevin Young, Ntone Edjabe, David Toop, Mikal Gilmore, Knox Robinson, Armond White, ZZ Parker, Sanyika Shakur, Alain Mabanckou, Kelefa Sanneh, Emily Raboteau, Ta-Nahesi Coates, Sandile Dikeni, the artists Tricky, Terence Trent D'Arby, Saul Williams, Keziah Jones, and so on, etching their eclectic and electric *Blackness* across Vibe's pages, yessah, Mr. Gilmore, too. What did Toni Morrison once say about Bill Clinton's cultural capital?

Ehe!

If I were to single out a writer who impacted on me deeply, largely because I have this funny itch that we both, separately and in different periods, owed healthy doses of influence to Amiri Baraka's performative, blues-funk manner of weaving words, the cadences, or attempts, of his Yoruba/Zulu/Mandinka/ Nuban dance of the ghosts on the page, Greg Tate comes to mind.

To single out this or that piece of work he has done, even in as niche a platform as *Vibe* is to shoot oneself on the foot. Well, the world with self-mutilated feet wounds. I will gladly join their ranks.

One piece he performed for the magazine that reacquainted me with the African healing gifts in my own family, a journalistic work that—against all odds—transported me back to my hollering, shrieking, quaking, rock 'n roll African village of initiates, seers and rain-prophets, is the profile he did on Carlos Santana.

Riding high on the back of a collaborations-feast of an album *Supernatural*, not to make light of the renewed mad love thirty years after the 1971 chart-topping *Santana III*, Carlos was enjoying his late career's second-act and maybe, truly his last.

Thing is though, he was a relic of a psychedelic age and only a few of the 1990s new urban culture arbiters truly knew of his place in the African-Tex-Mex pantheon.

Tate was one of the few and so was dispatched to talk to rock's shaman at his home in California.

The resulting piece in the September 1999 issue (the one with a moodier Mary J. red cover, and yes! Yes!), affirmed what I've always felt but unable to express about a certain strand of rock 'n roll. "I do not play [the] blues. I do not play rock. Neither do I play jazz nor Latin music. What I do is; I play African music. "

Santana and Tate in conversation? Initiates of shamanistic traditions of storytelling, be they carried through the media of song, or in a silent way that some of the most open minded writing sometimes manages.

Although Tate (to attempt a lame Tate-ass'ness) was one of a band of real bad *muthahs* on the magazine. Many of us growing into our own skin in the 1990s tended, like people in generations prior, and many after us will, obsess on the game of compare and contrast and reducing everything to winners and also-rans: great versus greatest, etc.

It's our weakness.

Hey I'm a former perpetrator of that narrow score-keeping, too: "Pac or B.I.G.? New Order or Joy Division?" Back in the early 1990s many tended to throw the quite distinct literary journalistic styles and hearts of, say Tate in some kind of race-track battle with Powell's. The one writer whose work I imagined hustled heart for affections on the very same scale as Tate's profiles and "Black Owned" columns in *Vibe* was Bönz Malone.

There just was some glorious bounciness: a Nobel Prize winning, dice rolling pimp-ology about this Duke of hip hop streets. Listen here: Have you ever read the short piece in which he dissected and almost tossed away John Singleton's entire career under the bus?

The night I read it I wept for Singleton as much as I wept joyously at the manner in which the man who called himself "The Concierge" separated progressive black love from the ever required, though in less supply, black self-critical engagement within our communities, globally.

"The Concierge" affirmed me. In not so many words, Malone's crit gently nudged me: go ahead and risk being unloved, if only momentarily, on your own.

VI

By the end of the second decade of the twenty-first century, *Vibe* was no longer what it used to be. Neither was I. I love to fib to myself, that today, I, cultured, Mr. Neogy. Did some of the editorial lights show the *way, your way, our way,* the way of "The Healers," too?

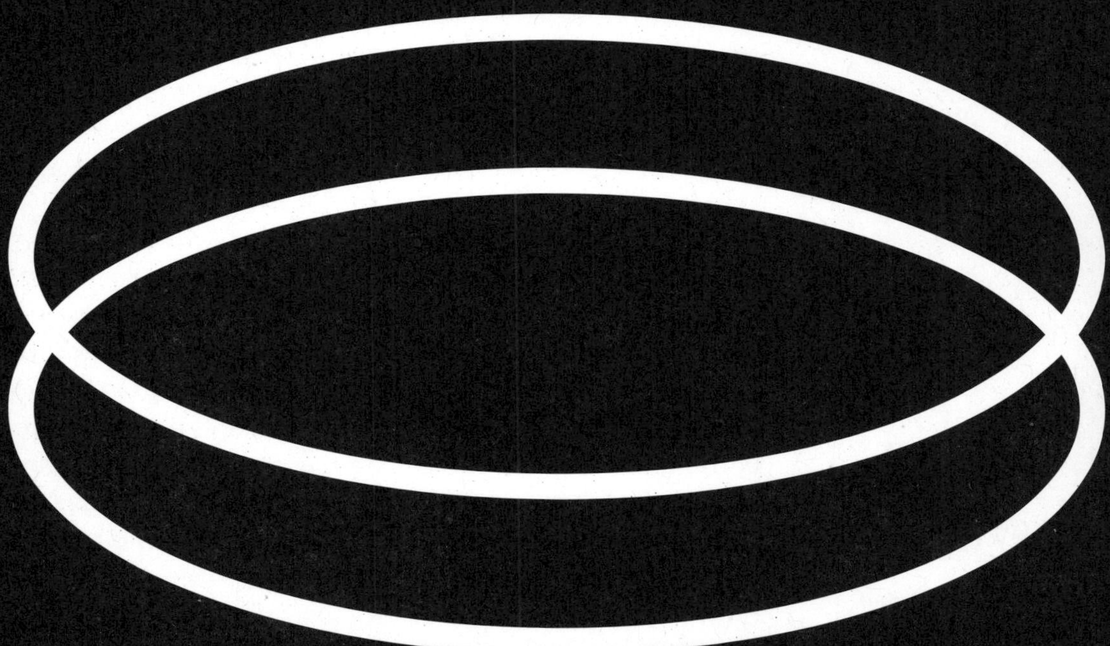

African Jazz:
A Mix by Max Annas & Gary Minkley

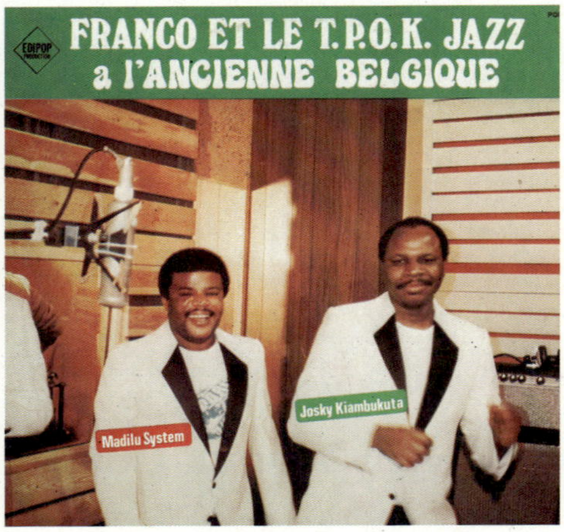

1
Franco et le T.P.O.K. Jazz
A l'Ancienne Belgique

It was 1984 when Franco and T.P.O.K. Jazz recorded this album in Belgium, named after a local hall where they had played. There are not many covers which talk so directly about the music they represent. The record is full of beauty and improvisation, sweet vocals and sax choruses, but the most sublime moments are produced by the work of the guitars. Gerry Diulangana is the official lead but only second after Franco. His role means that he is the first to answer to the Maitre's ideas and solos. Bass player Gege Mangaya and the third guitar of Deca Mpudi are building the foundation of beats and licks to shine on.

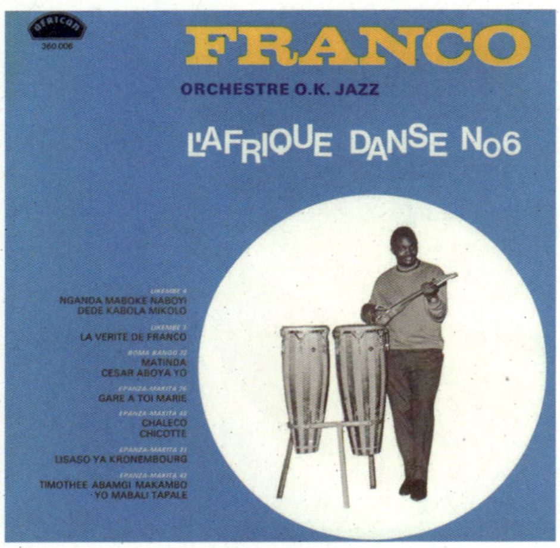

2
Franco Orchestre O.K. Jazz
L'Afrique Danse No 6

The cover of the compilation misrepresents the music. It suggests light sounds, a good mood and maybe a beer in the late afternoon. But Franco at that time had something else in mind. Most of the songs were recorded in the years after Mobutu Sese Seko declared himself president of the country now called Zaire. That was in 1966. And Franco's music and his storytelling reached a depth that was new to Congolese popular music. Every guitar solo told a story, as did every vocal chorus and any intervention of the saxophone. Under suspicious political circumstances Franco reinvented the format and the soul of Congolese rumba—but the cover avoids telling that story.

3

Le Mystère Jazz de Tomboctou

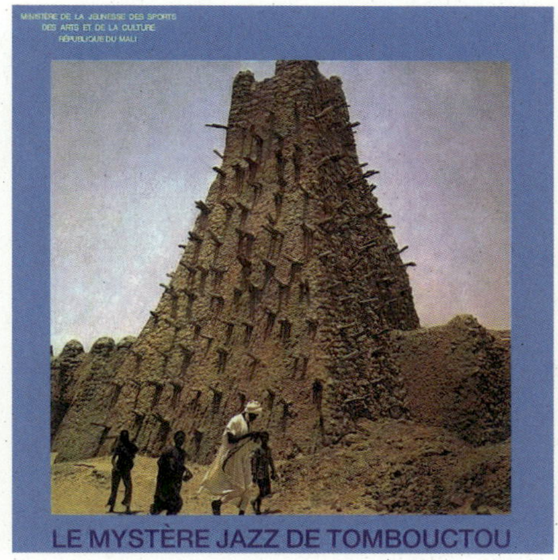

Avoiding any genre, this band of non-professionals created a record that showed the radicality of Malian popular music at its time in 1977. With roots deep in the local culture of Northern Mali, the band with the two guitars and the brass section of a sax player and two trumpets is full of astonishing breaks, attacking guitar playing and the horns trying to deliver a louder response to the guitars' already loud call. Saxophonist Baba Napoleon certainly has listened to the avant-garde of jazz sax players in the U.S. and gives their idea of sound a completely new meaning in a completely new environment. The long out-of-print album was reissued at the time when Islamist forces terrorized Timbuktu and destroyed any cultural expression they could get their hands on.

4

Ry-Co Jazz

Dansons... avec le Ry-Co Jazz

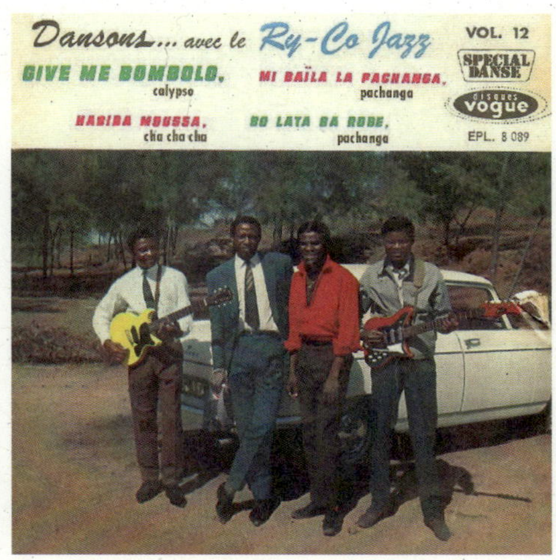

Ry-Co Jazz was one band among many in Kinshasa, one of too many. Because of the competition the musicians moved in every direction, but no band moved as far as Ry-Co Jazz, which in the beginning, in 1958, meant *Rythmes Congolais*. While others ended up in Kampala, Nairobi or Dar-Es-Salaam, Ry-Co Jazz moved west along the coast up to Senegal where this EP was recorded and the photo with the Peugeot 404 was taken. That was in 1963. They did not stop there. They crossed the Atlantic and spent four years touring the Caribbean islands, recording with legendary producer Henri Debs in Guadeloupe. In 1971 they moved to Paris and disbanded.

5

National Service Jazz Band & Baba Mkwe

We We Rafiki

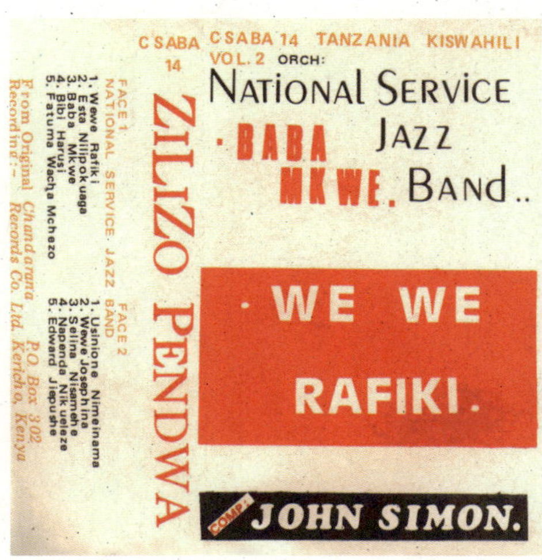

Listening to "Tenderly" or "Leap Frog" of the U.S. Army 76th AG Band where Albert Ayler survived a couple of years before the Free movement gave him an opportunity to express himself, answers—in a way—the question if there ever could be a connection between jazz and the army. What Ayler was playing with the army band is not what we see as jazz, because jazz is determined by more than the melody itself. In Tanzania it might have been a bit different, but it certainly was about money too. This cassette, influenced by Congolese rumba and played by a largely unknown band, might be the output of musicians sponsored by the army. Instruments were expensive, so support was welcome. There is one similarity between the music of the US army band and the band from Dar. They both do not play jazz.

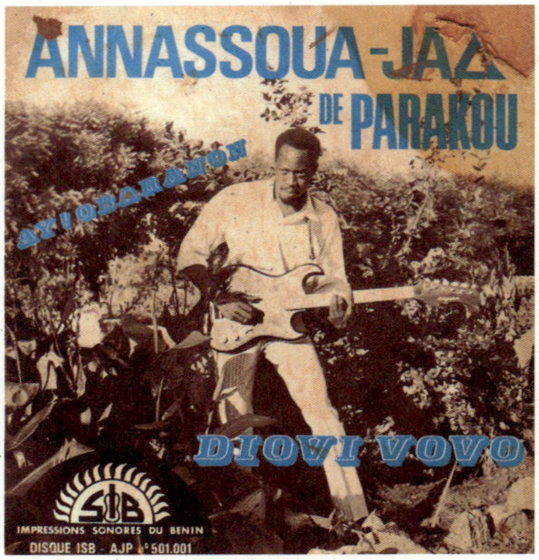

6
Annassoua-Jazz de Parakou
Diovi Vovo, Ay! Obaranon

Rock'n Roll. With a strong element of Afrobeat. This EP from the city of Parakou in Central Benin is the product of a cultural initiative that started with opening a pressing plant called SATEL (Societé Africaine de Techniques Electroniques) in Dahomey, Benin since 1975, on the highway between Cotonou and Porto Novo. In the 1970s there was a growing demand for new music and there were lots of opportunities for local bands to release their music commercially. Alidou Boukari who led Annassoua and later Orchestre Anos Band de Parakou took influences from all over the West African subcontinent and transformed them into one of these hybrids which characterized so much of popular music from that small West African country with that enormous output.

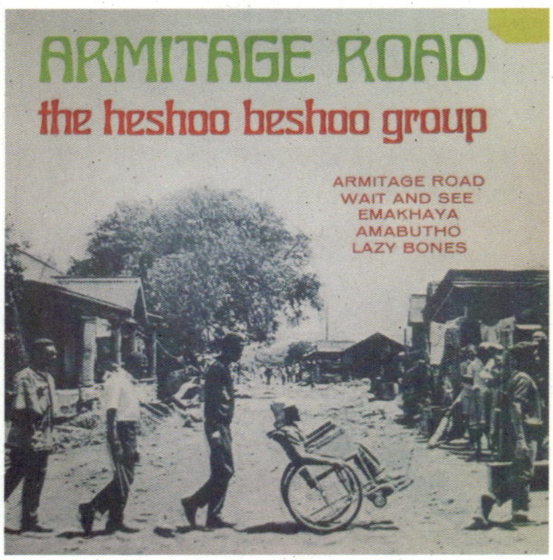

7
The Heshoo Beshoo Group
Armitage Road

The only cover in the series where the term jazz is missing. The only band in the series which was actually playing jazz. Fusion is maybe what we would say today. The beat is steady and keeps on going, but the solos contradict the idea of a sound that only wanted to please the drinking audience. It is still the 1960s, and these solos are rougher than the laid-back design of the sound would prepare you to expect them to be. They show an aggressiveness and an edge that the genre had lost with the many jazz musicians who had left the country. The cover shows the road in Orlando, Soweto that gives the album the title.

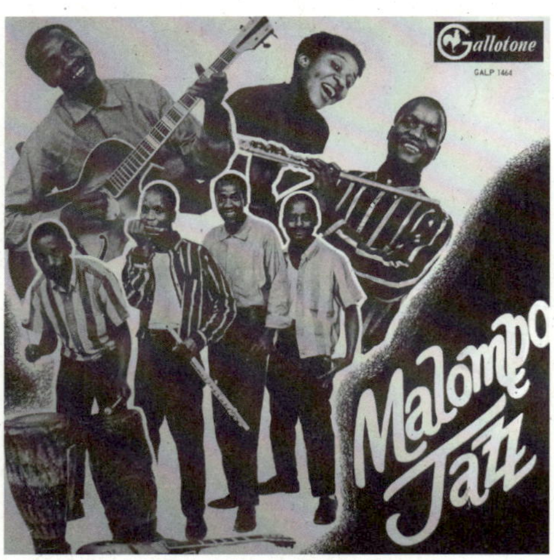

8
Malombo Jazz Makers
Malombo Jazz

A highly creative music that needed a label. The Malombo Jazz Men split into Malombo, led by guitarist Philip Tabane, and The Malombo Jazz Makers, led by drummer Julian Bahula. The dense communication between the drums, the flute or harmonica and the guitar doesn't rely on any kind of imported style or role model. But jazz was the sound of the 1960s in South Africa, so why not make this unique music part of the movement? Sometimes, especially when the harmonica dominates the song, you want to think of the music as a local, a South African version of the blues. But then... It is too much just its own music, its own style. Perhaps the most distinctive sound the country has ever produced.

9
The Soul Jazzmen
Inhlupeko (Distress)

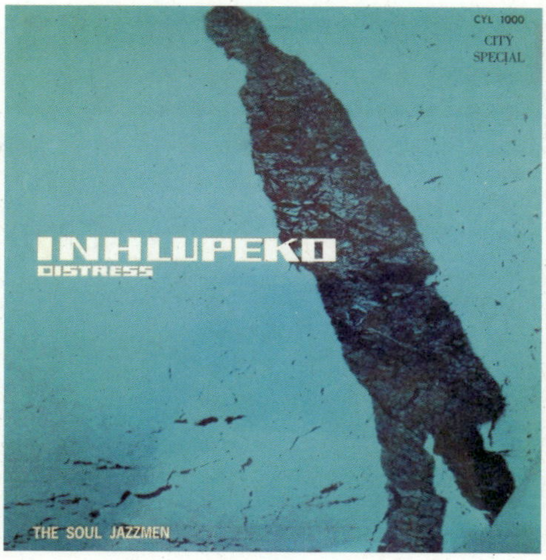

Saxophone colossus! The Sonny Rollins cover. It comes to mind amidst the shadowy granite like figure. And that's perhaps, not just the coincidence of our eye. Perhaps these are some of the first rare recordings of one of South Africa's saxophone colossus. On this recording, January 1969, it is Duke Makasi, joined by members Tete Mbambisa, Psych 'Big T' Ntsele and Mafufa Jama. But there was also Nick (Nikele) Moyake in the Soul Jazzmen. He is considered in some circles to be the godfather. He taught Makasi and Dudu Pukwana. Johnny Dyani called him *the influence.* And if part of the cover recalls a sense of the colossal, the title—distress—and the shadow perhaps also recalls Moyake's untimely tragic death before the making of this album. Perhaps as South African jazz found forms of the free in their hands, so too did they hold a legacy of sadness that comes to define jazz here.

10
Bembeya Jazz National
Regard Sur Le Passe

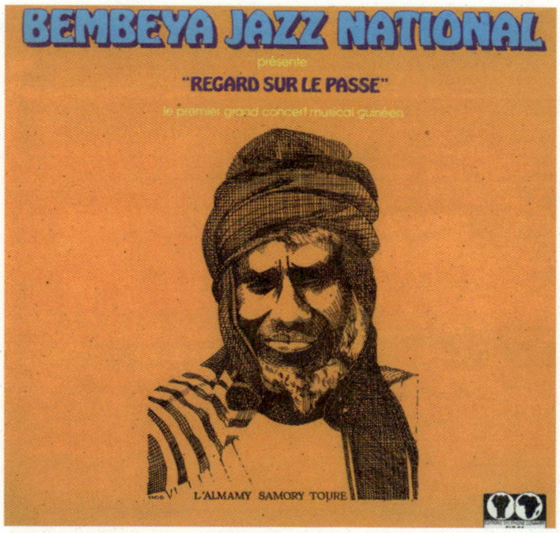

Bembeya Jazz National are a Guinean group. They emerged in the 1960s as part of Sekou Toure's replacement of private dance bands with state supported ones. Identified as an "orchestra moderne" they reworked Manding classic tunes into popular music with a feeling of jazz. *Regard Sur Le Passe*, released in 1969, is based on the epic of a great African emperor, Samory Touré who resisted French colonialism for more than twenty years. The illustration on the cover is of Samory Touré. He is also the grandfather of the guitarist of Bembeya Jazz, Sekou Touré. Two tracks. Epic. Heroic. Serious. The cover conveys this in its illustration of Touré and in titling him as such. Jazz here, reclaiming a tradition and an opposition to forms of white colonial worlds; jazz here then, one of those names and ways in the world.

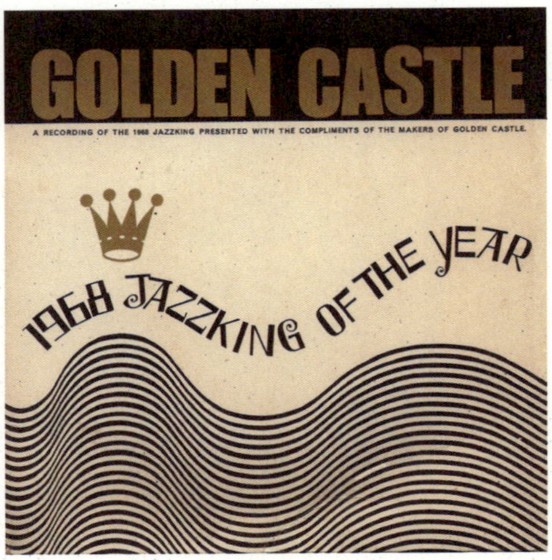

11
Golden Castle
1968 Jazzking of the Year

An album cover and a puzzle. Who is Golden Castle? And the 1968 jazzking of the year? And an album cover with the pretensions of the modernist covers of the famous jazz label Blue Note. But in the end it is what it is—an advertisement cover for Castle Lager beer, promoted to an imagined prospective new black drinking public by South African Breweries (SAB) through the sponsorship of annual Cold Castle festivals and other attempts to get and be connected to jazz. In 1968 Winston 'Mankunku' Ngozi was awarded that title and this is the free promotional single that went with it. There is no information about the artist or songs on the album cover. Both sides are bookended with a SAB jingle (You're a king with a Golden Castle). In 1968 Mankunku also released the seminal SA jazz album *Yakhal'Inkomo.* Much more than a jingle or a designated king by a brewery company, it would certainly have been worthy for a Blue Note issue and one of Reid Miles's designs. Surely, then we would have seen the sound of South African jazz in a very different way.

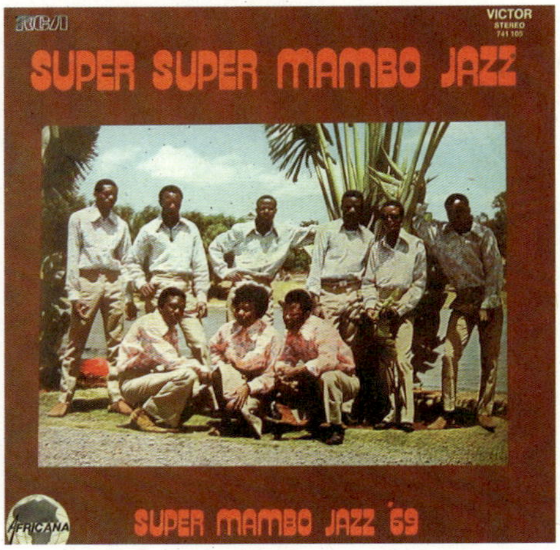

12
Super Mambo Jazz '69
Super Super Mambo Jazz

On the beach on this benga/ rumba/ mambo/ swahili soul hybrid in 1972. The cover reminds us of wedding photographs from the 1970s. It is one of the few album covers to feature a woman. Yet she almost disappears in the uniformity of the band. An overdressed uniform for the beach at that, or on the grass verges overlooking East African seaside lagoons. And the music follows suit. Dance music for weddings. Pink and blue floral shirts and matching khaki pants (and skirt). Flash 1970s dance shoes. And the photograph itself. Follow the band members from left to right and you have a staggered, sequenced dance move going on, with the band member on the left about to swirl out of the shadows of the wild *strelitizia* (wild banana) tree and arrive on the back cover ready to move again. And yet it is also a curious photograph for the "Super Super Mambo Jazz" emblazoned across the cover's top. There is a strange conservatism to it and a sense of the out of place between band, album title and album image. The band don't seem to be having much fun.

13
KZ Morogoro Jazz Band
Mfululizo wa Muziki

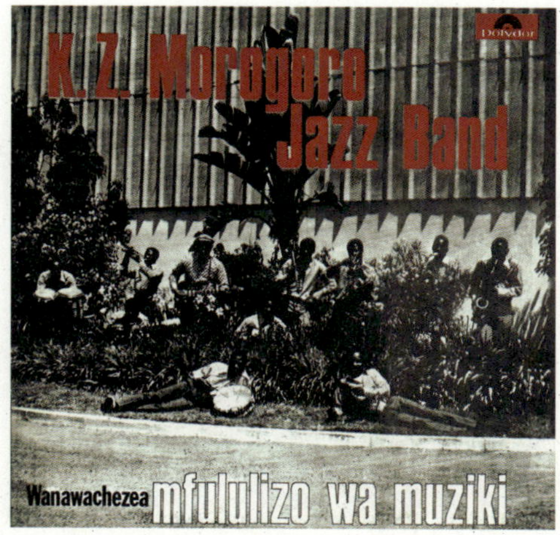

One of the few Tanzanian muziki wa dansi (dance music) bands not based in Dar es Salaam, the band played at the Morogoro Hotel in Morogoro. Very popular in the 1960s and 1970s, they received major airplay on Tanzanian radio and it was through these broadcasts that they were largely able to record. Influenced by Congolese rumba, jazz and the music of Cuba, mixed with taarab and Kenyan benga. It is generally more laid-back, with the music built around two or three guitarists backed by bass guitar, percussion and a horn section. How many guitarists can you spot on the cover? It is an extraordinary cover. It's 1972 and the band, all dressed up, matching blue shirts, are in the Morogoro Hotel public road garden. A day time shoot for a nighttime hotel dance band. Or perhaps jazz in the Tanzanian afternoon, all laughter and movement in the time of *ujamaa*.

14
African Jazz and Variety
South African Institute for Race Relations (SAIRR) presents African Jazz and Variety

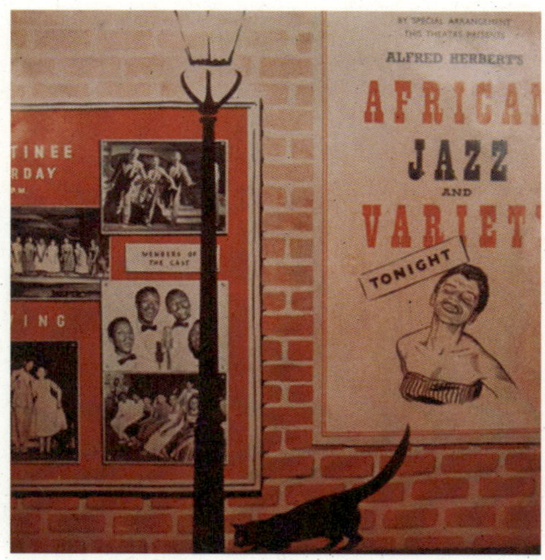

In 1952, white promoter Alfred Herbert organized his first African Jazz and Variety Show in South Africa at Johannesburg's Windmill Theatre (together with the SAIRR). This rare 10 includes two songs by The Woody Woodpeckers ("Fanagalo" and "Gumdrop"), a group around South African songwriter and musician, Victor Ndlazilwane. During his early career, Ndlazilwane was part of the legendary Woody Woodpeckers group as well as the Jazz Ministers, both of which were signed to Gallo Record Company. While the Jazz Ministers were the first African jazz band to perform at the prestigious Newport Jazz Festival in New York, the troupe itself was described as performing "...ragtime, Negro spirituals, jazz vocals, and syncopated African hymns and satirical comedy sketches". A sign of its times, with white promoters, racial depictions, "black face" and the almost obligatory lamppost and back cat. Dark and dangerous! Sexy? "We had to have bodyguards, because we were dressed in short African attire and it was very sexy" remembers Dolly Rathebe.

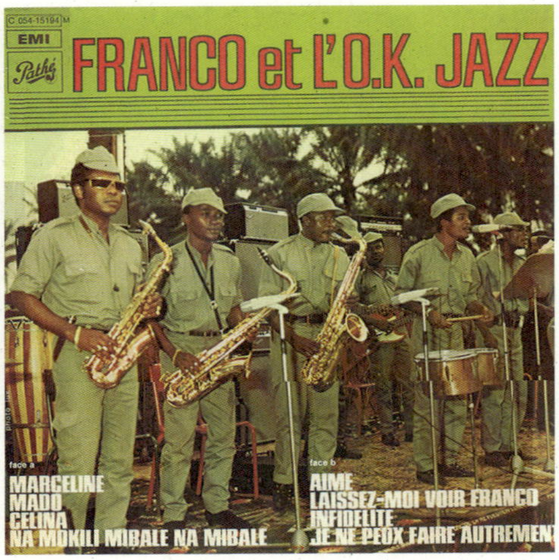

15
Franco et L'OK Jazz
(Marceline)

Recorded around 1970 the original name came from the OK Bar (owned by Oscar Kashama). With the title of their first album, which became the band's slogan "*On entre Ok on sort KO*" (You enter Ok and leave KO'd [knocked out]) defining a music for the masses and their asses, this is an extraordinary cover. Never a military band, a closer look shows OK Jazz in the uniform of Mobuto's Mouvement Populaire de Révolution. This is scary stuff, Mobuto a violent dictator. So what do we make of this? And where is Franco? For it is his guitar, particularly on Mado, the second track on the first side that links Franco to jazz—as he innovatively and improvisationally works over old traditions, refocuses trends and changes the way the music lives and breathes in strange new ways. Never just Mobutu's "Authenticité", the cover stands in stark contrast to what's inside.

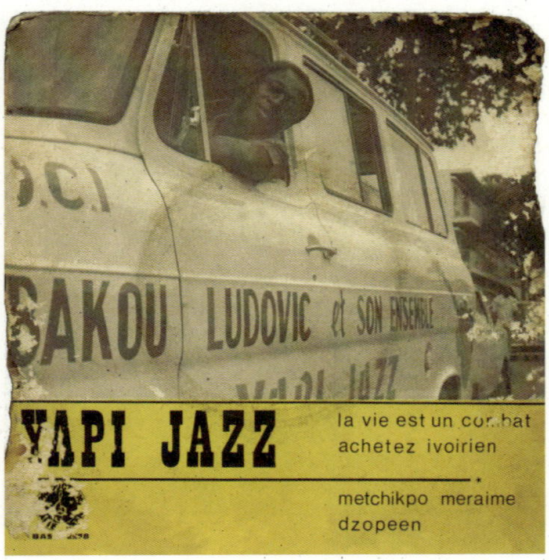

16
Mobio Angakou Ludovic
et Son Ensemble (Yapi Rene)
Yapi Jazz

Cotê d'Ivoire. The 1960s. Abdijan is about to become a cultural beacon in West Africa as the energy of the postindependence cocoa economic miracle fuels a new urban music. The cover photograph holds this moment: the band's bus in an Abdijan street on the way to the Oasis du Desert bar to perform with Amedee Pierre. Singing in the languages of the street—in Bete or Dioula—echoing independence as they replaced Spanish and French as the language of music. And who is the driver? Mobio Angakou or Yapi Rene? Does it matter? The expression of nonchalant freedom, named as the owner of Yapi Jazz heralds the arrival of this Ivorian "jazz" which reflects what Mamadou Doumbia famously sang in his first song in Dioula in 1963—"destiny is a slate you can write on and rub out".

The Black Elegance: Escape from the '80s

Charles Tonderai Mudede

The Crepuscular '80s Dub

The 1980s were the end of a world. Its hours and days detailed the sunset of the twentieth century, which opened in 1917. The nineteenth century, which ran from 1789 (the French Revolution) and closed with the end of the First World War and the birth of the Soviet Union, was the platform from which the dreams (and consequent nightmares) of the twentieth century were launched. These dreams (and nightmares), rocketed by the militarized and mobilized super powers, each imagining itself to be "the legitimate heir"[1] of the nineteenth century, came to end in 1989 with the fall of the Berlin wall—an event that was accompanied by other great events of that astonishing year: after twenty-seven years of imprisonment, the releasing of Nelson Mandela; the first bursts of the Japanese bubble; the Soviet withdrawal from Afghanistan; the Tiananmen Square massacre; and the release of the swan song of the hypermasculine revolutionary black male, Public Enemy's "Fight the Power."

When people say that we entered the twenty-first century on September 11, they are gravely mistaken. Despite the scale of the destruction, 9/11 was mostly just that: massive destruction. It was the collapse of two massive buildings but not the collapse of the prevailing ideological edifice of our new times.[2] The buildings went down but the ruling ideology remained erect. It is no accident that the towers were annually spiritualized by nearly 100 search lights, the Tribute in Light. The thing of each tower is gone but not the more important thing-in-itself: the post-Bretton Woods economic order of floating currencies, shareholder maximization, financial deregulation, and the *satellization* of financial flows.[3]

9/11 was the deepening and intensification of what was already there, the twenty-first century, in all of its significant features, which Deleuze succinctly describes in his "brief and enigmatic essay, 'Postscript on the Societies of Control'"[4].

Published at the dawn of the twenty-first century, 1990 (indeed, the first year after the very short twentieth century), "Postscript on the Societies of Control" outlines the primary shifts and new directions that were to shape what President George Bush Sr., famously called The New World Order: the "breakdown of all sites of confinement" that defined "disciplinary

1 In *Dreamworld and Catastrophe: The Passing of Mass Utopia in East and West*, Susan Buck-Morss writes: "The great cold war enemies, while having been truly dangerous to each other, appear as in fact close relatives. Their common descent from the French revolution (which Lenin constantly stressed, but with the understanding that since October 1917 only his own regime was the legitimate heir)."

2 In *Lenin and Philosophy*, Louis Althusser writes: "[Ideology according to Marx is] an Imaginary assemblage (bricolage), a true dream, empty and vain, constituted by 'the day's residues' from the only full and positive reality, that of the concrete history of concrete material individuals materially producing their existence."

3 Jean Baudrillard called this stage of capitalism *Transeconomics*: "Our only reality is an unchecked orbital whirl of capital..."

4 From Michael Hardt's essay "The Withering of Civil Society," which is published in *Deleuze and Guattari: New Mappings In Politics, Philosophy, and Culture.*

society" (prisons, schools, barracks, and so on); the diminishing role of the nation state in controlling the desires of capital (the Japanese management guru, Kenichi Ohmae championed this as "The Borderless World" in his bestseller *The Borderless World: Power and Strategy in the Interlinked Economy*, which was also published in 1990); the merging of Third and First worlds within the same geographic space (characterized by the growing similarities between cities like Los Angeles and Mexico City or, more physically, San Diego and Tijuana—as noted in Mike Davis' 2000 *Magical Urbanism*—and also, more globally, described as uneven development in David Harvey's 2006 *Spaces of Global Capitalism: Towards a Theory of Uneven Geographical Development*); the end of distinct economic right and left positions in politics.

In the way that Hiroshima accelerated the twentieth century, 9/11 accelerated the twenty-first century. The parts that were gathering to give the era its final shape and meaning were rushed closer to their defining center when the second hijacked jet plane hit its tower. This is why the term "new war" so easily replaced the term "new economy"—they were, as Hal Foster says in another context, "expressions of a particular period": meaning, concepts conditioned and fashioned by the same historical moment or materials. We must turn to the 80s to see the end. Objects in the 90s are exposed to the strange light of dawn; objects in the 80s are rounded and caught in the diminishing light of dusk.

Dub: The Final Events

Chic releases "Good Times"; Margaret Thatcher takes power in the U.K.; the Soviets invade Afghanistan; the Space Shuttle program is launched; the Three-Mile Island meltdown occurs; Ayatollah Ruhollah Khomeini's exile ends and the Iran hostage crisis is born; Skylab, America's first space station, launched in 1973, reenters the Earth's atmosphere, showering fiery fragments over Australia; The failure of Operation Eagle Claw brings an end to President Carter's reelection hopes; former Hollywood actor Ronald Reagan is elected the 40th President of the U.S.; the Volker shock kills high inflation and initiates the management of interest rates as the sole economic policy for the U.S.; the nuclear reactor core of Cosmos 1402 returns to the earth, leaving a radioactive trail through the atmosphere; Argentina and Britain declare war over the Falkland Islands; a Soviet jet shoots down Korean Air Flight 007; Jimmy Jam and Terry Lewis begin working with SOS Band; Chernenko dies and is replaced by Mikhail Gorbachev; U.K. miners strike; China initiates the second phase of an economic program launched by Deng Xiaoping a month before the first year of the last decade of the twentieth century; the crack epidemic hits every American city with a large black population; one of the reactors at Chernobyl explodes and releases into the atmosphere thirty to forty times the radioactivity of the atomic bombs dropped on Hiroshima and Nagasaki; Public Enemy drops "Don't Believe the Hype"; the Challenger Space Shuttle explodes in the sky; the core of what was to become Mir Space Station is launched; the Iran-Contra hearings start; Cosmonauts Vladimir Titov and Musa Manarov spend 366 days in Mir setting a record for the longest time any earth-born creature has spent in space; the Pan-Am Lockerbie crash occurs; SOS Band completes its last hit with Jimmy Jam and Terry Lewis, "Borrowed Love"; Cuba withdraws from Angola; a fatwah is issued on the author of *Satanic Verses*; Ayatollah Khomeini dies; the Berlin Wall falls; the Strategic Defense Initiative program is aborted; Soviets withdraw from Afghanistan and the Taliban take power; Public Enemy opens "Fight the Power" with the words: Nineteen Eighty Nine.

"The Clock Keeps Turning—A Remix"

In 1979, Chic's "Good Times" opens with this line: Happy days are here again. The "happy days" the singers have in mind are located in a time before the processes of de-industrialization began sucking the economic life out of urban cores, transforming, in city after city, black neighborhoods into the "hoods" that Mel Melle described in hiphop's first major social statement: "The Message" (1981). Like the TV show, *Happy Days*, *Good Times* is nostalgic. What it longs for is what the Chicago school of sociologists in the 1930s and '40s called "the black metropolis," which, though considerably poorer than white neighborhoods, still had recognizable leaders, a class pyramid (from the many indigent to a relatively stable working class to the very few affluent), homeowners, and storeowners. This was the time of "the jitterbug," a time when "boys could be boys" and "girls could be girls." In the black metropolis, a father brings home the bacon and a mother cooks it. This world of factory work was in fast decline by 1974 (the year of the first showing of *Good Times*, a sitcom set in a Chicago housing project), and all but gone by 1979 (the year of the last showing of *Good Times*).

Inspired by Roxy Music, Chic introduces black elegance, the fashion of escapism. Black elegance is the hot air that lifts the balloon of black pop over the economic devastation of the final Reagan years. By the time hip hop begins its descent from space (or electro funk) to the streets (in 1981), R&B has long departed from Motown for the sky—and it stays up there until Mary J. Blige collaborates with rap to negotiate a return to the "hood", which by the mid-1990s is on the verge of being wiped out by a Clinton-era wave of redevelopment capital. This wipeout is the subject of August Wilson's last play, *Radio Golf*.

A Mix of Time and Chic

With black elegance, two streams become one during the '80s. The source of the first stream was Chic, and the source of the second stream was Time. From Time we get Jimmy Jam and Terry Lewis. From Jam and Lewis we get the SOS Band. The SOS Band draws its cosmopolitan look from Chic and its post-disco sound from Time, whose lead singer is Morris Day, Prince's arch-rival in *Purple Rain*.[5]

5 Though connected with Time, and coming from the same city, Minneapolis, Prince has never been part of the black elegance movement, which on principle never blurs the line between male and female roles. The women in black elegance aspire to be ladies, and the men aspire to be gentlemen. The sex codes are stable. Prince, as Steven Shaviro has pointed out in *Doom Patrol*, is not stable; he is not altogether black or altogether white, nor altogether a woman or altogether a man. Prince is mixed and androgynous, and his look and music constantly disturb clear codes, clear roles, clear borders. "If I Was Your Girlfriend" is a prime example of how well he blurs the border between the sexes.

The Floating World of Black Elegance

In 1983, the SOS Band releases the album *Rise*, which is produced by Jimmy Jam and Terry Lewis (former members of Time) and contains the hit single "Tell Me If You Still Care." The video for that single captures the essence of black elegance, a mode and mood inaugurated by Chic's "Good Times." In the video, immaculately dressed members of the SOS Band fly through the clouds in a dream of a blimp. Far down below are the too painful postindustrial, post-white-flight, post-Watts, post-Treaty of Detroit, post-New-York-Drop-Dead, post-black-metropolis realities/ blues of the hoods ("Temporary lay-offs," "Easy Credit rip-offs"); up in the blimp are the transitory pleasures of sex, pop music, and designer clothes. It is this disco-funk escapism that modern hip hop (1987 to 1992) rebels against. Often, this rebellion is hypermasculine, as it attempts to resuscitate the black power movement which, in pop music, collapsed under the contradictions of Bob Marley's internationalism. Public Enemy leads the reconstruction effort with new sampling technologies. The crew, which enters the mainstream in 1988, borrows heavily from the sermonic tradition, the industrial-era images of black male militancy, and focuses on urban economic development. In an effort to keep things real, hip hop, in general, replaces the business suits, fedoras, and champagne of black elegance with tracksuits, sneakers, and 40 ouncers. The black elegance dream blimp crashes in 1992 when Mary J. Blige makes a truce with the street. (Note: black elegance must not be confused with the Clinton-era cult of bling-bling.)

The Economics of Black Elegance

In 1986 Gwen Guthrie releases the economic doctrine of black elegance: "Ain't Nothin' Goin' On But The Rent." To stay high in the air, to stay way above the neoliberal demolition of social housing and New Deal guarantees, Guthrie abandons love as it has been known in the West since the twelfth century (also a massive period of social change); for her, love is "too mysterious" and what is clear, what is understandable, what everything in life boils down to is paying the rent. Because the government no longer provides a security net, and it's now all up to the individual to make or break; from here on out it's "no romance without finance," no sex without a wage. Nothing only produces nothing. You must have some money if you want to get some.

This is not a joke. This is a serious and blunt declaration. And in 1988, hip hop, with its growing obsession with being, staying, keeping it real, which usually takes the form of a street reality that produces what LA's NWA calls "street knowledge," confronts Guthrie's doctrine and the excesses of black elegance as a whole. The year NWA releases *Straight Outta Compton* (which means: "Straight Out of the Realities of a Postindustrial Black Neighborhood") Three Times Dope, a Philadelphia crew whose lead rapper, EST, has the dopest fade, declares in "Funky Dividends" that enough is enough. For the trio, the ultimate substance of a relationship should be once again love and not money. (Public Enemy is not at odds with this view. And to make their case, they, like Chic's "Good Times," turn to the happy days, the days of their moms and pops, the age of the "black metropolis"—Keynesian-era black neighborhoods that were stabilized by a large working-class stratum.[6] Back in those days it was about the heart, about the kind of love that made its first appearance in the West in the High Middle Ages; these days it's about staying paid. Indeed, maintaining one lover is so expensive that you can't afford to have two. "This is getting ridiculous!" yells Three Times Dope's beat-maker, Chuck Nice. "That's the third dress this week!"

The split between hip hop realism and R&Bs escapist elegance is finally resolved in 1995 when Mary J. Blige, who first brought R&B down to the street level in 1992, makes a commitment of ghetto love to hip hop's Method Man on "I'll Be There for You/You're All I Need to Get By"—a *hoodization* of a black-metropolis-era tune "You're All I Need to Get By." R&B and hiphop, which have been separated since "Good Times" (the tune that introduced black elegance and hip hop—"Rapper's Delight"—to the world) are reunited, in the video for "I'll Be There for You/You're All I Need to Get By," on the very same spot that the rapper Intelligent Hoodlum first "bust a nut," the project roof.

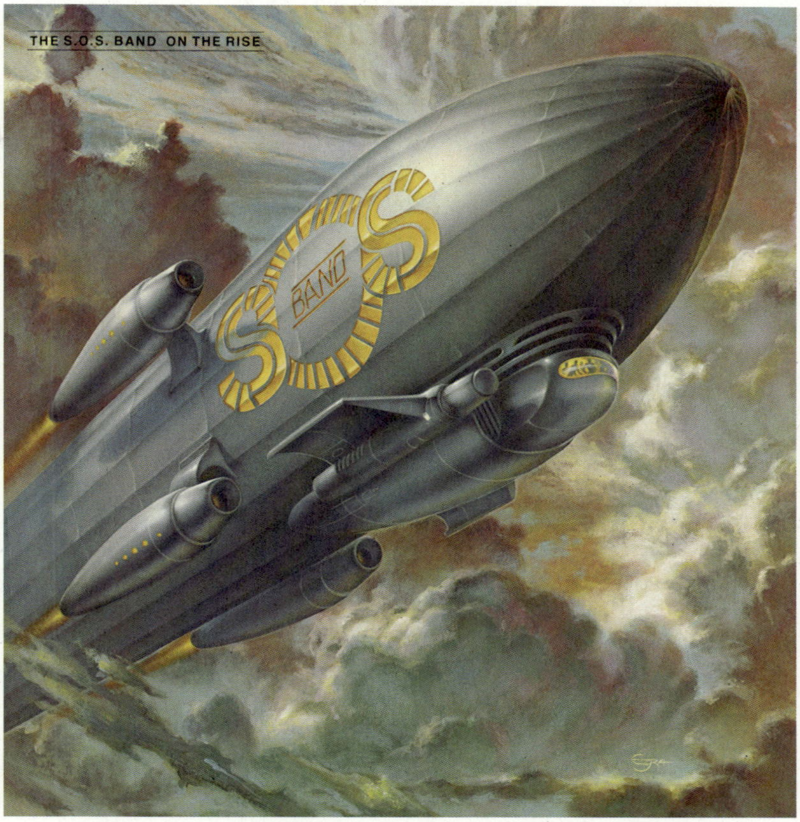

Cover of the SOS Band, *On the Rise*, 1983. Cover illustration by Ezra Tucker. Reproduced by permission of Demon Music Group Ltd.

The Pain of Too Much Pleasure

With the SOS Band, the acronym stands for "Sounds Of Success", and not, as one might expect, considering the period of time that the Atlanta-based group experienced its peak, the early to mid '80s, "Save Our Souls". Despite the consolidation (Reaganomics) and globalization (Structural Adjustment Program) of neoliberal policies, the federal and banking disinvestment of the inner city, and the rise of a violent drug market (globalization ghetto style) organized around what Cornel West described as the quintessential postmodern drug, crack. SOS Band decides to abandon reality and spend some of the harshest years in post-slavery, black American history dreaming of fine clothes, champagne bubbles, and private clubs that float high above the city. Video after video ("Just The Way You Like It," "Tell Me If You Still Care"), we see ordinary, working-class people zapped out of reality and zapped into

6 The sociologist Wilson Julius Williams explains in his seminal study *When Work Disappears: The World of the New Urban Poor* that in the industrial black metropolis of the '50s and '60s, 77 percent were employed, whereas in the postindustrial hood of the '80s, only 23 percent were employed.

fantasy clubs where the only kind of pain they might feel is "the pain of too much pleasure."

In their most stylish and cinematic video, "Borrowed Love," SOS Band is not in the sky or in a dream but dancing in the ruins: The hot sun appears to have just set, the cooling sky is pink and dark blue, in the distance is a black massif, and in the ruins of an apartment building is the band, dressed in garments that flow over swaying bodies. The men and women express no emotion; they have perfected the aristocratic art of class indifference.

The editing is as smooth as the movements of the dancers. The camera pans across, glides over, slides toward, pulls away from the ruins of a building that was destroyed not so much by time but by a wrecking ball. And we cannot disassociate this wrecking ball with the one that begins demolishing Robert Taylor Homes in 1998.[7]

Unlike Benjamin's *Angel of History* (who "sees one single catastrophe which keeps piling wreckage and hurls it in front of his feet..." and wants, "to stay, awaken the dead, and make whole what has been smashed"), in "Borrowed Love", black elegance is so self-confident, so unfazed by what the British dub poet Linton Kwesi Johnson, with Thatcherism in mind, described as "destruction all around," that it has the imagination (no, the audacity) to project itself into the twenty-first century and persist in the aftermath of the U.S.'s complete break with the social form of urban development. As Mary Davis sings about "the emptiness, the emptiness," we realize that it's not the fall of dusk, the mood and moment of the '80s, but the rise of dawn, the new millennium, that's brightening the sky above the massif, the desert, the ruins of the hood.

7 From *The Wall Street Journal*, December 2000: "[F]or months [Ms. Hewitt, a 23-year-old Taylor Homes resident] has listened to a wrecking ball taking bites out of the building behind hers. Through her window, she can see moving trucks backing up to her building, which is known only by its address: 4444 South State. Her building is next, yet she hesitates to go."

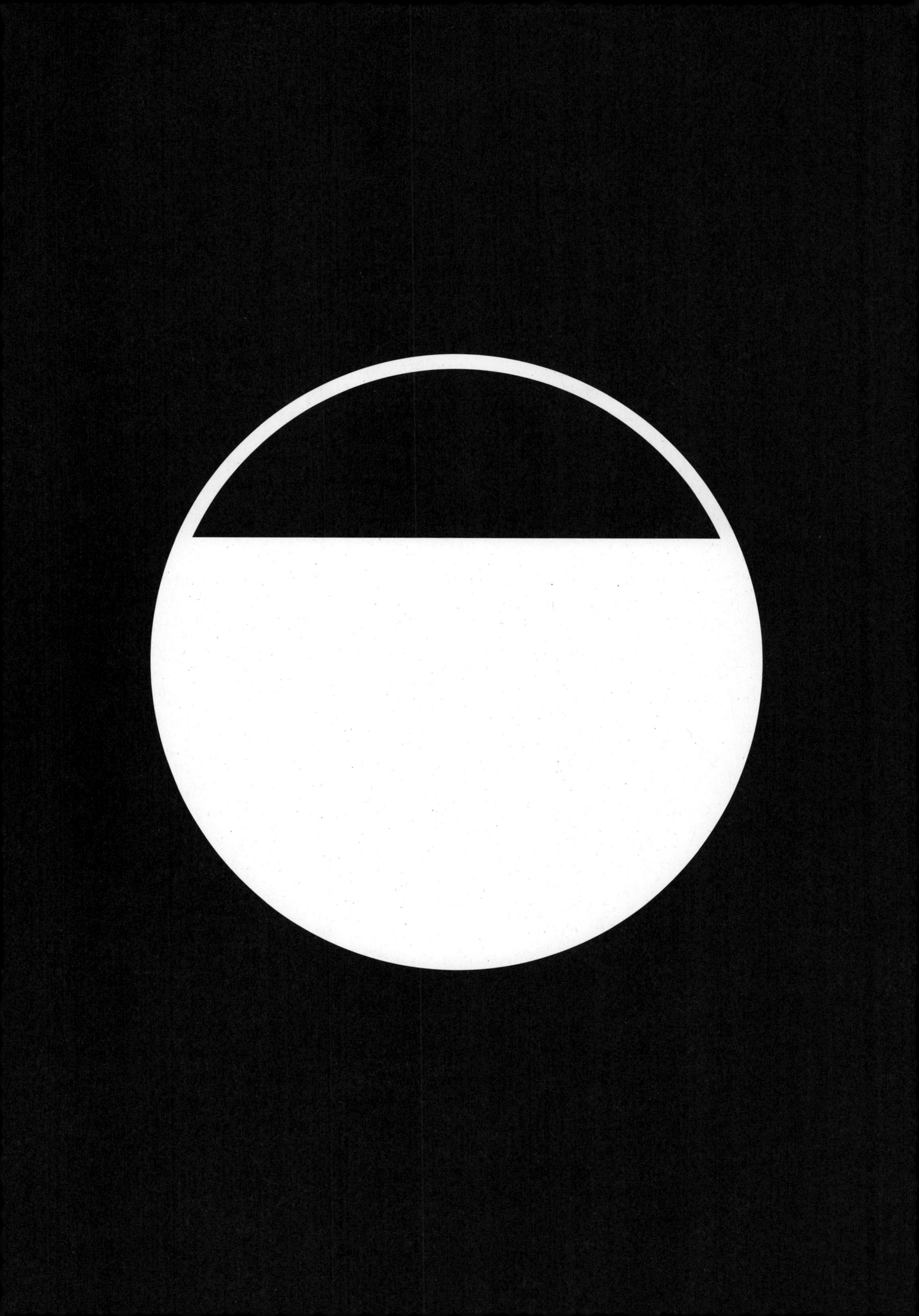

History Does Not Repeat Itself, but It Does Rhyme

Fred Moten

... the ethical text sustaining our demands for recognition and legal redress should become the object of radical critique.[1]
—Denise Ferreira da Silva

I want to make a plea for insovereignty. More specifically, if surreptitiously, I want to approach a meditation on and in the irreducible blackness of poetry by way of a specific theoretical challenge to the notion/delusion of the sovereignty of the poet who has been figured, depending upon the preference of whoever seeks the state's properly invested embodiment, either as executive, legislator or jurist. The relation of blackness to sovereignty is characterized by flight and fight, and that is where blackness and poetry converge.

The problematic of historical rhyming is further evidence that there's a question concerning poetics that lies at the heart of the matter of insovereignty. I've been reading a lot about the Asia-Africa conference held in Bandung, Indonesia in April of 1955, and for the past year I've been thinking a lot about sovereignty, about modernity as the era of what Angela Mitropoulous calls "the democratization of sovereignty" or what Gerry Simpson calls "the diffusion of sovereignty." If anticolonial mobilization, given and instantiated in wars of or for national liberation, is a claim upon sovereignty, then I have been trying to consider what it is that my forebears claimed. This has led me to a kind of uncomfortable question, one that could be said to exemplify history rhyming with, if not repeating itself, as Mark Twain once said (and I thank Annett Busch for alerting me to Twain's formulation): Vijay Prashad's book *The Darker Nations* gives a kind of annotated timeline of anticolonial, anti-imperial struggle in the interest of reviving it, in the interest of reconfiguring the geography of collaboration (which refers not to a place, he says, but a project) called the Third World. But what if the Third World's timeline also includes The Peace of Westphalia and the Berlin conference of 1884–85? Deeper still, what if the project of the Third World is always already stunted by the concept of world and the structure of time[line], the illusory coherence in/and spatio-temporal constitution of sovereignty. This is not just to ask whether the postcolonial condition is as much a function of colonialism as it is of anticolonialism. This is to inquire, rather, about the possibilities of a radical discontinuity that remains unclaimed even though it is, at the same time, embedded in the history we do claim. This discontinuity, its deconstitutive force, has to do with how a kind of theoretical irruption and interruption is lived and how we discover clues of/for that living. How do we access and claim the insovereign modes of life that make possible and even instantiate the critical displacement of sovereignty?

1 Denise Ferreira da Silva, "NO-BODIES, Law, Raciality and Violence," *Griffith Law Review* 18, no. 2 (2009): 234.

Let me proceed by way of two more quotes from a brilliant essay by Denise Ferreira da Silva:

> *Self-determination and self-preservation [are] the sovereign's distinguishing attribute and highest duty.*[2]
>
> *...raciality assumes that, everywhere and anywhere, across the surface of the planet, that ever-threatening 'other' exists because already named; as such, it is an endless threat because its necessary difference consistently undermines the subject of ethical life's arrogation of self-determination.*[3]

I'm interested in the (more + less than) ones da Silva refers to as the NO-BODIES, "whose existence spreads beyond the juridical borders of any given state and the ethical borders of every nation." They are the ones whom the state can put to death in the interest of its self-preservation without any explanation; the ones whom the sovereign can dispose of or dispense with or disperse or disburse, again, in the interest of self-preservation and self-determination. They are the ones who are in passage, not just from this world to the next but from world to earth, world to ground or underground; world to water or underwater. Da Silva charts the trajectory of their externally imposed determination as non-self-determining, as there for and under the dominion of a masterful subject whose capacity for reason and reflection allows him not only to suppress or subordinate his own impulses and appetites but also obligates him to control those who are supposed to have no such capacity. That masterful subject is privileged and obligated to control all that shows up for him in the world of things. On the other hand, things are without impetus and have no internal volition. They are affectable. The paradox is that the affectable ones must immediately be considered dangerous in their supposed total lack of armature precisely because the condition of affectability is contagious given the irreducible desirability of affectability's indiscreet non-being. This is to say that affectability, which is the essence of social life, is the condition of possibility of desire, as such. What can be more terrible than bearing the projection of affectability as the primary object of the impossible subject's desire and fundamental instrument of the impossible subject's disavowal of desire? What could be more dangerous than the constant enactment of the subject's impossibility. What could be more beautiful than this insistent indiscretion given in and as the fleshing out of this general and generative affectability. Eternally endangered danger, serially sacrificed savior, always overrun, NO-BODIES always run amok in always overrunning every border.

Within this violent proximity, a distinction is operative as the de/generative condition of self-determination, the sovereign's being and not being there, his material and symbolic bodies: that between persons and peoples. The self-determination of peoples indexes the creative/preservative/destructive ethico-juridical power of the nation-state; the self-determination of persons depends upon the legal restriction of that power. Self-determination is mired in this antagonism, wherein the state preserves peoples by endangering persons, enlarges persons by dimin-

2 Ibid., 212–36, here, 233.
3 Ibid., 235.

ishing the power of peoples to protect themselves. Has the sovereign ever been able to bear this strife? The sovereign's inability to distance itself from mere flesh can be said both to mark and to instantiate a radical incapacity, an already given undoing that tends toward its own redoubling.

Or, put another way: There are two figures over against which stands the sovereign—two iterations, two semblances, two coalescences, of the NO-BODY: dead flesh, sold flesh. Against these inevitabilities of imposed embodiment—for the body must die, and must be sold—the incoherence of self-determination trying to preserve itself stands, in free fall. Internal self-determination ends in the disintegration of the sovereign state. The state's exercise of self-determination, which is an external imposition upon its citizens endangers the sovereign person. Sovereignty moves by way of its own degradation, is enthralled by its own irreducible vulnerability, incompleteness, decay, which it enacts at the intersection of expansion and expression, the constant violation of its own integrity, on impulse, as if it were driven. The ongoing murder of flesh, the ongoing regulation of its exchange, is sovereign activity.

What if self-determination inheres not in the Hegelian relation of subject and object but in the Kantian distinction between persons and things? What if the distinction between the subject's mind and the object's body is displaced by that between these—in their systemic interrelation—and (no)thingly flesh? Hortense Spillers allows and requires us to think flesh as a theft of body perpetrated within and alongside a general imposition of body—its supposed and impossible coherence and enclosure; the submission of its experiential functionality to transcendental imperatives. At the same time, she also allows and requires us to think flesh as a stealing away from and within that theft that is, paradoxically, paraontologically, the very constitution of that theft and its subject; as militantly fugitive flight, in immanent hapticality, from the imposition of ownership and severalty.[4] Flesh instantiates the ones Da Silva call's NO-BODIES as something more + less than a construction of sovereign power. It opens out onto a broader instrumentality so that the imposition and ascription of affectability, which we must claim, is not what instantiates by both exceeding and falling short of the false universality of the sovereign; it is, rather, the actual universality of the insovereign.

This stealing away from theft in theft is something Senegalese filmmaker Ousmane Sembéne brilliantly shows in his rendering of the fate of the captives at the beginning of *Ceddo*[5]—what lives in substitution of one's interest, or even one's place, is aligned with their radical non-alignment, their disappearance, (their transfiguration of) the gun they become. Having been moved, the Pan-African shi(f)t is already given there as back-

4 Hortense J. Spillers, "Mama's Baby, Papa's Maybe: An American Grammar Book," *Diacritics* 17, no. 2 (Summer, 1987): 64–81. In using the term "severalty" I refer to the Dawes Severalty Act of 1887 in which the United States Congress imposed a system of of private land ownership on an indigenous population that traditionally held an inhabited land in common. It's not just that severalty and sovereignty imply one another within an ontologic of what Edouard Glissant refers to as "single being"; it's that the imposition of severalty on the indigenous population was understood by U.S. lawmakers to constitute, by way of brutal absorption, a mode of genocide. For Glissant's formulation see Édouard Glissant, "One World in Relation: Édouard Glissant in Conversation with Manthia Diawara," trans. Christopher Winks, *Journal of Contemporary African Art* 28 (Spring, 2011): 5.

5 *Ceddo*, 120 minutes, 1977, Senegal.

drop and precursor and this is given for us, in a slight and all but unmentionable way in these figures—refuse, without refuge, in refusal—whom I'd like to imagine Charles Mudede would claim under the rubric of the inhabitant. What I want to try to approach is, if not a politics without the state, then something like a counterpolitical or extrapolitical stateless sociality, given in lives that are normatively considered unnatural, given in the unnaturalizable lives of the sub-subject; the insovereign, the un(self-) determined. This is not meant to romanticize the lives of those who are not the masters of their fate but to think their lives as platforms for the study of the destruction, as opposed to the reversal, of mastery. What is it to be the servant of fate? This is a question we can ask the stranger or even, in a more pointed formulation, which Sembéne gives in *Xala*,[6] the *métèque*, the non-citizen, the one who is subject to, but not a subject of the state. In ancient Greece, the *metoikos*, the one who is outside of the house, the one who changes houses or households, is usually the freed slave, the former slave. But the history that is intimated in the figures we see in that film declares that there is no such thing as the former slave. The former slave persists as (no) (such) thing. What if this is a field or a relay? Why must I feel like that? Or what if we think of the interplay between Flora M'mbugu Schelling's *These Hands*[7] and Djibril Diop Mambéty's *La Petite Vendeuse de Soleil*[8] as representing an Afro-diasporic formation: having been moved, after the death of Samora Machel, Mozambican women working practically underneath the building trades are stateless in a way that reflects and reflects upon the statelessness of Sili, *la petite vendeuse*, "her" "disabled" "body's" generative and degenerative incompleteness. M'mbugu Schelling works the incompleteness of Mambéty's scarred, amputative trilogy, which moves as if the living embodiment of Afro-pessimism, in the "original" sense that indexes the continent as a collection of failed or abortive states/polities/civil societies. These films are dismissed as avatars of hopelessness by some, but what is lost in that dismissal, when hope will have been given in and as the announcement of functional governance under viable states and their apparatuses? See, I want to begin with this proposition: that the lived experience of the *citizen* is most accurately characterized as statelessness. What would it mean to acknowledge and, then, to embrace this condition?

To consider the political economy of placelessness is only to begin this approach. It's not about making a claim upon global passage as a Smithian right of labor; it's not about passage as an end; it's not about some locally instantiated claim upon the universal right to be and to determine the end(s) of man. It's about the means of passage and the recognition that we are means; it's about the undercommon fugitivity of means, of debt, of the hapticality of our mutual instrumentality. Attunement to difference is not a citizenly obligation but is, rather, happily, what disqualifies one from citizenship. Consider Sili, the insovereign sociality

6 *Xala*, 123 minutes, 1975, Senegal. For a powerful exploration and explication of this formulation, which informs and allows the present essay, see Brent Hayes Edwards, "Introduction: The Genres of Postcolonialism," *Social Text* 78, 22, no. 1 (Spring, 2004): 1–15

7 *These Hands*, 45 minutes, 1992, Tanzania.

8 *La Petite Vendeuse de Soleil*, 45 minutes, 1998, Senegal.

of her flesh, which moves with the interior in(ter)dependence of a drummer, Tony Allen flown in the trap set, and the external in(ter)dependence of a rhythm section, where everyone is held by the ones they carry.

Ultimately, happily, fugitive affectability manifests itself in/as our undercommon opacity, our open secret. Poetry is always and only a matter of collaboration—a geography of collaboration: an earth writing, an earthy, airily undergrounded writing; an earthly, as opposed to worldly, writing. Its necessary opacity, its irreducible and necessary blackness, is a function of collaboration: that held, insistent rub. It's not about solitary expression, the composed delineation of a view of the world, the assertion of worldly (self-)possession: it discomposes and dispossesses that: it's the transmission of the earth and the (no-)things of the earth. John Akomfrah speaks of the opacity of his *Transfigured Night* needing support. What emerges is a pedagogical imperative, the responsibility of Pan-Africanism, which is yet to have been fulfilled, to produce a pedagogy of blackness, "schooling in the ways of the coming of the demos."[9] Akomfrah says the primal scene of Pan-Africanism is the cabin of the plane to Bandung (which Richard Wright describes and narrates in *The Color Curtain*[10]). It's not that this is not true. It's just that it was first true in another place and time that constituted the radical displacement and radical arrhythmia whose iteration Wright describes. The primal scene of Pan-Africanism is the hold of the ship; and what was true before that is that the primal scene of Pan-Africanism is narrated and described by Sembéne at the beginning of *Ceddo*; and that, somehow, both before and after that, in the slow and broken circle of the blackness of time, the primal scene of Pan-Africanism is Sili, the little girl the sun sold, NOBODY, insovereign, dancing her anarepetitive rhyme.

9 John Akomfrah in the conference as part of the exhibition "After Year Zero: Geographies of Collaboration," October 5, 2013, Haus der Kulturen der Welt, Berlin.

10 Richard Wright, *The Color Curtain* (Jackson, MS: University Press of Mississippi, 1956).

Artists

John Akomfrah
Kader Attia
Balufu Bakupa-Kanyinda
Kudzanai Chiurai
Jihan El-Tahri
Theo Eshetu
Yervant Gianikian
& Angela Ricci Lucchi
Ruy Guerra
Walter Heynowski
& Gerhard Scheumann
Kiluanji Kia Henda
Daniel Kojo Schrade
Sana na N'Hada et al.
The Otolith Group
Yann Le Masson
& Olga Poliakoff
Kidlat Tahimik
Qes Adamu Tesfaw

John Akomfrah

Exploring the many facets of migration, human experience, and political struggle, John Akomfrah and Lina Gopaul's films, gallery installations, documentaries, TV productions, and video works challenge and redefine traditional modes of filmmaking. John Akomfrah OBE, and Lina Gopaul co-founded the seminal film and video group Black Audio Film Collective and the more recent production company Smoking Dogs Films. Their long-standing partnership has won them over thirty-five international awards and over one hundred official film festival selections. Akomfrah's *Transfigured Night* (2013) is a two-screen cinematic reinterpretation of Richard Dehmel's poem *Verklärte Nacht:*

> *There's a kind of cult of twins across West Africa. They are sort of omenic: they are both harbingers of something good, but also something not very good. I didn't want to make something that is all symbolic, I wanted something which is not a metaphor but an actual metonymy. I was searching for material and I just came across these archive images of twins conjoined in the 1950s. And you watch the film and they do the operation and you think "ok they've got everything they need to both stay alive." But there was one organ that they didn't know about, that one didn't have, so one died. And this sense of twinning is something I have been preoccupied with a lot, it's something I just made a piece about called* Transfigured Night. *It's based on a piece by Schönberg,* Verklärte Nacht, *based on a poem which pretty much tells you everything about my obsession with twins. The poem is about two lovers who are walking through the woods on a moon lit night and the woman says to the man "my love, I am yours but I need to confess to you on this night that I'm carrying someone's child and it's not yours." The man says "ok, my love, do not worry because tonight the moon will transfigure our love. From this moment, we will be one and this love will bring this child into the world." Something about the nature of the postcolonial movement reminds me of that. The postcolonial state goes to the postcolonial subject and says "I love you, we're gonna be together but I carry these weird postcolonial elements inside and I promise you they won't get in the way," and the citizen says to that "we love you too." Of course this love doesn't last. The dream of unity, of being twin, of being identical, having an interest that is absolutely the same, seems to me to mark that moment of independence. For that reason I have always been fascinated, other than for folkloric reasons, in twins and especially because these are siamese. They really are joined, but they can't survive without that space of relative autonomy.*
>
> *I think necrophilia is absolutely central to how the diasporic imaginary works, and by implication for its filmmakers. When you think about it, in everyday speech, part of the urgency that informs black militancy—"Ahm shoutin, you fucked my people, and now we need justice"—the invocation of the dead made in this speech is one that requires endlessly to look to the dead for sustenance, for legitimation. For me that is a kind of feeding off the dead. And it is there throughout, it is part of the diasporic imagination, because you are aware of this moment of rupture and break, and if you are a new world diasporic figure that moment of rupture is marked by the triangle. If you listen to the spirituals and the gospels, they are infused with this necrophiliac imaginary. But I think filmmakers become even more in tune with it—so much of what I've done is about the dead. Figures who are no more. So much of the authority of the films comes from this act of mourning. Which in visual terms is a kind of consumption of those figures.*[1]

1 This is an excerpt of a conversation between John Akomfrah and Stoffel Debuysere held on June 25, 2014. Available online at http://www.diagonalthoughts.com.

In "AfterYear Zero" Berlin, John Akomfrah showed *The Unfinished Conversation*, a three-screen "narrative construction" of the multiple realities of Stuart Hall, one of the world's most eminent thinkers. As a theorist of cultural identity and difference, Hall exerted great influence on Akomfrah and the collective movement in which he was involved. Hall arrived in the UK from Jamaica (then still a British colony) in the 1950s, graduated from Oxford, and became a decisive voice of the New Left along with intellectuals such as E. P. Thompson and Raymond Williams. *The Unfinished Conversation* focuses on Hall's "formative years" in the 1950s and 1960s.

John Akomfrah, born in 1957 in Accra, lives and works in London

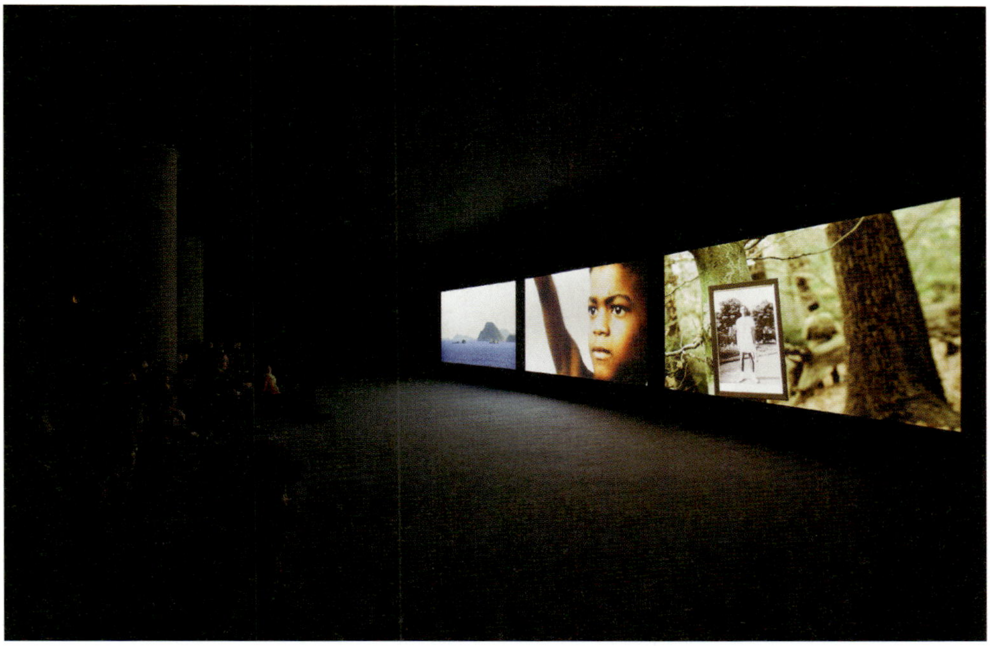

John Akomfrah, installation view— *The Unfinished Conversation*, "AfterYear Zero" (Haus der Kulturen der Welt), 2013.

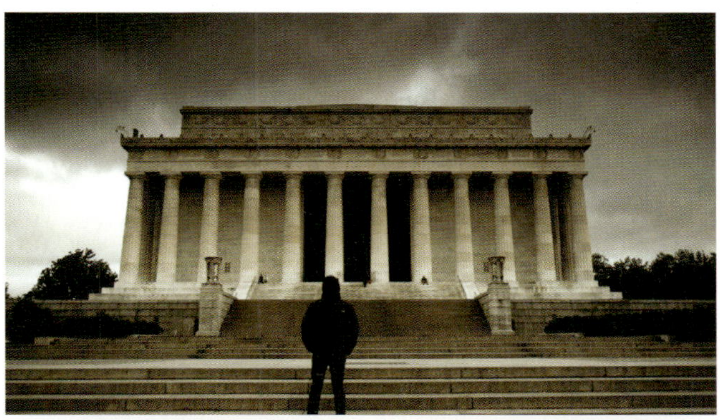

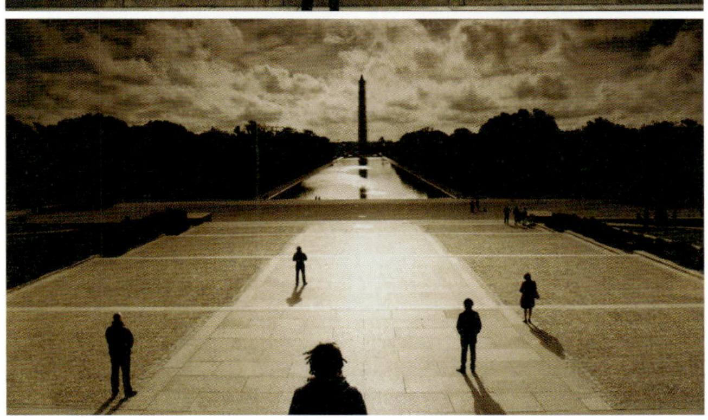

John Akomfrah, detail from— *Transfigured Night*, 2013.
Double channel HD video installation, color, sound, 30 min.

Kader Attia

In Kader Attia's works "repair" is approached as a strategy situated in identity politics. In his research Attia adopts an almost ethnographic and archaeological gaze to trace back the influences and lineages that have shaped cultural appropriation, bearing witness to the cultural repercussions of Western hegemony in non-Western cultures, as well as the counter-appropriations of a colonizer's culture by the colonized.

The video *Silence's Injuries* (2014) shows a series of West African LP covers dating from the African postindependence period till the early 1990s. Attia reads the history of blues, already a history with no definite consensus, against the grain. Commonly it is narrated as an Afro-American story, imported to the U.S. by African Slaves and developed on Southern plantations in the area around New Orleans. The rhythms of blues are associated with the cadence of working songs, giving blues a very distinct sociocultural background. In this work, Attia adds a new layer to the traffic of appropriation in the history of blues by looking at how, after African independence, blues was reimported into West Africa, where it copied from North American blues but got also mixed with other African styles to become a true creolized genre. In this transformation, after being connected to a bleak episode in the history of slavery, blues was reborn and in its reimported shape became the sound of hope, joy and liberation.

In the installation *Dispossession* (2013) shown in "After Year Zero" in Berlin, Kader Attia confronts the imagery of ethnographic objects kept in the collection of the Vatican with interviews on the practice of collecting African art and artifacts. The interviews accompanying the photographic images discuss aspects of the trade of ethnographic artifacts and artworks. As in some of his previous works, Attia approaches the question of the shifts in meaning of art and artifacts as part of a colonial and countercolonial geography of appropriation. These geographies, manifest as a contradictory tension in the respective objects, shed light on the historical production of the divide between the Christian and the pagan idolater, a division that turned into the colonial separations made between the ideology of scientific objectivity versus primitive fetishism, and between art that was embedded in cult and ritual versus that which was secular—modern art.

Kader Attia, born in 1970 in Dugny, lives and works in Berlin

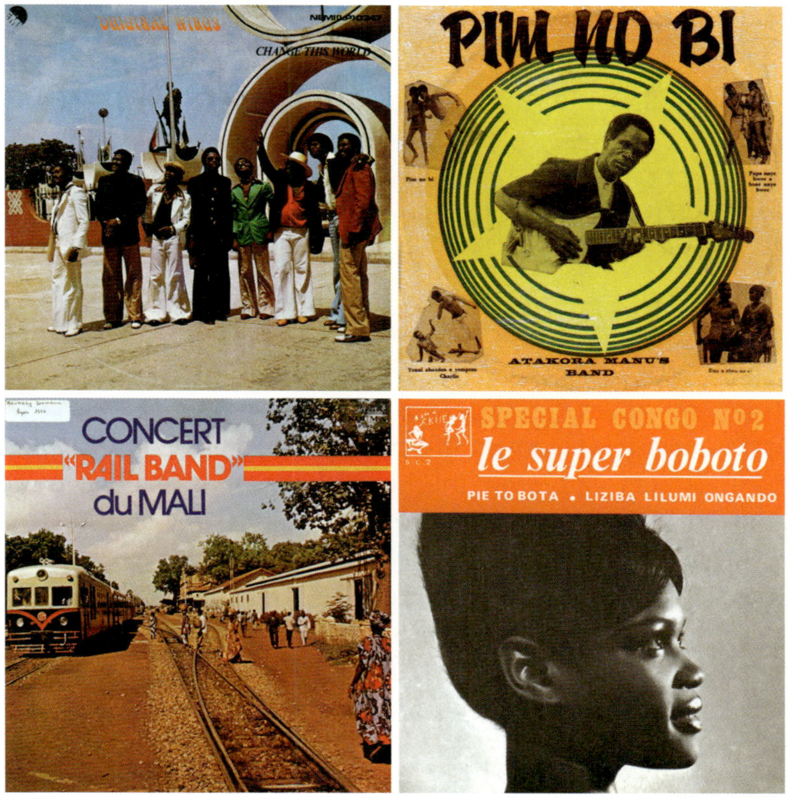

Kader Attia, detail from—*Silence's Injuries*, 2014. Video, color, sound, 13 min. 51 sec. Reproduced by permission of the artist and Gallery Lehmann Maupin.

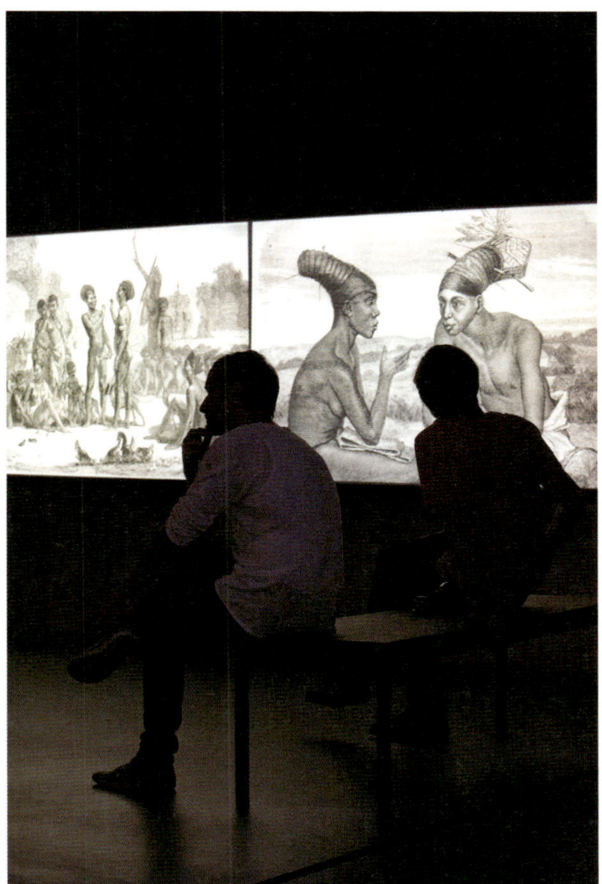

Kader Attia, installation view—*Dispossession*, "After Year Zero" (Haus der Kulturen der Welt), 2013. Installation with double slide projection (2 × 80 color slides), video (color, sound, 13 min). Photograph: Jacob Hoff.

Balufu Bakupa-Kanyinda

Balufu Bakupa-Kanyinda starts things right in the middle. He doesn't explain—if there was something to explain it could be found in the eye of the other. There is something courageous in the decision to start a filmmaking career with two pieces devoted to friends—friends in politics as well as in cinema—Thomas Sankara and Djibril Diop Mambéty. Bakupa-Kanyinda maintains a distance by kind of "writing history" through film. It will be six years before his highly commended *The Draughtsmen Clash* is out in the world. The film is a bitter satire about a character named Mobutu Sese Seko, formerly known as Joseph-Désiré (!) Mobutu. It's an intimate play about playing checkers and a dangerous play with authority—just a play, a deadly one.

How Bakupa-Kanyinda enters criticism of the dictatorial regime doesn't come from a superior point of view, but from asides. The picture begins with the guards playing checkers while insulting each other with explicit verbal barbs. Later, when the peoples' champion plays checkers with the dictator, and, somehow stoned, not only starts winning but insulting "Papa National". On walkie talkies outside, the same guards comment on the game that the peoples' champion is going way too far. A middleman reminds his colleagues that talking harshly against an opponent is part of the game. With an internalized belief in the "righteousness" of the reigning powers, the other guards insist that speaking against authority is not permitted. They know all too well that this kind of speech can only be punished by death. The slapstick and the comic would be just too dangerous.

Balufu Bakupa-Kanyinda was born in 1957 in Kinshasa, he studied sociology, history and philosophy in Brussels, Belgium. He was trained in cinema in France, the United Kingdom and the United States. As a writer and a poet, he produced an analysis of African Cinema. He also teaches cinema and has been invited by New York University to lecture in the NYU-Ghana campus in Accra. He made his first documentary, *Dix milles ans de cinéma* (1991), and returned two years later with *Thomas Sankara* (1993). *The Draughtsmen Clash* (1996) is his first fiction film.

As in his documentary, the UNESCO financed *Afro@Digital* (1999), Bakupa-Kanyinda wouldn't have any interest in using images as illustrative material, as proof or antithesis; but neither does he trust the image as such. Still, it remains difficult to describe the slight differences. Explaining his montage in an interview with Olivier Barlet he refers to *kasala*, the language of the Kasaï griots:

> *The kasala are very moving to listen to, especially when you understand how they function—not through emotions, but through images that the narrator conjures in you, the images of a brave past, of the present and future. Unlike the Malian griots, kasala performers do not glorify a person. They position him in a lineage, or a territory in a lineage. I thus wrote my texts starting out from a sculpture that is very close to the intertwined structures of the kasala. I applied this to my film Dix mille ans de cinéma. I first of all wrote it as you would a kasala, by trying, on a visual level, to weave what is said into what is filmed. Within the narrative sphere, I constantly tried to create this weave, which appears unstructured, but which becomes structured because that is how it's meant to be. John Akomfrah from Ghana manages to create this same weave.*[1]

Balufu Bakupa-Kanyinda, born in 1957 in Kinshasa, lives and works in Brussels

1 This is an excerpt of a conversation between Balufu Bakupa-Kanyinda and Olivier Barlet held in Berlin in February, 2000. Available online at http://www.africultures.com.

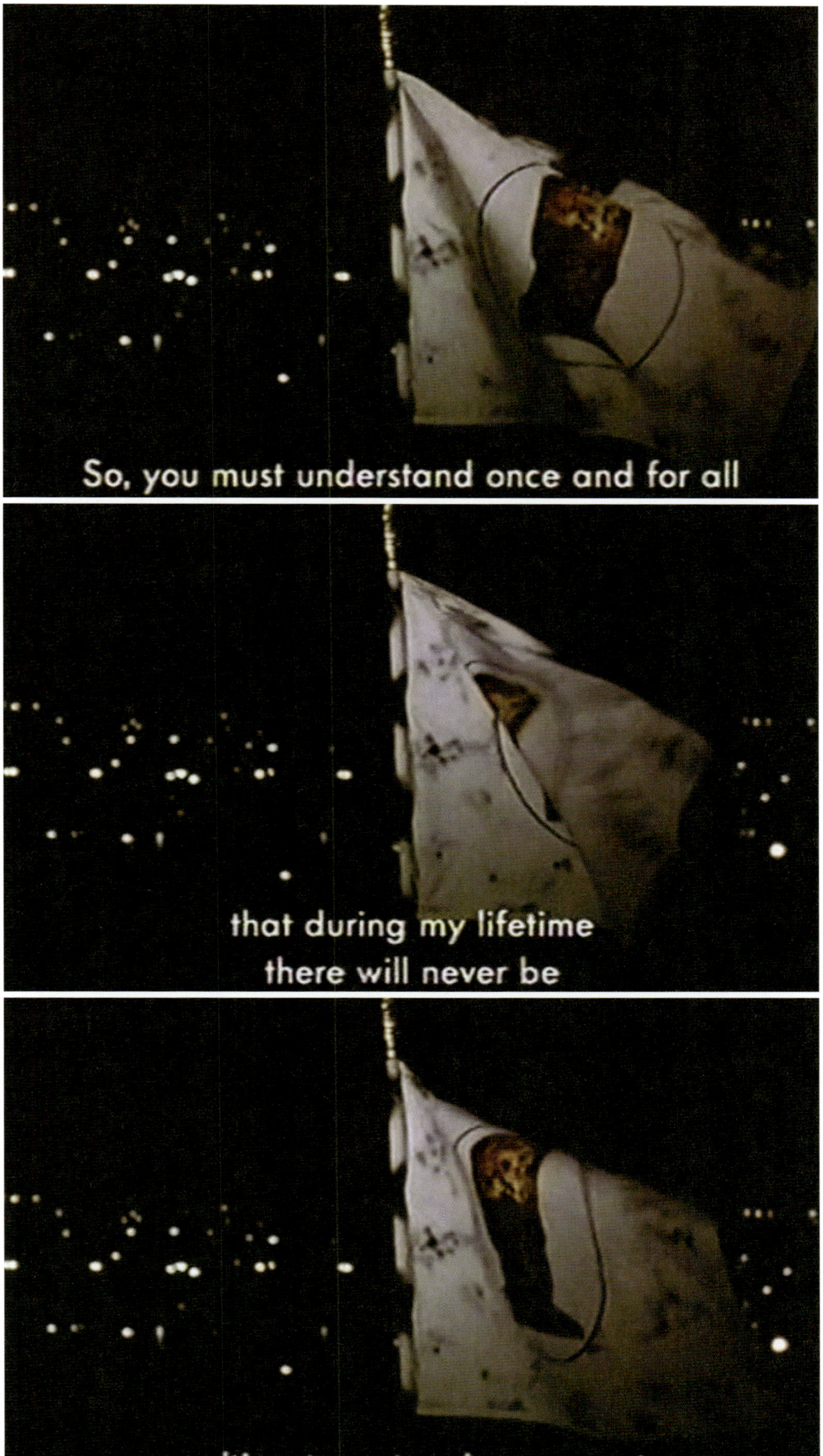

Balufu Bakupa-Kanyinda, detail from—*The Draughtsmen Clash*, 1996. Video, color, sound, 40 min.

Kudzanai Chiurai

The photo series *Revelations* is part of Kudzanai Chiurai's 2011 work *State of The Nation*. This body of work represents an exploration of the relationship between the notion of "state" and "nation". In this project, Chiurai creates a fictional new nation, with a woman as head of state. The 2011 exhibition that took place in Johannesburg featured a speech by the head of state, as well as hip hop concerts. The work includes a photo series that plays on rituals of power, staging a political theatre of surreal scenes alluding to ghetto aesthetics of U.S. hip hop. The artist stated the following about his 2011 exhibition:

> *On a continent that has experienced more violent conflict than any other, this exhibition follows an individual's narration of events that lead up to the inaugural speech by the first supposedly democratically elected prime minister. This leader, styled on many of our existing African leaders, retells the history of a people from another time, but still Africa's time...*

The photographic images are dramatized and stylized stagings from the scenes of collective memory: snapshots of different moments on the timeline of several African countries going through the volatile amalgam of colonization and decolonization, followed by a series of civil wars that were actually covert global wars, making Africa a battleground for interests that come from both inside and outside the continent. This perceived global within the perceived local creates a blurring of borders between that which is private and that which is public, one being a projection of the other. The images thus speak about power issues on the level of the state as well as male-female power relations and the quest for credibility both on the local street corner and in the office of state.

Kudzanai Chiurai, born in 1981 in Harare, lives and works in Johannesburg

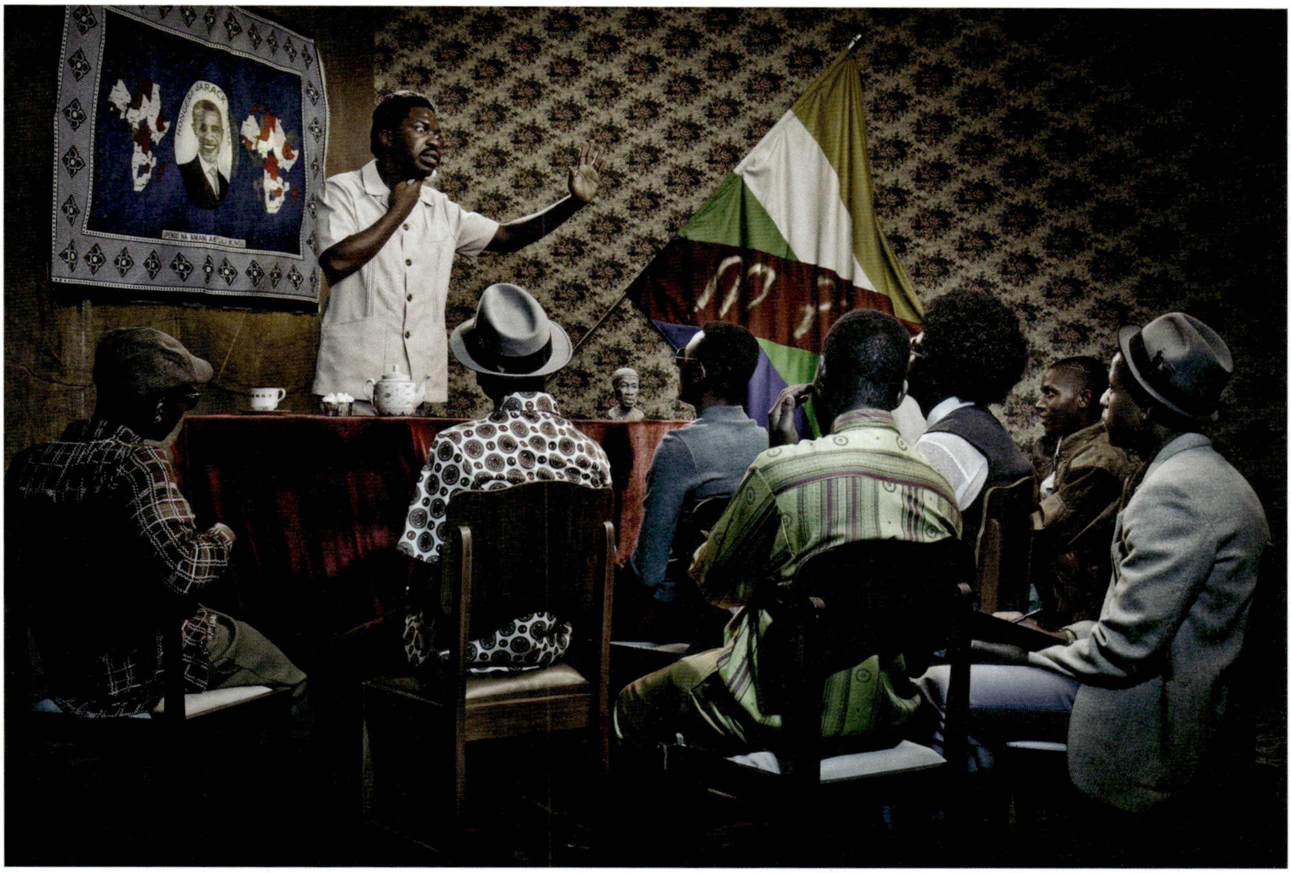

Kudzanai Chiurai, *Revelations 10*, 2011. Print, ultra chrome ink on Innova photo fibre paper, 100 × 150 cm. Reproduced by permission of the artist and Goodman Gallery, Johannesburg.

Jihan El-Tahri

> *I was born in Beirut where my father served as an Egyptian diplomat. My childhood was spent changing countries, schools and languages. Adapting was the key word! Politics was the main dish at home, so when I graduated from the American University in Cairo with an MA in Political Science I joined the Egyptian Foreign Service. That only lasted three weeks because I was told that I ask too many questions and that I should obey orders until the time came for me to be the one giving the orders... Just obeying orders is not my strong point! So, journalism was the route. At least no one would complain that I asked questions. I worked for Reuters,* The Sunday Times *and then the* Washington Post *and* US News & World Report. *I was a war correspondent in general but specialized in covering the PLO. After the Gulf War in 1990, it was time to figure out my own identity... Times had changed and believing that I was simply a citizen of the world was no longer an option. I moved to France and into political documentaries... mostly about Africa where my heart lies.*

El-Tahri has since directed more than a dozen films in which she seeks to understand the geographies produced by movements and individuals and their ideological resources, the often implicit framework being conditions of a global dimension, and the anatomy of power as it has played out in postcolonial states. Her contribution to the exhibition consists of newly produced filmic and documentary montages, mainly two outtakes from previous films, extended interviews with two exemplary independence leaders from Egypt and South Africa, General Moukhtar Hallouda and Victor Moche. She explains her interest in these figures as follows:

> *After the 1952 revolution in Egypt, General Moukhtar Hallouda was among the first Egyptian Army officers to work on creating a locally designed and manufactured missile defense system. The secret missile project was launched with the help of a number of German engineers who had sought asylum in Egypt after the Second World War. Gamal Abdel Nasser, the strong man of the military regime, believed that producing the weaponry needed was the only route towards real independence.*
>
> *I was particularly fascinated by how Hallouda described the Army as the backbone of Egypt's postcolonial development. As a firsthand eyewitness, he detailed how the integration of the military into civilian life and into the fabric of the new state structures did not happen by chance. Postcolonial military rule was designed to stay. In the process it altered the nature of power in the newly independent states.*
>
> *The ANC (African National Conference) became practically a full-fledged State in Exile during the 1970s. The government in exile had its own ministries and its own diplomats. Victor Moche was among the key figures in the liberation movement's building of its infrastructure both in its headquarters in Zambia and later as its representative in Germany and Canada. His reflections about how the history of a liberation movement affects the nature of the new state after independence are particularly telling. He unravels how the secret networks functioned while working underground and how these very same unseen networks survive in the foundation of the new state. It is rare to get a firsthand look into the psychology of power. His reflections go a long way to a better understanding of the upheavals that have recently tainted the South African political scene.*

Jihan El-Tahri, born in 1963 in Beirut, lives and works in Paris and Johannesburg

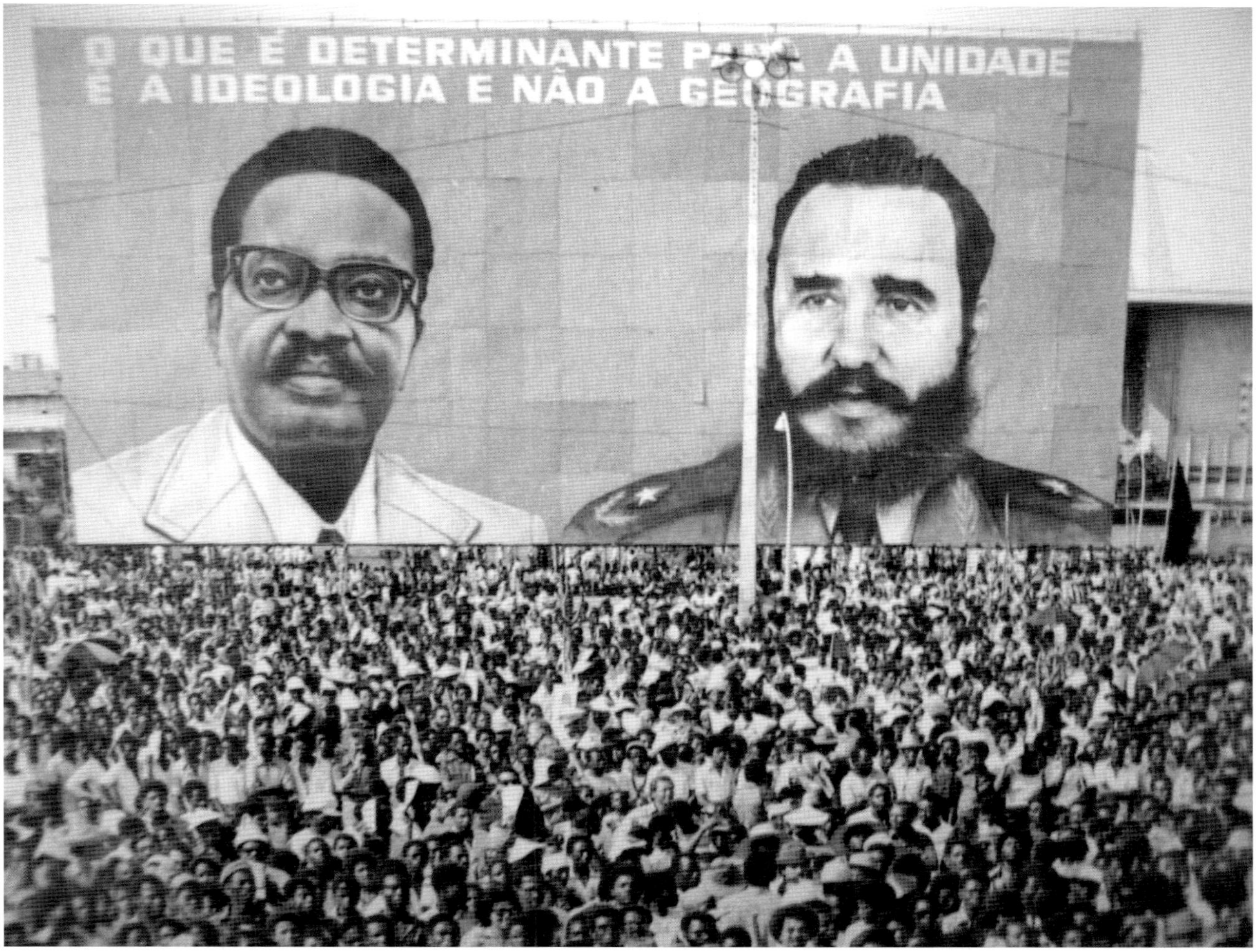

Jihan El-Tahri, a detail from—*Cuba, an African Odyssey*, 2008. Video, color, sound, 118 min.

Theo Eshetu

Trip to Mount Zugualla *(2006) is the testimony of an experience and an attempt to translate it into images and sounds. Every year, pilgrims, as well as beggars and the curious out for a day of fun, meet on Mount Zugualla—approximately 100 kilometers south of Addis Ababa in Ethiopia—to celebrate the saint who in the third century converted the animist population to Christianity. To this day, animists and Christians meet to celebrate this event. I visited this site with Professor Alula Pankhurst, head of the anthropology department of Addis Ababa University, who as part of his MA program has been studying the events on Mount Zugualla. Little can be said about why this tradition still exists, its reasons are lost in time, but the gestures are still left for us to see.*

Trip to Mount Zugualla *presents an unabashedly African view, both in form and in content, of a subject that usually has its roots in European culture. Contrary to common knowledge Christianity was integrated within Ethiopia before it was adopted as a religion in Rome, so the aim of the installation is to create a relationship between different cultural systems.*

The ritual is not photographed simply for its aesthetic properties, but as a form of dialogue between the act of seeing and the significance of what is being enacted. The dilemma within a photographic image is that it is a visual statement absent of lived experience, and its aim is to transcend appearances to reflect an inner reality. It is the very experience and the sensations of our physical presence in a place that often needs to be communicated and expressed.

On Mount Zugualla, animism—the belief in the natural elements and in that which appears before our eyes—is being transformed to Christianity, the belief in a spiritual divinity within mankind. It is exactly the realization of this passage, this transformation from one state to another that leads some participants to go into a state of trance. Of course it can also be argued that it is the desire to belong to a larger community that provokes a self induced trance, as a form of initiation or maybe it is something else that we just don't know and through art and ritual itself, try to understand.

Theo Eshetu, born in 1958 in London, lives and works in Berlin and Rome

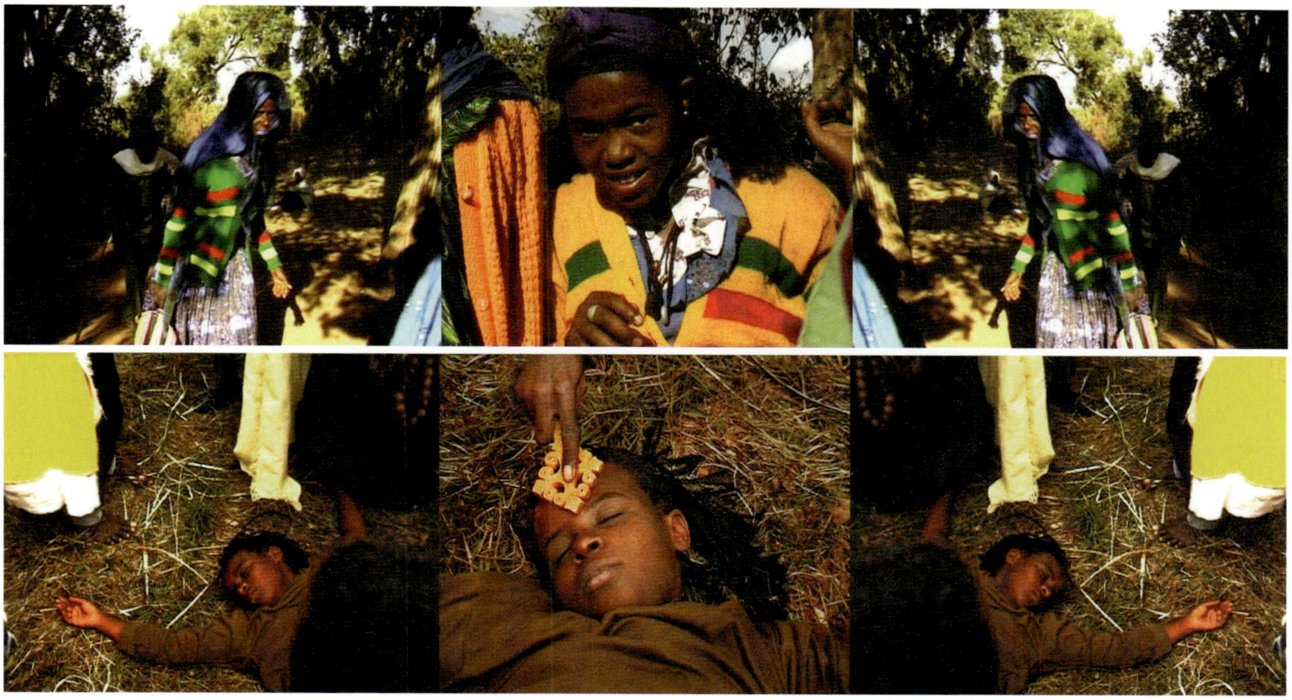

Theo Eshetu, detail from—*Trip to Mount Zugualla,* 2006. 3-channel video transferred to single channel video, color, sound, 7 min.

Yervant Gianikian & Angela Ricci Lucchi

Since the 1970s, Yervant Gianikian and Angela Ricci Lucchi have been pioneers of a cinema based on the cinematic ready-made. They work with lost and salvaged archives and collections of both film and photography, mainly public and private documents from colonialism, the wars of the twentieth century, and fascism. They refilm everything they use in their work, steep those images in colors and manipulate them in sequences. The historical image in their work is both forensic evidence, and a haunting, hallucinatory presence of the past.

The film *Pays Barbare* (2014) is a chronicle of the attacks fascist Italy conducted under Mussolini in Abyssinia and Libya in the 1920s and 1930s. In an attempt to create a New Roman Empire, the forces of Italy first "pacified" Libya and then attacked Ethiopia, which would be incorporated as Italian East Africa in May 1936 (forty years after the historical defeat of Italy in the battle of Adwa that had secured Ethiopian sovereignty during the last stage of the scramble for Africa). This second Italian campaign was notorious for its brutality, including the use of mustard gas, admitted to by Italy only in the 1990s. The materials Gianikian and Ricci Lucchi use are sourced mainly from the private archives of soldiers, workers, and bankers who traveled along with the colonial mission and worked closely with the general Rodolfo Graziani and Count Galeazzo Ciano, Mussolini's son-in-law. Organised in several chapters, the film is a reflection not only on colonialism and fascism, but also on the propagandistic use of images and their function in the great collective lie of colonialism in which Europe has been, and continues to be steeped. This archaeological investigation of the rise of "fascist man" points to the continuities between colonialism and fascism, and entangles the viewer in a web of complicity.

Pays Barbare is the latest in a series of works by the artists that engage with the continuous presence of colonial mythology in Europe and Italy, in particular. Among others, *Pays Barbare* is interspersed with images from *Diana's Looking Glass* (1996), a film on Lake Nemi, a mythical place in Italy where the sanctuary of the antique goddess Diana has been situated. The Roman emperor Caligula built two large ships on Lake Nemi, floating palaces that later sank in the lake. In 1926, his "Napoleonian year", the "Duce" decided to drain the lake in order to recover Caligula's ships in 1928. The destruction of "Diana's mirror" was a hugely symbolic gesture: not only to establish continuity with the Roman Emperors, but also to destroy, in an appraisal of patriarchal, fascist power, the temple of the feminine goddess of birth. Nemi had a wider significance in European mythology, as icon of premodern "primitive" magic. The story of the succession of the priest-kings at Nemi was core "enigma" around which Sir James Frazer's *Golden Bough* was built, a, massive and hugely influential work of anthropology that influenced countless modernist artists and writers since the late-nineteenth century. For Frazer, Nemi symbolized the pagan, oriental, and African roots within Europe. The recovered ships of Caligula were accidentally burnt by German soldiers during their retreat from allied forces in the Second World War in 1944.

Yervant Gianikian, born in 1942, lives and works in Milan
Angela Ricci Lucchi, born in 1942, lives and works in Milan

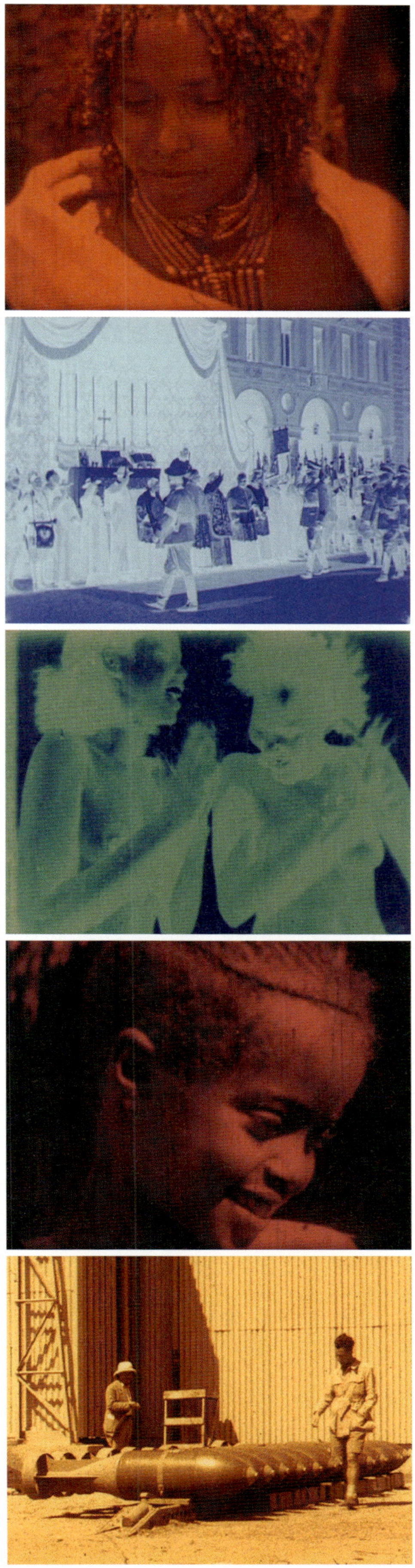

Yervant Gianikian and Angela Ricci Lucchi, detail from
— *Pays Barbare*, 2013. Video, color, sound, 65 min.

Ruy Guerra

Reenactment, historical documentary, political fiction, ethnographic film—all these genres are evoked, at first glance, by *Mueda, Memória e Massacre* (1979). The historical issues at stake in *Mueda* point to a genealogy of Mozambican cinema interwoven with the country's political project. The founding film of Mozambican cinema, since it launched the formal and expressive conditions of its birth, *Mueda* would be reedited without Guerra's direct supervision after being awarded the Prizes "Film and Culture" and "People's Friendship Union" at Tashkent Film Festival in 1980.

Guerra, who had lived in Brazil since 1958 came back to Maputo on the invitation of the INC (the National Institute of Cinema). At this moment, Guerra had already directed some of his most remarkable works, such as *Os Cafajestes* (1962), and *Os Fuzis* (1964). Guerra's international reputation as one of Cinema Novo and Latin America's leading cineastes would legitimate Mozambican cinema while his presence in Maputo would mark the birth of national cinema. He participated in the cinematographic foundation of Mozambique not only training technicians at INC, but also cinematographically reconstituting the collective memory of one of the most significant episodes of resistance against Portuguese colonialism, the Mueda Massacre, the subject of *Mueda.* Guerra was also involved in the failed project of taking cinema to communal villages, a project similar to Godard's intended program, except that it only involved the reception of moving images and not their production by the population.

Guerra chooses to shoot an oral and improvised play, never set down in writing, in which Mueda's people incarnated simultaneously the colonial administration's characters and the demonstrators. The film intercuts images from this mise-en-scène with documentary interviews with survivors and witnesses of the massacre. The theatrical and carnivalesque performance of the massacre was based on the homonymous theatre play by Calisto dos Lagos, who is also quoted as the film's screenwriter and dramatic director. Mueda overrides all efforts at generic classification, thus opening the category of cinematographic œuvre, as a cultural form, to new dimensions that include cinema, theatre, collective memory's modes of expression and dynamic performative cultural forms such as the *mapiko*, a traditional masked dance of the Makonde, which constitutes an example of a dynamic cultural practice reflecting historical processes. At the same time, the film's diegetic structure reveals a complex intertextual conception of the historical narration—and of the film object as a form of historical representation—questioning the operative categories of documentary and fiction's validity, giving new meanings to the film practices of re-enactment. According to Guerra, the film, as a process, is a "documentary directly written with the image", conceived in the frame of "a cinema of experimentation".[1]

Raquel Schefer

Ruy Guerra, born in 1931 in Maputo, lives and works in Rio de Janeiro

1 This text is a short abstract taken from "Fictions of the Liberation Struggle: Ruy Guerra, José Cardoso, Zdravko Velimirovic" in *Kronos* 39, vol. 1, ed. Rui Assubuji, Paolo Israel, Drew Thompson (Cape Town: Ravens Press, 1981). Reprinted with the permission of the author.

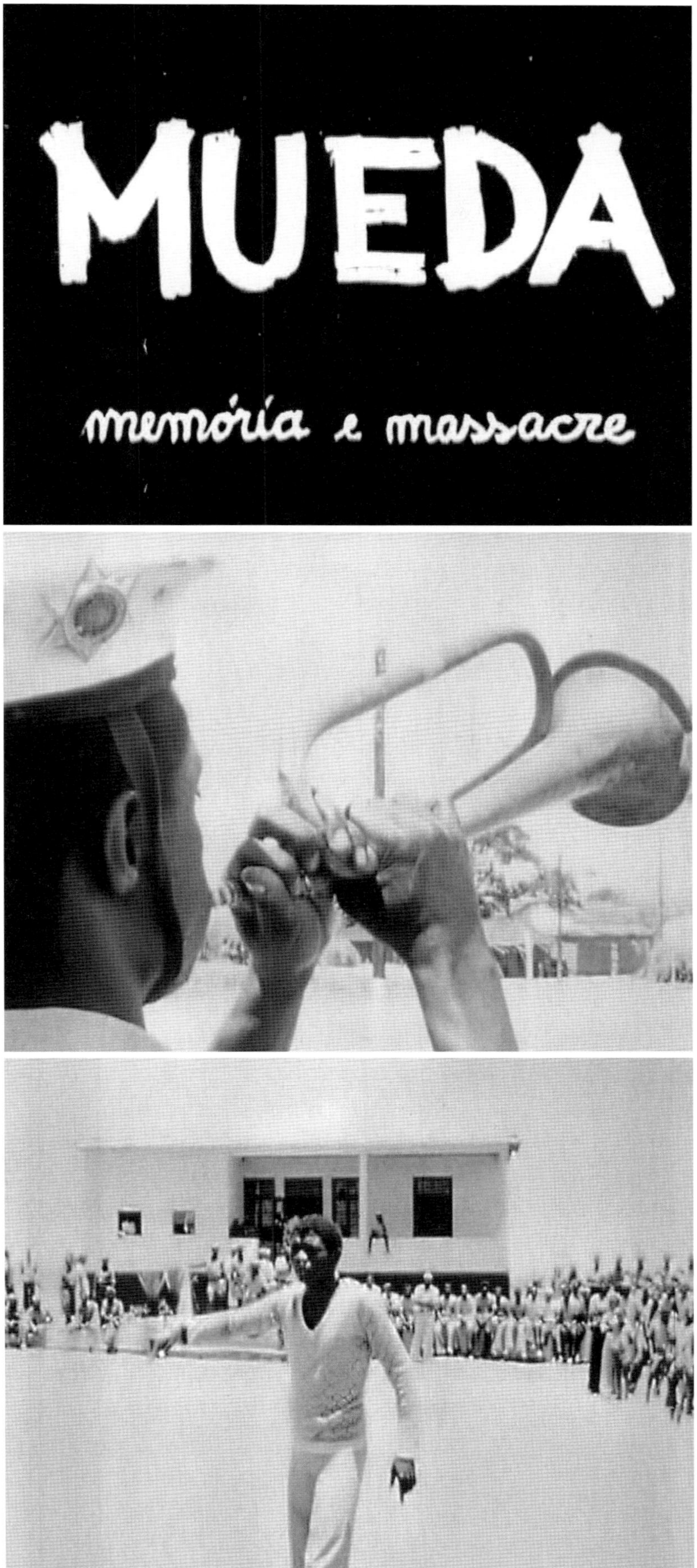

Ruy Guerra, detail from—*Mueda Memória e Massacre*, 1979. Video, black and white, sound, 76 min. 58 sec.

Walter Heynowski & Gerhard Scheumann

Outside the GDR, *The Laughing Man* (1966) is probably H&S Studio's best-known film. Posing as *Stern* reporters, Heynowski and Scheumann interview one of the most notorious mercenaries of his time, Siegfried Müller, who happened to be off duty in Europe after one of his "missions." Müller who had arrived for his interview with an Iron Cross pinned to his jacket, felt very confident before the camera.

> *"Herr Müller, a frank question. Can one say that you are known throughout the world? After all, you can claim that the press of the world reported about your Congo activities." "That's right, from Peking to Washington." (laughs) "Has this worldwide interest given you a special name? Can you tell us any particular name that you're called?" (laughs) "Yes, in Germany they call me Ko-Mü, Congo Müller." (laughs) "Congo Müller." (laughs) "Congo Müller, yes". "Otherwise I can't say. Major Müller is known in Belgium, in France I'm very well known, and American papers wrote a lot. In Congo everybody knows me, everyone knows where Major Müller is, just write Major Müller, Congo and it'll arrive." (laughs) "Well-known." (Ein Begriff also) "Well-known, yes." (Ein Begriff, ja.)*

Wearing a smile that combines a too-obvious modesty with self-contained arrogance, a chain-smoking man gazes at his interviewer. Major Siegfried Müller, in a good mood and politely answering the questions posed to him, is clearly enjoying his Pernod as well as the attention he is receiving. In this interview, filmed in 1966 by Walter Heynowski and Gerhard Scheumann, the fascist leader of commando troops and mercenary known as "Congo Müller" recalls with a surprising nonchalance his path to becoming the great military strategist he claims to be.

While speaking, Müller creates an illusion of being a charming man of the world, an illusion of being a defender of the Western world and its freedoms. However, by laying a trap of questions for Müller to fall into, the ingeniously paced interview nevertheless shows what is underneath, as the interviewee gets increasingly drunk. The gruesome contradiction between his smile and his past actions is revealed when secretly obtained photos and audiotapes are used as pieces of evidence against him.

> *"Then at the beginning of September 1964 came the order from General Mobutu." "Head of the forces?" "He was head of the forces. He was also for a time head of the Congolese government". "Yes, he is again today." "He said he urgently needed an effective group for the Equatorial Province. And he said, Müller, you have volunteered and if you like, you can go. And I went. I went out and asked which men I could have. Whoever you like. So I chose the paratroopers because I particularly like paratroopers. And Mike Hoare told me to take the Germans too. Naturally I took the German."*

The Laughing Man has a mysterious, even hypnotic appeal to it. The camera observes Congo Müller's face almost all the time, but as the interview subtly progresses the facade built by Müller is brought down and the audience is provided with an insight into the mind-set of this infamous mercenary.[1]

Walter Heynowski, born in 1927 in Ingolstadt, lives and works in Berlin
Gerhard Scheumann, born in 1930 in Szczytno, died in 1998 in Berlin

1 Compiled by Aryan Kaganof. Available online at http://www.kaganof.com

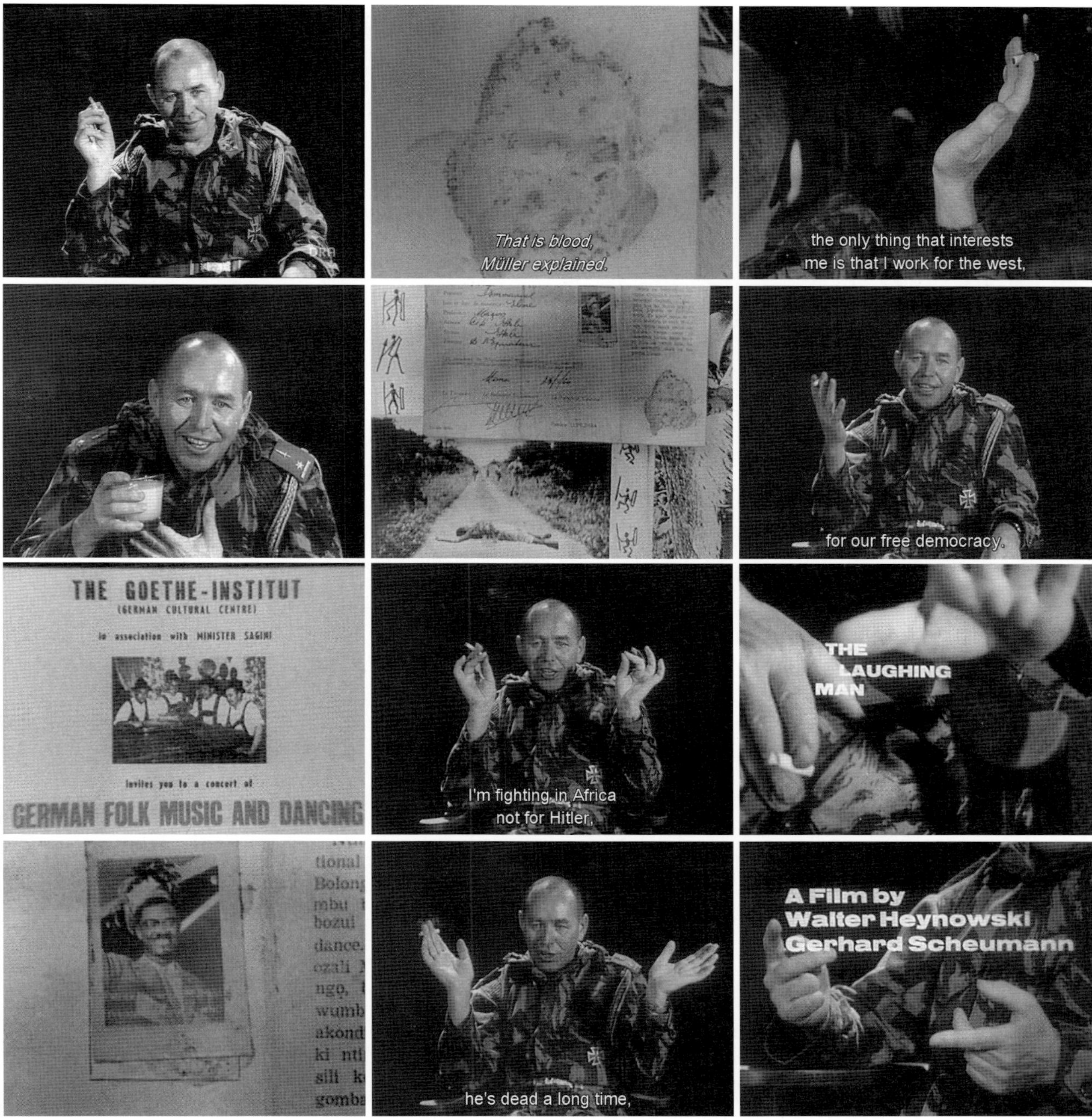

Walter Heynowski and Gerhard Scheumann, detail from—*The Laughing Man*, 1966. Video, color, sound, 66 min.

Kiluanji Kia Henda

The son of a former government official, Kiluanji Kia Henda is a member of the bourgeoisie who has come to reject monocular visions of Angolan society. Born in 1979, Henda has lived his entire life—until 2002—in a war torn country, learning his craft from photojournalists documenting the Civil War.[1] The process of an artist in Angola in many ways mirrors the liminal nature of Angolan culture, a society with the possibility of being born anew. Just as the artist invents new worlds and composes new realities, so too have Angolans required flexibility and inventiveness to survive. Henda describes being "original" as an artist as a "huge challenge," particularly "in a country where every[one] has to be creative to overcome many problems. It's like improvisation as a way of living."

Redefining the Power rewrites the semiotic force of past monuments, "those self-aggrandizing, heroic monuments that utilize their physical remove from daily life to reinforce the static and eternal history they articulate," and makes apparent that the actors who will create and define Angola's future may very well originate from the ordinary creativity of the everyday.[2] The temporal life of Henda's monuments—as brief as the click of a camera lens—are counter-memorials which allow the "active negation of presence" to shift the political work of memorialization onto public discourse itself. That is, Henda's photographs encourage speculation as to whether or not certain monumental pedestals in central Luanda should remain vacant.

Henda's work suggests that, as in Bamako, Mali, these new national *lieux de mémoire* could be places "wherein citizens, especially young people, can engage in the performance of a shared history and national purpose".[3] These yet to be realized sites will be interrogated by new sets of interpretive practices, engaging in a cyclical process of historical interpretation that allows evolving cultures to continually revisit unanswered social questions. Henda's series *Redefining the Power* represents an intermediate, catalyzing step between forgetting the past and imagining the future. As Achille Mbembe explains, the "future" is both a political and an aesthetic category with a profound role to play in postcolonial societies. "Futurism is a form of imagination that in practice is becoming a foundational dimension."[4] The capacity to imagine the future is necessary for genuine collective agency because it keeps open the possibility of its own existence. If societies are constituted by means of controlling oneiric functions, as Mbembe argues, then by denying basic infrastructure, Angola has curtailed Luanda's citizens' temporal imagination by restricting their bodies to daily struggles, reducing them to a purely biological life. The creative fields, with their capacity to demonstrate, or "try on," different guises of the future like so many different clothes, is key to the revitalization of Angola's shared cultural dreaming functions.[5]

Dariel Cobb

Kiluanji Kia Henda, born in 1979 in Luanda, lives and works in Luanda

1 Lígia Afonso, "'Kiluanji Kia Henda to me,' Interview with Kiluanji Kia Henda," *BUALA*, April 8, 2011.
2 Thomas Stubblefield, "Do Disappearing Monuments Simply Disappear?", *Future Anterior: Journal of Historic Preservation History Theory & Criticism* 8, no. 2 (2011): 1–11.
3 Mary Jo Arnoldi, "Bamako, Mali: Monuments and Modernity in the Urban Imagination", *Africa Today* 54, no. 2 (2007): 2–24.
4 Achille Mbembe, "Introductory Lectures 1, 2, and 3 to 'African Future Cities.'" Lectures presented at Harvard University, Cambridge, September 4, 9, and 11, 2013.
5 The text is an excerpt of *"Luanda's Monuments"* ed. Achille Mbembe, Megan Jones and Stephanie Bosch Santana, Johannesburg Workshop of Theory and Criticism 7 (2014). Available online at http://www.jwtc.org.za.

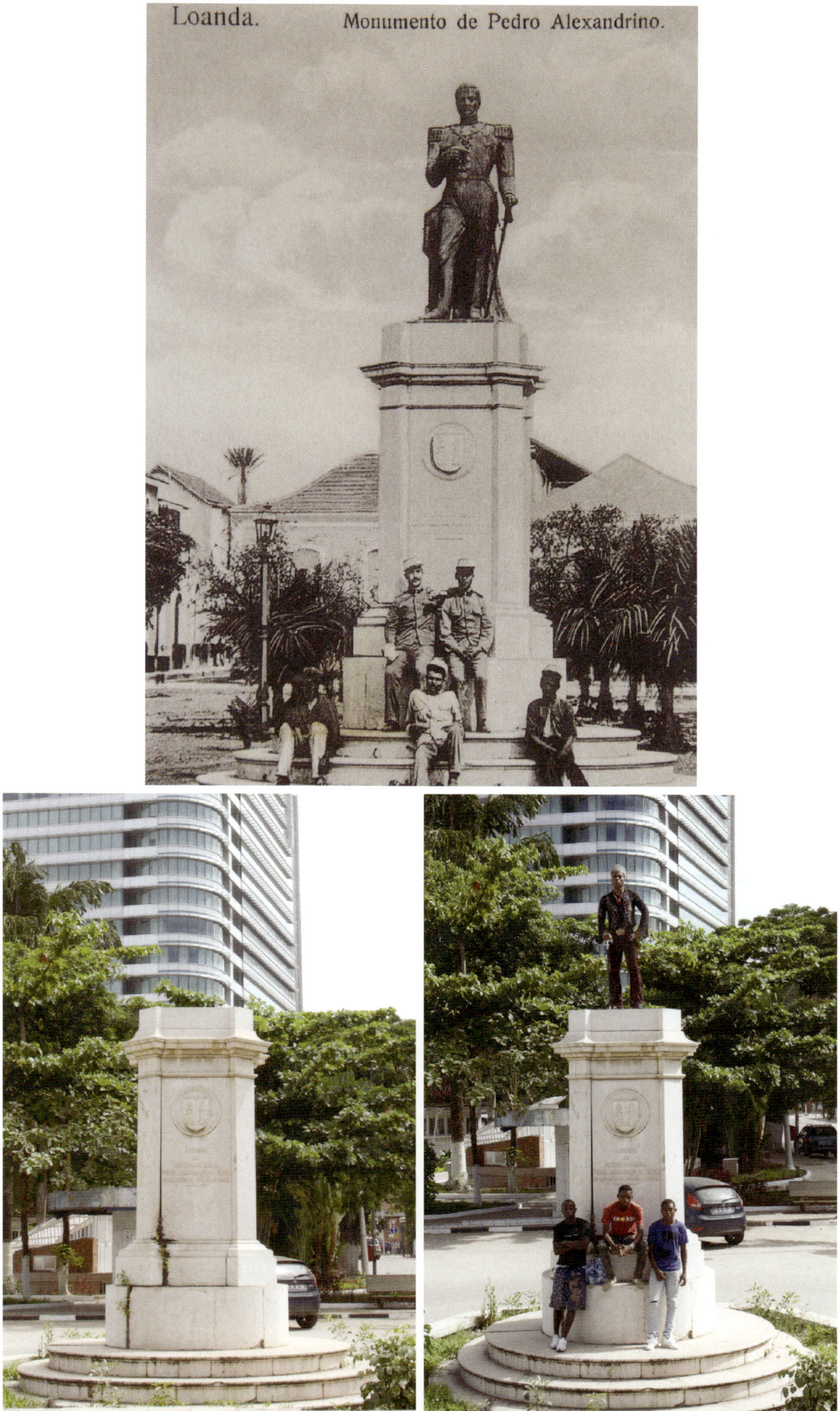

Kiluanji Kia Henda, *Redefining the Power III (series 75 with Miguel Prince)*, 2011. Photo print mounted on aluminium, 80 × 120 cm (× 3).

Daniel Kojo Schrade

Henriette Gunkel: *Daniel, you have been thinking around and working in the realm of Afrofuturism for a while now. The figure of the Afronaut, for example, appears in a number of your works. It is also the title of a series of paintings you have produced. How did that series come about, what inspired you?*

Daniel Kojo Schrade: That was around 1999, after I had done a series of works and paintings with titles like *DuBois*, *Made in Diaspora* or *Brother Beethoven*.[1] The *Afronaut* series arose under the influence of a number of things, such as the work of musicians like George Clinton, Sun Ra, and Lee Scratch Perry, whose performances in outfits with mirrors, antennas, and helmet-like objects on his head in a way bring together the trickster and shaman with the space voyager. An interview with Henry Louis Gates that I read in 1998, about his *Encyclopedia Africana*, also played a role. In the conversation, the journalist made fun of the project, questioning the point of an *Encyclopedia Africana* when there existed already an *Encyclopedia Britannica*. Gates expressed really beautifully why he was going to present Ludwig van Beethoven, the European cultural icon, as an Afrodiasporic time traveler in his *Encyclopedia*. It is an important subject.

My Afronauts are dislocated characters who create and control their image spaces themselves. They claim the power to renegotiate ascriptions of identity. The roots of my painting lie in gestural abstraction, and the presence of Afronauts in these otherwise homogenous paintings has an unsettling effect. It transforms my work into painting that comes from the "spaces in-between." The Afronauts often function as elements that operate in the liminal space between foreground and background. At a certain point, the viewer is left alone with their own "reading ability." The Afronauts are an important projection surface not just in my paintings, but in my performances too.

H.G.: *In your paintings, you don't simply work with various materials. You also apply these in different layers—a practice that doesn't just make reference to the in-between spaces that you describe, but also produces a complicated temporality. In addition to this, you work with archive material that, in a sense, you dig up, expose, and incorporate in the piece, but also cover over again. This means that various temporal levels come together in your paintings, and that the futuristic element is always permeated by the past. Can you tell us about this retro-futuristic approach?*

D.K.S.: Yes, there is a really practical connection there, between painting and these temporal levels. I work in countless layers of paint. Every single layer has a memory, each layer continues to have an effect in, or an influence on, the next one. And the structure that grows out of this is infused with different layers of time which, superimposed on one another, can take on greater meaning. The idea of the palimpsest is very fitting here. Then there is the materiality of the paint, which through the continued layering builds up three-dimensionally, relief-like. It forms a landscape, so to speak, that can store much more information, more memories, than a two-dimensional surface.

As I mentioned, these memories are inspired by a broad spectrum of Afrodiasporic music: Lee Scratch Perry, George Clinton, Sun Ra—and of course Drexciya, DJ Spooky, and Butch Morris, who conducts an orchestra without a score by creating a piece out of the moment. That is not exactly true; you can't say out of the moment, because this moment—and this is the case with

1 http://www.danielkojoschrade.com

my painting, too—is so permeated by the past and by the future, by expectation, that you don't need things like notes or a fixed palette of shapes and colors. In literature, the works of Samuel Delaney and Octavia Butler, as well as, for example, the traditional Ghanaian stories of *Anansi the Spider*, convey dramatic, nonlinear concepts of time and space. The *Anansi* stories were basically already Afrofuturistic a thousand years ago.

H.G.: *My last question is aimed at how you conceptualize technology, one of the central aspects of science fiction and Afrofuturism as last word. We are talking about, for example, the synthesizer, the beatbox, the human-machine interface. Your Afronauts seem to be able to do without this kind of technology. Instead, other objects appear, for example the umbrella, the iron, simple antennas?*

D.K.S.: Exactly. To me, an umbrella or an iron can be a high-tech communication tool. When one of my Afronauts holds an umbrella in their hand, that is a code for a kind of communication that utilizes this high-tech level, but also a more complex, spiritual communication level. They're tapping into survival strategies that were, and still are, existential in the depths of the (black) Atlantic, in outer space, or in social spaces that aren't clearly defined—in spaces in-between. The Afronaut expands the technology by cultural and spiritual means in order to navigate the countless terrestrial and extraterrestrial in-between spaces.[2]

Daniel Kojo Schrade, born in 1967 in Schienen, lives and works in Amherst

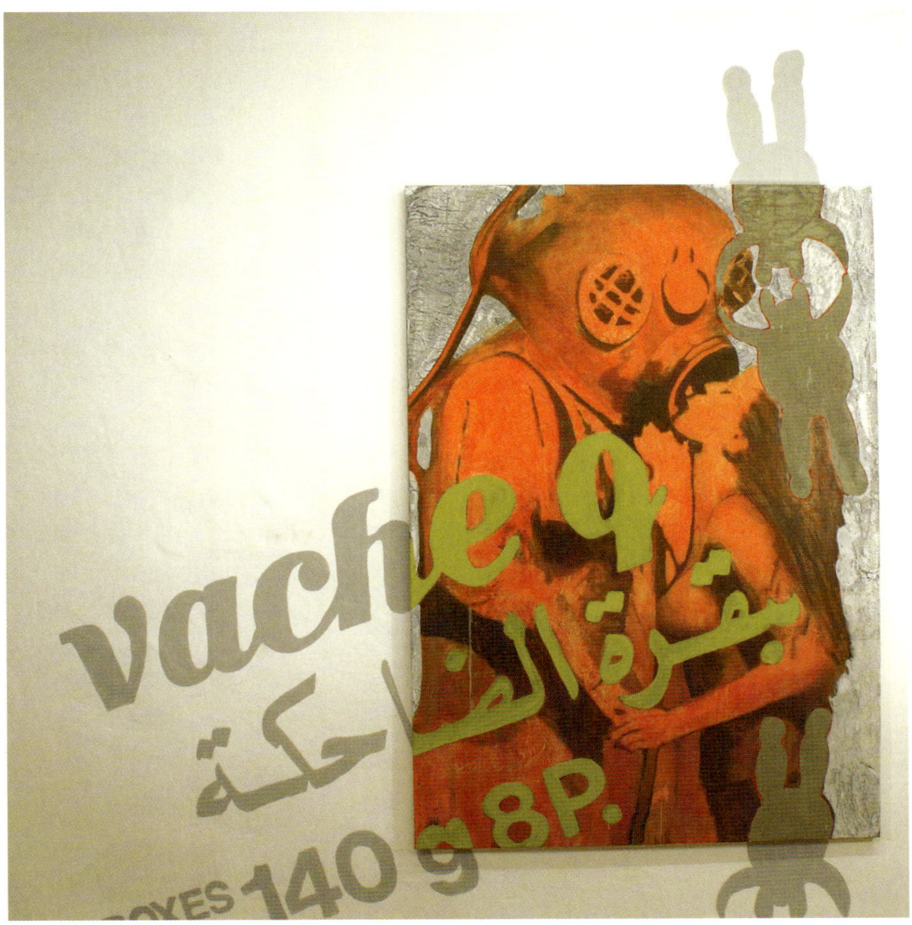

Daniel Kojo Schrade, *Afronauts (Francophone)*, 2010. Painting installation, acrylic on canvas, mixed media, 240×240 cm.

2 The interview was published in German online at http://www.malmoe.org, December 2014, and printed in *Malmoe* 69.

Sana na N'Hada et al.

This collective film, *O Regresso de Amílcar Cabral* (1976), was the first production realized by Guinean filmmakers after the liberation of Guinea Bissau from Portuguese colonialism in 1974. According to Sana na N'hada the original aim of this film was to call upon the Guinean diaspora back to the newly free nation. In fact, the film documents the translocation of the remains of Amílcar Cabral from Conakry (where he was assassinated in 1973) to Bissau the capital of the country. This event was edited with Guinean songs, and archival material framing Cabral addressing freedom fighters during the guerrilla war. The convocation of lament in this film is a gesture to provoke a multiplicity of returns.

The history of Guinean cinema starts during the eleven-year-long war for independence with Portugal when Amílcar Cabral, the leader of the PAIGC (African Party for the Independence of Guinea and Cape Verde), sent four young Guineans—Flora Gomes, Sana na N'Hada, Josefina Crato and José Bolama Cobumba—to the Cuban Film Institute (ICAIC) to learn cinema. Cabral's propaganda vision was to make his people and the world aware of the ongoing struggle, making use of the audiovisual to create a new national identity. Aligned with militant cinema culture, these productions were meant as a political tool, a way to establish the pillar of a collective memory and to promote the development of a national cinema Film production in Guinea-Bissau thrived for many years following independence, however, with the coup d'état of 1980, the concept of a national cinema was deemed unimportant by governmental authorities (the exception to this period is one of the most important Guinean productions, Mortu Nega [1988] by Flora Gomes). With the outbreak of civil war in 1998, state-sponsored for funded state-funded cinema was completely abandoned.

Today, all that is known to have remained from this period of production is an archive of films and unedited footage and sound tapes made between 1972 and 1980 and stored in Bissau at the INCA (Instituto Nacional de Cinema e Audiovisual). Assembled with this material are other films and news reels originating from countries which supported the Guinean struggle (Cuba, Sweden, the GDR, Senegal, the USSR, Holland, France, India and Algeria), productions by Portuguese filmmakers struggling against colonial politics as well as copies of several films left by Chris Marker during his visits to Guinea-Bissau in 1979.

In 2012, all the fragmentary remains of this archive, including the film *The Return of Amílcar Cabral*, were digitized by the Arsenal—Institute for Film and Video Art, Berlin, in the context of the research *Luta ca caba inda* [The struggle is not over yet]. This collaborative ongoing project—named after an unfinished film in the archive—focuses on experimental ways of keeping the archive open, giving access to its kaleidoscopic imaginary potencies through live commented screenings, mobile cinemas, workshops, discussions and other encounters.

Filipa César

Sana na N'Hada was born in Enxalé in 1950, lives and works in Bissau

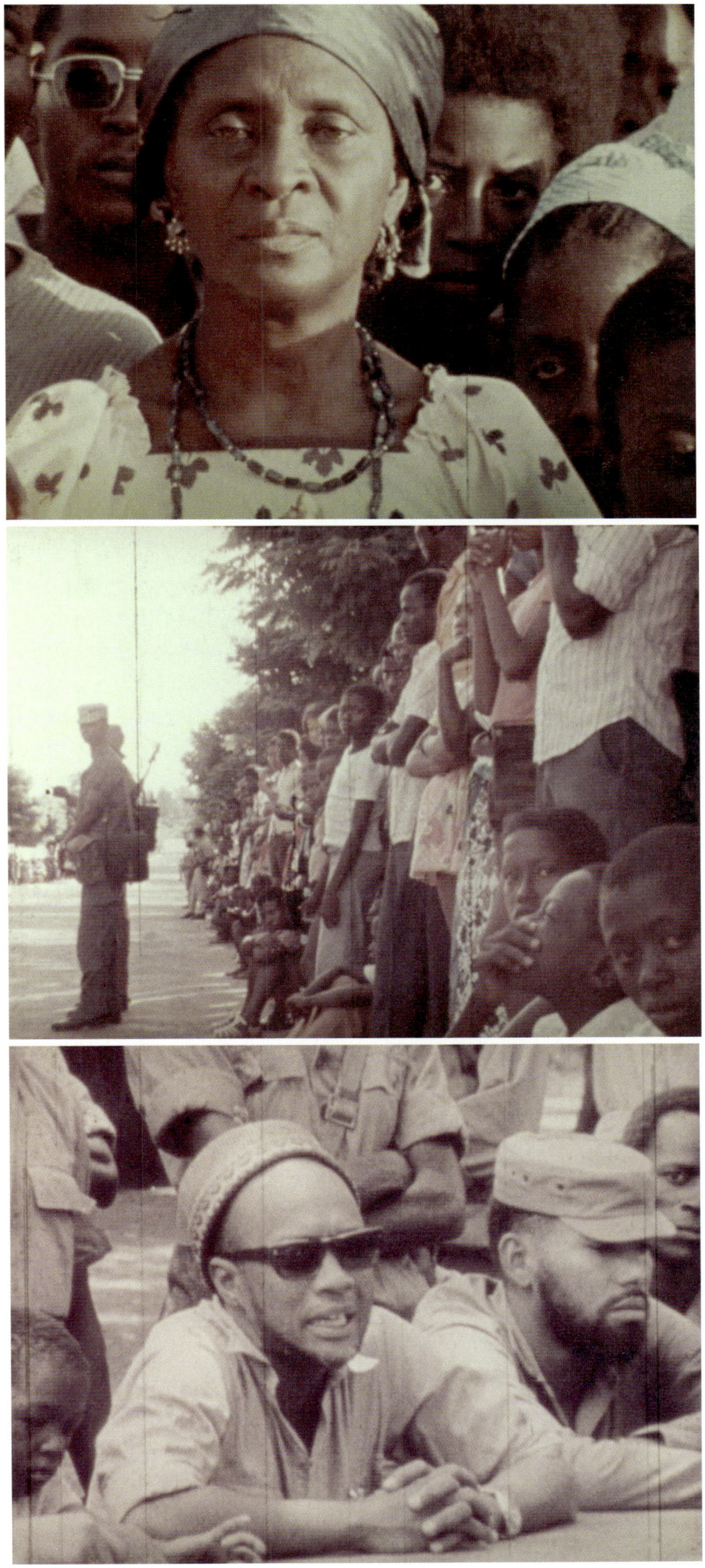

Sana na N'Hada, José Bolama Cobumba, Josefina Crato, Djalma Fettermann, Flora Gomes, detail from—*O Regresso de Amílcar Cabral*, 1976. 16mm film transferred to HD video, color, sound, 31 min. Reproduced by permission of INCA.

The Otolith Group

In the Year of the Quiet Sun[1]—The Otolith Group's thirty-four minute film essay on the fragile dream of Pan-Africanism—is neither quiet nor sunny. If anything, it resounds with a melancholic sombreness, born of hindsight and hope—a series of echoes and reverberations that seem to animate and agitate the totems of the past so that they are no longer still or silent. At the heart of the film is an astronomical conceit. It relates to an intermittent solar phenomenon—occurring in an eleven-year cycle—when the sun's surface cools sufficiently to allow scientists to study it. During one such period, between November 1964 and November 1965, many countries, including emerging independent African states, issued commemorative stamps to mark this significant moment. These spheres of saturated yellow and red with spiky, radiating rays—reproduced in the film—seem to shine a beneficent light onto the orbiting earth. But down below, despite similar philatelic symbolization—stars, spheres, roundels and flags proliferate on the commemorative and celebratory stamps of decolonization and independence—the territorial and political transformation of the unquiet continent far exceeds the capacity of these miniscule propaganda prints to adequately tell its tale.

It is this disjunction between the minute materiality of the postage stamps and the epic events they commemorate that the film dramatizes so brilliantly. Taking its formal cue from the period-specific design and display value of these small but significant prints, *In the Year of the Quiet Sun* blows up the scale of the stamp, allowing it to fill the screen. Stamp and screen become one, flattening out and filtering the archival and documentary footage with which it is interwoven and juxtaposed. The stamps themselves are interesting: we notice their schematic design, the simplified graphics of 1960s commercial art and advertising; and the standardized lettering and modernist fonts which situate them firmly in the American context from which they were generated and distributed. Why, asks the narrator, are the symbols of Pan-African liberation and decolonization designed on Wall Street? Who is the "New York Philatelic Society?" What is the Pan-African Pop that the stamps seem to symbolize and suggest? These are not only issues of design and decorum. They point to the question of power and the fraught issues of allegiance and alignment for the emerging African nations, poised during the early years of the Cold War between their old colonial occupiers (from which they needed to liberate themselves, mentally and economically) and the new power brokers of East and West, each vying for prominence and influence. At the same time they signal the formal and symbolic languages through which Pan-Africanism found its robust, if short-lived, voice.

Tamar Garb

The Otolith Group was founded in 2002 in London by Anjalika Sagar and Kodwo Eshun

1 This text is a short abstract taken from "Of States and Stamps: The Otolith Group at the Delfina Foundation," published online by contemporaryand.com. Platform for International art from African Perspectives. Reprinted with the permission of the author.

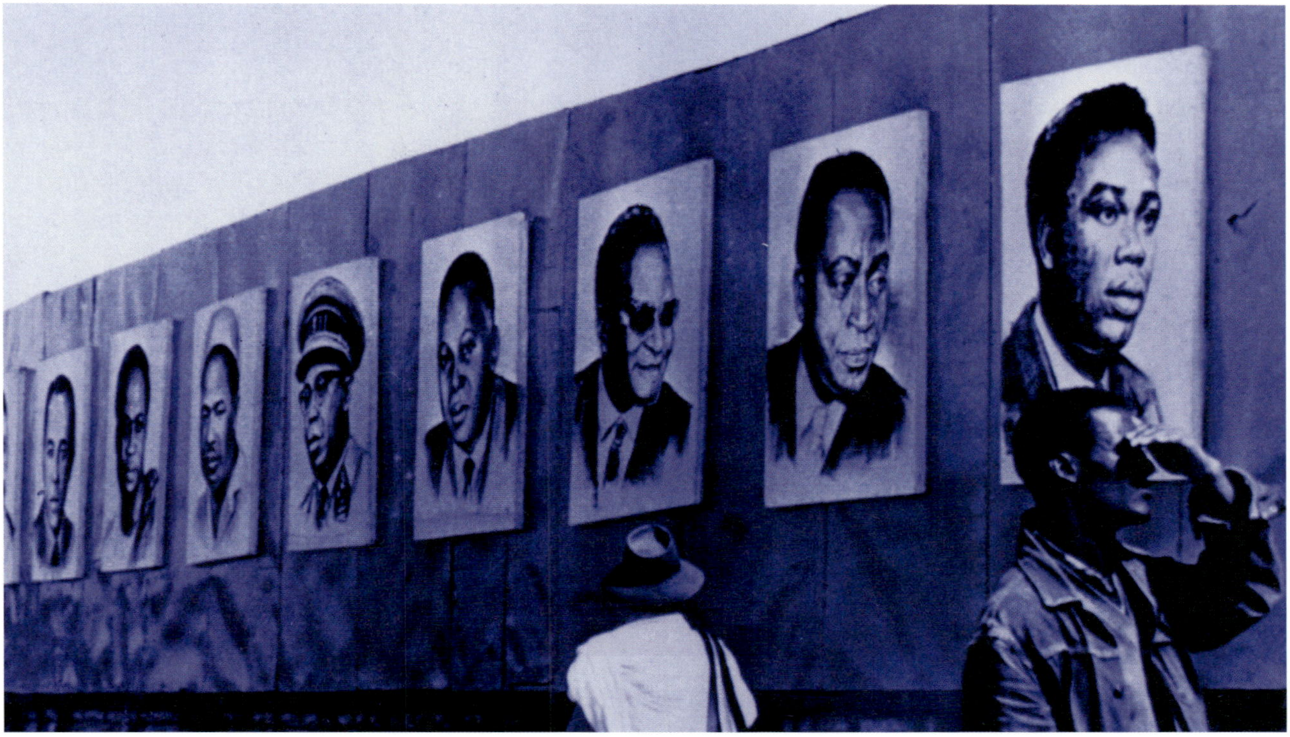

The Otolith Group, a detail from—*In the Year of the Quiet Sun*, 2013. Single channel HD video installation, color, sound, 33 min. 57 sec. Reproduced by permission of the artists and LUX, London.

Yann Le Masson & Olga Poliakoff

The short film *J'ai huit ans* (1961) by Yann Le Masson and Olga Poliakoff was prepared by Frantz Fanon and filmmaker René Vautier as Fanon was working with Algerian child refugees in Tunis, experimenting on a therapy that involved visualization of trauma. René Vautier was responsible for collecting the drawings for the film. When the film was made in 1961, the number of Algerian refugees in Tunis had reached 175,000 and many of them were very young. The film starts simple and serene, with short filmic portraits of young boys that are all apparently eight years old. Later, children's drawings of tanks and guns enter the frame together with children's voices that talk about what they witnessed during the Algerian War, including accounts of the killing of family members and attacks.

The film was banned in France and existed in French consciousness only by word of mouth. It is striking to see how informed the Algerian refugee children in the film show themselves about the causes of the war, one child stating for example that France's presence in Algeria is driven by the lucrative oil business.

J'ai huit ans is a highly stylized documentary with a clear mission in the same way that Fanon's *Wretched of the Earth* has a simple and clear set-up. The central focus is the look of the child, it is a look that affronts the camera, as the children's narratives speak of a stunning level of awareness. Hardly ever portrayed in combination with war at that time, the children are treated as resisting subjects not used as victims—a filmic strategy quite incompatible with the feel-good charity events of our times.

"Another indispensable way to help the Algerians and to denounce the role of the French army in this war, was to use another weapon I had learned to master: the camera. In collaboration with Olga (Poliakoff), and thanks to René Vautier who had procured the Algerian children's drawings for me, we created a little anticolonialist 'agit-prop' film,"[1] stated Yann Le Masson about his artistic approach.

The French state refused to give the film an "exploitation visa", necessary for legal projection in France, and the French police seized it at least seventeen times before it gained authorization in 1973, eleven years after the Algerian War had ended.

Yann Le Masson, born in 1930 in Brest, died in 2012 in Avignon
Olga Poliakoff, born in 1928 in Pancevo, died in 2009 in Villejuif

1 "Kharon at his oar: An Interview with Yann Le Masson" by Paul Douglas Grant, April 13, 2010, Avignon, France. Available online at http://www.lafuriaumana.it.

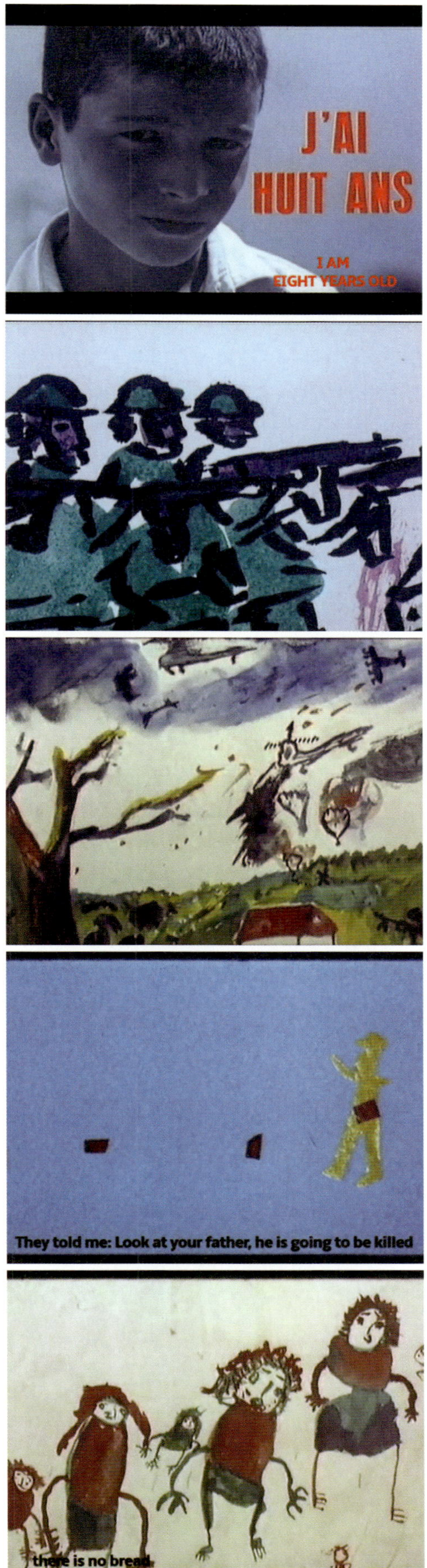

Yann Le Masson and Olga Poliakoff, detail from—*J'ai huit ans*, 1961. Video, color, sound, 9 min., 12 sec.

Kidlat Tahimik

The slave's story was in no way 'a story to be filmed'—in the classical sense of a character to be embellished from historical accounts. The filming itself was a story to be lived out—for the next three-and-a-half decades. (Kidlat Tahimik)

"Balikbayan"—the word Kidlat Tahimik chose as the title of his film—is the Tagalog term for guest worker. Many Filipinos from the huge underclass of their developing country work in affluent Asian countries. Their employment is usually precarious and based on temporary contracts, some of which are extended for a long time. While women from the Philippines often work as housekeepers, nannies or nurses, many male Filipinos work as builders or drivers on building sites in the Gulf States, as workers on oil platforms or as sailors on oceangoing ships. The protagonist in Kidlat Tahimik's long unfinished film *Balikbayan #1 Memories of Overdevelopment Redux III* (2015), who appears simultaneously as a victim and beneficiary of Europe's colonial expansion, is also a "balikbayan": Enrique Melaka, a slave of Ferdinand Magellan. The Portuguese seafarer, who undertook several expeditions to Asia on commission from the Spanish crown, thereby not only paved the way for Spanish colonialism; his journeys also finally proved that the earth is round. Magellan almost became the first person to circumnavigate the globe but shortly before the end of his last journey, warriors of the tribal chief LapuLapu killed him in battle on the island of Mactan, which is part of the Philippine archipelago.

A few brief passages in the notes of Magellan's ship's chronicler Antonio Pigafetta, make it seem possible that Magellan's slave Enrique succeeded where his master failed: in traveling all the way around the world. Magellan had bought him on an earlier expedition in Malacca (today a state in Malaysia) and brought him back to Portugal. Magellan's next voyage was to the "Spice Islands" of Southeast Asia—but this time in the opposite direction, westward across the Pacific. In his testament, Magellan ordered that Enrique, who had served him as valet and interpreter, should be freed. If Enrique returned to Malacca after Magellan's death, then he was in fact the first person to sail around the world. Kidlat Tahimik deduces that Enrique originally came from the Philippines thanks to a detail that chronicler Pigafetta mentions in his log of Magellan's expedition: when the Spanish ships reached Cebu, Enrique was able to make himself understood by the natives.

The extant historical sources cannot conclusively prove the claim that Enrique was a Filipino and also the world's first circumnavigator, but they don't conclusively refute it either. Kidlat Tahimik uses the resulting narrative possibilities to stage a fascinating thought experiment: what if a paradigmatic victim of early colonization accomplished a historic, pioneering achievement? Did a man purchased as a servant by a Spanish conquistador on the slave market in Malacca, who interpreted for him and had to serve him at table, play a role in history comparable to that of Marco Polo or Columbus? In the film, Enrique (played by the director himself) does not appear as the object of European exploitation, but rather as a kind of shrewd cosmopolitan from the Global South. Kidlat Tahimik began working on his film about Enrique Melaka in 1979, but for personal reasons never completed it. Not until more than three decades later has he now been able to finish it, almost without a budget but partly thanks to new developments in media technology (some of the new footage was shot with an iPhone).

Tilman Baumgärtel

Kidlat Tahimik, born in 1942 in Baguio, lives and works in Benguet

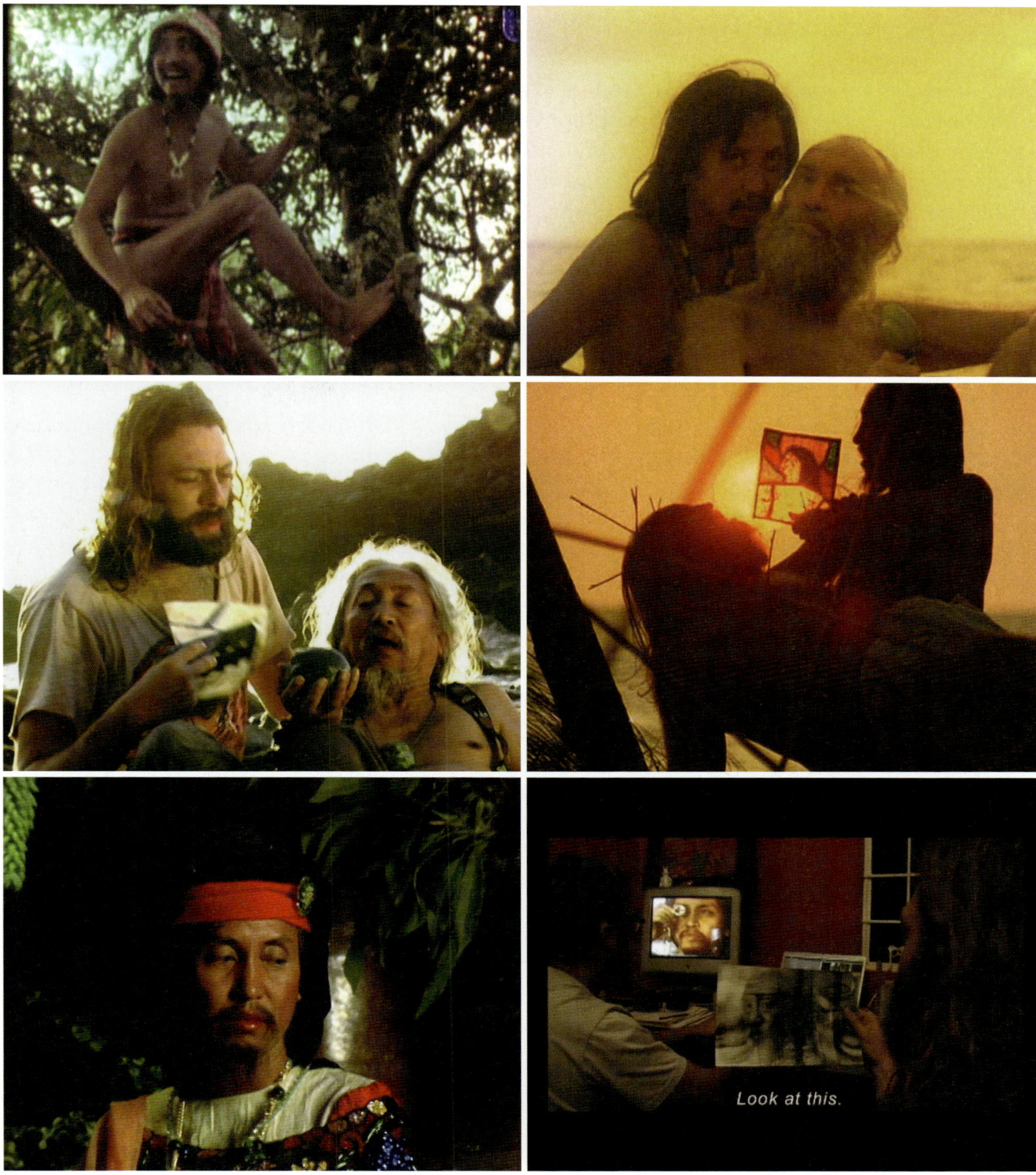

KidlatTahimik, detail from—*Balikbayan #1 Memories of Overdevelopment Redux III*, 2015. Video, color, sound, 145 min.

Qes Adamu Tesfaw

Ethiopian painter Qes Adamu Tesfaw paints in a typical style that developed around the eighteenth century capital city of Gondar to convey theological and poetry interpretations and was later refined in the nineteenth and twentieth century. This style fits seamlessly into the artist's biography as the artist was trained as a priest in the Ethiopian Orthodox Church and as such gained the prefix "Qes" to his name, which translates as "priest". His personal style, however, is characterized by a very free interpretation of canonical conventions, both in subject matter and in his use of color, which makes his work closer to the category of contemporary painting. Expressive hues of pink, green and yellow are used for secular paintings that depict subjects which range from public health issues to depictions of state visits, while religious depictions are painted in a limited palette of muted tones.

The long titles of his works—in this case *Haile Selassie's Visit to Jamaica (2003)*—function as captions for what is depicted. The visit of Haile Selassie to Jamaica took place on April 21, 1966, and was a key moment for the Jamaican Rastafari movement. The Jamaican Rastafari movement took root in Jamaica after the Jamaica-born early Pan-Africanist Marcus Garvey had predicted in 1927: "Look to Africa when a black king shall be crowned, for the day of deliverance is near." When Haile Selassie was crowned king of uncolonized Ethiopia in 1930, it was he who the Rastafarians recognized as their messiah and this would fuel the movement to grow exponentially. By 1966 the Rastafarian community was vast but also very maltreated in Eurocentric Jamaica, especially by the police. In 1963, merely three years before Selassie's visit, dozens of Rastafarians were killed by security forces in the Coral Gardens Massacre.

The visit caused unseen scenes as an estimated 100,000 Rastafarians went to the airport in Kingston to greet their Messiah—Selassie himself was so overwhelmed that he had to be convinced to disembark the airplane after he had tried a first time but returned back inside. However, the visit brought about a significant change. The fact that Selassie, the spiritual leader of the Rastafari movement was granted an official visit and was given the keys to the city, recognizing him as an important figure in world politics, led to the first steps being taken towards the recognition of the formerly ostracized Rastafarians. The movement celebrates April 21, Grounation Day, as the second most important holy day in their calendar.

Qes Adamu Tesfaw, born in 1922 in Bichena, lives and works in Addis Ababa

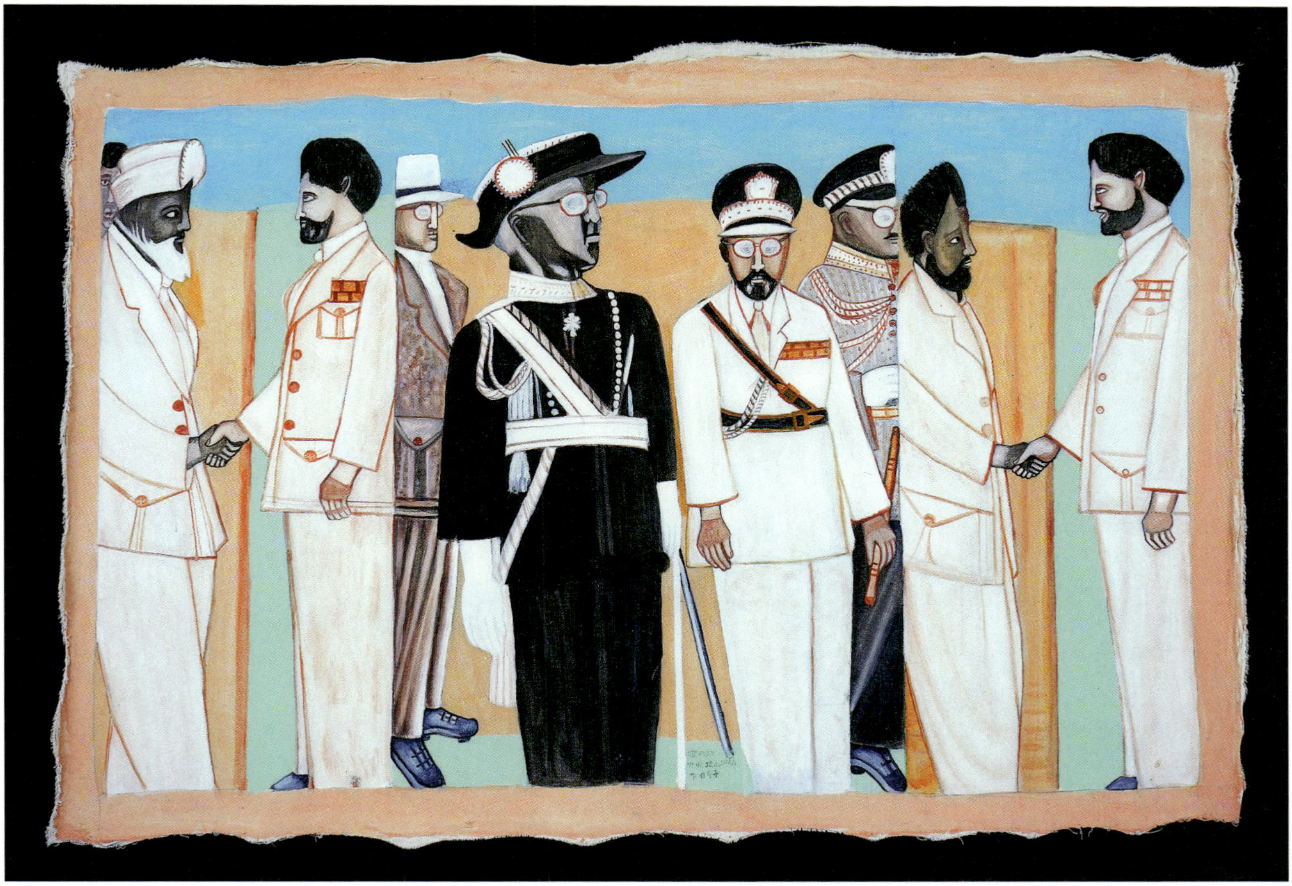

Qes Adamu Tesfaw, *Haile Selassie's Visit to Jamaica*, 2003. Paint on canvas, 94×148 cm. Reproduced by permission of Leah Niederstadt.

John Akomfrah
The Unfinished Conversation, 2012
3-channel HD video installation, color, sound, 46 min.

Transfigured Night, 2013
Double channel HD video installation, color, sound, 30 min.
Courtesy the artist and Carroll/Fletcher.

Kader Attia
Dispossession, 2013
Installation with double slide projection, (2× 80 color slides) and video (color, sound, 13 min.)

Silence's Injuries, 2014
Video, color, sound, 13 min. 51 sec.
Courtesy the artist, Galerie Nagel Draxler and Gallery Lehmann Maupin.

Balufu Bakupa-Kanyinda
The Draughtsmen Clash, 1996
Video, color, sound, 40 min.
Courtesy the artist.

Kudzanai Chiurai
Revelations 10, 2011
Print, ultra chrome ink on Innova photo fibre paper, 100×150 cm.
Courtesy the artist and Goodman Gallery.

Jihan El-Tahri
Flag Moments, 2013
Single channel video, color and black and white, sound, 6 min. 39 sec.

Interviews with Mokhtar Hallouda, Victor Moche, 2013
Single channel video, color, sound, 47 min. 51 sec.

The Price of Aid (Excerpt), 2009
Single channel video, color, sound, 11 min.
Courtesy the artist.

Theo Eshetu
Trip to Mount Zugualla, 2006
3-channel video transferred to single channel video, color, sound, 7 min.
Courtesy the artist.

Yervant Gianikian & Angela Ricci Lucchi
Imperium, 2013
Mixed media installation with 4-channel video, color, sound, 3 min. 10 sec.

Pays Barbare, 2013
Video, color, sound, 65 min.
Courtesy the artist and Les Films d'Ici.

Ruy Guerra
Mueda, Memória e Massacre, 1979
Video, black and white, sound, 76 min. 58 sec.
Courtesy INAC, Instituto Nacional de Audiovisual e Cinema de Mozambique.

Walter Heynowski & Gerhard Scheumann
The Laughing Man, 1966
Video, color, sound, 66 min.
Courtesy Deutsches Rundfunkarchiv.

Kiluanji Kia Henda
Redefining The Power III (Series 75 with Miguel Prince), 2011
Photo print mounted on aluminium, 80×120 cm (× 3).

Concrete Affection—Zopo Lady, 2014
HD video, color, sound, 12 min. 30 sec.
Courtesy the artist, Galeria Fonti and Giorgio Fasol.

Daniel Kojo Schrade
Afronauts (Francophone), 2010
Painting installation, acrylic on canvas, mixed media, 240×240 cm.

Afronauts C07Afl, 2012
Mixed media on canvas, 132×182.8 cm.
Courtesy the artist.

Sana na N'Hada et al.
O Regresso de Amílcar Cabral, 1976
16mm film transferred to HD video, color, sound, 31 min.
Courtesy arsenal—institut für film und videokunst e.V.

The Otolith Group
In the Year of the Quiet Sun, 2013
Single channel HD video installation, color, sound, 33 min. 57 sec.

Statecraft: An Incomplete Timeline of Independence Determined by Digital Auction, 2014
Lightbox display system, encapsulated stamps. Dimensions variable.
Courtesy the artists.

Yann Le Masson & Olga Poliakoff
J'ai huit ans, 1961
Video, color, sound, 9 min. 12 sec.
Courtesy the artists.

Kidlat Tahimik
Balikbayan #1 Memories of Overdevelopment Redux III, 2015
Video, color, sound, 145 min.
Courtesy the artist.

Qes Adamu Tesfaw
Haile Selassie's Visit to Jamaica, 2003
Paint on canvas, 94×148 cm.
Courtesy Leah Niederstadt.

Biographies
Colophon

John Akomfrah lives and works in London. An artist, lecturer, and writer, as well as a filmmaker, his work is among the most distinctive in the contemporary British art world. Akomfrah is well known for his work with the London-based media workshop Black Audio Film Collective, which he co-founded in 1982, together with Lina Gopaul, Avril Johnson, Reece Auguiste, Trevor Mathison, David Lawson and Edward George. Since 1998, Akomfrah has worked primarily within the independent film and television production companies, Smoking Dogs Films (London) and Creation Rebel Films (Accra).

Max Annas is the SARChI Chair in Social Change at the University of Fort Hare in East London, South Africa, working on a project on jazz in South Africa, with a particular focus on The Blue Notes. He has published, edited and co-edited non-fiction books on African film, anthropology, food production, right wing youth culture and the African American struggle for liberation. His first novel, *Die Farm*, was published in 2014.

Lotte Arndt is based in Brussels and has taught at the art school l'École d'art et design in Valence (France) since 2014. In 2014, she coordinated the research program "Karawane" that accompanied the making of the Belgian pavilion of Vincent Meessen and Katerina Gregos at the 56th Venice Biennale (in collaboration with *l'erg*, école de recherche graphique, Brussels). In 2013, she finished her PhD entitled *Postcolonial Negotiations in Paris Based Cultural Magazines Referring to Africa* (Humboldt University Berlin/Paris VII, Diderot, 2013). She is part of the artist and writers group *Ruser l'image*.

Tilman Baumgärtel is a writer. He lives in Berlin and teaches media studies at Hochschule Mainz. Previously he was a professor at the University of the Philippines in Manila (2005–2009) and at the Department of Media and Communication at the Royal University of Phnom Penh (2009–2012). He has written or edited nine books on various aspect of media culture, including internet art, computergames, the aesthetics of loops and the director Harun Farocki.

Annett Busch (ed.) works as a freelance curator, writer and translator. She was an editor for *SPEX—magazine for pop-culture* (1997–2002) and co-edited the book *Ousmane Sembéne—Interviews* for the University Press of Mississippi. She co-curated (with Florian Schneider) "Of a people who are missing" an exhibition and ciné-club on films by Danièle Huillet and Jean-Marie Straub in Extra City Kunsthal, Antwerp, 2009. Together with Anselm Franke she co-curated the exhibition "After Year Zero" at the Haus der Kulturen der Welt, Berlin, 2013. Currently she works at the Trondheim Academy of Fine Art/NTNU on the research project "Electronic Textures", which revisits twentieth-century modernism by reading through vanguard Pan-African, transcultural, and international magazines.

Filipa César explores in her films, essays and installations, the fictional aspects of the documentary genre and searches for experimental forms of accessing historical events. The places and events César has exhibited at include: Tate Modern, London, 2007; International Triennale of Contemporary Art, Prague, 2008; 12th International Architecture Exhibition, Venice, 2010; 29th São Paulo Biennial, 2010; Manifesta 8, Cartagena, 2010; MUDAM, Luxembourg, 2012; Jeu de Paume, Paris, 2012.

Dariel Cobb is a PhD candidate in the History, Theory, and Criticism of Art and Architecture at Massachusetts Institute of Technology. Her current research interests include postcolonial expressions of national identity in Southern Africa; Afrofuturism and the technological body in Africa; juridical definitions of space. She would like to thank Achille Mbembe for the course that led to the paper quoted here.

Clare Davies received a PhD from the Institute of Fine Arts, New York University in 2014 for a dissertation entitled *Modern Egyptian Art: Site, Commodity, Archive, 1891–1948*. She is the recipient of the inaugural Irmgard Coninx Prize in Transregional Studies, *Forum Transregionale Studien*, Berlin. In Fall 2015, she will join the Metropolitan Museum of Art, New York as Assistant Curator of Modern and Contemporary Art from the Middle East, North Africa, and Turkey.

Denis Ekpo is Professor of Comparative Literature and Director of the Comparative Literature Program, University of Port Harcourt, Nigeria; a cultural theorist who developed the concept of Post-Africanism; member advisory board of *Third Text* from 2004 to 2012; a guest editor of *Third Text*'s special issue *Beyond Négritude*; the author of two books namely, *Neither Anti-imperialism nor the White Man's Tears*, and *Philosophie et litterature africaine*. He is currently working on a Manifesto for a Post-African art.

Kodwo Eshun is an artist and theorist. As co-founder of The Otolith Group, his work has been presented in solo exhibitions at Casco, Office for Art, Design and Theory, Utrecht, Museu Serralves, Porto, and Bergen Kunsthall, Bergen, and group exhibitions at Museum of Modern Art, New York, Haus der Kulturen der Welt, Berlin, and dOCUMENTA (13). He is the author of *Dan Graham: Rock My Religion* (2012) and *More Brilliant than the Sun: Adventures in Sonic Fiction* (1998) and co-editor of *WORLD 3* (2014), *The Militant Image: A Cine Geography: Third Text 108:* (2011), *Harun Farocki: Against What? Against Whom?* (2009), *A Long Time Between Suns* (2009) *and The Ghosts of Songs: The Film Art of the Black Audio Film Collective* (2007). Eshun is Lecturer in Aural and Visual Cultures at the Department of Visual Cultures, Goldsmiths, University of London.

Anselm Franke (ed.) is Head of Visual Arts and Film at the Haus der Kulturen der Welt in Berlin where he developed, among others, the exhibitions "The Whole Earth" (co-curated with Diedrich Diederichsen), "After Year Zero" (co-curated with Annett Busch) and "Ape Culture" (co-curated with Hila Peleg). He curated the 2014 Shanghai Biennale titled "Social Factory" and the 2012 Taipei Biennial, titled "Modern Monsters, Death and Life of Fiction". His critically acclaimed exhibition "Animism" has been traveling worldwide since its inception in 2010 and has been shown in Antwerp, Bern, Vienna, Berlin, New York, Shenzhen, Seoul and Beirut. Franke was artistic director of Extra City Kunsthal in Antwerp from 2006 to 2010.

Tamar Garb is Durning Lawrence Professor in the History of Art at University College, London. She writes on sexuality, race and gender in modern and contemporary art and is the curator of "Figures and Fictions: Contemporary South African Photography" (V&A, 2011) and "Distance and Desire: Encounters with the African Archive" (Walther Collection, 2013–2015).

Nida Ghouse is a writer and curator. Her on-going projects include "Emotional Architecture" and "Acoustic Matters". She is presently the director of Mumbai Art Room.

Marie-Hélène Gutberlet studied Art History, Philosophy and Film Studies in Frankfurt/M. and Basel (DPhil) and works as an independent curator, writer and film scholar. She is the co-initiator of the "Migration & Media" project which involves symposia and exhibition projects, most recently "Shoe Shop" (Johannesburg, 2012) and "The Space Between Us" (Berlin and Stuttgart, 2013–2014). She is currently the artistic co-director of the project "Visionary Archive" in Berlin, Bissau, Cairo, Johannesburg and Khartoum, and the editor-in-chief of the online publication *Future Memories*.

Stacy Hardy is an editor of the Pan-African journal *Chimurenga* and a teacher in the MA in Creative Writing program at Rhodes University. Her short stories have been published in numerous literary journals (*Black Warrior Review, Evergreen Review, The Literarian, Bengal Lights, Chimurenga* and many more) as well as in books, literary anthologies and catalogs.

Tobias Hering is a freelance curator and writer whose work focuses on experimental documentary forms and the politics of the image. Since 2011, he has been a member of the selection committee for the Kassel Documentary Film and Video Festival (dokfest). Tobias Hering also lectures and publishes on the topics of his curatorial research and has recently edited the essay collection *Der Standpunkt der Aufnahme—Point of View: Perspectives of political film and video work* (2014).

James T. Hong is a filmmaker and artist based in Taiwan who has been producing thought-provoking, unconventional, and occasionally controversial films and videos for nearly twenty years. He has produced works about Heidegger, Spinoza, Japanese biological warfare, and racism. His current research focuses on nationalism and disputed territories in East Asia.

Bongani Madondo is a senior writer and social critic on mid-career leave from the South African licensee of *Rolling Stone* magazine, where he served as resident rock critic. He published monographs on media, culture, style and politics in South Africa, Europe and the U.S. His first book *Hot Type: Icons, Artists & God-Figurines* was the African recipient of the National Endowment of the Arts. His latest book, *I'm Not Your Weekend Special* an anthology on Brenda Fassie is out now from Picador Books. SABCTV aired *Roots of Shangaan Electro,* a documentary film he produced and narrated on the Shangaan people of South Africa and Mozambique.

Gary Minkley currently holds the SARChI Chair in Social Change at the University of Fort Hare in East London, South Africa. Minkley's research interests are in South African history and the dynamics of social change, in public, sound and visual histories and around the question of social acts.

Fred Moten is a poet and student of the Black Radical Tradition. He is author of *In the Break: The Aesthetics of the Black Radical Tradition, Hughson's Tavern, B. Jenkins, The Feel Trio, and The Undercommons: Fugitive Planning and Black Study* (with Stefano Harney). He lives in Los Angeles and teaches at the University of California, Riverside.

Charles Tonderai Mudede is a Zimbabwean-born cultural critic, filmmaker, and film editor for *The Stranger*. Mudede collaborated with the director Robinson Devor on two films, *Police Beat* and *Zoo*, both of which premiered at Sundance, *Zoo* was screened at Cannes. Mudede has contributed to the *New York Times, LA Weekly, Village Voice, Black Souls Journal, CTheory, Cinema Scope*, and is on the editorial board for the *Arcade Journal* and *Black Scholar*. Mudede has lived in Seattle since 1989.

David Murphy is Professor of French and Postcolonial Studies at the University of Stirling. He is the editor of the collected writings of Lamine Senghor, the interwar anticolonial militant (*La Violation d'un pays et autres écrits anticolonialistes,* 2012), and he is currently preparing a biography of Senghor to be published in 2016. He is also the co-editor of several collections of essays with Charles Forsdick, including *Francophone Postcolonial Studies: A Critical Introduction* (2003) and *Postcolonial Thought in the French-Speaking World* (2009).

Joanna Mytkowska is a curator and art critic. Since 2007 she has been director of the Museum of Modern Art in Warsaw. Formerly she worked as a curator at the Centre Pompidou, Paris. She is also a co-founder of the Foksal Gallery Foundation. In 2005 she curated the Polish Pavilion at the 51st Venice Biennale, exhibiting *Repetition* by Artur Żmijewski. Other exhibitions she has curated include: "Alina Szapocznikow, Sculptures Undone 1955–1972" (Centre Art Contemporain Wiels in Brussels, Hammer Museum Los Angeles, Museum of Modern Art in New York, 2012–2013), "Les promesses du passé" (Centre Pompidou, Paris, 2010), "Awkward Objects" (Museum of Modern Art in Warsaw, 2009), "Les Inquiets. Cinq artistes sous la pression de la guerre" (Centre Pompidou, Paris, 2008), "Le Nuage Magellan" (Centre Pompidou, Paris, 2007), "Oskar Hansen. A Dream of Warsaw" (Foksal Gallery Foundation, Warsaw 2005). She has edited the following publications: *Henryk Stażewski. Economy of Thought and Perception* (2006), *Edward Krasiński* (1997).

Shirin M. Rai is professor in the department of Politics and International Studies. She directed a Leverhulme Trust funded program on Gendered Ceremony and Ritual in Parliament (2007–2011). Her research interests are in gendered performance and politics, gender and political institutions and gender and the political economy of development. She is the author of *The Gender Politics of Development* (2008) and editor of *Democracy in Practice: Ceremony and Ritual in Parliament* (2014) and *The Grammar of Performance and Politics* (2015).

Raquel Schefer is a filmmaker, a film curator and a PhD candidate in Film Studies at Sorbonne Nouvelle, Paris 3 University, where she is finishing a dissertation about Mozambican revolutionary cinema. She published the book *Self-Portrait in Documentary* in 2008.

Bernd Scherer has been the director of Haus der Kulturen der Welt since 2006. Scherer came to the HKW from the Goethe-Institute. He has curated and directed major art and cultural projects such as "Das weiße Meer", "Rethinking Europe", "Water-agua" (in Mexico), and "Über Lebenkunst". He is the co-editor of books such as *"Das Marco-Polo-Syndrom", neue bildende Kunst* (1995); *Alexander von Humboldt-Aufbruch in die Moderne* (2001); *Das vermessene Paradies. Positionen zu New York* (2007); *Feindbilder. Ideologien und visuelle Strategien der Kulturen* (2007); *Die Alte und die Neue Welt* (2008); *1989/Globale Geschichten* (2009). He has written numerous articles on cultural philosophy and aesthetics.

Bisi Silva is an independent curator and the founder/director of the Centre for Contemporary Art, Lagos (CCA, Lagos) which opened in December 2007. She was recently appointed as the Artistic Director of the 10th Bamako Encounters: African Biennale of Photography taking place in November and December 2015.

Łukasz Stanek is Lecturer at the Manchester Architecture Research Centre, University of Manchester. Stanek authored *Henri Lefebvre* on Space: *Architecture, Urban Research, and the Production of Theory* (2011) and edited Lefebvre's until-then unpublished book *Toward an Architecture of Enjoyment* (2014). His current book project is focused on the work of architects from socialist countries in West Africa and the Middle East during the Cold War. Stanek taught at the ETH Zurich and Harvard Graduate School of Design.

Colophon

After Year Zero: Geographies of Collaboration
This volume accompanies the two exhibitions "After Year Zero" organized at the Haus der Kulturen der Welt in Berlin (September 19 to November 24, 2013) and at the Museum of Modern Art in Warsaw (June 12 to August 23, 2015)—both curated by Anselm Franke and Annett Busch in collaboration with research curator Heidi Ballet and (at MoMA Warsaw) Magda Lipska (curator). "After Year Zero" was based on a series of workshops held under the title "Matters of Collaboration" in 2012 in Algiers, Dakar, Paris, and Johannesburg in cooperation with the Goethe-Institut in Brussels and with funding from the Excellence Initiative of the Goethe-Institut.

Editors: Annett Busch, Anselm Franke
Editorial assistance: Heidi Ballet
Research assistance: Meagan Down
Translations: Michael Dills (from German to English),
Łukasz Mojsak (from Polish to English),
Colin Shepherd (from German to English)
Transcription: Mandi Gomez
Copyedited by: Erik Empson
Proofread by: Meagan Down
Publishing co-ordination: Katarzyna Szotkowska-Beylin,
Syelle Hase, Sonja Oehler

Graphic Design by Zak Group
Lithography and print supervision: Noviki Studio,
Katarzyna Nestorowicz, Marcin Nowicki

Printed by
ARGRAF Sp. z o.o.
ul. Jagiellońska 76, 03–301 Warszawa

ISBN: 978-83-64177-25-5

Publisher
Museum of Modern Art in Warsaw
Pańska 3
00–124 Warsaw
www.artmuseum.pl
Chairman of the Museum Board: Andrzej Turowski
Director: Joanna Mytkowska

Museum of Modern Art in Warsaw is supported by
Zwierciadło Foundation and CMS Law-Tax:

Co-publisher
Haus der Kulturen der Welt
John-Foster-Dulles-Allee 10
10557 Berlin
www.hkw.de
Haus der Kulturen der Welt is a division of Kulturveranstaltungen des Bundes in Berlin GmbH (KBB).
Chairwoman of the Supervisory Board: Monika Grütters
Director: Bernd Scherer
General Manager: Charlotte Sieben

Haus der Kulturen der Welt is supported by

Federal Government Commissioner for Culture and the Media
Federal Foreign Office

Distributed by
The University of Chicago Press
www.press.uchicago.edu

Thanks to:
aarc (Algerian Agency for Cultural Influence), Adekeye Adebajo, Nabil Ahmed, John Akomfrah, Fatma Alioua, Stefanie Alisch, Andy Amadi, Kristine Andersen, Max Annas, Lotte Arndt, Kader Attia, Enoka Ayemba, David Barton, Pascal Bianchini, Nicholas Bussmann, Jacqueline Cabaço, Garnette Cadogan, Aziz Cissé, Andrée Davanture-Taleg, Elsa de Seynes, Yasmina Dekkar, Souleymane Bachir Diagne, Rama Salla Dieng, Aissatou Diop, Boris Boubacar Diop, Emily Dische-Becker, Ntone Edjabe, Brent Edwards, Bassam El Baroni, Jihan El-Tahri, Kodwo Eshun, Pia Entenmann, Ute Fendler, Berthold Franke, Pier Paolo Frassinelli, Miriam Greiter, Günter Gretz, Marie-Hélène Gutberlet, Henrike Grohs, Adam Haupt, Lien Heidenreich, Nanna Heidenreich, Rangoato Hlasane, James T. Hong, Michael Jeismann, Keyti, Philippe Lacote, Malika Laïchour Romane, Susanne Leeb, Koyo Kouoh, Brigitta Kuster, Anna Leon, Bongani Madondo, Peter Makurube (1956–2015), Olivier Marboeuf, Vincent Meessen, Kerstin Meyer, Thokozani Mhlambi, Gary Minkley, Fred Moten, Charles Tonderai Mudede, Museum of Yugoslav History, Simon Njami, Nana Oforiatta-Ayim, Adebayo Olukoshi, Birgit Plank-Mucavele, Nataša Petrešin-Bachelez, Janina Prossek, Shirin Rai, Laurie Robins, Tim Roerig, Katharina von Ruckteschell-Katte, Catherine Ruelle, Markus Ruff, Jay Rutledge, Anjalika Sagar, Ebrima Sall, Arfang Sarr Crao, Davina 'Satori', Lisa Scheibner, Dierk Schmidt, Raymond Silverman, Rose Skelton, Dirk Snauwaert, Anna Schneider, Lucy Steeds, Territorial Agency, Michael Vasquez, Francois Venter, Cédric Vincent, Klaus Walter, Ibrahima Wane, Anne Marie Youm, Leo Zeilig, Andreas Zürn